IDEAS AND EVENTS

IDEAS and EVENTS / Professing History

LEONARD KRIEGER

Edited by M. L. Brick
With an Introduction by Michael Ermarth

The University of Chicago Press
Chicago and London

Leonard Krieger (1918–1990) was, at the time of his death, University
Professor Emeritus in the Department of History at University of Chicago.

The University of Chicago Press, Chicago 60637
The University of Chicago Press, Ltd., London
© 1992 by The University of Chicago
All rights reserved. Published 1992
Printed in the United States of America

01 00 99 98 97 96 95 94 93 92   5 4 3 2 1

ISBN (cloth): 0-226-45302-2

Library of Congress Cataloging-in-Publication Data

Krieger, Leonard.
    Ideas and events : professing history / Leonard Krieger ; edited
by M. L. Brick ; with an introduction by Michael Ermarth.
        p.   cm.
    Includes biliographical references (p.   ) and index.
    1. History—Philosophy.   I. Brick, M. L.   II. Title.
    D16.8.K72   1992
    901—dc20   91-48097
                                                       CIP

⊗ The paper used in this publication meets the minimum requirements of
the American National Standard for Information Sciences—Permanence of
Paper for Printed Library Materials, ANSI Z39.48-1984.

History remains for us . . . an inimitable way of rendering comprehensible modes of humanity which must otherwise remain incomprehensible. . . . [W]hen such heterogeneous relationships cannot be understood by the logics of either propositional thinking or the analytical sciences, they may still be manageable by a kind of thinking that makes sense of arranging things, however incongruous, along the time line. . . .

For the historical sense refers precisely to the understanding that the human combinations that have been struck through time, however ill-sorted or incongruous they may be, derive a meaning simply from their having actually happened in conjunction; that this meaning is inimitable; and that each instance adds its increment of this meaning to the general feeling for the way men circumstantially behave.

The historical sense is a cumulative wisdom. It grows with the reading of history that aims beyond history. There are no substitutes. There are no shortcuts.

Leonard Krieger
Ranke: The Meaning of History

Contents

Editor's Note

While compiling the essays in this volume for publication, I aimed to construct a comprehensive review of Leonard Krieger's thought as an American historian of Europe and European and American intellectual history. Inevitably, in the course of getting the work to market, this aim had to be narrowed, if only slightly.

Professor Krieger's academic interests, always interrelated, were so many and so varied that a single volume proved incapable of accommodating them all. (For a bibliography of his writings see the end of this volume.) Long-standing interests like European and American liberalism and nationalism, which a follower of Leonard Krieger's career might well expect to find here, threatened to make the collection unwieldy. Cuts simply had to be made.

Nonetheless, by drawing together under a single cover those essays of obvious lasting importance, I have attempted to throw fresh light onto the thought and career of one of this century's foremost American historians. Toward this end I have placed a series of brief excerpts from Professor Krieger's writings as prologue to each part of this volume. Each excerpt was chosen to underline the sense of historical perspective and prescience with which he wrote.

For example, the excerpt which introduces part 4 on twentieth-century German history was penned in 1957, only to be realized in 1989. The excerpt introducing part 2 on the history of intellectuals paraphrases Professor Krieger's response to a question I put to him as a first-year graduate student, namely, "What is intellectual history?" The reader must judge whether my aim was true throughout. Together with the essays they introduce, these excerpts should lead to Professor Krieger's many books and help the reader weigh the great unity of purpose and perspective that sustained him as an historian.

In the course of completing a project such as this I accrued many debts, and I want to thank everyone who has had a hand in publishing this work. I especially want to thank Professor Michael Ermarth of Dartmouth for his fine introduction to this volume as well as for his critical comments and contributions toward its completion. Thanks are due as well to the University of Chicago Press and especially to Douglas

Mitchell for their long-standing commitment to the success of this project.

A personal debt of gratitude goes to Andy Bouvet and to Professor Krieger's son Nat. Andy gave freely of his time to clarify numerous references and was always generous with his criticism and advice. Nat demonstrated a dedication to his father and his father's historical legacy that is as rare as it is selfless. He has my deepest admiration for his tireless efforts on his father's behalf, and to those sentiments I want to add my sincerest gratitude.

Last, and most important, I want to thank Professor Krieger himself for the opportunity to act as editor of this volume, and for everything that he has done for me. It was my great pleasure to work closely with Professor Krieger during his last years, as graduate student, teaching assistant, and amanuensis on the manuscript for his next-to-last book, *Time's Reasons*. Without his help and guidance, the present volume—his last work—could not have been completed with the same degree of success. Needless to say, any errors or oversights in this work are attributable to the editor; the book itself benefits at every turn from my having been able to consult with Professor Krieger as problems and questions arose during the editing process.

Leonard Krieger's thought and example have helped to shape my knowledge and sense of history. I can only hope that my efforts on his behalf, as represented by this volume, will leave his intellectual legacy in good historical stead.

M. L. Brick

Introduction

Leonard Krieger (1918–1990) has aptly been called a historian's historian. This is not because his work is intramural or narrowly professional but, rather, just the reverse: because it calls his readers to a twofold reflection that reaches both inward and outward. The inward direction engages the basic assumptions with which we approach history; the outward direction confronts the past as something different from ourselves and our assumptions. These dual tendencies work together to enlarge our human outlook, yet enable us to maintain a critical awareness of the determinants of that outlook. In this sense history is not merely the inert record of what has happened but an active ingredient in what continues to happen.

The person thinking about history is inevitably in history. Since we cannot think ourselves free of our specific existence into some pure theoretical consciousness, the effort of knowing the past is bound to be conditioned by influences and conditions that are not directly under consideration. This situation puts historical inquiry not so much at cross-purposes as in a creative tension between efforts toward engagement and toward detachment, between "outer" objective cognition and "inner" subjective recognition. Leonard Krieger summons his readers to the rewards and demands of this tensile relation: history remains an avenue conducting us toward deeper acknowledgement of our present condition, while at the same time demanding that we think beyond the bounds of our own situation to explore other assumptions, institutions, ways of life, and habits of mind.

No one is more skilled than Leonard Krieger at bringing out the interplay between the suppositions we carry with us through life and the matters we encounter in history. For this reason he might just as well be called a philosopher's historian or, more aptly, a layman's or an everyman's historian, insofar as such a person bothers to think seriously about what is undertaken in the name of history. Krieger professes a form of history that goes beyond the bounds of academic specialties and subspecialties to engage the fundamental question of how and why we have come to think historically at all—and where such historical thinking has taken us.

The rewards of such thoughtful history are not in the form of grand sweeping lessons, precise predictive models, or insider tips for the next eventuality. Such history does not provide the security of an ironclad view of the world, nor does it merely instill the opposite, dizzying reminder that most things change most of the time (although Krieger, in stressing the "historicity" of historical knowledge, shows that history has been used for such purposes, and others too). The multiple sorts of meaning in history cannot be encompassed at the extremes of the overriding rational finality of a Hegel or the all-pervading opaque contingency of Sartre's *La Nausée*. Human knowledge of human history remains of a different order, at once humbler and more strenuous.

In one sense the study of history would seem to present us with a relatively accessible subject matter: the tacitly familiar, "natural" course of human affairs conducted forwards over time—the matter-of-fact, "matter-of-course" human life in so many ways like our own, even if surveyed backwards from a later time and a different place. This sort of history is the accommodating, familiar discipline beloved among college students as the academic "course of least resistance." However, with a moderate realignment of our assumptions, the historical vantage point may also present us with a strange, alien order of things that confounds our ordinary notions and evaluations. Whether in the casual or confounding sense, we who undertake a study history are bound to employ a mental pattern in trying to grasp the pattern of thoughts and actions in the past. We are at once agents and interpreters of history's complex patterns.

For his readers Leonard Krieger leaves no doubt about the quickening value of history, especially intellectual history. Here the patterns of intelligibility are, so to speak, built into the subject matter from the ground up. He certainly does not contend that all history is "essentially" intellectual history or somehow resolvable into ideas, concepts, or forms of consciousness; it is rather that intellectual history prompts us to the joint inward/outward movement in an especially concerted manner. It goes directly—and discerningly—to the core of what Henry James said of history as such: "History is never, in any rich sense, the immediate crudity of what 'happens,' but the finer complexity of what we read into it and think of in connection with it."[1] Here there are no "simple" atomic facts or discrete idea-units. (The very concept of "atomic fact" is anything but atomic, being already an episode in the fertile intellectual history of modern thought.) In Krieger's simple but far-reaching definition, "a historical 'fact' usually proves to be a network

---

1. Henry James, *The American Scene* (New York, 1946, c1907), 182.

of relations extending the outer shell of its external appearance to the inner core of its meaning" (see below, p. 149). The historian remains implicated in the network he is trying to discern and trace. This implicative, "networking" effect in human affairs is clearly evident—or most readily recognized—in the domain of intellectual history.

Intellectual history serves to encourage integrative thinking and rethinking in a world of proliferating, specialized data and informational overload. It deserves to be esteemed as more rather than less important in our contemporary "information society," since it confronts hectic factual profusion with a strong imperative toward coherent comprehension over the longer term. As a branch of history with its own distinctive lines of development, it has always stressed "thinking through" its material along several lines and levels rather than mere fact-finding compilation or updated paraphrase. It is, after all, ideas and mental patterns that give the world its basic intelligibility—and intellectual history makes us take stock of these patterns with fidelity, rigor, and coherence. If we acknowledge that categories and mental forms define our actual experience, our cognition, and our very media of communication and exchange, then intellectual history deserves to be regarded as eminently fundamental rather than as remotely ethereal.

This is the sort of fundamental history Leonard Krieger professes, as will become evident throughout the present volume of essays. Here, as well as in *Time's Reasons: Philosophies of History Old and New* (1989), he offers a cogent answer to the searching question posed by a kindred mind, the French social thinker Raymond Aron: "What remains to be determined is the relation between the history that men live, the history historians reconstruct, and the history that philosophers substitute for the historians' reconstruction."[2] There is not—and will never be—a simple, fixed configuration for this shifting relation. Indeed, as is evident here, Krieger's own triangulation of it does not remain unchanged through the course of his own thinking and writing. But for all the daunting difficulties of formulating and tracing it, this crucial, if intractable, relation will go on having a profound bearing upon any sense we try to make of ourselves and of the human past.

The essays in this collection are diverse but hardly sundry: they are linked thematically and chronologically. The unifying theme of the entire volume is the role of history in Western thought. Stated briefly, this

---

2. Raymond Aron, *History and the Dialectic of Violence,* trans. Barry Cooper (New York, 1976), 142.

role can be said to have shifted from an older belief in the natural or divine continuity *behind* events to a modern belief in a man-made continuity *among* events, then verging into twentieth-century assertions of discontinuities and ruptures *within* human affairs (and *between* these affairs and the inquiring mind), these latter ruptures being said to be so radical that the "stuff" of history and the forms of its representation fall asunder. Primary patterns of meaning that were once thought to be either "found" or "made" have over time become un-founded, un-made, and even "un-thought." This dual rupture of fundamental connections within history (as that purported to exist between ideas and events) and between history and the historian has so transformed its earlier matter-of-course qualities that the very possibility of historical meaning is put in question. While Krieger does not use the term "postmodernism" or any of its cognates, this is the crux of the so-called "postmodern condition" being discussed today in several of the humane disciplines, especially the time-bound, historical ones.

Krieger's constellation of concerns is conveyed in the main divisions of this collection. The distinctions among these sections remain important to his effort to reconcile variety with coherence in the study of the past. This introduction can serve only to indicate some of the main lines of that effort. To begin with, he distinguishes between history of ideas, intellectual history, and the history of intellectuals and provides an argument for each different endeavor. These areas obviously overlap, but they are separable fields of inquiry. Intellectual history, he says, "has been more comprehensive than history of ideas in two dimensions: it has included inarticulate beliefs, amorphous opinions, and unspoken assumptions as well as formal ideas; and its primary unit of historical concern has not been the set of these notions as such but rather their external relations with the larger life of the people who have borne them" (see, p. 161). The historian can inquire after all sorts of past notions that were not held by persons who can be considered intellectual, just as one can pursue a history of intellectuals that emphasizes matters other than their own explicit ideas in their own chosen terms.

In a similar analytic vein Krieger differentiates between an activating ideology, its doctrinal variants and offshoots, and its individual adherents. Consequently he separates Marx's own thinking, the several main varieties of Marxism, and individual Marxians. The same analytic rigor yields several varieties and phases of Western historical-mindedness (i.e., "historism" and a later and more radical "historicism," both being stages within generic historical-mindedness or historical consciousness). The point of such analytical typologies is not to engage in scholastic term-splitting, but rather to set forth visible markers in the network of ideas to be traced along more concrete lines for the reader. Such terms function as knots in the interpretive network: they are the historian's "secondary" index points for actual but once removed "primary" tendencies of thought that develop for their part within a web of already existing beliefs. Such patterns may hold sway even after intellectual tendencies become outright doctrinal "isms," with their own supposedly self-sufficient grounds, special terminology, and avowed partisans or schools.

The first part of this volume, "History of Ideas," may conjure up for the reader the venerable academic tradition of this name. It was a distinct approach within—or alongside—intellectual history, with its own distinguished advocates, journal, and even dictionary. Over the years it was closely identified in this country with Arthur Lovejoy and his followers at Johns Hopkins University, as somewhat later and more loosely with the University of Chicago, well before Leonard Krieger's arrival there. Krieger demonstrates that this approach can be pried out of its somewhat rigid and disembodied mold and deployed more inclusively and concretely. As with the older approach, Krieger does not shrink from treating ideas in ways that may disregard unconscious motivation, psychic make-up or personality, vested social interest, or even immediate circumstance. For him the linkage of ideas and events remains the prime connection. This linkage forms the axis of his own characteristic method of multiple contextualization.

While the older approach usually treated the evolution of ideas without much concern for engendering or ensuing events, he is at pains to show the relation of ideas to public actions and institutions. Human ideas not only have "moving parts" but also moving meanings and shifting applications. Krieger cannot readily be assigned to the ranks of "internalists" (stressing the immanent "logic" or system of ideas) or "externalists" (stressing connections to setting and context), for he works precisely at the junction of these two dimensions. With respect to thought and culture, he remains equally interested in the internal "logicality" and external "porousness" of its manifestations. As he puts it in terms of examples: "Giotto's art can be seen as the product of a new use of space or of a new city-state environment. Hegel's *Phenomenology* can be seen as an answer to Kant or an answer to the French Revolution. But the problem is: how can either be seen as both?" (see below, p. 198). This difficult but fascinating "both" is what impels Krieger's blend of perspectives and sensitivities. It makes him—and his readers—into "hybrid historians" of multiple susceptibilities.

The ideas in this first part (freedom and authority) are treated over a long span of time, from the canonically ancient to the distinctively modern. From a base in the classical idea of freedom, this section weaves a pattern of its own as the core ideas mesh into an emergent relationship of historical derivation and dependency. The history of ideas, as Krieger practices it, is hardly a geometric demonstration, but neither is it just the random iteration of one idea after another, nor the same idea over and over. The transparency and habituality—perhaps even banality—of these key ideas bear testimony to their continuing core of common meaning. Yet this meaning is shown to be not static but dynamic: it changes discernibly over time and place.

One of the most striking effects of Krieger's approach lies in showing the transformation of beliefs accepted as "common sense" in different epochs. Sometimes this transformation is so gradual as to seem almost imperceptible, as in certain stages in the evolution of the idea of freedom. But he also shows that the unraveling of the tensile network of meaning that links ideas can happen quite suddenly and irreparably. The knots in ideational networks can be tightened, loosened, or severed by events themselves. The essay on authority, to give an example, was clearly prompted by the crisis of legitimacy of institutions felt in the Western industrial (and academic) world in the late sixties and early seventies. Without gloating or hand-wringing, Krieger confronts the reader with the stark possibility of "the demise of authority as we have known it" (see below, p. 50). It is a possibility that presents itself rather differently now than it did twenty years ago, although as Krieger himself shows, there are certain key elements that hardly change over decades—or centuries, for that matter.

The second part, entitled "The History of Intellectuals," treats several master thinkers who have recast the horizons of reflection upon personal existence, collective politics, social institutions, and reason itself. The underlying theme of this section is the transformation of the notion of intellectual "engagement." Krieger stresses quite differing views of engagement among nineteenth- and twentieth-century thinkers, and he disputes the facile view that intellectuals are destined to be either critics or apologists of their age and surroundings. Modern intellectuals have sought a form of engagement that avoids conformity to society or submergence in reality but that also acknowledges the pervasive influence of social reality upon the workings of mind, whether personal and individual or public and collective. Intellectuals have always wanted to think or act beyond present conditions: if there was no state, they proclaimed the state; if there was a state but no nation, they extolled the nation; if there was nation, then they held to something beyond the nation. Western intellectuals have tended to view society as both the matrix of personal existence and the collective means for moving beyond such a situation. The mind's involvement in real conditions and events can be seen as either a matter of descriptive fact or a matter of prescriptive value—in Kantian terms, as both an empirical "is" and a normative "ought." The difficulty comes in negotiating the balance between these conditions, without one co-opting the other.

On the Herculean topic of "Hegel and History," Krieger makes for an interesting match, as his historian's analytic distinctions are clearly at odds with the German philosopher's dialectical transformations. While sympathetic to the genuine concreteness in Hegel's notion of "spirit", Krieger finds that the vast continuities of his system are purchased at the price of even more colossal inconsistencies. Hegel elevates to preeminent status an important dimension in historical thinking, but only at the cost of denaturing human history itself. In rationalizing to the point of irrationality, Hegel's mode of "rational" understanding inevitably distorts what is understood. After Hegel's ambitious, speculative account of "time's reasons," we more modest and more modern mortals must acknowledge that a later human perspective may not succeed in encompassing an earlier one—or even in securing partial access to it. In the end Hegel's view of history indicts itself as a case in point about the futility of total history, as it remains striking for its balkiness for the modern temperament. In a contrasting vein, Krieger's sympathetic essay on Jean-Paul Sartre traces the impact of events of the thirties and forties in fostering Sartre's "conversion to history" and his revision of earlier existentialist premises. Here the larger question at stake is not simply the degree of internal coherence in Sartre's own intellectual development, but the function of history in contemporary thinking in general.

The eloquent tribute to Hanna Arendt in the essay "The Historical Hanna Arendt" invokes history in the double-barreled manner characteristic of Krieger, that is, "both as a measure of [Arendt's] status and as a dimension of her work" (see below, p. 126). Arendt is judged "an original" by virtue of the manner in which she invoked classical traditions against modern ideological positions—especially those she saw fatally converging in twentieth-century totalitarianism. She herself belonged to no identifiable ism or school of thought (including "political classicism") but rather to a company of thinkers across the ages, who thought against the grain of their times and against a backdrop of protracted cultural crisis. She belonged with the "men in dark times," to use her own title, borrowed from Bertolt Brecht. In this essay Arendt is shown to pit herself against the very same conceptions of history that Krieger has elsewhere delineated: presumed civilizational progress, Hegelian hybris, socio-economic determinism, and "heroic" decisionism. Arendt argued in favor of an older but uncomplacent conception of the "human condition" that underscored man's participation within a larger co-order of Being. In a vein akin to that of Karl Jaspers and Martin Heidegger, she argued against the tandem modern notions of hermetic subjectivity and "radical world-alienation" which together produce a modern condition that has rendered pre-modern ideas of nature and history no longer conceivable, thereby undermining our main sources of belief in binding traditions, and even in reality itself. A brave new world in which everything becomes man-made is a world fitted totally to human purposes, but it is not thereby fit for man, human habitation, and genuine political participation. Arendt castigated modern ideologies and philosophies of history as pretentious pseudo-thinking; Krieger gently shows that she herself required an equivalent philosophy of history in order to criticize the dominant ones of her own age of "dark times."

The third part, "Intellectual History," brings into sharper analytical focus a set of related themes that have previously figured more vaguely in the background: the history of history, the valences of historical thinking, and the specific differences between what is often indifferently called "historism" and "historicism." To these crucial but will-o'-the-wisp notions Krieger brings a rigorous and searching clarification: what was before obscurely on the horizon is now brought into close view. This part of the book explores the separate strands of pragmatic, aesthetic, and scientific historical thinking, and how they have combined in the academic professionalization of the discipline. Given the current importance of "historicism" and even the "new historicism," not only in academic history but in virtually all of the humane disciplines, including philosophy and literature, Krieger's treatment becomes highly topical.

In Krieger's view, historism emerges not as a narrow, school concept of largely nineteenth-century Germanic (and academic) descent but as a more general, enduring tendency of Western thought to present human affairs according to a developmental dynamic of becoming. It became the self-conscious stance of modern historicism around the turn of the century with figures such as Dilthey, Simmel, Croce, Meinecke, and Troeltsch, when the question of values was brought to the fore. For the latter thinkers, crucial categories and values that had previously been deemed above or below the vicissitudes of change were now brought into the process of becoming: thus, historicism became embroiled and ultimately submerged in relativism and scepticism. Krieger traces the crucial transition from historism to historicism by showing the encroachment of historical approaches upon the notions of state, society, science, and even civilization itself. But in all this unsettling transformation, the underlying historism cannot be said to devour or exhaust itself as an episodic thing of the past (i.e., by becoming historicism!), for it must continue to remain an abiding concern of any self-reflective person, branch of learning, or culture in general. Historism will endure because it is an intrinsic dimension of human awareness and of human reflection as such. The Marxian legacy itself falls within the scope of historism insofar as historism's cognitive aspect takes on moral significance. By way of confirming Krieger's point about the moral dimension of historism, it need only be said that we are presently in the midst of vehement debates about the historizing of all sorts of crucial episodes and experiences—the Nazi past, the Cold War, the Viet Nam War, or Marxism itself.

Krieger probes the entire range of implications of historical thinking as historism/historicism. He brings a welcome combination of rigor and scope to these troublesome but recurrent isms, which in the hands of commentators such as Karl Popper, Leo Strauss, and Allan Bloom have the annoying habit of shifting into their opposites. On balance Krieger tends to dwell less upon historism's vitiating effects and more upon its positive impulse toward recovering integral individualities, with the salutary reminder that such recovery can never be fully objective or perfect. He argues that historism is not so much apologetical or skeptical as critically "re-constructive" in its basic impulse. At its core is neither all-devouring scepticism nor all-preserving conservative awe for continuity, but a decent "liberal" respect for otherness—and not the least for interpretive categories other than one's own. Thus, both of the positions Krieger delineates put a high premium on human "difference" and cultural "diversity" long before these terms entered contemporary use as crusading slogans to resist homogeneity and subordination. The current invocations of "difference" and "alterity" (or otherness) are not so different from past positions that emerged periodically within the Western tradition of historical-mindedness. (Krieger's interpretation of one of the major nineteenth-century focal points in that long tradition can be found in his *Ranke: The Meaning of History*, (1977). Historism has proven its worth in enhancing broadly human susceptibilities in a special way: although it remains without specific ethical content, historicism harbors ethical significance as an affirmation of human autonomy and indelible individuality—with regard to epochs, persons, or works.

Both forms retain a measure of emancipatory, humanizing potential that is grounded in respect for the concrete and particular.

The fourth part of the book, "History and Natural Law in Early Modern Europe," places modern ideas about the legal and political order in an illuminating half-light, a sort of chiaroscuro of familiarity and surprise. Early modern thought mingled bold claims to "worldly" realism with very old assumptions about a fixed hierarchy of norms: the result was a different force field of ideas from what had prevailed previously and what would prevail afterwards. Krieger shows the close and reciprocating interconnections among the domains of law, politics, and history at work in writers as different at Grotius, Hobbes, Clarendon, Pufendorf, and Leibniz. They were all respectable, if indeed official and semi-official, historians by avocation, who felt compelled to defend a kind of middle-order human truth lying somewhere between pure rational demonstration and revealed religious truth. Krieger does not slight important differences among these figures, but remains intent upon illuminating the common background beliefs of the entire early modern age. Here Krieger shows that his brand of intellectual history does not dictate obsessive preoccupation with unique individualities: "What distinguished Pufendorf was his articulation of the implicit relations among ideas which were generally shared" (see below, p. 231). This shared seventeenth-century background is explicated at greater length in Krieger's study, *The Politics of Discretion: Pufendorf and the Acceptance of Natural Law* (1965).

Krieger examines the function of natural law in justifying the study of history and the sociopolitical order, a function previously exercised largely by religion and later by science. The justification for history shifted gradually from theology to jurisprudence, as legal precedence supplanted divine providence as the preeminent source of legitimation for both order and change in the world. The essay "The Distortions of Political Theory: The XVIIth Century Case" makes the point that "the historian is, in fact, a logician of distortions," usually making inferences from the exceptions that prove the rule. The brilliant essay "Kant and the Crisis of Natural Law" shows how history and current politics—most notably, the French Revolution—produced fundamental realignments in Kant's systematic thinking. In all Krieger presents natural law not as a closed, static concept that served its time and now rests embalmed in the past, but as a continuing reference point for ongoing issues. It will become clear to the attentive reader that Krieger does not interpret natural law and historism as inherently antithetical positions, as is often argued by both European and American scholars. If one wishes to use ideas as polemical bludgeons to attack opponents of straw,

Krieger's treatment offers hardly any reinforcement, as he forces one to think beyond such stereotypical notions.

The fifth part of this volume, "Marx and Engels and History," is acutely pertinent to the current state of ideas and events in the world today. Established, state-sponsored Marxism has been moving precipitously along a course of extinction far different from previous expectations of either supporters or detractors and, one might add, even of noncommital observers. Marxism as a historical perspective is itself suddenly coming into an unexpected kind of historical focus—a sort of focus by sudden jeopardy. This inverted "fate" of Marxism, so contrary to its own teleology, palpably illustrates Krieger's point about the historicity of larger views of history, and how they can change with the rapidity of events themselves. Marxism's unique linkage of theory and practice, of idea and event, has come home to haunt it: the "dustbin of history" that Marx confidently set out for capitalist society is seen to be roomy enough to hold multiple varieties of Marxist theory and practice. There is a huge irony here, whose effect in the West should compel serious reflection rather than smug satisfaction. Too great a gulf between theory and practice—between binding "ideas" and attending "events"— spells the undoing of fundamental convictions and support for any social system. The reader of these pages will find that the durable bridgework of "classical" Marxism that made it one of the few systems of thought to span the two halves of the nineteenth century, and then the nineteenth and twentieth, may preclude its further extension from the twentieth to twenty-first. But Krieger also reminds us that dialectical "revisionism" is the very element of Marxism whereby one aspect may come to offset another: the aesthetic to offset the scientific, the personal to offset the collective, and—significantly for the present—the future-invoking, chiliastic aspect to offset the historical aspect, including the sheer dead weight of past failures. After reading Krieger intently, one would be less surprised at Marxism's collapse, but also alert to the sources of its potential revival.

Krieger's essays provide the conceptual framework for such a serious stock-taking of different strands of Marxian ideology. He turned the theoretical tables on Marxism long before the practical failures of major communist states came to dominate headlines and public discussion. This conceptual turn about (which he calls a "relativizing" and "deflowering") does not arise from a reflexive anti-Marxism, but is rather undertaken within broader historical categories. The task of assessing Marxism must include comprehending its longevity in the light of its repeated disconfirmation by events and by institutional evolution. Marxism may fail as a school system and as a "totalization" of history, but still remain compelling as a higher-order synthesis of modern developments precisely because of the way its central moral imperative has been couched within that very historical development: "What intrigues us about Marx is his capacity to find an essentially ethical rationale running within and across the centuries at the very same time that he perceives the diversity and complexity of human existence" (see below, p. 280). In this light Krieger shows that the histories written by Marx and Engels were not simply heavy-handed applications of a preconceived theory, impervious to the force of facts, but a subtle weave of ideas and events. Krieger slights neither Marxism's incongruities and absurdities nor its power of illumination, motivation, and self-transformation.

The final part of this volume, on German history and historiography, is also remarkably discerning in light of Germany's recent reunification. His overall perspective on German history is not cast along lines that some observers might expect, for he remains chary of full-bore theories of German exceptionalism or strong versions of the so-called *Sonderweg* thesis. Generally he does not dwell upon allegedly unique features of German historical development, but rather sees German history synoptically in the wider frame of Continental patterns. As Krieger phrases it, internationalism in Central European history is not simply a separable point of view but remains an ingredient of the subject matter itself. This is especially true of German history, wherein swings between nationalism and internationalism have been disruptive and at times catastrophic. Krieger's "networking" and contextualizing approach to the German past remains thoroughly historical, without falling into the "bad historicism" that in its awe for individuality refuses to compare, let alone to judge and evaluate.

The backdrop for this entire final section on German history is not only several essays that appear earlier in the present volume, but the author's monumental study *The German Idea of Freedom* (1957). This oft-cited work traces over three centuries the intersection of intellectual currents with political, legal, and cultural institutions. It remains unsurpassed as the single most comprehensive examination of the German *Rechtsstaat* from its remote post-Reformation origins through national unification under Bismarck. In this tangled intercourse of ideas and events, Germany showed a distinct pattern of development, wherein feudal-particularist ideas of German *Libertät* were infused into more modern universalized ideas of freedom to produce the unstable amalgam that persisted into the twentieth century.

The German conception of the state invested it with a moral-cultural mission, grafted on to a cumbersome "feudal-federal" structure. This conception aligned the domains of state, society, and individual quite differently from prevailing Western coordinates, as evident in the persistent distinction between negative "freedom-from" and positive "freedom-to". The conditions of freedom in Germany were imposed by state authority as legal stipulations for a modern social order long before there emerged any widespread popular spirit of civic individualism. Obedience to existing hierarchies became a condition of the "state of law" itself, as Germany continued the legal function of mediating bodies (orders, estates, corporations) after they had faded away elsewhere. The history of German political ideas and institutions showed a kind of constitutional "law of the included middle": the tendency to posit bridging entities where the Western pattern tended to find unmediated alternatives. Germany's difficult history of "wanderer between two worlds" has constitutional roots, as well as philosophical-religious and geographical foundations.

Krieger shows that Germany was for a long time either a vaguely cultural "nation" without a state, or multiple states without a nation; its relatively brief period of congruent nation-statehood has been precarious and threatening. The imbalance of socioeconomic forces in Central Europe led to their explosive accumulation rather than their phased resolution in serial installments. The concomitant German sense of lagging behind more advanced nations produced the combination of "overcontrol" at home and "overreach" abroad. Here too, historical thinking played a constitutive role in the German question: the penchant for partisan historism re-inforced the sense of a special German "moment" in the larger "world destiny." Such would be the explosive legacy of nineteenth-century developments to the twentieth century.

It should be added, however, that Krieger finds a fundamental difference between Nazi totalitarianism and previous forms of German authoritarianism. He does not indulge in facile continuities and extravagant parallels, and nowhere is this sobriety more apparent than in his treatment of Nazi totalitarianism. Totalitarianism arose from a predicament that looms large only in the twentieth century: the condition in which large numbers of persons in a beleaguered social order come to surrender their individual freedom in the hope of recuperating some single incarnate meaning as members of an exclusive community of race, a cultural mission, or ultimate ends. Totalitarianism is thus shown to have genuine intellectual and ideational foundations, as well as socioeconomic ones. Among other noxious effects, Krieger shows that it perpetrated bad historiography, since it reduced the past to a prologue for its own exclusive mission in a foreordained future. Among its terrible simplifications, Nazism compressed all history into an auxiliary of itself.

The masterful essay, "Nazism: Highway or Byway?" assumes an almost impossible but unavoidable task: to show the implications of the shift from Nazism's earlier status as "massive, central reality" and consummate German "finality" to its latter-day status of circumscribed stage in an ongoing history of Germany and a larger Europe. Krieger is intent upon showing the meaning of Nazism's historization: here the stakes in the "history of history" are exceedingly high and manifestly more than purely academic. He uncovers a central dilemma at work in the prevailing historical interpretation of Nazism: an "unwitting revisionism" ensuant upon the historian's urge to specification and specialization. These otherwise laudable professional tendencies work at cross-purposes with their overall intent by diminishing Nazism's thrust toward radical totalization and uniformity. Some recent interpretations of Nazism thus represent an antinomy or "mismatch" in historical reason, showing themselves to be hapless instances of the categorical difference between "the modalities of contemporary existence and historical events" (see below, p. 356). Krieger's approach resists the attenuation of scaling-down of the total claims and actions of Nazism: its inevitable "graying" in time should not entail any blanching or muting of its central dynamic. In Krieger's view, Nazism remains a "monstrous provocation" that compels the question, "What is the meaning of a historically resurrected integral Nazism for ages outside its epoch?" (see below, p. 359). It is an urgent question that Krieger's terse formulation will remain in the forefront of historical attention precisely because it takes seriously the passage of time and the inevitable transformation of meaning in history.

Leonard Krieger's style of history requires active, parallel thinking on the part of the reader, but it repays the effort with interest to spare. Complexity of detail and mordant wit are woven together with an urge to higher order. He obviously agrees with Leibniz's dictum: "as much variety as possible, but with the greatest order possible." He does not shrink from instancing "two levels of reality, doubly related." The observant reader gets a return on this extra investment in the text. For Krieger also inclines to what he calls the "advantages of a bargain rate— the understanding of two types at the cost of only one study" (see below, p. 245, 104). In order to trace relations that are important but indistinct for their lack of contrast, he freely employs "the shuttling devices that are the stock in trade of the historian to move quickly back and forth between the universal and the unique, each time narrowing the gap between them (see below, p. 248).

Krieger keeps his readers alert to the constitutive and often unrecognized role of language and categories in all thinking, including historical thinking. In this vein he observes that "connections [often] become perceptible through pejoratives." Likewise he uses the difference between subjunctive and indicative moods in grammar to show shifts in Kant's thinking. He distinguishes between the "adjectival" (derivative or dependent) and "substantive" (self-sufficient) stages of Sartre's existentialism. But he does not allow the latent networking effect of language itself to carry off his account into spirals of reflexive theoretical jargon. He is often terse and direct: "Marx came to economics via the proletariat and not the other way around." Even subtly implicated points are conveyed with brisk economy: "The historian does not so much treat of unique events as treat uniquely of events. . . . History differs from the other disciplines in having an approach and not an area of its own" (see below, p. 152).

There are passages of wry humor, used to press and enlarge a fundamental issue. With his last *Critique of Judgment* Kant is said to "add a wing" to nature to augment his previous systematic critiques. In a similarly droll avian image, Hegel is said to be given to "nocturnal bird-watching for Minerva's old owl." Krieger colorfully contrasts the "grain-of-sand" and "atmospheric" approaches in historiography, a figurative contrast more compelling than older descriptions of "lumpers and splitters," or "hedgehogs and foxes." He compares the history of ideas to "travel in outer space, where deflections of a small degree get magnified into fateful discrepancies covering vast distances." In matters of interpretation he is obviously no slave of authorial intention or self-ascription. He finds that we can validly interpret an idea, text, or policy differently from the intentions and ascriptions of its progenitors: "Never, in short, ask an intellectual figure to classify himself, for we must assume that he knows not what he does" (see below, p. 180). In keeping with this tenet the relation of existentialism and historicism can be succinctly stated as one of "rival siblings, spawned in the same cultural matrix" (see below, p. 103). As few other historians, Krieger is capable of evocative flashes of brilliance that mobilize rather than stabilize the thinking of his readers: "When viewed historically an event is less particular than it is in itself, and when used historically a principle is less general than it is in itself" (see below, p. 152).

These matters of style often turn out upon further thinking to be matters of substance, and we can agree with Krieger that style in history is inseparable from philosophy of history. Such has been the stress in much recent theoretical treatment of historiography at the hands of literary theorists. Krieger remains fully aware of this rhetorical dimension of the historian's craft: such awareness, for example, prompts his pithy observation that Marx's "lifelong addiction to the rhetorical converse [was] his way of placing what he considered to be the false diversions from existence back within the sphere of existence." In Krieger's view, style in history is hardly an extraneous embellishment but rather the very "weave" of the historian's network.

This being acknowledged, it would be a natural and intriguing, if also difficult, undertaking to extract Krieger's own philosophy of history from his style, or from his account of others' style and weave of categories. He himself did this with Ranke, with the result that the style and substance of his history come into clearer and more expansive focus. But for Krieger, this would be a daunting task. Directly autobiographical digressions are few and far between in these pages. Aside from brief remarks in prefaces and epilogues, he has provided no explicit, sustained account of his own substantive philosophy of history, if indeed he can be said to have one in the careful terms he sets out. Such a philosophy of history remains tacitly vested in his writing and the reader will have to perform an added reflection to summon it forth.

Here it must suffice to say that his philosophical premises are pluralistic and his political convictions unswervingly liberal. While alert to the ethical dimension of all historical thinking, he is not given to moralizing, in keeping with the deliberate restraint of his subject Pufendorf: "If the moral is to be drawn from history, the reader must supply what the historian does not venture to write" (see below, p. 237). Without resorting to platonic strap-hangers, he clearly wants to save historism as an ingredient of our common heritage from the vitiating coils of historical relativism and nihilism. Freedom, or more specifically, human autonomy remains fixed at the center of his concern, but this freedom is a "tensile" autonomy that always makes its appearance within a social foreground and a historical background. Human reason, as Krieger employs it and traces it, does not play favorites by stacking decks left or right, for either sheer affirmation or sheer negation of what exists.

He does not predispose the tensions in his historical writing to one side or the other. He strives for strong conceptual coherence on the assumption that such coherence is a goal worth striving for; yet at the same time he underscores what thereby inevitably eludes our clumsy nets of conceptualization. "Recalcitrant" is a term which appears often on these pages. He presents ideas and events according to broad schema of phases, zones, types, and orbits, but such demarcations serve as guideposts, not votary monuments or prophetic zodiacs.

Most emphatically, Krieger does not seal off the domains that have recently been held to be self-contained "systems," "modes of discourse," "meta-narratives," or hidden "agencies." He acknowledges but does not hypostatize the gaps between idea and actuality, structure and event, language and experience. Although attentive to the reception and trans-formation of ideas, he has little use for the sorts of wrenching "creative anachronism" and farfetched re-contexualization now practiced under the historian's newfangled semi-poetic license. He values fidelity to the entirety of the text and to the integrity of time and place. He views so-cial theory along with philosophy of history as inescapable, but con-stantly in need of reality checks and even "theory checks" by means of contending theories.

There is a palpable Kantian-Weberian rigor (and tension) in Krieger's views: the autonomy of persons (as well as disciplines) is often secured at the cost of antinomies in thought and action. He finds it especially neces-sary in historical inquiry to remain alert to "the vagaries of assumptions which in any case determine our judgment even of the empirical fact." He emphasizes a crucial gap between the stability of discrete general ideas and the transitive pattern of particular actions undertaken in their name. Reigning ideas do not precede or trail after some "really real" bedrock of reality, nor do they hold uncontested sway over the course of events, at least not for long. Ideas are a dynamic human force among (and around) other forces, but they do not timelessly enclose or superintend them. He finds the conjunction of practical interests and loftier ideals to be an espe-cially potent mix in history, one that can rapidly rupture or even suddenly explode its conventional and institutional vessels: "This combination of the visible and invisible has ever functioned as the most explosive com-bination for human activity."[3] Historical thinking must remain adept at shifting bifocally between perspectives of the shorter and longer term.

Krieger has long defended the autonomy of historical inquiry, but he has also stressed its hybrid and "hyphenated" character. His focus upon "idea and event" does not confine history to a closed conceptual court-yard bounded by hard data and rigid categories, for genuine historical thinking must reach across to other disciplines, especially in order to fathom the "slow-moving, or even unmoving structural aspects of an

3. Krieger, "Nationalism in America," in *Amerikanische Gelehrtenwoche, 19–24 Juni 1961* (Munich, 1962), 146.

age, which are expressed in relationships rather than actions" (see below, p. 150). These crucial structural relations are not always expressed in ideas—nor, for that matter, are they necessarily evident in events.

Krieger argues that the exigencies of the present have a direct and often unrecognized role in stimulating our historical sense, but he does not take this condition as a warrant for all-out presentism. He insists on critically sorting out hindsight from foresight, with the valuable reminder that "in intellectual as in other kinds of history, men have acted in response to their own concerns rather than to the questions that historians would later ask of them" (see below, p. 251). He certainly does not hold that the latest historical interpretation (his own included) is necessarily the best. Whether as written or lived, in Krieger's vigilant sense the historical past remains more than merely the prehistory of ourselves and our view of things.

Krieger concluded his recent book *Time's Reasons* with a point about the present-day "un-historical" climate of thought and opinion. This passage bears repeating here, for it stresses the urgency of professing history properly without the hysterical sense of "high" cultural crisis that has beclouded this question: "Paradoxically, the less history is worth in the present, the more indispensable is its view of the past because we continue to believe that knowledge of the past is required for living in the present and because history was once highly regarded in the past. But, for both reasons—that is, the kind of past knowledge that is now useful and the ground for history's earlier popularity—it is the specific embodiment of life's coherence that matters rather than the usefulness of past facts. It is to the rehabilitation of historical coherence that the proposals for the revitalization of history must be addressed."[4] Where and when historical thinking becomes a genuinely vital matter— in being challenged for the high office of conveying moral, civic, and cultural values—there Krieger's perspective shows its true worth, in its openness as well as its firm foundations.

The historically conscious individual does not readily forget his debts to others. This applied in full measure to Leonard Krieger himself, who made clear his gratitude to teachers, colleagues, and students over the years. He always remained especially committed to the spirit of Hajo Holborn. Krieger was among a remarkable cluster of students of Holborn's at Yale University, of whom a large number went on to become leading lights in their respective fields. What Krieger said of

---

4. *Time's Reasons: Philosophies of History Old and New,* (Chicago, 1989), 171.

Holborn's influence and perspective can certainly be applied to Krieger himself: "He saw every human reality stereotypically, bearing a twofold truth: the truth of its meaning—that is, of what its relation with other realities made it; and the truth of its existence—that is, of what it was inimitably in itself."[5]

Such conjoined perspectives—and compound intellectual debts— have in their turn been felt by Krieger's own students over the years, who have benefited from the stimulating, refining force of his intellect and person. As teacher, historian, and thinker, he cultivated the search for autonomy in his students, just as he has traced its larger story within the vicissitudes of the past. In manifold ways Leonard Krieger bore witness to the truth stated best in his own words: "By its very nature, history is not the mere memory of humanity but the reformation of its memory" (see below, p. 156).

Michael Ermarth

5. From Krieger's introduction to *The Responsibility of Power: Historical Essays in Honor of Hajo Holborn,* eds. Leonard Krieger and Fritz Stern (Garden City, New York, 1967), 1–2.

1 HISTORY OF IDEAS

History must be true and it must make sense.
From the Epilogue to *Time's Reasons*.

1 Stages in the History of Political Freedom

Recent writing on the nature of freedom has served to underline a crucial gap in our academic experience. This writing testifies to progress along three lines. First—and most obvious—the concept of freedom has been modernized by its explication in terms of contemporary institutions.[1] Second, as an antidote to proliferation a new approach to the problem has been pioneered in the construction of typologies of freedom.[2] Finally, the awareness of the variety in the concepts of freedom has been paralleled for the practice of freedom by the consideration of the whole tumultuous history of Western man as the involved story of embodied freedom.[3] What is missing is the relating of the concepts to the actions of freedom. To be sure, this relation has frequently been established for particular notions of freedom. Many of the philosophical analyses—especially recent ones like pragmatic and existentialist—have been predicated on actualities of human behavior, and, on the other hand, many of the classic histories of freedom—Hegel, Bury, Ruggiero, and Laski, to list some ill-assorted samples—have traced the real development of a definite kind of freedom. What we do not yet have, however, is the connection between the recently emphasized variety in our concepts of freedom and the variety of our historical experience. Adler's *Idea of Freedom* has neither a practical nor an historical dimension, while Shotwell's *Long Way to Freedom* lacks a conceptual framework.

What follows is an attempt to use history to join theory with practice and to provide genetic continuity between the varieties of freedom. Such history must be both schematic and thematic: it must organize the historical manifold into categories if this manifold is to be made fruitful for concepts, and these categories must form a connected series through

1. Thus Paul Weiss, *Man's Freedom* (1950); Ernst Cassirer, *Determinism and Indeterminism in Modern Physics* (1956); Frank Knight, *Freedom and Reform* (1967); Karl Mannheim, *Freedom Power, and Democratic Planning* (1950); Christian Bay, *The Structure of Freedom* (1959). See also the valuable bibliography of recent anthologies on the idea of freedom in Mortimer J. Adler, *The Idea of Freedom* (1958), pp. 652–658.
2. See Adler, *Idea of Freedom* and Isaiah Berlin, *Two Concepts of Liberty* (1959).
3. James T. Shotwell, *The Long Way to Freedom* (1960).

First published in *Liberty: Nomos IV* (Yearbook of the American Society for Political and Legal Philosophy), ed. Carl J. Friedrich (New York: Atherton Press, 1962), 1–28.

3

the ages if the varieties of freedom are to have a developmental logic. Moreover, if the categories are to perform their synthetic function they must be formal concepts whose contents are the resultants of the total historical material organized for its bearing upon the area defined by the concepts.

The focus will be on the political field of freedom, because, in Western history, politics has been the most constant barometer of the civilization: more than any other single field of activity it has provided the central arena wherein impulses from the whole range of human interests have crystallized into perceptible and commensurable forms. The basic categories of this field are furnished by the concepts of liberty and order: the nature of the freedom characteristic for each age can be assessed through the kinds of liberty and order that are existent and esteemed and through the prevalent relationship between the two poles; the process of freedom may be reconstructed through the sequence of these assessments.

Obviously such an essay is too ambitious to be definitive. All synthetic judgments in history do violence to particulars, and given the unevenness of one man's knowledge, the tenuous line between the approximate and the arbitrary may well be breached for any single judgment. Again, the ultimate use of the historical process of freedom for a final definition of freedom must be left to the philosophers. What will be attempted here is simply a model for the reconstruction of historical experience into forms usable for general knowledge.

The initial problem is posed by the necessity of finding a working definition of essential terms that will function as a criterion of relevance without stacking the cards a priori. With all due recognition that no definition of freedom can be entirely neutral, we can probably strike a satisfactory balance between the exclusiveness required of any theme and the inclusiveness required of any historical treatment if we consider freedom to be simply the participation in the control over the conditions of one's own living. Such a definition posits the individual person as the locus, activity as the mode, and autonomy as the status, but it is flexible enough to permit of degrees, to admit of either intellectual or practical control, and to avoid the thorny problem of freedom as means or end. Political freedom in its generic sense, accordingly, will mean participation in the control over the common external conditions of one's living. In this sense it includes both civil liberty, which refers to individual control over such conditions, and political liberty (i.e., political freedom in the narrow sense), which refers to participation in the common control over such conditions. Juxtaposed with generic political freedom are personal freedom, which refers to the individual control over conditions that are both internal and particular, and social freedom, which refers to participation in a common control over conditions that are either internal or particular. The distinction between "common" and "particular" is obvious, but the distinction between "external" and "internal" conditions is not. External conditions are those situations which relate the area of freedom to the areas of nonfreedom; internal conditions are those situations that relate different loci or aspects of freedom to one another.

Finally, we must specify conventional definitions for a pair of concepts which have had a constant relationship with political freedom throughout its history. *Authority* is participation in the control over the conditions of another's living. *Order* lies between authority and freedom and refers to the organization of the conditions of living into some kind of system or unity, whether rational or existential.

When freedom is considered as an historical theme, such definitions can be multiplied indefinitely. What has been selected for discussion here should be viewed as representative types of freedom, and they will be treated for the two facets of meaning toward which history can make a contribution: the process through which the interaction of different kinds of particular activities generates a representative concept of freedom, and the temporal logic involved in the succession of such concepts.

I

Let us take our initial stand on a familiar promontory—the period around the beginning of the sixteenth century which is usually adjudged to introduce the modern era. This is not to say that Western man was unconcerned with the assertion of his freedom in the classical and medieval periods: in one form or another, the value of freedom was a constituent of the Greek city-states, the Roman Republic, and the law of the Empire; and later it entered into the tribal structure, the feudal arrangements, and the municipal constitutions that traversed the medieval period. Yet, the context of freedom which has characterized the modern era is so different in kind from what went before that only it seems directly relevant to our own concern. Free general conditions distinguish the modern experience and provide analytic support for the instinctive tendency to begin the story with the Renaissance and the Reformation. First, it is only from this point in time that freedom became a continuing rather than an occasional issue in Western history. Second, it was only then that freedom became a dynamic rather than a stabilizing force—i.e., that it was directed toward the extension rather than the preservation of control. Third, it was then that the institutional framework of freedom moved from the local to the regional level of organization. This shift implied more than a mere change of setting, for it worked a mutation in the existential status of freedom. The visual and personal connections which had made freedom, authority, and security natural adjuncts of a controllable local order were sprung, and gave way to the distant and abstract relations within which areas of control must be established. Fourth, then, the Renaissance and the Reformation mark the beginning of the process in which freedom develops into a distinct value and institutions which embody it into autonomous bodies. Fifth, they mark the beginning of the process of multiplying the agents of temporal freedom. Freedom in the abstract had certainly been recognized for all humanity long previously, but the exercise of freedom had been recognized only for identifiable representative or authoritative individuals. By questioning the former loci of freedom, the protagonists of Renaissance and Reformation initiated the expansion of the figurative "people" to an ever greater inclusion of the anonymous individuals constituting the literal people.

If, then, we take our stand at the Renaissance and Reformation as the starting points of the continuous process of freedom in these senses, the prior development of freedom in the West takes the form of assorted discrete traditions among which men picked and chose until around the middle of the seventeenth century. For the characteristic feature of the century and a half, the primary movements of which can be subsumed under these two general labels, was a dissolution of the system or the general order of institutions and traditions which yet left these institutions and traditions themselves still vital. From this vantage point, the familiar debate about the new and the old in the Renaissance and the Reformation, with its conflicting implications for the liberal or authoritarian nature of these movements, can be resolved into the interpretation that men sought a new ordering of the old ingredients and that their freedom was extended to the limited extent that they could choose among the alternative authorities to whom they would owe their primary obedience.

The traditions which continued to supply the materials for public life during this period were myriad, but two from classical antiquity and three from the middle ages may be singled out as particularly relevant to the history of human freedom.

From classical antiquity:

1. *The city-state tradition*. The main emphasis here was on the asso-

ciation of the freedom of the citizen with the independence and power of the local community in which he was a participant. Primary redounded to political freedom in the narrow sense, but this took two variant forms: democracy on the Athenian model, in which individuals were identified as equal members of the community, and mixed government on the Roman model, in which independent authority became the function of mutual freedom and political rights served to commit the citizens to loyalty vis-à-vis a community conceived as more than the sum of its parts. In either form, the individual was integrated into collective freedom.

2. *The tradition of the higher law.* The chief vehicles of this tradition were Roman Stoicism for the theory and the Roman Law for the practice of legislation. The emphasis here was on personal and civil rather than political freedom. In its origins this tradition can be traced back to Plato and Aristotle who, writing during the decline of the Greek city-state, questioned the natural coherence of individual and collective freedom and imposed a higher moral and metaphysical goal upon individual and collectivity alike. The Romans ultimately dissociated the goal from the city-state and gave it the form of law; in this form it was mediated to the sixteenth century. It prescribed private rights but subordinated them to social and political responsibilities. Recognizably, this is the origin of the "older" natural law whose main functions were to separate the private sphere from the public, to define private freedom as voluntary endorsement of the moral law and public freedom as the right to be governed well, to prescribe policies rather than institutions, and to guarantee private freedom by the autolimitation of the public powers.

What early modern man received from classical civilization, then, were two separate traditions: a tradition of political freedom with a local base and with no guarantee of private freedom, and a tradition of private freedom with a universal base with no guarantee of political freedom. Both traditions were perpetuated as such through the middle ages, in the shape of the commune and Christian theology; but medieval men sought also to bridge the local and the universal, and in the process they created practices and ideas which were to remain in the sixteenth and seventeenth centuries as an additional set of traditions.

3. *The tradition of chartered freedom.* The function of this tradition may be called the universalization of localism. Its origins lay in the necessity of recognizing local rights along both horizontal and vertical axes relative to the classical urban locus—that is, both in the fragmented units of a ruralized society and on the supralocal levels of politi-

cal organization which the dispersion of the older local centers of population and power made essential. The complex of chartered freedoms, then, was the response to the paradoxical situation in which the diffusion of local power, through a variety of rural and urban authorities, called for the construction of territorial, national, and even universal arrangements of order which would yet acknowledge the local bases of authority. The essence of chartered freedom was its special, or bilateral, character. This particularity had two functions: it preserved the local conditions of freedom through a series of parallel and ascending arrangements, and it broke down the distinction between freedom and authority by defining freedom in terms of authority. Bred by circumstances which confirmed local variety, corporate endeavor, and the demand for tangible order, freedom became the function either of the social authority of the group or of a political immunity which grounded the liberty from superior authority in the authority assumed over inferiors. The institutions of chartered freedom, then, bequeathed a tradition of myriad rights, infinitely variable in degree and in kind, extending indiscriminately across the religious, social, economic, and political interests of men, with the one common denominator that the variety of liberties made sense only as a hierarchy of authorities.

4. *The tradition of the divine order.* If the medieval experience built out and up from the local tradition of the city-state, it also built out and down from the universal tradition of the higher law. Not only did the Christian dispensation add substance and sanction to the classical tenet of a rational *telos,* but it institutionalized universalism. The Holy Roman Empire, to be sure, was never a reality as an institutional authority, but the Church was, and its power spread in conjunction with the attenuation of the Empire. The diffusion of clerical offices and prescriptions established the fundamental coherence among the variety of local institutions and, since men find meaning in unity, the manifestations of a single divine order supplied a basic mold for the medieval tendency to conceive of their liberties as claims to place in the hierarchy of authority. The role of the Church in this respect was to endow particular authorities with the validity of a general system.

5. *The tradition of spiritual individualism.* Contrapuntal to its authoritarian function, the Church developed a set of attitudes and practices which stemmed from the faith in the integrity of the individual soul before God. This tradition not only postulated, for the pure realm of spirit, the ultimate independence of the individual from all authority, secular and clerical alike, but also influenced the temporal realm, albeit in a highly diffracted form, by sponsoring the division of that realm

among the various autonomous institutions which embodied the integrity of the various interests of man. The most obvious expression of this tradition was the assertion of independence by the Church as the prime guardian of man's spiritual sovereignty vis-à-vis political authority, but for the full extent of the tradition it should be realized that every social and economic institution made a similar claim for activities authorized by God for the soul's own progress toward salvation. The tradition, in this general form, had two effects: it lent validity to the actual conflict of authorities with one another, and particularly with those who sought to direct the supreme system of authorities; and it established a pattern of freedom which consisted in the choice among authorities.

However different their inspirations and their forms of expression, the Renaissance and the Reformation may be considered jointly as breaking points for the tensions embodied in these traditions, and the history of the century and a half which these labels cover may be regarded, consequently, as essentially a series of struggles among particular authorities for domination over the general order of authorities. Liberal impulses entered powerfully into the process, to be sure, but what is more important is the role of the traditions in channeling these impulses into the support of one or another authority. For when the five traditions are taken together it becomes apparent that their chief function was to make authority represent freedom and that their chief means was to validate a plurality of representative authorities. The breaking point came when the demands for a supralocal scope for freedom and an infrauniversal center for authority met and destroyed the consensus which was grounded precisely in the conjunction of the local and the universal.

Superficial impressions notwithstanding, the Renaissance is less important than the Reformation for the history of political freedom. Its chief contribution may be summed up as the revitalization of the classical traditions—city-state and Roman law—only to the point at which they could be juxtaposed with the still vital medieval traditions. The Italian city-states ran through the cycle familiar to the local republics of antiquity, with the medieval guilds replacing the ancient clans as the primary organization of a citizenry which continued to form a small minority of the total population. The use of the labels "Guelf" and "Ghibelline" long past the period in which they had substantive political meaning testified to the role which Christian universalism continued to play as the repository of ultimate political values. In the north, the chief political effect of the Renaissance was transmitted by jurists who utilized the reinterpretation of the Roman law in "the French mode" to establish the ecclesiastical independence and secular superiority of territorial rulers vis-à-vis church and feudality without rejecting the legitimate functions of either. For both the southern and the northern cases, the result was rather to rearrange the hierarchy of authorities, hallowed by tradition, within an accepted framework of order, than to essay new functions for political freedom. The political relations of the Renaissance are perhaps most clearly articulated in its theories, which exhibit a common pattern through all the differences of substance. The pattern reveals an uneasy combination of traditions brought to tension by the pressure of reality and resolved or evaded through the appeal to regional authority. Classic republicanism and mirror-of-princes lay unresolved in the Italian humanists and in Erasmus. The Platonically modelled local Utopia remains isolated in the thought and activity of that pious royal chancellor Sir Thomas More. Civic republican virtue and the perception of princely power could not be reconciled by a Guicciardini. Pioneers like Machiavelli and Bodin could fight their way out of this complex of traditions only by an appeal to a princely savior, whereas Rabelais and Montaigne resolved their simultaneous addiction to humanistic libertinism and Christian piety through their voluntary subjection to the territorial political order.

During the Renaissance, men did indeed break through to new expressions of human freedom, but not in the realm of politics. We may say only that the conflicts of authorities which reflected the equalization of the older traditions of subordinate freedom in the new arena of a regionally organized society provided the tensile political and social context out of which the new cultural freedom sprang.

The Reformation was spawned by the same constellation of traditions and real pressures, and it exhibited the same fundamental tendency to channel men's demands into the relations of plural authorities, but where the Renaissance men juxtaposed authorities and could only appeal for a *de facto* resolution of their incompatible claims, the religious movements of the Reformation developed their claims into conflicting systems of authority and ultimately broke through the whole over-arching framework of order which had encompassed them. The validity of the respective claims to religious liberty by the various confessions is irrelevant to the theme of political freedom in this period, for the main effort of each major cult went into the construction of its own solitary religio-political system of authority. The role of temporal freedom within each system remained unchanged. What was new in temporal freedom was the possibility of choosing the true religio-political order from a plurality of such orders, and this affected political freedom only in the pragmatic context of conferring a right of opposition against a political authority aligned in an opposing system of order— not to the end of a permanent recognition of political rights but to the end of establishing an alternative authority. The assumption of leadership by princes, aristocracies, and oligarchies in the external struggles of all the major parties of the religious movements manifests the practical side of this development; the political conservatism of both the first-generation reformers and the later monarchomachs represents the theoretical side. If it be objected that there existed on the left wing of the Reformation spectrum groupings like the sectaries and individual spiritualists who were antiauthoritarian, the objection serves only to confirm the thesis, for these were precisely the groups that were most indifferent to politics.

Equally irrelevant were the social and political convulsions that took on a religious coloration and were merged into the early stages of the Reformation in Germany, Switzerland, France, and the Netherlands. Not only were the popular agents of these movements—lower nobility, peasants, artisans—essentially conservative or even reactionary in their goals, but in the course of the historical process of the Reformation these popular elements were strained out. Either they signed on as clients of established subordinate or superior authorities or they were smashed by these authorities. "World history is a world court of judgment."

To conclude. From the middle of the fifteenth to the middle of the seventeenth century, men continued, as they had for centuries, to prosecute their claims in the name of traditions which prescribed the rightful exercise of authority and defined their liberties as specifiable shares in the chain of authorities. Fundamentally, freedom continued to be conceived as the capacity to realize a pre-established good. But with the organization of the formerly diffuse and unfocused frictions into the definite conflicts denoted by the labels Renaissance and Reformation, two innovations developed important specifications of freedom within the persistent general meaning of the term. First, the shift from the vague coherence to the direct opposition of traditions added a range of choice to the function of freedom. When choice had lain simply between an organic good and a disorganized evil, freedom had been attributed not to the act of choice but to the result of it—that is, freedom was a function of the good. But with the erection of rival systems of goods, a *de facto* element of choice was added to the idea of freedom, and therewith a primitive beginning was made in the process which led to the consideration of freedom as the quality of an act rather than of a condition. Second, both the Renaissance and the Reformation supported the new status of their authorities by proclaiming far more emphatically than previously the freedom of the spirit as the function of right choice, and if this emphasis had no direct temporal extension, it did supply a general foundation for particular chartered liberties with the indirect effect of universalizing the internal limitations upon authority to match the long-standing universal sanction of its power.

Both departures, limited as they were in this period, were to develop in the next era.

II

The second stage in the history of modern political freedom, which extended from the middle of the seventeenth to the middle of the eighteenth century, can be labeled "the generalization of subordinate freedom." Out of the welter of struggling particular orders, each claiming universal validity, there emerged in practice and in theory a single general order, still exalting authority as the prime desideratum but grounded now in the recognized general rights of all individuals. The process through which this order was established witnessed a thorough reorganization of man's cosmos. The scheme which had characterized the first stage was organized vertically into a plurality of religio-politico-social orders, each of which linked heaven at the top and ordinary individual humans at the bottom in a particular dispensation with a universal mission. Since conflict and stalemate among the orders had blunted the universal claims of each and proved subversive of the general order which was the common goal, the goal was achieved by organizing the cosmos along the other dimension. Horizontal lines of division were drawn through all the vertical orders, separating the political sphere out from the particular religious dispensations at the one end and from particular social liberties and privileges at the other. So delimited, politics was assigned the function of general order as such; particular religious and social ends became ancillary to this prime function, and only those aspects of church and society that were relevant to communal order were relevant to the exercise of political force. Within the political arena, then, the old vertical lines of religious and social division were attenuated; they were subordinated to common membership in the political community, and they were confirmed only insofar as they were deemed contingent contributors to the order of the community. The total conflict between the older composite vertical orders gave way to limited conflicts between the newer specialized political orders in the name, now, not of God, but of security; but since these wars of states were more intermittent and more external to the lives of ordinary men than the former struggles, they were accepted as abusive of rather than inherent in the new system. The institution which incorporated this new independence of the political function was the sovereign state, and the emphasis during this period on the expanding powers of the sovereign organ within the state—usually, although not necessarily, an absolute monarch—testified to the preoccupation of the age with the establishment of a commonly accepted authority as the indispensable agency of the new order.

Given the concern for order and the emphasis upon authority, the role of political freedom during this period continued to be a subordinate one, but in three important ways its relationship to authority and, consequently, its internal meaning underwent a decisive change.

In the first place, with the weakening of the specific religious and feudal bases of rulership—i.e., the weakening of the external relations of politics—the validation of political power was attributed to the original political rights of the governed themselves—i.e., to the internal relations of politics. Concomitant with the intellectual tendency of the age to deny substantial forms and to engage generals directly with particulars, the dominant political ideas postulated individual humans rather than corporate groups as the bearers of these elemental rights, and therewith the older school of natural law gave way to the new school of natural rights.

Second, the older local integration of freedom and authority, which had associated liberty from a higher power with the exercise of authority, through corporate participation or subordinate magistracy, over lower powers, gave way to the radical distinction between freedom as such and authority as such.

Third, the effect of the new relationship with authority was to generalize the idea of freedom. The standard of the chartered freedom fell, and with it the particularized character of freedom, both in the sense of the variable attribution to it to discrete groups and in the sense of the variable kinds of freedom granted in each charter. Freedom now became general in the sense that it originally redounded to all men alike and in the sense that it was applicable—albeit not applied—to all spheres. The restrictions upon freedom were certainly far-reaching in this authoritarian age, but they were no longer deemed special restrictions inherent in each liberty. Rather, they were general restrictions imposed from the outside by an authority enforcing the general rules of a political order. To be sure, these restrictions varied in intensity with the area of freedom—absorbing frequently the whole of political freedom and proportionately lesser amounts of civil and personal liberties—but this was only the specific application of general laws which had a general freedom as their counterpart.

The new role of political freedom is readily apparent in the political theories of the period, for, starting with Hobbes and running through the jurists and publicists of the early Enlightenment, the new school of natural law, which emphasized the derivation of authority from the free rational faculty of individual men, supplied the ascendant categories of formal political thinking. But it is more difficult to recognize the new relations in political practice, since monarchical absolutism, the popular predilection for ideas of divine right, and the persistence of feudal survivals were all standard for the age. The English revolutions did provide a real handle for the theorists, but even with these events in mind it cannot be denied that the categorizing of experience in terms of the prevalent rationalism made for a distortion of political reality in political ideas. Yet the fact remains that what the theorists made categorical were the implications of a real change in the political order of the West which gradually developed these implications in action. The overt agents scarcely changed, but their fundamental relationship did. From a plurality of authorities striving for unity there developed a unified authority seeking to accommodate plurality. This accommodation could take place only on an expanded basis of political action which recognized the political relevance of all subjects and postulated direct and reciprocal connections between them and the sovereign. The extension of mercantilist policies from the struggle to control existing corporate institutions to the direct stimulation and regulation of individual entrepreneurs is characteristic. Ostensibly, to be sure, what were taken into account were the interests rather than the rights of the collectivity of subjects, but even practicing statesmen came in time to root these interests in an original freedom. The enlightened absolutism, which became the representative form of monarchy toward the end of the period, registered this recognition. There has been dispute over the validity of the term "enlightened absolutism" if "enlightened" be defined as liberal or benevolent, but there can be no dispute over the term if it be taken as the growing consciousness in rulers of their service function and of the ultimate grounding of this function in an original right of those for whom the service was performed.

The period of absolutism presents the paradoxical picture of a political freedom that had diminished in quantity and increased in status. From a set of bilateral relationships in which political freedom had been enmeshed with sundry other liberties and declared valid only in the degree appropriate to particular local conditions, it was now reduced to a single act; but as such it was declared to be that distinct aspect of a general system of freedom whose voluntary surrender guaranteed the rest. Since men had to account for a kind of political freedom that contained both a constituent act and the subsequent attribution of the effects of the act to the definition of an irrevocable authority, another dimension was added to the meaning of freedom. Freedom within the scope of political society continued to consist in the realization of the good— i.e., voluntary obedience to law—but for the original act of political freedom and for those civil liberties that lay outside the political relationship, the notion of freedom as the natural capacity to follow one's own bent was also received as valid. Both of these meanings are in Hobbes, Spinoza, and Locke, who manifest the political form of the ambivalence that inheres in the general problem of ethical freedom patent during the Enlightenment from Leibniz to Voltaire. In politics as in ethics a temporary bridge was constructed across the meanings of freedom in the shape of locating freedom in a reason that was homogeneous for the individual, nature, and society and that integrated the individual's control over his own actions into the intellectual acknowledgment of the natural and social processes incumbent upon him.

III

The crowded and tortuous revolutionary era that reached from around the middle of the eighteenth century to the closing decades of the nineteenth was, for the theme of political freedom, a simple one. Its dominant motif was the attempt to organize an order of general freedom. The period marked the crucial turn in the history of the West, for it witnessed the development of freedom from a subordinate to a dominant value. Whereas freedom had been a postulate of order, order now became a condition of freedom. The rupture of the age-old relationship between freedom and authority was produced by the increment of political freedom in the narrow sense—defined variously as constitutional or democratic freedom but requiring in either case the participation of the governed in government by right—which was now added to the cognizance of personal and civil liberty. For this addition meant not simply the inclusion of another kind of freedom but the development from the postulate of a general freedom to an explicit system of general freedom. Where the realm of politics had been an authoritarian order guaranteeing nonpolitical freedom, the attribution of state law to consent (viz. Kant) now subjected political and nonpolitical realms alike to the requirements of freedom. It was precisely this homogenization of freedom, brought to completion by the synthesis of political with civil rights, that elevated freedom into an independent universal.

Abstract as this process seems in its categorical formulation, it formed the central thread in the concrete political practice of the age. Not, of course, that men were interested only in the acquisition of constitutional rights to individual personal and civil liberty and to participation in the sovereign authority. Not only did authoritative monarchies survive through the period, with the active support of rejuvenated aristocracies and the passive support of the majority, but socialist and communist movements took their rise with their claims to a social reorganization that transcended both civil and political rights. But if constitutional claims were not exclusive, they were authoritative. In part, this primary status corresponded to the quantitative bulk of political liberals and their middle-class backers in the public conflicts of the era, but more important was the qualitative function of this numerical weight in establishing the constitutional mold which shaped in its own image the diverse claims of the respective groupings.

The tone was set early in the period, in the last third of the eighteenth century, by French aristocrats and American moderates: to defend their privileges, the former shifted their position from feudal exemption to political participation in a limited monarchy, whereas the latter moved from the acceptance of a *de facto* autonomy to the demand for consent in tax legislation. And so it went throughout the period. Monarchs—and conservatives, generally—tended to shift the basis of their authority from the legitimacy and the serviceability of their prescriptive order to their leadership of a nation that was constituted by the rights and values of the people. Again, when socialists were not utopian, the cynosure of their struggles was political democracy: however vague or explicit their collectivist goals, Chartists, Karl Marx, Ferdinand Lassalle, and the British Lib-Labs carried through the nineteenth century the postponement of the social claim in favor of the immediate concentration on the libertarian political constitution.

But the most telling evidence in support of the actual enthronement of freedom as a system is furnished by the two main political processes of the period: the dismantling of absolutism and the stabilization of revolutions. The struggles against absolutism all developed from particular claims upon authority to a general attack upon the primacy of authority as such, as the remnants of the old chartered freedoms proved inadequate to sustain the conflict with the generalized authority of the state sovereign and responded by growing into an equally generalized system of freedom. In both of the great upheavals of the eighteenth century—

the American and French Revolutions—the claims of colonies and nobility, respectively, the chartered privileges blossomed into the assertion
of the priority of freedom for the whole society. The revolutions of the
mid-nineteenth century started from particular claims to expanded suffrage or to liberal princely policies and blossomed into changes of system grounded in democratic or national self-determination. In each
case there were two basic reasons for the conflict: the vague definition
of the line between the political and the nonpolitical—i.e., between the
dimension of order and the dimension of rights—and the special confusion of these dimensions caused by the irritating persistence of chartered liberties which, with their commingling of particular political,
social, and civil rights, were always the most obvious points of violation
and consequently were initiators of the struggle over infringed bound-
aries. In the eighteenth century the agents of these liberties tended to
line up on the revolutionary side against encroachments by the sovereign; in the nineteenth century they tended to line up with the sovereign, where their privileges afforded a prime target to the action of
the revolutionaries against the social and civil encroachments of the sovereign. In both cases the only alternative to encroachments by the sovereign lay in the attribution of primacy to a general system of freedom
which would validate political participation in the sovereign power.

Even more striking as evidence of the new priority assigned to the
value of freedom was the tortuous process of the three revolutions that
were the fundamental political events of the age: the American of 1776,
the French of 1789, and the European of 1848. In each case the history
of the revolution can be seen as a series of attempts to construct political
order out of freedom itself. In the American case the solution was to
balance two levels of political freedom—the state and the federal—
against each other. In the French case the temporary solution was to
deposit the problem with that archetype of the uprooted individual,
Napoleon Bonaparte, and follow his embodiment of freedom in a national order. In the European case no solution was found, and the
requirements of political freedom had to be vested with the old authorities for realization in small doses.

Here, then, were the origins of that process which Erich Fromm has
labeled, for the twentieth century, the "escape from freedom," and this
process can hardly be understood if it is not realized that in its
nineteenth-century phase, it was not an "escape" at all but rather an attempt to find an immanent order in freedom which would both permit
its coexistence in the great mass of variegated individuals and endow it
with meaning by providing a unitary direction for its exercise. By the

closing decade of the nineteenth century, a consensus had been reached on the parceling out of discrete areas of freedom to all persons, but there was no such consensus on the scope or the general ordering of these individual realms of freedom. Nationalism and socialism seemed to furnish alternative ordering principles which took individual freedom as their base, but their essential incompatibility with this kind of freedom was revealed in the failure, during this period, of all purely liberal national and socialist movements. The solution everywhere tended to lie in the *de facto* union of the national and the social motifs with the traditional structure of the sovereign state and in the consequent empirical compromises, variable according to circumstances, between the rights of individuals and the powers of modernized authorities. The vogue, in the last third of the century, of representative constitutions which finessed declarations of rights and, indeed, any statements of common ideals, and which simply reflected the existing balance of forces in the society, testified both to the common recognition of functional individual liberties and to the absence of a general system for them.

What was tendency in the political practice of the age became articulated into categorical ideas for its theorists. From Montesquieu through Marx freedom became the central value, and the order of freedom the central task.

The initial position, which prevailed during the revolutionary era of the late eighteenth century, completed the adaptation of the system of natural law as the structure for general freedom by adding the natural rights of political and economic liberty to the already recognized extrapolitical liberties of conscience and of thought. The coincidence of Jefferson, Paine, and Condorcet with the Physiocrats and Adam Smith showed clearly that the new emphasis upon political liberty was simply the capstone of the process which included the material as well as the spiritual world in the sphere of a general freedom.

No sooner had this system been constructed than it became immediately apparent that the natural law which had been appropriate to the relationship of a spiritual freedom to a material authority was inappropriate to the newly claimed general freedom. The juxtaposition of moral freedom with a physically determined nature which plagued Enlightenment thinkers was tolerable, logically inconsistent as it was, as long as it paralleled men's actual experience of free thinking and bound actions. But when Bentham, Rousseau, and Kant faced squarely the implications of general freedom, the old order of natural law was strained to its breaking point.

Doctrines of utility were a characteristic feature of the Enlightenment, and Bentham was representative of his age, both in the importance which he came to attribute to extrapolitical freedom—on the grounds that each individual was the best judge of his own happiness—and in his subsequent development into a political libertarian who viewed democracy as the means of collective control by the individual over the common conditions of this freedom. From the start, however, he rejected the system of natural law and natural rights, which his contemporaries posited as the sanction of utility, on the ground that no general substantive norms were binding.

For both Rousseau and Kant, the agency of integral freedom was not knowledge but the will to action, and for both men the theoretical knowledge of the natural order bore only a negative relation to freedom. They became explicitly concerned with the construction of an order that would be internal to the act of freedom itself. This effort underlay the characteristic doctrines of the general will and the categorical imperative. But neither Rousseau, nor Kant, nor the subsequent doctrines of the nineteenth century can be properly understood if their innovations are taken as a wholesale reprobation of prevalent ideas. Rousseau and Kant agreed with their contemporaries that the integrative activity of freedom was political; they agreed, too, that the form of freedom must be rational and that there is a possibility of integral freedom in the order of nature. In short, after they had broken the old theoretical combination of nature and morality in order to make way for active freedom, they recombined them in a new political way in order to give reality to this active freedom. At the heart of this reinterpretation was the notion of *potency:* nature is susceptible to the action of freedom, and the act of freedom thereby becomes an act of rational self-recovery. Clearly, there is something here of the traditional notion which postulated freedom as the realization of the good, but now the good was not something given. Rather, it was the immanent form which freedom gives to itself.

From these breaks in the Enlightenment pattern the characteristic nineteenth-century lines of thought developed. Common to this thought was the twofold recognition that a higher order was necessary for freedom and that all previous forms of this order were antithetical to freedom. Early utilitarians and early romantics did try to do without such supraindividual principles but, significantly, both proved to be unstable positions.

Representative nineteenth-century thinkers tended to espouse supraindividual principles of nature or society which were recognized to be indifferent to freedom but which were loosened sufficiently to make possible its accommodation. Two alternative schema of such ordering principles became particularly influential. One scheme drew a radical distinction between the orders of nature and of society and redefined freedom as the conformity to one against the other. Thus for Comte and the classical economists freedom consisted in the positive knowledge of necessary natural laws as against the arbitrary constructs and will of men, whereas for John Stuart Mill freedom came to consist, conversely, in social arrangements that would neutralize the natural obstacles to individual freedom. The other scheme, typified by Hegel and Marx, continued the juncture of natural and social orders but turned necessity into dialectic and potency into history. Men's freedom remained partial, in conformity with the self-contradictory order of things, until such time as the rational unity of the order would bring with it the complete freedom of control over it. Obviously, these schema often appeared in mixed form, as Comte's philosophy of history and Marx's scientism attest, and these blendings emphasize their common feature: the persistence of belief in a total order which comprehended man's freedom not simply as a constituent but as a dynamic element.

This nineteenth-century thought both reflected its age and transcended it. In its take-off from individual freedom and its struggles to construct an order in which freedom would be an essential and real ingredient, it underlined the actual aspirations of ordinary men in this period. Those writers, on the one hand, who, like Humboldt, Ricardo, Tocqueville, Mill, and Spencer, held that in the last analysis freedom within the natural and social order could be asserted only as individual spheres of freedom, were particularly in tune with the actual conflicts of the day. On the other hand, however, the insistence by writers like Comte, Mazzini, and Marx on the extension of individual freedom into a social freedom which would simultaneously perfect individual freedom and transform it from an exclusive sphere into a joint co-operation undoubtedly went beyond the consciousness of their age and anticipated the future. The connection with the preoccupations of their contemporaries lay in the homologous relationship of the pioneer social freedom to the prevalent notions of political and national liberties, for both involved the mutual community rather than the reciprocal delimitation of rights. But where the political and national freedoms were generally viewed as guarantees of individual personal and civil liberties and might or might not be deemed as essential extensions of freedom in themselves, the new application of collective freedom to extrapolitical activities endowed it with a prime value, even superior to individual spheres of liberty, which were deemed at best insecure and often oppressive.

The theoretical divergence between the justification of individual economic liberty and the innovation of collective social freedom mirrored the dual impact of the nineteenth-century industrial revolution: by opening the possibilities of economic activity it removed the control over such activity from the stabilizing hold of custom, corporation, and regulation to the enterprise of individuals; at the same time, the requirements of division of labor and concentration of capital placed a new premium on the voluntary co-operation of emancipated individuals. Both these lines were picked up by theorists, but the first remained dominant, during this period, in practice.

Thus the democratic, the national, and the industrial transformations that made up the revolutionary era between the middle of the eighteenth to the end of the nineteenth century were all channeled into two lines of force for the development of freedom: they created systems of liberty which were carved up into discrete spheres of individual autonomy, and they created forms of collective participation which purported to integrate this heterogeneous freedom into the unitary order of society and the universe. But behind these varieties of freedom lay a common assumption about its nature: freedom was deemed an integral status of man, in which the capacity to realize desire and the capacity to realize the good were joined. The medium of this synthesis was the emphasis upon the locus of freedom in the control over the external—i.e., political and social—conditions of life, whether by individual or collective means; the agency of the synthesis was the emphasis upon human *activity*, which served both to remove hindrances to the fulfillment of desire and to make the autonomy of ordinary men the motor of a higher order. The general consensus on the centrality of political freedom rested precisely upon its integration of empirical and moral liberty.

IV

It is precisely the breakdown in the integral status of freedom that has characterized the present stage of its history. This breakdown, during our century, has taken three main forms:

1. The first quarter of the twentieth century witnessed the triumph in political practice of the democratic principle which has persisted in the states of the Atlantic community. This principle has taken a form which combines the divergent theoretical emphases of the previous period—it has exalted political freedom as the instrument of balancing

social control against individual rights. But with the comprehension of individual and collective spheres of freedom within a single political system the unity which was based upon alternative applications of an integral idea has been shredded. It has given way to the concept of concentric levels of freedom, each appropriate to a different area of activity and each postulating a different type of freedom. In short, integral freedom has yielded to a plurality of freedoms.

Originally, in the form that may be epitomized as "Wilsonian," these levels of freedom were deemed compatible with one another. Freedom, under this dispensation, stretched from the sacred sphere of individual immunity through the balance of individuality and collectivity in the liberty of association through co-participation in democracy—i.e., political freedom—and national self-determination vis-à-vis other collectivities. Implicit here was the common acknowledgment that the physical orbits of men's activities had become too intensively involved with one another for them to be delimited into exclusive individual rights-of-way. For such common spheres the exercise of freedom in the sense of a share in the communal enterprise, which might or might not coincide with individual desire, now became not simply a political instrument but an ultimate and valid type of freedom alongside the type of individual sovereignty. But there was more in acceptance of collective freedom than the mere juxtaposition of liberties. Since the actions of collectivities were now deemed wholly a function of freedom, the progressive investment of the individual in all units of the species extending from the person to humanity took on the aspect of a structure of liberties as the model through which freedom finally created its own order.

The model has persisted in the West, but its internal relations have shifted under the grinding pressures of a world depression, recurrent recessions, two hot world wars, and a cold one. In the light of this sobering experience, which revealed the extensible powers of both the free association and the democratic state, the levels of freedom no longer seem to form a continuum. Faith persists in the authenticity of each level as an expression of freedom, but collisions between the levels are now accepted as inherent in the plural system and permanent procedures of compromise and adjustment are now validated as essential to the exercise of freedom.

2. Outside the Atlantic circle of peoples, the unraveling of nineteenth-century integral freedom has taken another form. In the extra-Atlantic societies this integral freedom, based on the autonomous activity of individuals, had been institutionalized only as modifications of conservative regimes, and although their intellectuals had accepted it in theory the col-

lectivist version was more prevalent than elsewhere. Basic to this constellation was the felt necessity of using the fulcrum of order—whether of traditional authority or of revolutionary collectivity—to mobilize the individuals of undeveloped societies—whether for competition with the West or for the realization of the common libertarian ideal. When, in fact, the conservative regimes crumbled under international competition and internal social development, they were already well into the twentieth century, and the subsequent democratic regimes, faced with the intensified national and social pressures of this century upon an inadequately institutionalized liberal base, were short-lived. The postdemocratic fascist and communist regimes based themselves, both in idea and institution, on the concentric levels of freedom which form the common universe of political discourse in our century. But in the totalitarian context the internal relations both among and within the levels of freedom assumed a categorically different form from those in the West. Where the West accepted, under pressure, the permanent conflict of freedoms, the totalitarian regimes which had been established under similar pressures insisted upon the subordination of individual to collective freedom—to the rights of the state, of the nationality, or of the society. In form, this converted the concentric levels of freedom into a hierarchy of freedom, but the effects of the dislocation were much more far-reaching. Since the collective levels of freedom provided the order in freedom, the restriction of individual liberty to co-participation in the collectivity made it simply a constituent of a new kind of order. Individual activities and representative institutions were validated, but only in their function of integrating individuals and groups continuously into a unitary collective will which, therefore, claimed sanction for authority in all the realms of freedom. In this form, then, the integral freedom of the nineteenth century developed into the integral order of the twentieth.

3. The intellectual temper of the twentieth century has contributed its bit to the demise of freedom as an integral status of man. The general rejection of the belief in total processes and total solutions, whether natural or moral, has had, as its logical consequence, the disbelief in total freedom. With the new appreciation of infinity and the new emphasis upon discrete occasions or relations, the notion of the concrete universal has lost its force. The faith in a general order of things, susceptible to activation by universal freedom, has yielded to the picture of plural arrangements contracted for special purposes and each equipped with its own modicum of freedom. In these intellectual circumstances, political freedom has lost its central position in the spectrum of liberties. Its centrality has been grounded in the common assumption of an

ultimate natural or moral order which men could prepare to realize through appropriate external activity. But now, with the assignment of discrete orders as well as liberties to human endeavor, the division between the external and internal has been attenuated, and all the various types and fields of freedom are ranged alongside political freedom in the general problem of creating a meaningful fabric of life. It has been through the vacuum left by the dissolution of meaningful coherence that the tendencies toward levels of hierarchies of freedom has risen.

As a result of these contemporary influences, a dominant conception of freedom, appropriate to our age, has emerged. According to this conception, freedom is a *dimension* of human thought and action. Since the task of men is now deemed the infusion of particular realities with the meaning lost by its suspension from any general coherence, all values, as well as the resistances by men and things, enter into the process. Freedom, then, no longer possesses an exclusive field or enjoys an integral status but, rather, is one dimension of this effort: its substantive character and extent become a function of the particular processes in which it is engaged. But there is a constant that defines the dimension of freedom—creativity. Given the ineluctable pressures that are recognized to crowd in upon man and the consequent obstacles to the consummation of a free thought or a free act, the touchstone of freedom becomes the capacity to endow these pressures and obstacles with a meaning they did not have previously, whether by an actual reworking, a mental reordering, or a rational understanding. In any case, freedom is now a form of endeavor in which the agent exercises control or participates in the exercise of control not by any definite kind of action or knowledge but by contributing a distinctive piece of himself to the world within or around him. Since freedom is the creative dimension of all endeavor, which is now deemed subject to analogous challenges in each of its fields, there is no longer anything distinctive about political freedom in its positive functions. But a distinctive negative function does remain: since totalitarian authority can legislate away the very possibility of freedom in all areas, political freedom now has as its particular function the preservation of the plurality without which freedom cannot be even a problem.

If we assume the validity of the foregoing sketch for the purpose of completing the model, three historical conclusions may be advanced for possible service in philosophies of freedom:

First, although the immanent requirements of philosophies have led to the articulation of the most varied conceptions of freedom in all ages, different notions have been particularly appropriate to different ages.

Second, these notions form an actual process of freedom in the modern era. This process starts from the idea of freedom as the realization of the given good in a period when the choice of traditional orders made freedom a relevant concern but the acceptance of traditional authorities limited its scope. It proceeds through the unresolved juxtaposition of freedom as the rational comprehension of the good and freedom as the realization of desire in an age which called for the grounding of a supreme but delimited political authority in an original freedom, to the synthesis of freedoms in the emphasis on a politically oriented freedom of action. Our own age witnesses the unraveling of the synthesis, the extension of the concern for freedom from politics to all the interests of man, and the reinvolvement of freedom with all the other values of life.

Finally, then, the contemporary problem of freedom, from the historical point of view, is twofold: to determine whether there is, through the varieties of historical experience, a common core of human freedom, and to redefine for our own generation the valid forms it may take in the myriad of relations into which it must now enter.

2 The Idea of Authority in the West

My reason for inquiring into the history of the idea of authority is neither an affection for authority nor the detection of a gap in historical knowledge that needs filling merely because it exists. Instead my purpose is to illuminate our much-discussed crisis of authority, the crisis which became particularly visible with its spread from the society at large into the groves of academe during the sixties and which is one feature of those tumultuous years that has survived the apparent return to normalcy.

This crisis of authority in which we now find ourselves is a crucial present concern for us all, whatever our political and social persuasion, because authority has been an essential means of controlling our collective destinies, and the crisis in it entails a crisis in our means of control by anyone and for any purpose whatsoever. It is a crisis, moreover, which is not only difficult for us to resolve with the means at our disposal, but is also difficult for us to understand with the knowledge at our disposal. Since the crisis of authority raises a problem of knowledge which apparently defies solution in contemporary terms, there would seem to be nothing left to do but to make a historical inquiry into the idea of authority for the purpose of shedding light on its present crisis. The social scientists, after all, have long told us that history is a residual discipline, so we might as well make the most of it.

Now let us make clear at once what the problem of knowledge raised for us by the crisis of authority is, since the nature of the problem determines the nature of the inquiry. The most obvious view of the crisis is to see it as the recent erosion of authority, and the object of an inquiry into it would be to watch it wear away. This view of the problem implies a quantitative approach to authority: either you don't have it or you do, and if you do you can have more or less of it. The history of people having less and less of it would tend to take the form of telling how every year a locust came and took another grain of wheat—a story which might be true enough but is neither very interesting nor very illuminating. It leaves open, moreover, the question of whether we are overreacting to a transitory ripple or witnessing a fundamental change, and

First published in the *American Historical Review* 82 (April, 1977), 249–70.

on this we find the contemporary evidence confusing enough to drive us back into history for clarification. Those who challenge authority both reject it as such on the ground that there is no valid distinction whatsoever among humans to justify it—a rejection which seems the logical conclusion to the fundamental process of democratization—*and* reject specific authorities on the ground of their "illegitimacy"—a rejection which implies a remediable aberration and essential acceptance of authority as such. Among those who resist this challenge we find the crisis depicted *both* as the ultimate revolt against free variety in human nature and civilized form in human creation—a depiction which implies the fundamental barbarization of the culture—*and* as another chapter in the long cycle of generational revolts of the sons against the fathers—a periodic surge made somewhat more violent than usual by the transitional effects of affluence, technology, and a noxious war.

What we look for in history to resolve these ambiguities about the essentiality or contingency of the contemporary challenge to authority are the projective tendency and the projectile force of the long-range process in which authority has been involved. To abstract this tendency and assess this force we need a history whose span is protracted enough and whose stages are continuous enough to yield an identifiable and measurable momentum. Authority certainly has the required range, since in its broadest sense it is as old as human community itself. But for the required continuity we shall focus on the *idea* of authority. Whether the real institutions of authority are continuous from age to age or are discontinuously created afresh by the people of successive generations is a matter of interpretation, and contemporary opinion increasingly supports the interpretation of discontinuity. The continuity of the idea of authority, however, is a matter not of historical interpretation but of historical fact. It has moved demonstrably with the transmission of language itself from generation to generation since the time of the Romans— not only within the same linguistic nationality, but with the historical diffusion of languages, from Latin into the vernaculars of the Romance tongues, and from French into English, and with the spread of Western culture, as spread from southwestern to northern and eastern Europe, and from Latinized terminology into Germanic and Slavic usage.

Obviously, the first step in an inquiry like this is to have clearly in mind what the idea of authority is, so that we may recognize it when we see it in its various historical guises and contexts. Now this is trickier than might at first appear. We can agree that authority objectively refers to a kind of relationship between members of a society and subjectively refers to a quality or capacity in certain of the members who are active parties in the relationship. But when we go further to ask what this relationship, quality, or capacity is we run into a real problem of definition—to wit, when we try to nail it down, the idea of authority seems to mean too many things to tell us much about our crisis or its background. Recourse to the dictionary does not help, for the common usages of the term, far from resolving, merely illustrate the problem of plural meanings. The verbal meanings range from power and dominion to influence and prestige. This span covers and obscures the distinction between force and persuasion, a distinction which is absolutely crucial both for the understanding of our own times and for the history of political and social ideas.

In the history of ideas generally, basic conflicts of principle often take the form of mere shadings of emphasis and proportion. In this sense the ethereal realm of the history of ideas resembles travel in outer space, where deflections of very small degree get magnified into fateful discrepancies covering vast distances when they are extended to actual contacts on this earth. Hence it will not do simply to expand our definition of the idea of authority to include what is common to all variations, since such a definition glosses over distinctions which must not be glossed over if the practical life of this world is to make any sense. If we combine all the meanings of authority into the definition of it as the acknowledged superiority of some men over others and write a history of it vis-à-vis the obviously contrary idea of the acknowledged equality of every man with all others, we shall miss the real historical problem in the idea of authority—that the choice of emphasis on the acknowledgment or on the superiority within the abstract definition of authority has entailed the use of the same idea to cover relationships both complementary to human liberty and opposed to it, both complementary to reason and opposed to it, both opposed to power and complementary to it. We need a definition of the idea of authority which will permit us to understand its internal dialectic.

Fortunately, historical definitions are available to give us the help which a categorical definition cannot give. In the early stages of the idea's development its predominant meaning was the acknowledged capacity of certain persons to evoke from others a voluntary submission to acts and opinions over and above the compelling force inherent in those acts and opinions themselves. In its later stages the idea of authority has come predominantly to mean the acknowledged capacity of certain persons to evoke from others submission to imposed acts and opinions by any means whatsoever. In its early form authority was an independent idea, lying between power and freedom in the spectrum of human relations; it was a pressure upon men to conform in ways to which they could not be ordered or compelled by the possessor of power and in things to which they did not freely consent or contract for good reasons or adequate compensation. Authority in this sense was, as has been well said by a famous historian of Rome, less than a command and more than advice. Those subject to this kind of authority, formally equidistant between power and freedom, tended to stress the side of authority which was distinct from power because it abjured force and which was complementary to free assent because it needed a *voluntary* obligation. In its later form, however, authority became a dependent idea, a quality of power connoting merely its legitimacy or rightful title to command and to compel obedience to its commands.

When we investigate it historically then, we cannot simply assume a constant idea of authority—say, as the acknowledged capacity to dominate others—and ask who claimed it, how people felt about it, and how men related it to other ideas, because the idea itself changed with the kind of people who claimed it and the way people felt about it. From a historical point of view we must rather look for the two basic forms of authority—the independent capacity to dominate without compulsion and the legitimate power to dominate, including compulsion—and understand the process that led from one to the other. Now it would be convenient if I could say that this process—the process from moral authority to authoritative power, to put it in a crude package—is *the* historical definition of the idea of authority and that our task therefore is simply to look for the moral kind of authority in the earlier stages of Western history, watch for the point of transfer, and then work with the definition of authority as a dimension of power.[1] This is generally our procedure in tracing historical change over *shorter* spans of time, but in the *longer* runs the historical process is not so conveniently linear.

Certainly there has been a strong trend of this kind leading from one kind of authority to the other, but it is a case of too much of a bad thing. The trend has been so strong that the autonomous idea of authority has developed into the mere legitimation of power not once, but several times. It has happened, indeed, in each of the major periods of our culture since Roman times, thereby adding a cyclical pattern to the overall development. Between these cycles, moreover, there has also occurred and recurred a reverse process, a kind of countercycle in which

1. The abbreviated reference to the early, independent stage in the idea of authority as "moral authority" should not be taken to imply that the contrary ideas of power and freedom did not have moral dimensions of their own. Neither these ideas nor their distinctive morality will be discussed here.

men shift their attention from the stabilized authority of power to the dynamic claims of an independent moral authority. This countercycle cannot be considered a part or stage of the main process, because it entails a process of an entirely different kind. Where the original cycle is a development, the countercycle is a mutation. What this historical pattern shows, in fact, is that we have to deal with two recurrent processes and two persistent ideas of authority. Because they are involved in two processes which are not only reverse but incongruous, moral authority and authoritative power have not been two stages of one idea of authority, but two different ideas of authority immersed in a variety of historical relations with each other. At any point in time the idea of authority is not *the* idea at all; it is actually a composite attitude based on the relationship that exists between the two ideas of authority at that time, and this relationship, in turn, is based on the respective stages which these ideas have reached in their separate histories.

If, then, we are going to bring history to bear upon the contemporary attitude toward authority, we have two ideas to follow in the past. Only when we have sketched them both, in their own terms, and matched the current impetus of each with the other can we draw lessons of history for our current crisis of authority.

Let us first establish the historical pattern assumed by the idea of authority that is familiar to us because it has become predominant in modern times. This is orthodox history in which we start with the endpoint of development—in this case a developed present idea—and ask the past how it grew. This idea of authority is an idea in the sense that it is a general notion that historical people actually and consciously held about authority. According to this idea, authority is simply constituted power—that is, any capacity to secure obedience or conformity that carries with it some title to do so. It is located primarily in societies which are overtly political or which harbor a coercive force akin to politics, since only there do people think about power directly. This idea of authority, then, is a solid idea—a nugget of an idea. For its past, one asks how it came to the idea of authority out of what was not the idea of authority, how big it was at any time, who held it, and what titles they gave for holding it. Its history is not a history of changes *in* the idea, since such a simple idea cannot change without becoming something else; it is the history of the initial crystallization out of the intellectual nebula *into* an idea and of the subsequent changes in the *external* relations of this idea with practical circumstances and with other ideas.

This idea of authority as a consciously constituted or legitimate power to command and to secure obedience is a modern idea—that is, it is one of the ideas whose distinct emergence during the sixteenth and seventeenth centuries have led historians to mark the period as the origin of modern times. Certainly men had acknowledged authorities *in practice* since the beginning of organized human society, but in too many contexts and for too many different purposes to require any thought about authority as such. Certainly too there had long been plural ideas of authority, connected with these specific institutional authorities and usually ensconced in traditions, which would persist in the form of corporate or constitutional notions throughout the modern period. The point about the generic idea of authority as legitimate power was not its prevalence but its appropriate innovation in the early-modern age.

At the beginning of the modern period, there was indeed a city-state tradition, which had been recently revived by generations of humanists and which perpetuated the classical notions of political power, but in a local context and with moral overtones which relegate it to the prehistory of the idea of authority. There was, similarly, a medieval territorial tradition which posited a harmonious order of superior, subordinate, and coordinate authorities, but within a general acceptance of plurality and a presumed cooperation for a common religious purpose that relegate it also to a prefatory state. Convulsive events of the early-modern period had the effect of dissolving the classical and medieval protective covers which had preserved the limited and fragmented power of authority. Machiavelli showed what could happen to the protective cover of the city-state's fabled civic virtue when political attention was shifted to the larger arena of the territorial nations which made it an anachronism. And later in the sixteenth century Jean Bodin showed what could happen to the protective cover of a common religious purpose when he developed the doctrine of a lawfully constituted, supreme, indivisible, exclusive, and purely political sovereignty in response to the raging wars of religion that were triggered by the conflict between Christian churches but fed by the espousal of a religious cause on the part of every authority with a claim to more power.

The natural-law writers of the seventeenth century—Grotius and Hobbes, most prominently—added the theoretical foundations to the definitions advanced in the sixteenth, and from this sequence of responses to the mutually destructive conflicts among the traditional hybrid authorities there emerged the modern idea of authority as legitimate power per se, distinct from any of the rights that constituted it or the ultimate ends to which it might be directed. It signified the segregation of politics as the sphere of common interests on whose uniform administration the community could agree, because such unified control was a necessary condition for men's pursuit of the various social and spiritual ends on which they could no longer agree; and it signified the community's acknowledgment of power as *the* principle of this autonomous political sphere. Hence the modern idea of authority arose as the new built-in rationale of political power to replace the divisive social and spiritual purposes which used to justify it. In the period of its first definition—that is, in the sixteenth and seventeenth centuries—modern political authority performed this function precisely, both in fact and in idea. It was a single crystallized point of generally accepted power, politically raised above the myriad traditional social and ecclesiastical authorities—aristocracies and state churches—which still persisted but whose power relationships the political authority now took over.

From that time forward the application of this modern idea has been steadily expanded, homogenizing the various types of hierarchical human relations into cases of authoritative power and polarizing the world of political ideas into systems of authority on the one side and of freedom on the other. For clarity's sake, we can mark off this gradual process of simplification into two stages. In the first, the social world was simplified down to two linked ideas—authority *and* freedom. In the second, it has been refined down to an ultimate choice: authority *or* freedom.

The first stage in the extension of the uniform modern idea of authority was the response to the two urgent questions raised by the explosive new definition of authority as justified power: what was the extent of such authority (that is, what was the boundary of the common political interest for which the exercise of power was collectively recognized?) and who would exercise it? From the end of the seventeenth to the end of the nineteenth centuries men devoted themselves to these questions, and beyond all the local permutations and combinations in the answers the general theoretical result was for thinkers to align their answers into whole systems of ideas under the primacy either of authority or of liberty. This categorical confrontation, streamlining authori*ties* into authority and liber*ties* into liberty, testified to the simplifying and expansive effect of defining authority in terms of power, in contrast to the plurality of traditional authorities with their obscure frictions against one another. Indeed, what demonstrated the universal resonance of the new idea of authority above all else was that even the opponents agreed essentially on what it was. Conservatives may have emphasized the legitimation more than the power and liberals the power more than the legitimation; and, of course, conservatives approved of authority while liberals feared it. But by and large they were on opposite sides of the same thing.

And yet this was only an intermediate stage in the expanding range of authoritative power. For if there was a general consensus that authority must have power within its due sphere, there was also a general consensus, on the part of authoritarians and libertarians alike, that the sphere of authority was but one of the two spheres which made up the social world and that the sphere of authority therefore was not by itself coterminous with this world. If we keep in mind the two patron saints of this period's intellectual conflict, John Locke for the liberals and Edmund Burke for the authoritarians, we get an accurate idea of the standard relations between the two leading ideological systems of this stage: the liberals sketched out a large sphere for political rights and civil liberty and a small sphere for a responsible authority, and the conservatives sketched out a large sphere for aristocratic—that is, independent—authority and a small sphere for freedom of enterprise and liberty of conscience; but both sides acknowledged some role for both the authoritarian and the liberal principle.

In the twentieth century this process of homogenizing ideas and polarizing the human world was taken one stage further to a logical extreme. In totalitarian fascism the principle of authoritative power became the principle of the entire human world. As Mussolini formulated it: "Fascism stands for liberty, and for the only liberty worth having, the liberty of the State and of the individual within the State. . . . It is the purest form of democracy if the nation be considered—as it should be—from the point of view of quality rather than quantity, as an idea . . . the truest, expressing itself in a people as the conscience and will of the few, if not, indeed, one. . . . Therefore the State is not only Authority which governs and confers legal form and spiritual value on individual wills, but it is also Power. . . ."[2] In the ideology of fascism, therefore, authoritative power did not reject liberty—since rejection would have implied the existence of an idea outside of authority to be rejected—but absorbed liberty into authority and converted liberty into a function of authority. Thus Hitler repeatedly insisted that in contrast to the rights of the majority in modern democracy, he espoused the principle of "old Germanic democracy, . . . which knows only an authority which proceeds downwards from the top and a responsibility which proceeds upwards from the bottom," and he defined this nomi-

2. Benito Mussolini, *Fascism: Doctrine and Institutions* (Rome, 1935), 11–13.

nally bi-directional process as a real hierarchy which subsumed the democratic responsibility under authoritative power. The leadership might recognize morally "as its supreme instance the authority of the German people as a whole," but actually this recognition contributed to the people's "blind obedience" in "following the leader, . . . a single will which issues its commands and which the others must always obey."[3]

Now the ideology, if not the reality, of totalitarian fascism died in 1945, and it might seem as if we have entered a post-mortem stage in the modern idea of authority—as if, that is, the trend which we have observed toward its continuing simplification has continued to the point where it has refined itself out of existence, along with the demise of all the other political and social principles caught in what has been called "the end of ideology." It is tempting for an age as quantitatively oriented in its thinking as ours to infer that a development going from many kinds of authority to one kind of authority will naturally conclude in no kind of authority as the simplest idea of all. And undoubtedly the contemporary view of our age as pluralistic, practical, negotiable, open-ended, on the one side, and materialistic, group-oriented, and self-alienated on the other would seem to leave no important place or function for the idea of legitimate or justifiable power.

But there is another possibility. There is in the postwar intellectual movement an indication that the modern idea of authority did not reach its climax in the overt totalitarian regimes after all—that the totalitarians' attempts to use the organs of state as their legitimate instruments for the exercise of total power over the society implied the persistence of a distinction between state and society, and to that extent did not carry the simplification of the idea of authority to its final conclusion. In the thinking of Herbert Marcuse, for example, the ultimate shape of the modern idea of authority emerges only during our own age, taking the form of a subtle power constituted in all of our social organizations and penetrating even into the contemporary "one-dimensional"—that is, submissive—individuals, who thus legitimate this single, pervasive, manyheaded authority within their psyches. Such a conception uncovers a crucial possibility in the modern political idea of authority which is easily overlooked. We are accustomed, perhaps from the historical origins which we have discussed, to think of politics as a set of definite things (that is, governments) operating in their own distinctive sphere—the public. But in the context of authority politics is

3. *The Speeches of Adolf Hitler*, ed. Norman H. Baynes (New York, 1942), 1:180, 20, 200–02, 543.

actually something more general which took this reified form in a definite historical period. The modern political idea of authority as such simply makes authority the principle of power over men. Consequently, when society gets politicized, as ours has been, it can take the overt totalitarian form of extending the coercive activities of governmental organs into society and thus enlarging the public sphere at the expense of the private, but it can also take the covert form of reorganizing voluntary associations into power relationships legitimized by the nominally voluntary base and thus of erasing the line between the public and private spheres so far as the principle of authority is concerned.

This is as far as we can go with the history of our *modern* idea of authority. It is an ending reminiscent of the story about the lady and the tiger. It leaves us with the choice of all or none. It leaves us, that is, with the knowledge that history, in the sense of the tendency in the past development of the idea, leads equally to either of the contemporary attitudes toward the idea of authority. This history supports both the idea that authority has expanded continuously until it has now become everything and the idea that authority has been focused continuously until in the concentrated form of post-fascist totalitarianism it disappeared into naked violence. The choice is rather important, since the first attitude toward authority fits a program of total revolution and the second attitude toward authority denies a moral target for any revolution. There would seem to be something wrong with a history that keeps saying "amen" to both of such choices. What we gain from this history is the understanding that there is historical reason for the confrontation. What this history does not tell us, since it is a history of the common idea of modern authority, is whether contemporary men are really talking about the same thing when they talk about authority or whether they actually have different ideas in mind.

As I indicated earlier, there is another idea of authority whose historical career has been quite the reverse of the modern one. Where the history of the modern idea shows a continuous development from obscure origins to a clear and definite concept, the history of the other, older idea of authority shows a recurrent pattern of regression from clear and definite origins to a present obscurity. Such a history means that we may well be carrying about with us connotations of authority which we are not quite aware that we have and that we may well be modifying the modern idea of authority with them in ways which distort our communication about it. To consider whether we are in fact bearing unbeknownst this burden of the past, we must do two things: we must return to the early period when this older idea of authority was most explicit in order to learn what the telltale signs are that we must look for in the present; and we must look into the subsequent history of the idea to determine the probability of its persistent underground effectiveness in our own age.[4]

For the seminal period in the history of this older idea of authority let us turn to the Romans, not because we necessarily believe that it was born there—although some scholars do believe that—but because the Roman use of one distinctive Latin term *auctoritas* for the several applications they made of the idea gives us the most convenient way of following what it meant for an ancient culture, and because the philological connection between Latin and modern authority makes the Latin version particularly available for infiltrating the modern idea of authority. Before we try to define what the Romans meant positively by authority, let us delimit it in general by specifying its two most prominent differences from the modern.

The Roman idea of authority evolved in contradistinction to power. The two most striking examples of this function were afforded by the Roman Senate and by Augustus, the first emperor. As opposed to the command power of the magistrates and the constituent power of the people the Senate was recognized as having only "authority," a term signifying the Senate's peculiar mode of domination which, unlike the other offices of the republic, had no legal status and no compulsory force, and yet in fact bound the Roman citizens to compliance far more definitively and extensively than did the other offices of the republic. As a further mark of this distinctive, uncoercive authority associated with the Senate, we may note that the Romans attributed "authority" to the Senators in their capacity as members of an advisory council of "fathers" or "elders," but preferred to use the idea of "power" for the domination of the father within his own family. After the conversion of the republic into an empire Augustus expressed the distinction between authority and power when he characterized his own position as equal in power with the other magistrates but supreme in authority. We may pause, in passing, to note the two different contexts afforded by these examples for the same idea of authority, since clarification now may avoid confusion later. Authority could be possessed both by men without official

---

4. For a more explicit and less analytical elaboration of the materials on which the interpretations in this section are based, see my entry on "Authority" in the *Dictionary of the History of Ideas*, ed. Philip P. Weiner (New York, 1973), 1:141–62.

power, like the Senate, or by men with official power, like Augustus, but in both cases it referred to the same kind of domination—a kind of domination which lay outside the exercise of power.

The second general distinction between the Roman and modern ideas of authority is that the Roman idea was multiple. It was a flexible idea with plural meanings and varied applications held together by an implicit common tendency. To revert to an earlier analogy, it was an idea with moving parts, which constantly shifted in their internal relationships with each other and in their external relationships with other ideas. We must be alert to these fluctuations as, in the course of time and changing circumstances, authority assumed new forms and acquired new sources.

For the *positive* content of this multiple idea we must also look to the Romans. They developed the three basic forms and the several kinds of sources of authority which recurred time and again in the history of the idea. The three basic forms of Roman authority were: authority as guarantee; authority as origin or creation; and authority as personal prestige. Sources of authority appropriate to it as guarantee were trustees who by declaration confirmed the acts of their wards and elders who by experience confirmed the acts of their people. Sources of authority appropriate to it as origin or creation were planners whose designs were carried out by others and initiators whose proposals were enacted by others. Sources of authority appropriate to it as personal prestige were nature's noblemen—that is, men of recognized moral or intellectual pre-eminence. At first glance, these groups would seem to have little to do with one another. People who merely add guarantees to something else certainly would seem entirely different from those who initiate or create something; and both of these groups, who were authorities by virtue of something they *did*, seem quite different from the third group, who were accounted superior by virtue of something they *were*. And yet it was from combinations of these apparently ill-assorted ideas that the Romans derived some of our most familiar applications of authority. From the combination of the authority that is due the initiator and the guarantee added by age and experience they derived the authority of tradition. From the combination of the authority stemming from an original design and the authority of personal pre-eminence they derived the long-lived idea of authority as the inevitable product of the natural inequality of men. From the combination of the authority due to intellectual pre-eminence and the guarantee of experience they derived the idea of the authority of the expert.

These Roman combinations, moreover, produced more than persistent general principles of authority; they also established long-lived concrete forms of authority. When the Senate combined the initiation of legislative proposals—still under the guise of extralegal advice—with its earlier function as an unofficial council of guardian elders, it became, despite its lack of power, the "principal" organ of the Roman constitution. This combination established the fateful double meaning of primacy in government that has endured: the right to act first in time is also the right to be first in rank; the authority with the function of initiative is the supreme authority. From the same combination of the original authority of the initiator and the added authority of the trustee the Romans derived the equally important concept of authorization, through which an original authority is not only transferable but is actually enlarged in the hands of the representative who becomes its guardian. From the second combination of the authority due a progenitor with the authority due the moral pre-eminence of a benefactor has come the influential application of natural hierarchy that has supported parental authority generically and paternal authority especially. And from the combination that produced the authority of experts as a class has descended the specific focus on the authority of the teacher.

These blends of authority are not only important ideas in themselves, but they indicate the connection underlying the apparently disparate forms of the older idea of authority. They all import some general claim on human trust into a social relationship in order to introduce an additional pressure for conformity beyond that which the relationship itself can exert. Indeed, we may say that, if obedience is the counterpart of power, trust is the counterpart of authority. What all these forms and sources of Roman authority have in common is that they are trustworthy. This is obvious in the case of the trustee and the personally honorable man, but a moment's reflection will show that it is also behind what the identification of the creator contributes to the execution of his design; that is, it provides the executors with a principal agent who can be held accountable.

Just as revealing of this idea of authority as these internal relations were the two things that happened to it in Roman history. The first was that Roman law established the connections between these highly variegated forms of authority and molded them into *an* idea. References to authority appeared in all spheres of Roman life, but it was law, the sphere in which Rome invested so much creative genius, that became the matrix for the organization of the several materials of authority into a new coherent idea.

The second development was the change that the idea underwent along with general changes in Roman conditions. The original Roman idea of authority proved to be unstable. While independent of other ideas, it was internally fragmented. Subjected to opposing pulls from the idea of power, to which the theme of domination in authority made it kin, and from the idea of liberty, to which the theme of voluntary, un-coerced compliance in authority made it equally kin, it did not succeed in maintaining the delicate and tenuous balance between them that was the condition of its autonomy. During the course of the Empire the idea of authority became increasingly associated in Roman law with the power of the Emperor, until it finally became a quality of his power, prefacing his formal decrees as a kind of verbal symbol of their legit-imacy.

Thus the Romans ended with the familiar, if to them still subliminal, idea of authority as authoritative power which we have inherited. But if we look more closely at the history which lies between them and us and if we look at it not for the further development of the familiar idea of authority they ended with but for the original idea of authority they started with, we find it reappearing time and again. If we look at this in-tervening history for a pattern of these recurrences we find that not only the result but the process of Roman history is relevant to us in the pre-sent. With each of the main creative surges of Western man, and in the specific field of the creation, the idea of authority was reborn as the means of diffusing the innovation among masses of routinized people and of organizing society in the light of that idea, but without violating the freedom of commitment which is in the spirit of each cultural cre-ation. And in each case this fragile idea of an uncoercive moral or spir-itual authority developed ever-increasing associations with the idea of power, until it became the moral or spiritual justification for the exercise of coercive force, thus stabilizing the idea of authority as a fixed quality of power until the next breakthrough.

We can identify three of these breakthroughs and subsequent stabil-izations between the Romans and the present—breakthroughs that re-produced the older idea of spiritual and moral authority successively in the spheres of religion, politics, and society, and stabilizations that turned them into additions to the modern idea of authoritative power.

The medieval Catholic Church *perpetuated* the connection of author-ity and official government in the law which it took over from the later stages of the Roman Empire, but it also *innovated* the spiritual authority of the Scriptures and the Church Fathers over the assenting souls of men. As authorized trustees of this divine tradition the Popes explicitly distinguished their dominion as "authority" from the Kings' as "power."[5] The Divine Incarnation which built God's warrant into the rules of the earthly order, the Divine ordination of the temporary and ecclesiastical offices which governed that order, the Divine creation of the hierarchy of superior to inferior beings which stretched from heaven through the earth as the unquestionable constitution of the cosmos— all these positions, which contributed to the power of superiors over their subjects, had their Christian origins in an authoritative conception of God, His Son, and His Word that was to be broadcast to benighted souls the world over and freely received by them. This kind of authority was deemed complementary to both tradition and reason. In early Christianity tradition, as an autonomous consensus of the generations on the meaning of Christ's message for human living, was one of the three roughly equal forms—along with Scripture itself and the episcopal office (including the Roman papacy)—taken by spiritual authority.[6] For St. Augustine authority and reason dovetailed in a consistent process of equivalent parts, whereby authority provided the definitions and the stimulus for the necessary role of reason in the formulation of the rules of faith.

But medieval conditions for propagating a unified faith among disparate peoples and medieval needs for the Church organization in secular life led to the growing association of Christian authorities with ecclesiastical power, to the overlap of ecclesiastical temporal categories, and to intellectual conflicts between the spiritual and the power-full ideas of authority in which the latter won out. The idea of authority was increasingly vested in the papal "power of the keys" which, with the aid of the canon lawyers and papalist theologians, made the definition of tradition a function of this power and in principle excluded reason from the formulation of the rules of faith.[7] By the fourteenth century not only were the papalists applying the Pope's "plenitude of power" to temporal as well as church government, but even the Conciliarists, despite the advocacy of corporate tradition in matters of spirit, were, in the writing of Ockham and Marsilius of Padua, deriving moral precept and external organization alike from the command, the will, and the power of both God and the community.

5. Especially in the famous distinction of Pope Gelasius I.

6. Karl F. Morrison, *Tradition and Authority in the Western Church*, 300–1140 (Princeton, 1969), esp. 33.

7. A. J. MacDonald, *Authority and Reason in the Early Middle Ages* (London, 1933), *passim;* Michael Wilks, *The Problem of Sovereignty in the Later Middle Ages* (Cambridge, 1963), 375–77.

The principal issue of the Reformation, both in the early opposition of the reformers to the contemporary forms of Catholicism and in the subsequent divergence of institutionalized Protestantism from the spirit of the early Reform, should be seen as a conflict not between religious liberty and religious authority, but between the two kinds of religious authority. It began as a restatement of the original kind of religious authority against the later imperious developments of the Catholic church and then itself recapitulated the Catholic evolution. Luther and Calvin climaxed the long line of resistance to the triumph of ecclesiastical power over the direct authority of Scripture, and they led this resistance in the name of a justification by faith and a literal reliance on Scripture which were simple theological terms for the direct and unimpeded flow of God's definitely defined spiritual authority to all kinds of men everywhere. But their apparent victory was shortlived, because their churches, too, quickly took on the usual pattern in the development of authority and grew from the pious spirituality of their origins into alliances with temporal powers that endowed these powers with the title of authority and ecclesiastical authorities with the instruments of power.

I have dwelt upon the Roman and medieval cases because both the original idea of autonomous, uncoercive authority and the historical process which changed it into a legitimation of coercion were overt in them and because these cases furnish keys to the recognition of both the idea and the process during the modern period, in which they have been obscured by the explicit and continuous association of authority with political power. The identification of authority with legitimate government is indeed, as we have seen, the paradigm of modern authority as such, but the gross association of authority with the right to exercise a public power should not blind us to the two kinds of relationship which have gone into the forging of this association. The production of the modern state between the sixteenth and the middle of the nineteenth centuries was a prime creation of Western culture, and, like the other cultural creations of the West, it was diffused first through its claims to an uncoercive authority before its establishment as a legitimate coercive institution. Although the process in this instance was confused by the circumstance that the cultural product was collective power itself, there remained nonetheless the crucial distinction between the early modern idea that an uncoercive authority was necessary to the very constitution of a political power and the nineteenth-century idea that an authority was simply the legitimate exerciser of a pre-existing political power.

The reliance of the early-modern state upon uncoerced and uncoercible compliance was attested by theories which grounded both the origins and the ultimate purposes of political power in a principle which lay between power and rights and was categorically distinct from both. Once Bodin, Grotius, Hobbes, and others of the dominant natural-law school set aside, as disorderly, the immediate derivation of the ruler's powers from divine ordination and the natural hierarchy and vested the origins of those powers in the consent of the community, they were confronted with the problem of the convertability between the community's right, which was an original power over itself, and the ruler's power, which was a derived power over it. The idea of authority became central to their scheme of origins as the voluntary general authorization of the ruler's function which made his particular powers different from the unaccountable to the corresponding constituent powers of the community. In respect to the ends of the state, analogously, the early-modern theorists grounded political compliance ultimately in a notion of the common good transcending the services which could be demonstrably secured by the sovereign's use of the collective power. The very ambiguity which has so often been noted in them between the compulsory peace and order they emphasized and the ideal moral unity of their final resort testified to the theorists' registration of an attitude toward the benefits of power that required the belief in a transcendent political moral authority to produce conformity even when the benefits of power were not forthcoming. As a principle of origins as well as of ends, authority was then built into the modern service-state as the indefinite appeal for loyalty over and above the services the state actually renders.

The form that political theory now took was to relate human freedom and authority internally as two sides of the same moral force. Thus, however much they differed in the specifics of their politics both Hobbes and Locke agreed that the supreme authority of the sovereign—in Hobbes the ruler, in Locke the legislature—is an authorization from the community as a whole, whose natural rights become the original authority through the authorization. The moral and spiritual basis of this original authority—that is, the liberty and rights of man—becomes explicit in Rousseau, whose idea of the general will is so mysterious and difficult precisely because it is the point at which men turn their various rights into a single authority, and is so spiritual that it is embodied in no earthly institution.

The method of this early modern political theorizing came from the mathematical mode of reasoning in the contemporary natural philosophy of the seventeenth and eighteenth centuries. Now reason as such—

especially deductive reason—has an ambiguous relationship to authority. The compulsive force of a deductive logic, where the conclusion follows necessarily from an axiomatic or previously demonstrated premise, is not authoritarian because it carries its own credentials. The mind does not submit to the rational conclusion but appropriates it fully and freely as its own. Power and freedom can meet in reason, to the exclusion of authority. But reason can be employed in the service of authority when the premises must be taken on trust. In the science and philosophy of the seventeenth and eighteenth centuries such employment, and especially the use of Aristotle for the purpose, was violently rejected in favor of rigorous methods grounded in self-evident premises which made the rational method an exercise of freedom for their subscribers but also made it the method of a new invisible authority for their detractors. There was a precise parallel between the idea of men using their freedom to create an authority which would presumably enforce the goals of their freedom and the method of using self-evident axioms as the basis of a necessary logic which would issue in inescapable conclusions presumably available to but actually not shared by every mind.

So this kind of rational authority, with its apparently compatible relations to liberty and reason, did not last either, but yielded to the same kind of displacement as had previously overtaken its predecessors in law and religion. As the foundation of rational method shifted, during the eighteenth century, from deduction to induction, from axioms presumably self-evident in all minds but actually propagated by an intellectual elite to concrete experience actually verifiable by every man, the older reason was seen as an alien authoritarian imposition and the newer reason, emphasizing tentative conclusions limited to the available evidence, was associated with the freedom of inquiry and lost all connection with the liberal idea of authority. In a parallel way the idea of liberty was detached from the idea of authority, which became attached to the ideas and institutions of conservative power.

The culture of the eighteenth century has long been known for its mixture of rationalism and empiricism. It should hardly be surprising, then, to find that the century was analogously transitional in its modulation of independent political authority, which was generally approved, to authoritative power, which was the target of conflict. From Locke through the physiocrats to Burke, historical revisions have supplied the missing authoritarian dimension to the traditional liberal caricature and a liberal, powerful dimension to the long-standing authoritarian label. But there could be no question about the direction to which the future belonged. From the liberal intellectuals of the Enlightenment to the philosophical radicalism of the young John Stuart Mill and Karl Marx at mid-nineteenth century, empiricism and naturalism in philosophy were commonly associated with a corresponding defense of political freedom against ideas and institutions of authority viewed equally as attributes of the established power. Elaborating on a selective vision of Locke's argument against innate ideas and for the derivation of all knowledge from "experience," the French philosophes—at least in the instance of a bellwether like Diderot—attached human rights to a categorical doctrine of epistemological sensationalism and dissolved political authority into a part that was a function of the community's liberty and a part that was a function of the ruler's power.[8] Around the same time Adam Smith was preparing for the laissez faire of his *Wealth of Nations* by dividing the idea of moral authority in his *Theory of Moral Sentiments* between "our moral faculties . . . within us," represented above all by the conscience of the individual, and "the commands . . . laid upon [man] by infinite wisdom and infinite power," enforced by "the punishment of God, the great avenger of justice."[9] Somewhat later the young Mill, in the same vein, denied the logical independence of the syllogism, subsuming it under a process of induction that started from duly verified particulars. Correlatively he became a political and cultural liberal in whose eyes "government is always either in the hands, or passing into the hands of whatever is the strongest power in society."[10] He grew up to see, moreover, and continued to see recent history as dominated by the conflict between liberty and authority—by which he meant authoritative power. Well might Bertrand Russell sum up this whole tradition with the simple assertion: "The only philosophy that affords a theoretical justification of democracy, and that accords with democracy in its temper of mind, is empiricism"—or, as he preferred to call it, "empiricist Liberalism."[11]

This evolution of the idea of political authority from its constitutive

8. Locke's grounding of his argument against the proponents of innate ideas could have stood as a literal model of the hostile connection between rationalist and political authoritarianism: "Nor is it a small power it gives one man over another, to have the authority to be the dictator of principles." John Locke, *An Essay Concerning Human Understanding*, ed. A. D. Woozley (New York, 1964), 87, 89; Denis Diderot, *The Encyclopedia*, ed. Stephen J. Gendzier (New York, 1967), 2–4; Leonard Krieger, *An Essay on the Theory of Enlightened Despotism* (Chicago, 1975), 53.

9. Adam Smith's *Moral and Political Philosophy*, ed. Herbert W. Schneider (New York, 1970), 160, 178, 192–93, 198–99.

10. John Stuart Mill, *Autobiography* (London, 1924), 121, 135–37.

11. *The Basic Writings of Bertrand Russell: 1903–1959*, ed. Robert E. Egnier and Lester E. Denonn (New York, n.d.), 462, 467.

independence in the early modern period to a function of established public power in the eighteenth and nineteenth centuries, indicated by the liberals of the latter period, was positively confirmed by conservatives who were their contemporaries and by osmotic concessions of liberals themselves in the second half of the nineteenth century. The conservatives' attitude toward authority was in part a reaction against the antiauthoritarian facts of the French revolution and in part a mirror image of the liberal attitude toward authority to which they were responding. In both cases the result was that conservatives in the nineteenth century endorsed the union of authority and power. Certainly this was true of the main pillars of Restoration political thinking—Joseph de Maistre, Adam Müller, and Ludwig von Haller. De Maistre, for example, insisted that authority was intrinsically antithetical to both the reason and the rights of ordinary men and identified it exclusively with the legitimate power devolved by the Divinity upon the rulers of state and society. He endorsed the sentiment: "Power on one side, weakness on the other: this constitutes all the bonds of human society."[12] It should not be surprising, then, to find a recent defense of Hegel against the charge of conservatism couched precisely in terms of his rejection of authority as authoritative power over the community and his polemics against the conservatives who so defined the idea of authority.[13]

A second sign of political authority's development into an adjunct of public power in the modern period can be seen in the reluctant acceptance of such authority after the middle of the nineteenth century even by those liberals and radicals who had originally shunned it because of its association with political power. The growing respect for traditional and intellectual elitism in government on the part of such qualified liberals as Tocqueville and Mill is too well known to bear extended repetition here, but two lesser-known examples of similar development taken by famous radicals who spanned the middle of the nineteenth century may be adduced now. Whereas the youthful Marx had used dialectical reason to deny any possible authoritative intermediary between the natural rights of the human community and the oppressive power of its alienated masters and thought of the coming Communist revolution in terms of removing "fetters," the subsequent exposition of Marxist political theory by the older Engels under the later challenge of anarchist

12. Joseph de Maistre, *On God and Society,* ed. Elisha Greifer (Chicago, 1959), 6; see also *The Works of Joseph de Maistre,* ed. Jack Lively (New York, 1971), 4–5, 207.

13. Shlomo Avineri, *Hegel's Theory of the Modern State* (Cambridge, 1972), 47, 180–83.

competition asserted the necessary role of authority as the title to raw power in the coming Communist revolution. He defined authority simply and brutally as "the subjection of another's will to our own." And he declared that the socialist party must itself use it, like all victorious revolutionary parties, to "force its will on another part" of the population through "the terror exercised by its weapons."[14]

But it was in Kierkegaard that the potent character of the authority finally conceded by intellectual radicals of the nineteenth century was most drastically displayed. After a decade (from the mid-thirties to the mid-forties) of writing about the paradoxical immediacy of the relationship between the existent human individual and the absolute God, to the total neglect (and implicit rejection) of any mediating principles like the original idea of authority, Kierkegaard apparently turned about to proclaim the necessity of authority as the remedy for the chronic spiritual illness of his age. But the apparent turnabout was more of a development from than a reversal of his earlier implicit ideas of what authority must be.

Actually it was not the original mediatory but the very different transcendent and potent idea of authority, as "paradoxical" as the fundamental God/man relation with which it was consistent, that he now explicitly espoused. Authority in this sense has nothing to do with genius or service or indeed with any substantive quality of the delivered message that might serve to relate the individuals who are the objects of the authority to its wielder; it has to do only with the unconditioned title to obedience, "which comes from another place." The true authority is founded on the "eternal, essential, qualitative difference" between God and man; it is exercised only "when God appoints a particular man to have divine authority"; and it consists, therefore, in the fact of this appointment pure and simple. Nor did Kierkegaard shrink from the awful implications of this kind of authority. The counterpart to the "authority" of the apostle is the "obedience" of the believers, and, although all earthly authority is "a vanishing factor" because of the inevitably egalitarian and interactive dimension in human relationships, the worldly model of true authority can only be the unquestionable authority in the king's command, "for this analogy demonstrates the compulsory character of an authority" that "prohibits all critical and aesthetical impertinence with regard to form and content."[15] Analo-

14. *Karl Marx, Early Writings*, ed. T. B. Bottomore (New York, 1964), 155–57; Karl Marx and Frederick Engels, *The German Ideology: Parts I and II*, ed. R. Pascal (New York, 1963), 70–71; F. Engels, "Über das Autoritätsprinzip," *Neue Zeit*, 32:1.

15. Sören Kierkegaard, *On Authority and Revelation*, tr. Walter Lowrie (New York, 1966), 108–17.

gously with other revisionist individualists of his age, the authority which Kierkegaard finally accepted was very much the same as the authority with which he earlier would have nothing to do.

The last of the completed cycles of authority in Western history was initiated by the creative surge which constructed industrial society and found ideological expression in the theories of society is spawned. As in previous cycles the new creation rejuvenated the older, autonomous idea of authority, attaching it to the independent reality which had just been acknowledged—in this case social relations as such—and for this purpose separating it from the political institutions of power which militated against innovations of this kind. In the words of a twentieth-century theorist who reinterpreted the democratic state to fit it for the society created by the industrial revolution: "Those rules which the state enforces cannot possibly be identical with the moral standard which ought to govern our lives, and the authority of the state cannot be the authority of that standard."[16] So we find in pioneers of the new science of sociology—in Spencer, Durkheim, Max Weber, Michels, and Pareto—notions of authority specifically appropriate to social relationships and specifically distinguished from political power.

However separate in principle the early stage of social authority and the later stage of political authority may be, the thinking of the sociologists shows that by the end of the nineteenth century the historical weight of the modern political idea of authority had become so impressive that the usual development from the moral to the political idea of authority was no longer a development from one to the other through time but a simultaneous vacillation between them. The political idea was very much in the picture even for the first generation of sociologists, including Max Weber himself, and what had previously been a clear development now became a confusing mixture. Thus the identification of autonomous social authority in industrial culture raised thorny problems for the sociologists—problems which reflect the fundamental problem of authority in the contemporary world. For the only kinds of distinctive social authorities identified by the sociologists were dead authorities—that is, charismatic individuals, "segmental societies," and traditional institutions, such as the military and the family, which were registered to be still existent in fact but atavistic in principle, by reference to modern society.[17]

When these sociologists of the early twentieth century undertook to

---

16. A. D. Lindsay, *The Modern Democratic State* (New York, 1943), 1:207–08.
17. For archaic "segmental societies" and their modern residues, see Emile Durkheim, *The Division of Labor in Society,* tr. George Simpson (New York, 1964), 174–81.

uncover a principle of social authority that was appropriate to contemporary industrial society and yet distinct from coercive political power, the result was what we might call essential ambiguity. Max Weber's distinctively modern authority—bureaucratic authority—was common to compulsory political and voluntary social institutions alike, and not only did he not decide on the priority of the political or social spheres but he did not even treat it as an issue.[18] Pareto defined elites in terms of general social capacity but then focused his discussion on the authoritative power of the governing section of those elites. Robert Michels demonstrated his "iron law of oligarchy," which was presumably to denote the authoritative structure of all democratic social organizations, by recourse to the modern party—the precise crossroads of society and politics in our culture.[19] In these theories both the identity and the confusion of the two ideas of authority are complete. Elites are the effects of the natural laws of societies and are therefore acknowledged naturally, without compulsion. But political power is also one of the natural functions of society, and elites are never without it.

In 1936, finally, the Frankfurt Institute for Social Research's monumental "Studies on Authority and Family" carried the same mutual, albeit anomalous, permeation of the social and the political dimensions of authority over into the empirical sociology and totalitarian conditions of the mature twentieth century. Max Horkheimer's epitomal essay hearkened back to the autonomous period of authority in early bourgeois culture, when the authority of the father in the family and the authority engendered in the society at large by "patriarchal education" were spontaneously related in a purely social interaction, and he contrasted it to the subsequent, contemporary period of bourgeois culture when the authoritarian family was rendered self-contradictory by being both persistent and politicized. Thus on the one hand the hierarchical family remained "indispensable," but on the other its independence was undercut by the state and has become "a problem of mere governmental technique." The only way, indeed, that Horkheimer could make sense of the family as a politicized structure of authoritative power that was buttressed by the inert remnants of an autonomous social authority was by resorting to that last measure of the rationalists's desperation when confronted with confusion and contradiction—the dialectic— attributing authority to a "dialectical whole" composed of "a unity of

18. Max Weber, *Basic Concepts in Sociology,* tr. H. P. Secher (New York, 1962), 115–18.

19. Robert Michels, *Political Parties,* tr. Eden and Cedar Paul (New York, 1959), 23–40, 390.

divergent forces."[20] The formulation may have been idiosyncratic, but the idea was a representative indication of the modern interpenetration of autonomous and compulsory authority.

What was ambiguous in these ideas was the infiltration of coercive powers formerly identified with governing sovereigns into the structures of presumably autonomous social authorities. What was essential about these ambiguities was their reflection of the democratic industrial civilization, with the effect of extending the effective areas both of power and of liberty at the expense of the autonomous authority which has been the traditional buffer between both. The obvious resolutions of the ambiguity have been effected by subsequent developments into totalitarianism and by the anarchism which has been the reflex response to it. Both movements denied the autonomy of authority and drew their respective conclusions from the permeation of all social relations by the political model of coercion.

We have two final questions to ask. How does our dual inquiry into the two kinds of authority clarify the historical riddles about the nature of authority? And what does this historical clarification of authority contribute to the understanding of our present crisis of authority? The continuing riddles in the history of authority consist in the opposite answers which men persist in giving to the questions of its relations with other crucial ideas. They have time and again pitted reason against authority, but speak of rational authority. They have insisted upon the limitation of authority by law, but speak of the authority of the law. They have opposed authority in the name of liberty even when the authority is that of an egalitarian majority, and they have opposed authority in the name of equality, insisting that liberty in the form of voluntary compliance is an essential condition of this authority. We can throw light on all these puzzles, if they are interpreted in terms of the different ideas of authority that have in fact been meant. Men have generally assumed that any act or belief commanded by reason is an exercise of freedom. Reason itself can never be an authority, therefore, but an educative authority such as Rousseau's Legislator, who transitionally imposes reason upon willing and capable recipients not yet ready for it, has a rational authority, while the prescriptions of a permanently ordained superior have regularly been deemed antithetical to reason when their authority was exercised through mental or physical compulsion. To law, analogously, authority has been attributed when the validity of

20. *Studien über Autorität und Familie* (Paris, 1936), 75–76.

the law was grounded in its rational content, and the authority was grounded in men's accessibility to it, but law in this sense has been opposed to authority when the latter was vested in the simple command of a superior. Equality, finally, has obviously been the antithesis of uncoercive authority, and liberty the antithesis of authoritative power.

These two kinds of relationship of authority to other values depend on which of the two main ideas of authority is in question. If we put together now the results of our two historical surveys of these ideas we may conclude that each creative burst of our culture has been accompanied by the elevation of authorities whose superiority is freely accepted by dint of their rationality and legality, but that our modern idea of authority as a title to domination however exercised is a teleological idea derived from the use of force, the hostility to reason, the superiority to law, and the opposition to liberalization which these authorities have cumulatively appropriated.

Where, then, do we stand with our crisis of authority after our historical inquiry? We may project the following possibilities.

First, the decline of authority—seen as an independent moral and intellectual way of getting people to do or agree to something before they can understand adequate reasons for freely doing or agreeing to it and without using compulsion or duress to make them do or agree to it—is historically deep-seated, and the idea of this authority is probably doomed in every one of the shapes familiar to us. This is not to say that the institutions of such authority, like the family and the school, will disappear at once, for social inertia remains a powerful force. But they will survive as facts, without the support of a sustaining idea. Like government, with which they have been connected in recent history, they become more and more institutions dispensing an ill-assorted mixture of welfare, barter, and coercion.

Secondly, independent moral authority has declined not only in favor of the equality which recognizes no superiors and requires men to act with complete freedom, on adequate reasons and for adequate returns, but also in favor of the political power for which it has furnished an ever more tenuous justification. But even if, then, the demise of authority as we have known it is deemed a good thing—and I, for one, welcome the demise of any hindrance to rational choice and free decision—we must recognize that this demise will leave freedom-seeking individuals directly confronting institutionalized power, separated only by the facade of responsible authority and actually bereft of their older authentic buffer.

Thirdly, the imminent demise of all the familiar kinds of independent authority does not mean the permanent disappearance of all possible kinds of independent authority. It has, as we have seen, recurred unpredictably and in unpredictable forms with every fundamental cultural innovation, and consequently its future recurrence at a time and in a shape we cannot foresee is also probable. Not only probable but, as a strictly temporary thing, desirable, since in its recurrent transitional role authority without power has persuaded men to accept innovations on trust and in a voluntary way leading ultimately to their full understanding and free commitment.

If, finally, we are to hazard a guess about the next arena of cultural emphasis and its accompanying hierarchy of acceptable values, we should probably look to the individual psyche, for there is contemporary evidence that the growing loss of belief in any valid authority *between* individuals is being compensated by a growing belief in a valid authority among the drives *within* the individual. The large audience for neo-Freudians like Norman Brown, Erikson, and Marcuse; the renewed attention to Jung; the vogue of existential psychology—these are a few indices of the new focus on the reordering of psychic priorities and on the organization, within the personality, of a unity for action which has always been the function of authority. Since, in this contemporary view, the centuries of social authority have wound up only with the production of authoritarian personalities and one-dimensional individuals in the very image of the coercive society, why not reverse the process and see whether self-integrated individuals can produce a rational social authority in *their* own image? The prospects are that, like other forms of innovative authority, the psychologically authoritative individual will indeed lead those not so well integrated as he without compulsion—for a while.

2 THE HISTORY OF INTELLECTUALS

Intellectual history can always be understood, among other things, as the history of intellectuals.

—Leonard Krieger, in response to the question,
What is intellectual history?

3 Hegel and History

It is doubly ironic that Hegel's views on history should be taken primarily from his *Vorlesungen über die Philosophie der Geschichte*. First, these lectures were published posthumously in their various editions, starting from the first publication by the Hegelian follower, Eduard Gans, in 1837, from the manuscripts of Hegel's lecture notes, to which the notes of reliable Hegelian students in the course have been added. The notes were all published after the philosopher's death in 1831, and the work that came to be known as the *Vorlesungen* (Lectures) was no part of the philosopher's responsibly published writings; hence the work is subject to the whole distinction between what a professor says and what he writes. Second, it is ironic because it is well known that Hegel changed his publishing plans from including the philosophy of history in them to deliberately excluding it from them. Notwithstanding explanations and justifications to the contrary, Hegel's original plan of publishing first, as the introduction to his system, the work that came to be known as the *Phänomenologie des Geistes* and then publishing metaphysical accounts of this system in its application to the existences of the world, was aborted by the revised status of the *Phänomenologie* as the subjective summary of the whole system (originally published as the first part of a "System of Science," *System der Wissenschaft*), leading to Hegel's decision to publish only the "Science of Logic" (*Wissenschaft der Logik*—1812–16) as the first part of his system, with the compendia of his lectures for his students to follow in the *Encyclopädie der philosophishen Wissenschaft im Grundrisse: Zum Gebrauch seiner Vorlesungen* and in the *Naturrecht und Staatswissenschaft im Grundrisse: Zum Gebrauch für Seine Vorlesungen* as well as in the *Grundlinien der Philosophie des Rechts,* in 1821.

These are formal reasons for adducing what Hegel says about history not from the *Vorlesungen über die Philosophie der Geschichte* but rather from his *Phänomenologie des Geistes* itself as well as from his compulsive and occasional (both published and unpublished) works such as the *Encyclopädie* and the *Rechtslehre* and from the political articles on the Württemberg and German constitutions and on the English Reform Bill of

This paper appears here for the first time in print.

1831. In other words, to the explicit statements about history which have been attributed to Hegel in his *Vorlesungen* (even when corrected by the recent Hoffmeister-Lasson edition, which distinguishes between the introduction, published as *Die Vernunft in der Geschichte: Einleitung in der Philosophie der Weltgeschichte* in a critical edition by Johannes Hoffmeister as volume 1 of the *Vorlesungen*), and in other volumes of the lectures labelled *Die orientalische Welt* (vol. 2), *Die griechische und römische Welt* (vol. 3), and *Die germanische Welt* (vol. 4), must be added his views of history as embodied in the aforementioned sources. These works are necessary to a recounting of Hegel's complete attitude toward history. They furnish necessary modifications of the explicit views expressed for teaching purposes in the *Vorlesungen,* and they help to solve the problem entailed by an apparent circularity of Hegelian reasoning about history in the *Vorlesungen,* a circularity which no amount of critical editing can break through.[1]

Hegel himself opined that these *Vorlesungen* were the best popular introduction to his philosophy, and although he did not mean it so, the boast holds for the problems as well as the achievements of his thought. In the historical dress given to the general doctrine of spiritual development from implicit potentiality to its realization, Hegel saw the example par excellence of "the basic principles" which underlie a "universal process." But in the disquisition which follows, where Hegel discourses generally on the beginnings of history and on the course of historical development, the same fissures between nature and spirit and between history and philosophy from which he started reappeared and vitiated his attempt to use history to resolve his own dualistic problems (*Lectures,* pp. 125–45). What there is of philosophical ratiocination in the *Vorlesungen* Hegel inserted primarily but not exclusively in the introduction, which has been edited separately and given its own title, *Reason in History,* and from which the bulk of the lectures, on the stuff of world history, putatively follows but actually both does and does not follow. The aforementioned reservations notwithstanding, taken together the introduction and the main body of the historical lectures still comprise Hegel's most serious and most extensive venture into history; and it is in reference to both of them—to the introductory lectures dealing with the philosophy of history as such and to the main body of the lectures dealing with the actual past of humanity—that what is prob-

---

1. See Duncan Forbes's introduction to the English translation of Hoffmeister's edition, Georg Wilhelm Friedrich Hegel, *Lectures on the Philosophy of World History,* trans. H. B. Nisbet (Cambridge, Eng., 1975), Introduction: Reason in History, p. vii.

lematical in Hegel's approach to history as well as what requires a more rigorously specified context appear.

For Hegel's lectures faithfully carried out the *kind* of history that he specified in the *Introduction*. They maintained both of the distinctions into which Hegel classified history. In the *Introduction*, as is well known, Hegel distinguished among original history, where the historian presents his contemporary account, either as actor or as eyewitness of the events of which he makes an historical representation, and reflective history, where the historian applies his own spirit—that is, his maxims, ideas, and principles—to the past as a whole, with the result that there are three variants of reflective history: universal or compiled history, consisting in turn of abstract representations or haphazard particular details; pragmatic history, consisting primarily in the representation of meaning, i.e. of inner continuity, with the attendant lifeless themes of necessary progression and moral reflections; and critical history, consisting mainly in the history of history, along with specialized history, consisting mainly in the fragmentary abstraction of a particular branch of activity from the wider context in accordance with a unified general perspective. The third distinct type of reflective history is then the philosophical history of the world, relating to the specialized variant of reflective history but without its foibles. Philosophical world-history thus shares with specialized reflective history both the approach through general perspective and the idea that there is no past but only an eternal present which subsumes the past; but it is unlike specialized reflective history in that the focus is not on a single aspect of national life but on the whole, and the general perspective is not abstract but concrete. The result is that the subject of philosophical history is spirit or the Idea, which is eternally and concretely present to itself and which directs the events of world history. Hegel's later lectures were appropriately entitled "the philosophical history of the world" (ibid, p. 25).

From the start, then, Hegel built two points of view into his philosophy of history. On the one hand, he recognized the empirical basis of history—"history . . . is concerned with what actually happened"—but on the other hand he insisted that the philosophy in his philosophy of history can be considered something that "approaches history as something to be manipulated, and . . . forces it to conform to its preconceived notions and constructs a history a priori"(ibid., pp. 25–26). Apparently, Hegel acknowledged both points of view by maintaining that the historian "brings his categories with him, and they influence his vision of the data he has before him," with the result that the actual portrayal of historical events demonstrates that "the history of the world is a rational process . . ., the rational and necessary evolution of the world spirit" for the simple reason that "whoever looks at the world rationally will find that it in turn assumes a rational aspect" (ibid., pp. 27, 29). In short, Hegel resolved his difficulty nominally by converting metaphysics into epistemology, by viewing the problem of history as the problematic procedure of the historian. The fact is that history offered to Hegel two notions that were of great usefulness in giving a nominal resolution to his inherent duality between absolute spirit and its human, historical embodiment. He defined the associated ideas of progress and development in such a way that they seemed to give a covering of historical unity to notions that actually manifested an essential division between the timelessness of absolute spirit and its embodiment in temporal notions.

But Hegel immediately took back this conversion and thereby reinstated his problem by insisting that the essence of the historical process was indeed rational, not only subjectively in an explicit sense but also, in an implicit sense, objectively. "Sure in the knowledge that reason covers history, philosophy is convinced that the events will match the concept. . . . Admittedly, philosophy does follow an a priori method insofar as it presupposes the Idea. But the Idea is undoubtedly there, and reason is fully convinced of its presence. The perspective adopted by the philosophical history of the world is accordingly not just one among many general perspectives. . . . Its spiritual principle is the sum total of all possible perspectives. . . . It . . . deals not with individual situations but with a universal thought which runs throughout the whole" (ibid., p. 30).[2] Thus Hegel distinguishes between the particular and the concrete, insisting that "the object" of the philosophical history of the world is both universal and concrete, for this is the essence of spirit.[3]

The realm to which world history belongs is therefore the realm of

2. See ibid., pp. 29–31, for the context of these remarks.

3. "The general conviction that reason has ruled and continues to rule the world and hence also world history" is justified for Hegel by the correct—i.e., "determinate"—application of the idea of divine providence, for in Hegel's view God actually uses Providence, and philosophy can know God through his providential revelation of Himself in world history. Indeed, Hegel made the connection between reason and divine Providence explicit: "our principle (i.e., that reason governs the world and always has done so) has a religious equivalent in the doctrine of a ruling providence. . . . When God reveals himself to man, he reveals himself essentially through man's rational faculties." Hence, the concrete events are the ways of providence, the means it uses, the phenomena in which it manifests itself in history. . . . "History is the unfolding of God's nature in a particular determinate element, so that only a determinate form of knowledge is possible and appropriate to it." Ibid., pp. 37, 39, 42. See also p. 33.

spirit, and to investigate spirit "the empirical approach is not adequate," for spirit is not an abstraction invented by man. If spirit is conscious-ness, which is human, it is also the object of consciousness, which is di-vine. Hence, in this sense, spirit makes itself its own object and its own contact. God is the highest form of spirit, for God is "the universal truth itself," and "the Spirit is the whole." Thus spirit is both human and di-vine, a relationship which expresses itself in the forms of dialectical con-tradiction, the idea of freedom, and the emphasis upon the nation. Both of the former qualities are obvious, but the last of these is discussed by Hegel at length, with his conclusion being that the spirit of the maker is the universal spirit in a particular knowable form. It is in this time of the spirit's self-knowledge that "world history is the progress of the con-sciousness of freedom" (ibid., p. 54).[4] Hegel affirmed that "the prin-ciples of the national spirits in their necessary progression are themselves only moments of the one universal spirit, which ascends through them in the course of history to its consumation in an all-embracing totality" (ibid., p. 65).[5]

Nonetheless, Hegel rejected the idea of progress as a principle of incessant change, defined by the "indeterminate concept" of perfectibil-ity. Instead he affirmed progress in its definitions as "a principle of de-velopment" with an "inner determination" that afforded it stability, as a principle of potential in a present condition which has to be realized. In this kind of development, "the spirit, whose theater, province, and sphere of realization is the history of the world, . . . is in itself the abso-lute determining factor. . . . The spirit . . . is only what it makes itself, for it . . . makes itself actually what it already was potentially." In this development of spirit, the process whereby its inner determination is translated into reality is mediated by human consciousness and will, but in this context the process of spiritual realization is unitary. "The con-cept of the spirit is such that historical development must take place in the temporal world. In the world of the spirit, each change is a form of progress. . . . Thus, world history as a whole is the expression of the spirit in time, just as nature is the expression of the Idea in space." Hegel explicitly compared this notion of history, with its apparent unity "as the successive stages in the [gradual] development of that principle whose substantial content is the consciousness of freedom," with the metaphysical phases in "the evolution of consciousness." Thus Hegel distinguished between a pre-historical period, where nature rules and

4. But see also the context, ibid., pp. 46–57.
5. But see also the context, ibid., pp. 58–63.

there is still a mere potentiality in itself, and a historical period, "where rationality begins to manifest itself in worldly existence." He also continued to distinguish, in interpreting the course of world history, between the "historical" or empirical means, which furnish "the factual details" at the basis of the generalized "distinctive principles" of nations, and the philosophical interpretation "of any determinate object in a universal sense" (ibid., pp. 125–45).

The problem with this bilevel approach to history, whereby the spiritual connections were conceived by reason and the specific acts were perceived by sense, was that admittedly they did not always mesh, and in these cases "individual empirical instances" had to give way. "For it is through reason that we apprehend the work of God" (ibid., p. 67).[6] It is, then, philosophy rather than history as such that is the medium for rational truth and the way to it. Although the passions of individual men that constitute the external and phenomenal world which confronts us in history are needed to impart vitality and reality to the "universal and abstract" nature of inner freedom or reason, that is, to the ultimate end of spirit, it is precisely this inner freedom or reason, in the form of "principle, rule, or law," that is the primary object of inquiry. "In relation to this universal substance [i.e., universal reason] which exists in and for itself, "everything else is in a subordinate position and acts only as a means to serve its interests. This universal reason exists as an immanent principle within history, in which it fulfills itself. . . . In the actual process of world history, seen as something as yet incomplete, we find that the subjective element or consciousness is not yet in a position to know the true nature of the ultimate end of history, the concept of spirit . . .; and although the subjective consciousness is still unaware of it, the universal substance is nevertheless present in its particular ends and realizes itself through them" (ibid., pp. 74–75).[7] Thus spirit can only realize itself through particular acts, and therefore the knowledge of spirit only through philosophy and the particular acts only through history.

Hegel attempted to reconcile the two procedures, the philosophical approach directly to spirit and the historical approach to the particular embodiments of spirit in part through definition, by implying that spirit could know itself primarily through its particular external embodiments and in part through his doctrine of the cunning of reason, through which the particular acts of historical individual added up to

6. But see also the context, ibid., pp. 67–73.
7. See also the general context, ibid., pp. 67–75.

universal effects that were perceivable by reason itself. But he acknowledged the persistence of difficulty in this theme by insisting upon the activity of not one but two universals, reflecting the continuation of the old problem. Above the universal that realizes itself in particular acts and raised particularity to universality is "a second universal which expresses itself in history as a whole" and which "is a moment of the productive Idea itself, of that truth which works its way on to its own realization" (ibid., pp. 81–82). If the recognition of the lower universal is the business of both philosophy and history, understanding the higher universal—"the universal idea," in Hegel's terminology—"is the prerogative of philosophy alone. Particulars have their own interests in world history; from the conflict of particulars, "the universal emerges, and it remains unscathed itself," through "the cunning of reason." There is, then, a difference between inner essences and their external embodiments that cannot simply be covered by empirical generalization. "This inner center, this simple source of the rights of subjective freedom, religion, and ethics, as intrinsically universal essences . . . remains untouched and protected from the noisy clamor of world history, and not only from external and temporary changes, but also from those produced by the absolute necessity of the concept of freedom itself. The right of the world spirit transcends all particular rights; it shares in the latter itself, but only to a limited extent, for although these lesser rights may partake of its substance, they are at the same time fraught with particularity." From the viewpoint of the absolute itself, then, Hegel admitted that "the problem becomes more complex and difficult, for now the relation of a mere means to an end disappears" (ibid., p. 92).[8] Thus the subjective will represents the truth of reality only insofar as it wills the universal, i.e., inhabits the state. The aim of all education, therefore, is "to ensure that the individual does not remain purely subjective but attains an objective existence within the state." Hegel's view is that only in the state does the gap between universal reality and external existence seem to be bridged, for only in the context of the state is the meaning of phenomenal existence not external and particular, but the phenomenon itself *is* the essential. The external and the internal are in this instance coextensive. "This spiritual content is a firm and solid nucleus which is completely removed from the world of arbitrariness, peculiarities, caprices, individuality, and contingency. . . . Thus the state is the more specific object of world history in general, in which freedom obtains its objectivity. . . . For the Law is the objectivity of the spirit." Thus the

8. See also the context of realization, ibid., pp. 92–104.

state, as "the totality of ethical life and the realization of freedom," is "the objective unity" of the two moments of spirit—the Idea of freedom as the absolute and ultimate end of history, and the subjective aspect of knowledge, volition, vitality, movement, and activity which constitute history's empirical means (ibid., p. 97). For although the two moments should be distinguished, they are also connected.

But implicitly Hegel repeated his dualism here, for he ascribed the same unitary function to religion, art, and philosophy, that he ascribed ostensibly to the state: "Of all the forms which this conscious union assumes, religion occupies the first place. In it, spirit in its worldly existence becomes conscious of the absolute spirit. . . . The second form which the spiritual union of the objective and the subjective assumes is art; art enters more fully into the world of sensuous reality than does religion, and its worthiest occupation is to portray, if not the spirit of God, at least the form of the deity, and the divine and the spiritual in general . . . : and this brings us to the third form of spiritual union, that of philosophy" (ibid., pp. 104–5).[9]

Although Hegel tried desperately to show that these three forms were "intimately associated with the principle of the state" and were but "abstract moments which occur within the concept of the state," his demonstration that the state is based on religion rather than the other way around, and that, "as against this ideal mode of existence" defined by religion, art, and philosophy, "the state has a second dimension in the content of its external appearance," reintroduced the distinction between the direct conception and perception of the absolute Idea, however determinate it may be, and the particular forms of the universal which were the state's preferred bailiwick (ibid., pp. 107, 113).

Moreover, even within the state itself, Hegel had to recognize the distinction implicit in the state as "an abstraction which has its purely universal reality in the citizens who belong to it." This distinction becomes explicit in Hegel's view of the problematic relationship between the government and the subjective rights of the individuals who are governed by it, a distinction between the ruler and the ruled in turn sponsors the distinction between republic and monarchy, and within the latter between "primary and secondary varieties of monarchy" (ibid., pp. 116, 123).[10] But neither is this confession of Hegel's of the difference between the philosophical approach to the present and the historical approach to the past simply a peroration. In the final analysis,

---

9. See also the general context, ibid., pp. 104–13.
10. See also the pages between these points, ibid., pp. 116–23.

the inexorable advance of the dialectic makes it impossible for universality as such, i.e., essential universality, or concrete universality, to be equivalent to generalization from particulars. For "thought, "insofar as it is universal in character, has the effect of dissolving every determinate content. . . . The preceding principle has been transfigured by universality; its present mode must be considered as different from the preceding one, for in the latter, the present mode existed only implicitly and had an external existence only through a complex series of manifold relationships. What formerly existed only in concrete particulars now has the form of universality conferred upon it; but a new element, another further determination, is also present. The spirit, in its new inward determination, has new interests and ends beyond those which it formerly possessed." Thus spiritual self-consciousness, "since it is of a universal nature, . . . is also ideal, and accordingly different in form from the real activity, the real work and life which made such an achievement possible" (ibid., pp. 146–47). The universal must always assume a determinate form, even if none is permanent. For the determinate is the concrete, and philosophical universality must always have some determinate form, even if it does so without historical particularity, in which there always inheres a natural principle that is different in kind from the universal spirit. This dialectic shows that Hegel took logic seriously, and, whether the logical process was universality or not, it fit the individual nature of human history. Logic leans toward the collective and should be applied to the individual in history.

But Hegel opined that it was contemporary history which supplied him with his categories and the dialectic with its.

But we are just as fully concerned with the present. Whatever is true exists eternally in and for itself—both entirely in the present, 'now', in the sense of an absolute present. . . . The Idea is of the present, and the spirit is immortal; there is no past or future time at which it did not exist or would not exist . . . ; on the contrary, it exists absolutely now. This in fact means that the present world and the present form and self-consciousness of the spirit contain within them all the stages which appear to have occured earlier in history. . . . What the spirit is now, it has always been implicitly. . . . The spirit of the present world is the concept which the spirit forms of its own nature. . . . It is all that the spirit has created for itself through the labors of world history, and all that was destined to emerge from these labors. This, then, is how we should understand world history, which presents us with the work of the spirit in its progressive recognition of its own nature. . . . In this connection, it should be remembered that every individual . . . must pass through various spheres . . . each of which has taken shape and developed independently at some time in the past. But what the spirit is now, it has always been. . . . Since we are concerned with the Idea of the spirit and look upon everything in world history merely as a manifestation of it, we are invariably occupied with the present whenever we review the past, no matter how considerable that past may be. For philosophy is concerned with what is present and real. Those moments which the spirit appears to have outgrown still belong to it in the depths of its present. Just as it has passed through them again in the present—in the concept it has formed of itself (ibid., pp. 150–51).

Whereas for Kant the components of his system were merely in and of reason, where history was seen as the climax of the system, for Hegel history was built into the very components of the system. World history, then, as the history of nations *is* limited by its relation to the past.

And the great contemporary world-historical event in the national-historical mold, an event with the character and the impact of a phenomenon (that quality being requisite to the determination of the categories necessary for philosophical understanding in the present), was the French Revolution. Indeed, it is in this context of dialectical relationships and historical actualities that Hegel's relation to the Revolution and, in turn, the Revolution's influence upon his developing philosophy must be understood. As a Hegel expert in the Philosophy of Right has recently commented, for Hegel the French Revolution is "that event around which all the determinations of philosophy in relation to its time are clustered, with philosophy marking out the problem through attacks on and defenses of the Revolution."[11] Indeed, Hegel grasped the notion of the freedom of the will as what was embodied in the Revolution. It also embodied the basis of the Rights of Man. All this most certainly took place at the level of world history. The Revolution even shifted Hegel's view of nature from that of a deistic view to a philosophical view, from the positive to the negative, as it were. Hegel thought of himself as a philosopher, but if he conceived by other means the historical method as the alternative to the philosophical method, then he also conceived of the development of concepts as the method of relating philosophy and history. For Hegel, the French Revolution was his starting fact and the symbol of factuality in his thought; but Hegel conjoined philosophy and world history by historizing his own political and social principles to express his end point.

This was the meaning of the Revolution for Hegel: that historization proceeds social and political principle. But this meaning comes across clearly only from Hegel's political writings. Thus another expert, less the parti prix of Hegel's all-subsuming connection to the French Revo-

11. Gerhard Ritter, *Hegel and the French Revolution: Essays on "The Philosophy of Right,"* trans. Richard Dien Winfield (Cambridge, Mass., 1984), p. 43.

lution, commenting on the political writings which Hegel wrote over the greater part of his life, confirms that "the French Revolution and its aftermath dominated Hegel's formative years," but not without the rider that "it is only from his letters that we learn the full extent and nature of the enormous fascination and influence which Napoleon exercised over his mind."[12] Thus for Hegel, Napoleon was a part of the Revolution in process, a particular individual representative of the national will, and not just an independent political phenomenon of unequal consequence in the determination of his philosophical concepts. The Revolution was the symbol of all historizing for Hegel, but the historical symbols he created were of his own philosophy of politics and social position; and this is where the impact of the historical individual can be felt within the concept. Hegel did what he did by emphasizing the character of particularity, subjectivity, and externality, which were the counterparts of the objectivity, universality, and internality which Hegel really sought. It was through the historical individual, mediated by the revolution, that Hegel set forth his conception of objectivity, universality, and internality. The concrete individual, conjoined with the dimension of historical time, aided the determination of the abstract universal. History is the concrete universal mediated from the abstract universal by the particularity of the historical individual. For Hegel, Napoleon was undoubtedly such an individual, just as the French Revolution was the preeminent world-historical phenomenon of the times; but only by mediating the one by the other did this universal, this world historical character held by both, emerge from and merge with Hegelian philosophy. Hegel's published summaries of "world history" in the textbooks, the *Encyclopädie der philosophishen Wissenschaften im Grundrisse* (1817) and the *Grundlinien der Philosophie des Rechts* (1821), and his essays on actual history in the context of his political writings on the German constitution, on the Württembergian estates, and on the English Reform Bill of 1831, confirm but do not resolve the problem of Hegel's duality in his approach to history.

On the one hand, Hegel cradles history, in both of these applications, in contexts that show the priority of extrahistorical, metaphysical and political concerns. "World history," the only kind of history that Hegel discusses in the *Encyclopedia* and in the *Philosophy of Right*, is subordinated to other considerations in its placement. In these works it is placed under the category of the ethical life, where the subjective and objective spirit meet, and it comes right after Hegel's analysis of "the

---

12. *Hegel's Political Writings*, trans. T. M. Knox (Oxford, 1964), pp. 9, 7.

outer law of the state" and, indeed, in the *Philosophy of Right* it is directly subordinated to "the state" as the "actuality of the ethical idea." In this context the moral idea is primarily the incorporation of the world spirit that frees the particular subjective individual, or peoples and states, from their particularity; it is the rational "unity of objective and subjective freedom," i.e., of the universal and the individual which history is supposed to realize in outer events.[13] The summaries of world history which Hegel gives, moreover, have to do at least as much with the progressive and ahistorically absolute investment of the Idea as it does with the historical realization of the spirit in external events. Thus, to combine both of these extrahistorical points of view, Hegel defined world history as just another one of the investments of the world spirit, which embodied itself in temporal history as well as in other, nonhistorical realities. As he wrote in the *Encyclopedia,* "the determinate world spirit, since it is actual and is also its freedom as nature, is finally also in time and has a development of its actuality in freedom determined by its particular principle—that is, it has a history. But as a limited spirit it passes into universal world history, whose events are represented by the dialectic of the particular national spirits, that is, by the world court of justice."[14] In both the *Encyclopedia* and the *Philosophy of Right*—that is, in both of the publications in which Hegel gave an explicit context to his history, the emphasis was on the idea of history as the realm for the smooth "development" of the spirit in a subordinate way, generalizing the course of particular individuals and nations and spiritualizing their national historical careers. "Because history is the formation of spirit in the form of the event, that is, of immediate natural actuality, the stages of development are present as so many *immediate natural principles,* and these, because they are natural, are like a plurality external to one another. . . . The concrete ideas, the spirits of the particular nations, have their truth and determination in the concrete idea which is *absolute universality.* . . . As spirit, it is only the movement of its activity to know itself and therewith to free its consciousness from the form of natural immediacy."[15]

When, therefore, he went on to discuss the successive realms of the

---

13. Georg Wilhelm Friedrich Hegel, *Encyclopädie der philosophischen Wissenschaften im Grundrisse und andere Schriften aus der Heidelberger Zeit,* Intro. Hermann Glockner (3d ed., Stuttgart, 1956), in *Sämtliche Werke,* vol. 6, pp. 281, 292, 299–301; *Grundlinien der Philosophie des Rechts,* ed. Johannes Hoffmeister (4th ed. Hamburg, 1955), in *Sämtliche Werke,* vol. 12, pp. 142, 207–9, 229–91. *Sämtliche Werke* is hereafter abbreviated to *SW.*

14. *Encyclopädie, SW,* vol. 6, pp. 298–99.

15. *Philosophie des Rechts, SW,* vol. 12, pp. 289–93.

spirit, the historical sequence from the freedom of the One to that of the Few to that of All was nowhere in evidence. Now there were four realms instead of three (ancient Rome now had a realm to itself), and each of the realms corresponded to a set of "principles" *(Prinzipien)* which had to do with the metaphysical destiny "of the spirit" in its universal historical investment. The unfolding of the four realms reads as follows: the absorbtion of individuality into the knowledge of spirit (to which the Oriental realm corresponds), the orientation of the knowledge of spirit to "beautiful ethical individuality" (to which the Greek realm corresponds), the intensification of the knowing spirit to "abstract universality" and thus to "opposition against spirit-forsaken objectivity" (to which the Roman realm corresponds), and finally the climax of spirit so that it receives "its truth and concrete essence in its inwardness" and "is reconciled in its objectivity," knowing full well "this truth as Idea and as a world of Lawful actuality" (to which the German realm corresponds). The upshot, for Hegel, is the development of "principle" from abstract inwardness through the opposition of barbarous subjectivity against an intellectual world which it makes "unthinking"; thereafter, spirit is against the world to the end of opposition and to true reconciliation thus making the state, finally, "the actuality of reason" and religion "the perception of spiritual truth as an ideal essence." In this characteristic formulation of the historical process by Hegel, the course of the world spirit is climaxed in that philosophical science which "knows truth as one in the midst of its multifarious manifestations in the *state,* in *nature,* and in the *Ideal world*" (ibid., pp. 293–97; Hegel's emphasis).

Analogously, in Hegel's political articles the history was never autonomous, but was always introduced as background of a present political point. At the start of his piece on the German constitution, Hegel admitted that "the thoughts contained in this essay can have no other effect in their public expressions save the understanding of what is."[16] In this article, which Hegel wrote to demonstrate that the contemporary German constitution formed no state, he invoked the past to show that the medieval empire "was built up in a life totally different from the life it had later and has now." "The course of time and of the culture which has developed in it has separated the destiny of that age and the life of the present sharply from one another;" and he invoked this history for the contrast it demonstrated between the viable empire of the

16. Hegel, *Schriften zur Politik und Rechtsphilosophie,* ed. Georg Lasson (Leipzig, 1913), *SW,* vol. 7, p. 5.

German past and the nugatory state of the present time—between, that is, a situation in which a plurality of European states was not the norm and the situation in which it is the norm. In this sense, "the later situation arises directly from the situation in which the nation, without being a state, did constitute a people" (ibid., pp. 7–8). In short, whether in developing contrast or in inertial opposition, the historical past was mined by Hegel to produce support for the political point embodied in his abstract definition of the state in the present.

In his essay on the Württemberg estates, Hegel specifically identified his labor with "history." But as he himself admitted in his introduction, "the historical events" in Württemberg which he treats of in this essay "do not contain such a considerable part of the past as a history of more remote ages" might, but rather it treats of "the large purposes and interests, as well as the smaller details" of what "still has a present" and consequently remains "peculiar to our age" (ibid., pp. 157–58). Consequently and consistently, as in the essay on the German constitution, the article on the Württemberg estates uses the past to prove that the estates do not act as if Württemberg is a genuine state, as Hegel defines its requirements. In general, Hegel tended to use history in the essay on the Württemberg estates in the same ambiguous way that he used it in the earlier essay on the German constitution, save that, conforming to the more explicit mention of history in his argument, he additionally contrasted the haphazard growth of history with the homogeneity demanded by the idea of the state.

Hegel's final important essay, on the projected English Reform Bill of 1831, employed history analogously again. Here Hegel expressly contrasted the "positive privileges" grounded in history with the "rational law of the State and the true legislation" which the current state required politically, to the detriment of the former. Without explicitly identifying the peculiarities of the English development as the history he was in fact treating of, Hegel rejected both the reactionary standpat attitude of the English aristocracy and the historically based but equally invalid doctrinaire approach of the English radicals by the measure of English constant national character—i.e., the "healthy common sense of the English people" and of political "principles . . . grounded on universal reason," that is, "ideas which constitute the bases of a genuine freedom" (ibid., pp. 292, 315, 320).

On the other hand, Hegel also paid his obeisances to history proper. In this philosophical context not only did he acknowledge that world history was one of the three equivalent subdivisions of the ideal state because it was the only subdivision that represented the State as "a universal idea," one that gave the State "absolute power over the individual state" and that gave "spirit . . . actualization."[17] In short, world history is necessary both as the universalization of particular spirits and as the only way in which universal spirit can get to know itself, that is, to gain self-consciousness, for "spirit makes itself the object of its own consciousness" (*Philosophie,* p. 289).

Similarly, in Hegel's political essays one side always paid full respect to the autonomy of history. Hegel acknowledged that history is sui generis in its capacity to evoke that which is particular and that which is changeful in the development of mankind. Thus in the introduction to his discussion of the Württemberg estates, despite the dominance of his political point of view, he justified history not by its older psychological investigation into the motives of human action or by its accumulation of details, both of which approaches he found to be anachronistic, but by history's endeavor "to present the course of substantial things and to know the characters of historical actors from what they do."[18] The actual history that Hegel adduces in these essays reveals another bifurcation that is analogous to the bifurcation in his philosophy of history and makes Hegel's whole approach to history similar to the anatomy of an onion. For if, on the one hand, Hegel stressed that "history" is "the basis" of the positive law of the constitution, and that therefore historical developments "constitute together an unformed and irrational whole" characterized by particularity and changefulness, on the other hand the same "history showed, primarily through the growth of the Idea of a State and therewith of its essential unity," when "a constitutional provision was rational" (ibid., pp. 160, 173). In short, the application of universality as the standard of the Württemberg constitution is a political criterion whose development lies both outside and inside the historical process, and Hegel applied the political principle both as such—that is, as a present, unhistorical idea—and as the end toward which history aimed. This dual approach to history, so analogous to that in his *Lectures,* enabled Hegel to tie expressly the specific history surveyed in what would be his historical *Lectures:* "The system of representation is the system of all modern European states. . . . It has emerged from the forests in Germany; it makes an epoch in world history. The coherence of world culture has led humanity, after oriental despotism and the rule of a republic over the world, from the decline of the latter into the middle between both, and the Germans are the

17. *Philosophie des Rechts,* pp. 212–13.
18. *Schriften zur Politik und Rechtsphilosophie,* pp. 157–58.

people from which this third universal form of the world spirit has been born" (ibid., p. 93). And so, in his late essay on the English reform bill, Hegel countered his general identification of English history with English positivity, with its particular and fortuitous nature, by investing the "rational law," which he saw as required by the idea of the State, in the recent history of states on the European continent (ibid., p. 291).

We are led, then, by the incapacity or the unwillingness of Hegel to resolve in his history itself the problem of his dual approach to history, to the *Phenomenology of Mind*, where Hegel anchored history in his general approach to reality; for it is now beyond doubt that Hegel saw history as both the timeless investment of the Absolute Spirit in time and the temporal and social process of a humanity struggling teleologically to realize the requirements of spirit, and furthermore, that this dualism was not resolved by Hegel's particular addresses to the subject of history. Now, Hegel's changed notion of the role of the *Phenomenology* (which began as the introduction to his system) and his later composition of the celebrated preface are interesting questions in themselves, but they have little to do with our problem itself, which deals with the resolution of Hegel's dual approach to history and which resorts to the *Phenomenology* because it is all we have of the balanced Hegel.

At first glance, the *Phenomenology* simply perpetuates our problem of Hegel and history. Jürgen Habermas has characterized Hegel's argument therein as frought with "ambiguity" *(Zweideutigkeit),* since the historical development of phenomenological consciousness presupposes the absolute knowledge at which it ends.[19] Herbert Marcuse called the *Phenomenology* Hegel's "first and last attempt" to take account both of the unhistorical character of absolute knowledge and the historicity inseparable from the concept of life.[20] Indeed, Marcuse proceeded to demonstrate, to his own satisfaction, the preeminence of historicity as a motif both of the *Phenomenology* and even of the *Logic* that followed, as did the famous lectures of Alexandre Kojeve in Paris and the sparse comments of Otto Poeggeler on the same work. This emphasis, however, is in contrast to that on the eternal transcendence of historicity in Hegel's concept of absolute knowledge that has been made especially by such commentators on Hegel's logic and metaphysics as

19. Jürgen Habermas, *Erkenntnis und Interesse* (Frankfurt am Main, 1968), pp. 18, 33.

20. Herbert Marcuse, *Hegels Ontologie und die Theorie der Geschichtlichkeit* (2d ed., Frankfurt am Main, 1968), p. 256.

Hartmann, Trendelenberg, Kroner, and Manheim.[21] And the *Phenomenology* itself seems to support both sides of commentators. Thus its concluding paragraph pays obeisance both to history as the necessary externalization of spirit and to philosophy as the absolute and therefore timeless comprehension of spirit as such. "Their [the spirits'] preservation, regarded from the side of their free existence appearing in the form of contingency, is History; but regarded from the side of their philosophically comprehended organization, it is the Science of Knowing in the sphere of appearance: the two together, comprehended history, form alike the inwardizing and the Calvary of absolute spirit, the actuality, truth, and certainty of his throne, without which he would be lifeless and alone."[22] Indeed, the entire *Phenomonology of Spirit* can be read either as a historical account whereby consciousness goes through all the stages of development from primitivity to modernity, with the famous chapter on "Lordship and Bondage" representing the principle of ancient Greece, and with the successive chapters on Absolute Freedom and Terror and on Morality representing the French Revolution and Kant respectively, or as a logical analysis of what Habermas calls the "phenomenological self-reflection," that is, the analysis of the implications of the "notion" *(Begriff)* which to Hegel delivers absolute knowledge to self-conscious spirit.[23] The same duality informs Hegel's belated preface to the *Phenomenology of Mind.* Here he holds both that the "universal individual" *(das allgemeine Individuum)* had to be led through the "process of coming-to-be" *(die Bewegung seines Werdens)* by which the pure notion becomes genuine spiritual knowledge—a coming-to-be that Hegel admits is described in the work at hand—and that for "the single individual" who is "incomplete Spirit" this past exis-

21. Nicolai Hartmann, *Die Philosophie der deutschen Idealismus* (1948); J. E. Erdmann, *Grundriss der Logik und Metaphysik* (new ed., Leiden, 1901); Erdmann, *Die Philosophie des deutschen Idealismus* (Leipzig, 1929); Friedrich Adolf Trendelenburg, *Logische Untersuchungen* (2d ed., Leipzig, 1862); Ernst Manheim, *Zur Logik des konkreten Begriffs* (Leipzig, 1928); Richard Kroner, *Von Kant bis Hegel* (Tübingen, 1921–24); for a recent analysis which sets Hegel's systematic philosophy above his history in a context which goes beyond his *Logik,* see Reinhard Klemens Maurer, *Hegel und das Ende der Geschichte: Interpretationen zur Phänomenologie des Geistes* (Stuttgart, 1945). For the superiority of historicity in Hegel see Marcuse, *Hegels Ontologie,* pp. 257–368, and Alexandre Kojève, *Introduction to the Reading of Hegel,* ed. Allan Bloom, trans. James H. Nichols, Jr. (New York, 1969), pp. 14–15, 183–86, 209–15, 259.

22. Habermas, *Erkenntnis und Interesse,* pp. 29–35, 42, 58.

23. Hegel, *System der Wissenschaft: Erster Teil, Die Phänomenologie des Geistes,* ed. Georg Lasson (3d ed., Leipzig, 1928), *SW,* vol. 2, pp. 24–31.

tence is the already acquired property of universal Spirit which constitutes "the Substance of the Individual," and hence appears externally to him as "his inorganic nature"—that is, "the single individual must also pass through the formative stage of universal Spirit," since "the Substance of the individual, the World-Spirit itself, has had the patience . . . to take upon itself the enormous labor of world-history."[24] Men must deal therefore both with historical and with philosophical truths.

Now most commentators are agreed that what seems like duality to us was unity for Hegel. For them, the essence of Hegel's dialectic was his desire to reconcile the multiplicity of life, including historical life, with the unity of the rational notion of absolute knowledge.[25] And to be sure, in the *Phenomenology* itself Hegel's emphasis is upon the historical development through which the notion comes to know itself and from whose appropriation absolute knowledge develops the logic of its implicit moments. The problem that concerns us here, though, is the fact that the working of a timeless, philosophical investment of the spirit in dialectical logic and the temporal, historical embodiment of spirit in an external process of its own realization are two commitments apparently at odds with one another. This fundamental difficulty of Hegel's lay behind the discrepancies between his introductory epitome of the historical lectures and the lectures themselves, and it is through these discrepancies that the problem must be approached. The discrepancies lie in the well-known formulations by Hegel on the different degrees of the knowledge of freedom, namely, "that of the Orientals, who knew only that One is free, then that of the Greek and Roman world, which knew that Some are free, and finally, our own knowledge that All men as such are free, and that man is by nature free" (*Lectures*, pp. 54–55). There are two kinds of discrepancies in this formulation: First, the tripartite schema is in the event overlaid by an analytical presentation of a continuous development in which the Chinese and the Indians are mediated to the classical world by a depiction of intermediate peoples like the Persians, the Egyptians, and the Hebrews, and in which, in turn, the classical world of antiquity is mediated to the modern Germanic world by a depiction of the barbarians, medieval Christianity, and the Reformation. Second, the theme of the lectures is not the quan-

24. Habermas, *Erkenntnis und Interesse*, pp. 18, 33.
25. E.g., Jean Hyppolite, *Genesis and Structure of Hegel's "Phenomenology of Spirit,"* trans. Samuel Cherniak and John Hickman (Evanston, 1974), pp. 39, 48–50.

titative extension of freedom but the progressive realization of the conditions of freedom in the emancipation of the spirit from nature, and in the recovery by an emancipated subjective freedom of its objects in the world.

A hint of these discrepancies was vouchsafed in the introduction itself, both through Hegel's emphasis on the casual nature of his summary and through the inconsistencies in the epitome itself. On the first count, he characterized it as "only provisional remarks thrown out in passing" (ibid., p. 55). On the second, he also characterized the Oriental "One" as "not a free man and a human being" at all, and he insisted that Greek freedom was "itself . . . only a fortuitous, undeveloped, transient, and limited efflorescence," as well as one that was based on the slavery that confined freedom to only some (ibid., p. 54). Moreover, when Hegel returned prefatorily to his threefold distinction in the context of comparing the historical development of spirit with its metaphysical development he neglected the quantitative dimensions of extended freedom entirely, measuring the differences between the Oriental world, the world of classical antiquity, and the Germanic or Christian world by the progression from the relationship between the spirit and nature to the relationship between the spirit and God (ibid., pp. 130–32). As Hegel apparently realized, such prefatory caveats made the problem of relating a priori metaphysical structures, as understood by the philosophers of history, to the "empirical reality" or the "external reality" of developmental metaphysical structures, as attended to by "ordinary historians," the theme which Hegel actually followed in his lectures on world history (ibid., pp. 131, 141).

In his lecture, Hegel characteristically ever seeks "the principle" behind the institutions of each culture, and thus, by typing the principle to the evidence he cited, especially the religious evidence of each culture, he mended in practice the disjunction which he affirmed in theory; and this was the basic discrepancy between his philosophical introduction and the actual historical bent of the lectures themselves. The principles under which Hegel marshaled his historical evidence were the fundamental philosophical categories of subject, object, nature, and spirit, and his success in the fit, as measured by the seamlessness of the juncture between them, was a sign of his practical reconciliation of the categories and the evidence. Thus, although he claimed to begin only with the historical stage of the world-spirit, excluding thereby everything pre-political and mythical from his purview, he insisted that China and India, even in the stages in which their past is a part of world history, themselves "lie, as it were, outside of world history," since in principle both lack the element of free subjectivity whose objectification in the state makes for the vital progress of world history.[26]

In China the spirit of the constitution agrees with the general principle behind the culture, which stipulates that the factor of subjectivity is entirely lacking. The substance in China is immediately but one subject, the emperor, but this limitation of substance to one despotic individual means that the element of subjectivity is lacking in general. Hence, not individuals but the family is the spirit which animates Chinese culture. Even the emperor exercises his powers patriarchally (ibid., pp. 288–89). Hegel then marshals evidence from the Chinese constitution, its administration, its jurisprudence, its religion, and its sciences to support and to be explained by the general principle of the culture. Thus the form of Chinese science is connected with the lack of genuine inwardness.

In India, the culture has remained as static and undeveloping as the Chinese, but the principle of Indian culture is otherwise the opposite of the Chinese: in India the lack of separation between the particular external item of reality and the universal absolute spirit—a merger embodied in the characteristic Indian principle which exalts the idealism of the imagination or the dreaming spirit—spiritualizes particularity pantheistically while abhorring individuality and demeaning spirituality, or God. Thus, whereas China celebrates the principle of despotic unity over equals, India's contrasting principle sees differentiation stemming from despotic unity. But in the caste system this differentiation comes back to Nature. No more than China, then, does India have individuality, or the free subjectivity of individuals; and no more than the Chinese is the Indian culture a part of history. Despite the contrasts between them, then, since the Chinese write history whereas the Indians write none, and the Chinese principle of prosaic universality is countered by the Indian principle of diversity, in both cultures individuals are enslaved—in China by the despot, in India by the dreamworld—and history, which gives to variety the form of universality and is thus the empirical way of producing universality, is ruled out. Thus Hegel surveyed the civilizations of the Far East, in which he included China and India, from the point of view of the history of spirit, as a process ending with his contemporary comprehension of spirit, when the absolute is also spirit, whereas the realization of spirit is not in immediacy but mediated through the universal in the thought of man.

26. Hegel, *Die orientalische Welt*, ed. Georg Lasson (2d ed., Leipzig, 1919), *SW*, vol. 8, p. 275.

Despite the absence of such a division in his epitome, in his historical lectures Hegel made a distinction in kind between the Far East and the Near East of Asia. Where he included the civilizations (which he called "nations") of China and India in the former, he began the latter with the Persians and included among them those Mediterranean peoples whom we usually associate with the cradle of Western civilization—the Zends, the Assyrians, the Babylonians, the Medes, the Phoenicians, the Syrians, the Hebrews and the Egyptians—identifying them as members of the Caucasian, that is, European race, characterizing them as continuous interactors with the West, stressing their contrast with Asians further to the east, and especially with the Indians, aligning them with the historical peoples. "The Persians are the first historical people. While China and India remain static and prolong a natural, vegetative existence until the present, this country Persia has undergone development and revolutions, which by themselves betray a historical condition" (ibid., pp. 414–15). Thus Hegel saw as the principle of the Persian world the "unity" which stresses "light" and allows the individual for the first time "freedom from the natural principle" (ibid., p. 417).

In Persia and the Near East generally, then, Hegel traced the course of the spirit in two principles that ostensibly formed the transition between the Oriental and the Greco-Roman world but that actually showed a greater development toward the ultimate modern end of spirit than did classical antiquity. The principles are these: first, the spiritualization of unity: unity becomes separated from nature and becomes wholly spiritualized; and, second, the recognition of men as individuals (ibid., pp. 418, 453). What separates these achievements from the modern stage of spirit to its Greek embodiment and thus to its self-liberation is the down-playing of both the Hebrew and the Egyptian achievements. In some measure it was a matter of perspective, for Hegel presented the Persian performance in a positive light, the Hebrew and the Egyptian negatively—in terms of what the Hebrews and the Egyptians had not accomplished toward the free spirit of modernity. Indeed, he literally identified Hebraic spirituality with "the principle of negativity" (ibid., p. 460). Although they came later than the palmy days of the Persian Empire (both in actual chronology and in Hegel's presentation), and although they both shared with the parent Persian Empire and civilization the separation of the spiritual from the natural, the emphasis was on the abstract character of the spirit and the consequent bondage of the individual subject in both the Hebraic and the Egyptian cultures. In Egypt, moreover, the unity so far lacks concentration as to

be a problem rather than a resolution of the problem, for the spirit here
finds its emancipation from nature problematical, seeking the embodiment of spirit only in art and for the rest constituting itself as but one
particularity among others. In both Judea and Egypt, history is consequently dubious, mixed as it is with miracle and myth. The deficiencies
of the Hebrews and the Egyptians in the final analysis get attributed to
the Persian Empire of which they are a part and betray the immaturity
of spirit in that Empire. For the essence of the Persian principle is that
free as the spirit is in it, universality also remains separate from spirit.
The result is that the Persian spiritual principle is not diffused among
the constituent parts of the Empire and therefore forms no whole but
only an aggregate of the most various individualities. As represented in
"pure light," there is something natural that still pertains to spirit in the
Persian dispensation, and this circumstance in turn leads, according to
Hegel, to the separation of universality from human freedom, as with a
pair of abstractions.[27] The fault is that of the historical state, not of the
essence, of the Persian version of absolute spirit. "The fault of the Persian principle is only that the unity behind the opposition between nature and spirit is not known in a finished form. . . . In philosophy the
opposition must always be limited by the unity."[28] His summary was
that the Persian principle contained "a breath of the spirit" (ibid., p.
417).

Hegel thus saved his transition from the Oriental to the classical
worlds and therewith the historical basis of his survey. But he had saved
historical continuity at the price of inconsistency, for his view of the
classical world was twofold: on the one hand, he showed that it manifested a progress over the Oriental world in the self-consciousness of
spirit; but on the other hand he was also negative in his prevalent attitude toward it because of what it lacked in the embodiment of the absolute spirit. Hence he carried over the dual perspective with which he
viewed the Oriental world into his portrait of the classical world, and in
the different claims placed by history and by philosophy his original duality emerged once more.

In good measure, Hegel's portrayal of this duality consisted in his
depiction of the duality between the Greek and the Roman worlds. For
Hegel's picture of the Roman world was one of spiritless domination
expressing itself in "the preponderance of violence over concrete indi-

27. Hegel, *Die griechische und die römische Welt,* ed. Georg Lasson (2d ed., Leipzig,
1920), *SW,* vol. 8, p. 662.
28. *Die orientalische Welt,* pp. 425–26.

viduality," which was the opposite of the joyful spirituality of the Greeks in the latter's declining phase.[29] And yet, as Hegel's notion of the Romans as the continuation of the Greek destiny shows, he read his duality back into Greek culture itself. For if the Greek principle achieved the dismantling of the abstractness of the universal by its emphasis upon the individual, if spirit here celebrates its "rebirth" for the first time, and if we therefore for the first time feel "at home" with the Greeks, it is true too that nature operated as the galvanizing force for the Greek's spirit and that therefore the natural factors, even if spiritualized, play themselves out as individualities within the spirit taking the form of subjectivity. The combination of subjective spirit and objective individualities seen as the transformation of nature, after all, makes for the exaltation of Greek art. Thus if humans honor the divine principle, they have also created it.

The God of the Greeks, therefore, is not yet the absolute free spirit, but it is spirit in a particular way, in human limitation, still dependent as a determinate individuality on external conditions. The divine spirit is not yet spirit for itself, but it is still sensuously manifested. On the one hand, the Greek spirit is as spiritual as the Christian; on the other, the Greek spirit is known only in its manifest form; and because the Greeks do not yet know spirit in its universality, they do not yet have subjectivity of spirit. Hence they know neither absolute nor individual spirit as such, nor the reconciliation between them. The Greeks remain on the middle ground of beauty and have not yet attained the higher point of truth. Hegel showed the historical development of Greece toward the decline of the Greek spirit, which led for him, in turn, to the dead hand of Roman power.

If, in Hegel's portrait of the Greeks, the bad, although perceptible, was outweighed by the good, in Hegel's Rome the opposite proportion held sway. Even at its best, the universality of the sovereign One and the subjectivity of the individual person were equally abstract, with the result that their reconciliation through philosophy was also abstract. It was, then, also dead and could not satisfy the living spirit, which demanded a higher reconciliation. Thus, "the Roman world enters world history with politics as power actually constituting the abstract universal destiny of man and limiting all moral individuals" (ibid., pp. 661–62).

But at once linked with and in contrast to this secular Romanism was the birth of Christianity in the Roman Empire, and Hegel's attitude toward ancient and medieval Christianity was analogously dual. Again,

29. *Die griechische und die römische Welt,* p. 662.

on the one hand, the Roman principle of subjectivity imprinted the idea of personality upon the Christian religion. The difference between secular Romanism and Christian Romanism was bridged by "the discipline of the world," which entailed "the renunciation of himself" by each secular person (ibid., p. 727). The higher destiny is still missing in the Roman world and must be sought elsewhere in the Germanic world, despite the destiny of the Germans "to be the bearers of the Christian principle" and despite "the 'appropriateness' of the principle of the German Empire to the Christian religion." This duality spawned the opposition of church and state, wherein the state represented worldly consciousness, distinct from the inwardness of subjectivity in that it was particularistic, and the church represented "the internality of the Christian principle." But in both worldly and religious matters Christian freedom is distorted into the opposite of itself, and "spirit must know itself as an Other, which stands outside itself."[30]

The medieval West emphasized contingency, complication, and particularity as opposed to the admittedly abstract tendency of the Muslims toward the integration of the whole. The medieval Germans recognized no political obligation, and hence there was the possibility of forming a constitution: relationships were only between individuals. With this perversion of the principle of Christian freedom, the absolute division of the spiritual and the world principle follows; since piety is outside of history, which is rather the realm of spirit realizing itself in its subjective freedom, "in the Middle Ages" where there is not yet this realization of the divine, the opposition between divinity and reality is unreconciled; in this period subjective spirit translates the absolute into sensory, external existence. Thus the medieval church was no longer a spiritual power but an ecclesiastical one. The medieval church is a reaction of spirituality against secularity, but in such a way that secularity is only subjected to the church and not reformed by it; during the crusades spirituality longs for this secular embodiment; through the crusades the church completes the displacement of religion and the divine spirit; it perverted the principle of Christian freedom to the unlawful and immoral slavery of souls (ibid., p. 764).

In general, Hegel's tone with respect to the Middle Ages was negative, despite the presence of the saving Christianity and his doctrine of the progress of the absolute spirit. Biographically, this tone was accountable to Hegel's famed indebtedness to the European Enlightenment, a debt which led him to conclude his historical section on the

30. Hegel, *Die germanische Welt*, ed. Georg Lasson (2d ed., Leipzig, 1920), *SW*, vol. 8, p. 763–64.

Middle Ages by celebrating the succeeding onset of modernity in the third period of the German Empire, signaled and symbolized by the Reformation of the sixteenth century as that day of universality which finally breaks in after the long, eventful, and dark night of the Middle Ages. But consistent with this biographical note was his intellectual conviction that the modern phase of Germandom witnessed the self-conscious stage of the absolute spirit, wherein it attained the unity of objective and subjective freedom, achieving reconciliation in the entirety of its essence. This was Hegel's dominant note, but it was accomplished by a subordinate disclaimer that even in the modern period the domination of philosophy meant the domination of abstraction, since philosophy is only abstract thought and not the concrete conception of absolute truth—positions between which there is an immeasurable difference. This is obviously true of Catholicism, including that of revolutionary France, but it is also true, even if less so potentially, of Protestantism, and of Protestantism in Germany.

But by and large, for Hegel, the modern, Germanic, Protestant era is the period in which the "truth and actuality" of the Christian principle "is first given," in which, that is, "the principle of the free Spirit is made the banner of the world, and the universal doctrines of reason develop out of this principle."[31] In short, for Hegel the temporal process and the eternal investment of spirit coincided in the modern period, and he prepared for this happy event by demonstrating the eternal work of the spirit in the other Western ages as well. This positive side of Hegel's historical treatment goes back to the origins of Christianity during the classical period of antiquity, when the Christian religion so grounded the principle of subjectivity that it served as the basis for the salvation of the world because it gave birth to spirit as absolute object, truth, and therefore grounded the principle of divine spirit which is the beginning as well as the end of history. For the expansion of this principle from the field of religion to that of all reality—that is, the concrete realization of objectivity in the world—is now a matter of the smooth "development" of history. In this respect "progress is the development of free particularity, . . . but so that the particulars remain in unity, in relation to one another." Thus the relationship of religion and reason is that of a distinction without a difference, for the business of history is only that religion appears as human reason, that "the religious principle which inhabits the heart of man is also brought forth as worldly freedom."[32]

---

31. Habermas, *Erkenntnis und Interesse*, p. 22. My translation.
32. H. S. Harris, *Hegel's Development: Toward the Sunshine* (Oxford, 1972), pp. 27–30.

From this positive point of view we may call the ages of modern man—
that is, in Hegel's terminology, the three periods of Germanic history
(classical, medieval, and modern in current terminology)—the "realms
of the Father, of the Son, and of the Spirit," recalling the course of earlier history, with Charlemagne compared to the Persians, the Reformation to Germany, and modern times to Rome.

With this ambiguous but characteristic comparison, which demeans
the present age as much as it sanctifies past periods, we leave our survey
of Hegel's view of world history as it is embodied in his *Lectures*. In
them Hegel exhibited two inconsistencies of the same kind: he summarized his historical lectures in his introduction through the wrong
terms, and his actual historical lectures were divided between two different perspectives. Both inconsistencies related to the apparent gap between the timeless, philosophical investment of the spirit in dialectical
logic, and the temporal, historical embodiment of spirit in the external
process of its own realization. These discrepancies pointed to other,
nonhistorical contexts for their resolution. That Hegel switched his
model state from that of France to Prussia did not mean that he
changed his political philosophy. He merely changed that philosophy's
application while maintaining the constancy of his philosophy. Our job
has been to show how this constancy is reflected in the lectures and articles, how the articles show the incompleteness of Hegel's shift to history, and how the analysis of the lectures shows the completeness of his
shift to history. The *Philosophy of Right* shows the incompleteness of
Hegel's transition to history; the *Lectures* show how constantly Hegel
refered to history while developing his philosophical concepts.

Yet the story does not end here, for we must still ask what lies behind
Hegel's claimed solution to the reconciliation of life and reason, of multiplicity and unity. The answer is one that Hegel himself gave in the
context of his definition of history in the *Phenomenology*. The problem in
the deciphering of what Hegel really meant in the treatment of history
lies in his background, for he seemed to use an inherited idea of history
that was not at all the idea of history that he actually used. From an
early age Hegel was interested in traditional history, and he took his
ideas about history from typical Enlightenment histories of humanity.
Now the point about Enlightenment history is that it took over from
the past of historical consciousness the "supra-individual," or the social,
or the public quality in the definition of history, and it passed on this
quality to Hegel.[33] But although Hegel seemed to adopt this collective

33. Harris, *Hegel's Development*, pp. 27–30.

quality in his early idea of a "philosophical history," actually he did not; and his idea of a human development through time implied a definition of history that was really indifferent to the social quality in the traditional idea of history. Hence Hegel's idea of history in the *Phenomenology* appears in his final chapter, on "Absolute Knowing," in the context of his philosophical discussion of time and the Notion *(Begriff)*— "Time is the Notion itself that is there"—and of Spirit's movement toward self-knowledge, for which time, the Notion (which is existent Spirit or *Geist*) and the "I" (the *Ich* or "self-identity," *die Gleichheit des Selbstes*) are necessary. Hence history, which is juxtaposed to the "Science of Knowing in the sphere of appearance," as something preliminary is to a final principle, has nothing inherently social or public about it.[34] In Hegel's mind, it comprehends the inner dialectical movement of the Spirit more than it does the traditional social story of mankind. Hegel's idea of a "philosophical history" becomes explicable by this confusion, which is a confusion in his *Lectures on the Philosophy of History,* but is no confusion at all as the idea of history that is embodied in his *Phenomenology of Spirit*. Hegel's Preface to the *Phenomenology* seals this relationship by discussing the peculiar status of Time in relation to the Science of Spirit while not discussing history explicitly in this context at all. Not only history but that which would help to constitute traditional history in his *Lectures,* "the singular detail" *(die Einzelheit)* and the share of "the individual" in *des Individuums,* were demeaned in comparison with the Science which "exists solely in the self-movement of the Notion, and 'Time,' which is the existent notion itself" (ibid., pp. 39–59).

For Hegel, history had as much to do with philosophical principles as it did with socialized human culture. This was the idea of history that made his notion of the movement of the absolute consistent with the social externalization of the Spirit in the public records of socialized human culture. The movement of time, in Hegel's view, was actually the internal movement of history.

34. *System der Wissenschaft,* pp. 557–64.

4 The Intellectuals and European Society

I

Recent evaluations have tended to pass one of two judgments upon the European intellectuals. It has been concluded either that they live in isolation from their society and say nothing relevant to it or that they are entirely submerged in the society and merely reflect it.[1] The facts to which these judgments refer are clear enough. On the one hand, intellectuals have adopted a critical position vis-à-vis all the important social and political forces of the day, which offer no foothold for their ideas. The continental middle classes have moved into confessional parties in which clerical and economic interests predominate; the secular liberal parties have been reduced to splinter groups of the Right; the working class adheres either to a communism which has a set, unalterable doctrine or to socialist parties which can no longer afford a clear theoretical basis; the organizations of the Resistance are dead—Sartre wrote their epitaph with his withdrawal from the *Rassemblement Democratique Révolutionnaire*, which he had helped to found in their image. On the other hand, intellectuals have adopted an apologetic position vis-à-vis institutional forces—state, party, church, or university—on which they are increasingly forced to depend for their livelihood and for their continued intellectual existence. The factors behind this development range from the bureaucratization of the intellectuals which has grown out of the shrinkage of middle-class inherited incomes and the financial instability of the general periodical—the disappearance of *Horizon* and *Die Wandlung* are outstanding cases in point—to the threat which the Soviet danger poses for freedom of expression as the intellectuals have known it.

These alternative conclusions are susceptible of two rather obvious explanations. The first is that the same phenomenon is judged by different writers from divergent points of view. A prevalence of esoteric

First published in *Political Science Quarterly* 67 (June, 1952), 225–47.

1. An excellent article which goes beyond these categories is by Kenneth Douglas, "The French Intellectuals: Situation and Outlook," in Edward Mead Earle, ed., *Modern France: Problems of the Third and Fourth Republics* (Princeton, 1951), pp. 61–81.

themes, for example, can be interpreted either as a product of intellectual isolation or as an evasion of responsibility accruing to the intellectuals' uncritical submergence in society. The second explanations is that the judgments refer to different groups of intellectuals: the liberal intellectuals are in general identifiable as the critics; Communist intellectuals, orthodox religious thinkers, academicians and civil servants are identified as the apologists. But despite the variant judgments and distinctions an important problem remains: what are the general conceptions held by the intellectuals which form the background of their social ideas and on which the judgments of them must be based? Interest in these general conceptions represents more than mere idle curiosity, for it is often the general outlook of an intellectual rather than his social position as such that defines him. Thus, the extent to which a Catholic, an academic, or even a governmental intellectual is subordinated to the institution with which he is associated may well depend not simply upon his association with that institution but also upon his ideas about the nature of reality in general, social reality in particular, and the specific role of his institution in it. This function of ideas permits a variety of social relationships for the intellectuals. Conceptions which allow or encourage intellectuals to find a secure haven with some recognized social or political organization are of little interest, for by and large they come to terms with official doctrines which are well known. Likewise, conceptions which influence intellectuals toward a total unconcern with society supply little substance for an understanding of European society. But those conceptions which imply a tension in the intellectual because they are addressed to social reality and yet are unable wholly to penetrate it—such conceptions are objects of general concern.

The importance of this kind of general conception lies in the promise which it holds out to men that ideas can build a platform out from the world into an absolute realm from which the world can be moved. For an age in which the unitary strands of social experience have tended to unravel and in which tinkering with the resultant parts has been relegated to the efficiency expert, the presence of total views which are somehow connected with experience seems to offer the only possibility of organizing and improving the elements of this concrete existence. To revert to a previous illustration, religious thinkers who seek not so much to rationalize the existing role of faith and the churches by exegeses of traditional doctrine as to interpret anew their function on the basis of the new general insights of the age, academicians who are not content to remain within the framework of their special fields but go beyond them to apply their knowledge and their methods to general problems of humanity—such men participate in the crucial issue before the modern intellectual.

However various its manifestations, this kind of problem may be accounted the problem par excellence of the liberal intellectuals, if liberal be defined for this purpose as referring to the habit of mind which manifests anxiety about the concrete organization of life, is yet dissatisfied with current forms of organization, and is ever open to new ideal impulses which seek to develop this organization beyond those forms. In this sense, "liberal" includes not only representatives of the familiar secular political tradition nor only the intellectuals free of all institutional attachment, but rather all those intellectuals who, whatever their mundane ties, are responsive to general currents which come from beyond those associations and create a tension in them.

The attempt will be made here to deal with some of the general attitudes which form the background for the social and political orientation of European intellectuals who are "liberal" in this broad sense.

II

Some background is required to give an idea of the direction in which European thinkers have been traveling, for twentieth-century thought is composed of such a peculiar mélange of old and new elements that only a historical analysis will enable us to discover what is distinctive about it.

Although there is some doubt as to whether the lay intellectual has his origins in the Roman rhetorician or the Italian humanist, we may finesse that issue. The story, for our purposes, begins in the eighteenth century. It is at this point that the social position of the liberal intellectual and the substance of his thought meet in such a way as both to make him an effective force in society and to create the problem which is his main concern today. The position of the intellectual combined two elements: he still carried over from the humanists his consciousness of being a member of an autonomous spiritual estate, with all the critical functions of the *clerc* attributed to this estate by Julien Benda (himself a good eighteenth-century type); but he was at the same time, usually by origin and almost unanimously by conviction, representative of the aims of the liberal aristocracy and the middle classes, so that the standards of his criticism were not simply those of the conscience of the society but entailed a program for a new order. This position of the intellectual manifested itself in the character of his message. In the first place, he had no need to concern himself with "pure thought," since the presuppositions of his thinking had been worked out in the metaphysical and scientific systems of the seventeenth century, and since, on the basis of this security, he could limit himself to what concerned human affairs. In the second place, the so-called rational synthesis of the eighteenth century was, in content, the perfect meeting-ground for the cosmos and the individual. The external frame of meaning and the goals of the individual were considered to be entirely consonant; reality and ideals were homogeneous. Hence there was no bar to the realization of ideals, and the instrument of this realization was the free society. Consequently, there was no hindrance to the intellectual's immersing himself in social reality, for it was to this arena that he was naturally led, without fear of corruption, even by his contemplation of the eternal verities. And so the intellectual sallied forth to do battle against those phenomena of existence which were malevolent and, in a sense, illusory, thereby fulfilling his traditional function while yet pointing the way for a specific social group with whose material goals he did not identify himself.

The collapse of this rational synthesis, manifested in Immanuel Kant and the French Revolution, brought a real crisis of conscience to the intellectuals. The world of existences had shown itself to be, whether through the Revolution or the reaction, infinitely more complex and less manageable than had been supposed. Nevertheless, despite an initial reaction during the early years of the nineteenth century in which the synthesis was replaced by a confusion of partial complexes of thought, such as romanticism and Destutt de Tracy's sensationalism, and intellectuals recoiled back before the problems of political and social reality (it is not entirely fortuitous that Destutt de Tracy coined the term "ideology" at this time), they soon returned to the charge, built up systematic world-views and operated socially within them. But their ideas and their situation had undergone a significant change. The external framework of man's activity was no longer considered homogeneous with men's purposes; but while not of the same stuff as these purposes, yet it was compatible with them. The cosmic pattern imposed certain limits upon man's activity but yet permitted and even encouraged men to achieve their goals within those limits. But this implied an ambivalent attitude toward the world of existence, and in a sense the emphasis on reality which has been called the hallmark of the nineteenth century was a function of the necessity for careful examination of and abstraction from this reality to secure what was usable for man in it—the rational for philosophical idealists, the lawful and pragmatic for positivists and scientists. History became essential even to systematic thinkers for the working out of the implicit conflict between the two aspects of reality—that is, the external world and the internal ideal.

The immediate consequence of such preconceptions, visible particu-

larly in the middle third of the nineteenth century, was to bring the systematizers into more intense participation in political and social reality
than ever before, for their systems demanded man's concrete activity to
work out the oppositions within the world (hence the difficulty of
classifying men like Comte, Marx, Mill and Spencer within any specific
field of thought). While conservative intellectuals appeared upon the
scene and underlined the complexity of reality, the bulk of the thinkers
continued to plug the same libertarian values, realizable through society, as had been advanced in the eighteenth century. However, as the
century wore on into the 70s and 80s, the ever-growing consciousness
of the multiplicity of reality began to takes its toll. With conflicting material interests coming to dominate the political and social scene in an
unprecedentedly unabashed form, the intellectuals tended to split up in
a way far more basic than the political or even the philosophical differences between them. One section, perceiving this arena to be impervious to their ideals, withdrew to the Olympian heights of general
criticism, while the others subordinated their theories to the interests of
the institutions with which they case their lot and became rooted in a
self-consciously middle-class society. The latter tendency was reinforced
by the development among academicians of a characteristic type of
scholar who lived off the new specialization of disciplines and addressed
himself to the study of isolated aspects of existence. Though neither
necessarily nor universally definitive of the academic profession, this development, by slighting the general relationships of particular studies,
has had the effect of excluding a sizable group of lay thinkers from the
ranks of the intellectuals.

III

Even allowing for the inevitable errors of perspective, the thinking of
our own century seems infinitely complex. The positions which Western
man has taken for the past two thousand years all seem to reappear
upon the scene and demand once more to be recognized as ultimate solutions. Religious thought in mystical, eschatological, or humanistic interpretations, rationalism, scientific materialism, idealism, are all in the
arena still, not simply as the remnants of intellectual traditions but re-
vivified, almost blatant in their present claims. But this very coexistence
bespeaks a common element in the intellectual situation in which they
spawn. A frame of reference which permits of so many divergent interpretations is hardly any longer a single frame of reference. Karl Jaspers
has said that complete systems of thought are no longer possible, that
there is no longer any possibility of comprehending the whole of reality.

What has happened is that the reality which was so ambivalently conceived by the nineteenth-century thinkers has lost that aspect which made it rational to man and compatible with his purposes. It has lost its cohesive power and has become fragmented; its total meaning has disappeared. And since reality in this sense is taken to include society as well as cosmos, it would seem that the tendencies exhibited in the latter part of the nineteenth century—hypercriticism, withdrawal, or subordination—have been carried through to their logical conclusions, that the ideas of the European intellectuals tend to escapism or to treason and their consequent position in society to impotence.

Certainly, this seems to be the reigning conception of the present status of the European intellectuals, one that is inherent in the mood of their literature and that constitutes the chief impression from current surveys of the situation.[2] Moreover, there would seem to be good evidence, aside from literature, for such a conclusion. An important segment of European thought between the wars was dominated by a combination of nihilism and activism, by the conception, that is, that a meaningless and mechanized world was closing down upon man and that the only possibility for man's self-assertion in such a world—and this possibility was limited—lay in the powerful deed, in which would be harnessed the primitive life-forces of elemental nature; the very fact of such deeds, rather than their ends, would be the triumph against the encroaching meaninglessness of which men's apathy and powerlessness were considered an integral part.

A corollary was the tendency to adhere to the social unit from which such power could be most effectively drawn and the hierarchical organization of society which would permit it to be utilized. This group, exemplified in the circle of *Die Tat* in Germany, was balanced by those who continued to believe in the values inherited from the eighteenth and nineteenth centuries but who, confronted with the utter imperviousness of reality to those values, could do little but talk of crisis. If the first group moved one step further along the road to immersion of thought in life, the second manifested an extension of the movement of late nineteenth-century criticism in the direction of withdrawal, since they had lost the notion of an essential system of reality which this criticism had had and consequently had lost the toehold in social reality from which to work.

For these movements to be understood aright it must be emphasized that they were reactions against the nineteenth-century systems and par-

2. For example, *Saturday Review of Literature,* January 13, 1951.

ticularly reactions against the form which those systems took during the early part of the twentieth century in their first attempt to accommodate themselves to the new conception of reality; for the period from about 1890 until just after the First World War witnessed the return of the older idealism, in both its philosophical and its general moral sense, to the attempt to impregnate a balky reality with value. This was, significantly, the period of the neo—neo-idealism, with both variants of a neo-Kantianism and a neo-Hegelianism, as well as a revisionism which amounted to a neo-Marxism, both of the Right and the Left.

This was the period, too, in which it was realized that the former conceptions of a rational reality which permitted the realization of the ideal must be replaced by a new synthesis in which the ideal had to be worked, through the intensified activity of man, into a reality which could no longer be conceived systematically and to which consequently concessions had to be made. Thus the new German intellectual liberalism, of the Max Weber-Naumann stamp, combining a social ethic with national power. Thus the Fabian marriage of convenience with trade unionism. Thus the French insistence, in an Alain, a Péguy, a Juarès, on justice and integrity not as qualifying but as replacing a general system of thought. And thus, on a philosophical plane, the tendency of the neo-Kantians to scrap the *Ding-an-sich* and to proceed to emphasize beyond Kant the activity of human consciousness and particularly the necessity of communal action for ethical ends. For these groups, the nature of reality no longer afforded a coherent totality, but society, which represented the mediating sphere between man and this general reality and partook of elements of both, was still accessible to man. It was the First World War and its aftermath which effectively brought this attempt at reintegration to a close, which lined up society on the side of alien power, and which consequently fed into the undercurrent of general skepticism which had been developing from Nietzsche and Pareto.

This is not the whole story of the period, however. At this point we must distinguish between levels of intellectual activity. The process described above—that is, the new attempt at the realization of ideals and the subsequent combination of disappointment, pessimism and activism—certainly reflected the climate of the age, but at the same time it represented what we may call the secondary stage of ideas: that is, it represented attempts at adaptation by original thinkers and attempts at application by publicizers of ideas developed in a previous period. Simultaneously, however, thinkers began to work on another, a primary, level: apart from the social and the material forces of their age, they began to develop new philosophies to interpret directly, rather than through the medium of older ideas and values, the general experience of their age. That this experience called for a new approach is perhaps evident in the fact that for the first time since Hegel men demanded that philosophy retrieve itself from the function into which it had fallen of examining the methods and assumptions of the special disciplines, notably in the relationship of positivism to the natural sciences, and undertake a new and fundamental examination of reality. Hence some characterization—however superficial—of these new philosophies is probably more appropriate to and revealing of the general assumptions of the age which has produced them than the general mood expressed on other levels of thinking.

What is immediately striking about the new lines of thought is the difficulty of defining them. Not only has none of them achieved any position of predominance but even within each general tendency individual thinkers diverge markedly, thereby testifying to the breakdown of any accepted general framework of reality or of thought. "Schools" of thought, then, in the strict sense, are not to be looked for. With this reservation, however, certain classifications of philosophies of recent vintage can be discerned. The phenomenologists and the logical positivists represent transitions from older types of thought into the present age, the latter, to be sure, only in the logical rather than the chronological sense of transition. Consequently, they contain elements like phenomenology's aim of establishing philosophy as a rigorous science and its assumption of the essential rationality of reality and like logical positivism's self-dedication to explicating the bases and methods of the sciences, which are not wholly typical of contemporary thinking. But in other elements they are truly representative: not only does the phenomenological method, which is radical and dynamic rather than analytic and static, receive widespread current application, but its attitude toward the world of existence, in requiring the suspension of existence for the comprehension of rational essences, recognizes both its potentialities and its obfuscations; logical positivism reveals an implicit tension in its superimposition of "convenient" systems of symbolic logic, for the explication of meaning, upon the empirical basis which is, for it, the only knowable reality and yet of which these systems are structurally independent.

Here these two kinds of thought fall into line with the types of thinking which are peculiarly characteristic of our time: first, the philosophies of experience or process or life, manifested variously in metaphysicians like Alexander and Whitehead, idealists like Croce and Collingwood,

and the philosophies of history associated with historicism, with or
without their neo-Kantian attempts at an absolute, but generally having
in common the rejection of stable concepts based upon an organized
reality in favor of approximations to autonomous entities somehow experienced or intuited or pragmatically comprehended in their flight
through time and history (the American counterpart would be pragmatism, and only here does this category show a genuine school); secondly, the familiar doctrines of existentialism, in its Christian and
secular forms. One might add, of the older schools which have been de-
cisively influenced by this newer thought, the Catholic personalism of
Mounier and Marcel,[3] and the Protestant writings of the Barth and
Tillich stripe.[4] What, for our purposes, can be said to be common to all
these modern philosophies?

The basic attitude which must be emphasized, because it is so contrary to the general conception of modern thought, is its confidence.
The fragmentation of reality, the loss of meaning, is to these schools
nothing absolute; it is not the mark of failure of nerve or of mind, but
rather is the result of errors of previous philosophy which posed a false
set of questions and emerged with a false set of answers the illusory

3. Catholic personalism represents the organization and development of a more general mode of thought going back to the latter years of the nineteenth century. Born in the
reaction against the dissolution of the individual by scientific empiricism (particularly in
psychology) and objective idealism, the explication of the integral "person" as a central
concept found its chief early representatives in Charles Renouvier and Wilhelm Stern,
and, in this country, at the University of California from 1919. The concept was taken up
by the group of French Catholics around Mounier and Marcel (Denis de Rougemont is
the one Protestant prominently represented) as a result of the world depression of 1929,
and in this form has found an organ in the periodical *Esprit,* founded in 1932; its German
counterpart can be studied in Walter Dirks and his *Frankfurter Hefte.* While this latest
form of the concept may be said to be responsible for the "ism" in personalism, the movement is not to be regarded as constituting either a philosophical system or a political doctrine. Its proponents view it rather as an approach, an attitude, with nothing exclusive
about it. What is characteristic of this approach is the equal emphasis upon the absolute
and the relative, the ideal and the material, the moral and the social, the individual and the
community. The "person," for these thinkers, represents the focal point for the necessary
interplay of these vital elements: as opposed to the concept of the "individual," now
tainted by scientific thought and classical economics, the "person" is the incarnation of totality in disperse and partial temporal history and consequently is the necessary center for
any action which is to be both ethically determined and practically effective.

4. It is, of course, arbitrary to lump recent Protestant thought together in this way.
Karl Barth's neo-orthodoxy, for example, is very different in its original from Paul Tillich's
religious socialism. In their later development, however, these two movements have
drawn closer together, with Barth's provision for a social theory and Tillich's construction
of a general philosophy.

character of which is simply being proved in our age. Abjuring systems and arbitrary distinctions, such as the subject-object distinction, upon which systems have been founded, contemporary thought begins from what it considers to be irreducibles—the individual entity and immediate experience. The character of the individual entities varies, of course, with the specific philosophy: in the theories of process and in logical positivism, they are the individual "occasion" and the individual sense-datum which is experienced; in phenomenology and existentialism they are the individual mind or consciousness which experiences. For our purposes, however, these distinctions are not decisive. What is decisive is the common surrender or at least suspension of the conviction that the grasping of reality must be sought through its total coherence in favor of the conviction that the individual entity is a microcosm and is therefore the proper and indispensable basis for a new approach to reality. Moreover, it follows that the very dissolution of reality through the destruction of the absolute subject by history and the destruction of the absolute object by the new science—this very dissolution of reality into process which throws the totality of the process into the realm of the unknown—makes possible an unprecedentedly certain grasp of the individual constituents of that process; for the knower and the known are integral in experience. Knowledge can be attained only through concrete participation in a life-process which is made up of autonomous individuals. Knowledge then comes, not from contemplation, but from creative activity; this activity concretizes being into individual experience. Thus free, concrete participation makes up, according to this view, the individual life-process which is the basic stuff of reality.

The problem raised by this conception is clear: how does the individual entity, immersed in its own process, get beyond itself, how does it come to a relationship with the other entities and the other processes and thereby attain some knowledge of the whole? How, in other words, is meaning infused into the experience of the individual entity? This, of course, is the decisive question; for, having attained some security of knowledge through transferring the basis of their consideration from the reality of the world in general to the arena of the individual world, this question involves the return to the traditional problem of the general coherence of reality. The issue is not shirked by modern thinkers, who are proud of having escaped, to their own satisfaction, the dangers of solipsism and who extend their feeling of confidence from the comprehension of individual entities to the possibility of building the general structure of reality on this basis. Thus the phenomenological method includes not only a process of reduction, but one of the "constitution of the world," while some logical positivists, at least, reject what they call the "reductive fallacies" of old-fashioned positivism in favor of an "attitude of reconstruction."

The acknowledgement of the problem, however, does not mean that complete solutions have been worked out, but the general lines which such solutions should take have been indicated. In general, the answers given in modern thought revolve around the concept of transcendence, a concept which has undergone a change in meaning along with the general shift in the locus of thinking. Whereas formerly transcendence referred to a reality beyond and above the whole cosmos known by man and was therefore simply descriptive of two realms of reality, it now refers to a reality to be known or created within the cosmos beyond the particular experience of individual men at a certain time and a certain place and consequently becomes not simply a description but an actual power in the lives of men, opening them to the possibilities of action in a meaningful world beyond the here and now. By reason, then, of the individualized basis of reality, the concept of transcendence has become central in modern thought, not only for the question of ultimate reality, but even for the question of this-worldly reality.

The specific interpretations of this concept vary with each thinker, but for our purpose we may distinguish two different types of treatment of the problem of transcendence. In the first type, transcendence is filled by God, in the second by man. In the first type, only faith in God gives assurance of the coherence of all process and consequently of a meaning which can give direction to the individual life-process; that is, which can draw each moment of the process beyond itself and thereby provide not only the goals but also the very basis of continuous creation. Most of contemporary thought expounds or assumes a transcendence of this kind. The second type of transcendence is represented primarily by Heidegger and Sartre: through "conscience" and "decision," man, by an exercise of his sovereign freedom, engages himself in existence, from his interaction with existence he establishes goals for his own action and thereby, by creating being, transcends his immediate situation, his immediate experience. It should be noted that for neither type is the substantive direction of the transcendence clear, save for the specifically Christian section of the divine transcendentalists who fill the gap with revelation. For the others, transcendence seems to represent simply the categorical imperative to go beyond the present; the substance of the absolute thereby postulated seems to be no more than the sum of the individual absolutes which by its richness and diversity manifests the value of human freedom.

IV

This has been a difficult and abstract excursion, but one necessary to un-cover the assumptions behind the kind of writing which the intellec-tuals have been doing since the war; for undoubtedly the chief issue for the intellectual has become that of engagement, and what this means can hardly be understood without reference to the total assumptions of the age. The external evidences of engagement are manifold. Not only do the general reviews intermingle philosophical, literary, political and social articles—with the purpose, as Dolf Sternberger announced in *Die Wandlung,* "of drawing Spirit into practical responsibility and il-luminating politics with Spirit"—but leading exponents of the new philosophies have come down into the publicistic and even into the po-litical arena (with the notable exception of Heidegger).

What we have called the primary and the secondary stages of ideas now meet on even terms in the discussion of European social and politi-cal problems. Most striking here have been the yearly meetings of the *Rencontres Internationales de Genève,* where philosophers like Karl Jaspers, Georg Lukacs, Nicholas Berdyaev, Merleau-Ponty, Guido de Ruggiero and Karl Barth and men of letters like André Siegfried, Julien Benda, Pierre Hervé, Georges Bernanos, Stephen Spender, Hans Paeschke and Denis de Rougemont have met to discuss problems which live in that intermediate zone of value between philosophy and society—problems like the European Spirit, Technical Progress and Moral Progress, Toward a New Humanism. The temper of these discus-sions is well illustrated by an incident which took place early in the dis-cussion of technical and moral progress. One participant arose and tendered to the assembly a piece of advice, taken, he said, from an old Eskimo proverb: when you want to hunt the seal in the sea, don't go whistling in the mountains. This admonition to present concrete pro-posals for action took the conference by storm, thereby revealing the deep-rooted desire of European intellectuals to apply themselves to the solution of political and social problems.

From an external point of view, then, it would seem that the most re-cent period of European thought has been characterized not so much by the development of new philosophies as by the general recognition of the necessity for the intellectual to engage himself in the political and social arena. This simple interpretation of engagement, however, does not suffice either to explain the concept as the Europeans hold it or to explain what, under its aegis, the intellectuals are trying to do. It might be mentioned, in the first place, that such an interpretation is hardly distinctive, for in the 1840s this kind of engagement was precisely the rallying cry of the Young Hegelians in general and of the young Karl Marx in particular for their revision of Hegel. But second, and more important, the injunction to engage in social reality seems rather superfluous to an age which has been thinking along the lines which have been analyzed above: when the individual is so immersed in process, in existence, it is hardly a contribution to tell him to immerse himself still further.

Actually, engagement means two things. First, it states the fact, implied in all contemporary thinking, that men *are engaged* in existence, willy-nilly, and that consequently contemplative, static thought is an illusion. But secondly, it means that men *should be engaged* to transcendence, that is, to the moral purpose which reaches out beyond man's immediate existence and in the light of which he undertakes the creative activity which gives meaning to his life. This double meaning is clear not only in Gabriel Marcel, who, incidentally, seems to have coined the term "engagement" in its contemporary philosophical usage, but in Heidegger as well. The implication of the double meaning of engagement is a dual attitude toward society.

In the first place, the individual *is engaged* in society; the existence of other individuals about him, the existence of social and political institutions, help to make up the total situation which goes to form the experience of the individual and hence to help make him what he is: in this sense, society is on the one hand necessary and on the other neutral or nauseous for the individual.

In the second place, however, the individual *should strive* to transform the original engagement to society into a moral one; through engagement to his own transcendent goal, he opens himself to an absolute (which he either attains or creates) which becomes the ground not only of his own personality but of his recognition of the personality of others and of his essential personal relationship to them.

The fundamental nature of this duality is reflected widely in contemporary thought, for society is seen increasingly as the arena in which the crucial struggles that are to decide man's destiny must be fought out: society is viewed both as an embodiment of the concrete existence in which man is immersed and as an instrument for the transcending of that existence. In the abstract form which much of contemporary German writing gives it, the duality appears in the prevalence of such themes as sleep, silence, phantasy, which are deemed to give man, apart from society, the continuity and the coherence which the broken-up rational articulation of society lacks and with which it must be supplied from outside itself. It appears too in such discussions as the one graced by the Eskimo proverb mentioned above; for, despite the acclaim accorded the demand for practical solutions, the subsequent debate was interrupted periodically by equally urgent warnings of the perils of unremitting social concretion and by demands for purification through discussion of philosophical principles. The duality is striking in Immanuel Mounier's idea of the basically dramatic quality of human history, of the eternal withdrawal and return of Christian faith, characterized at once by transcendence and incarnation, from and to human society, which alternately is fructified by that faith, attracting it into social participation, and corrupts it, repelling it into an extra-social realm for its self-purgation. The duality is evident too in the many current spiral conceptions of human history, which bespeak the alternation between man's creative transformation of his social world and the oppressive weight of this world upon man's freedom. Indeed, in these ideas the infinite drama, with its implications of ultimate imperfection and incompleteness, is not only necessary but desirable, because it provides an ever-recurring challenge to man's assertion of his freedom and of his creative capacities. This line of thought is closely associated with the conception of man's self-alienation and self-recovery which are present in the thought of Hegel and emphatic in the thought of Marx. It is the present relevance of this conception which helps to explain the recent revival, in France at least, of interest in the young Hegel and the young Marx. It helps to explain too why the same climate which leads intellectuals toward existential forms of thought leads so many also to Marxism.

V

Given the emphasis upon engagement, the concern of the intellectuals with specific social and political issues follows naturally, but, since the concept of engagement is part of a general attitude and not of a philosophical system, the applications are not logically consequent. The content of such applications is not given in structured social and political theories. If the ideas in this field contain a pattern, it must be elicited from a series of concrete proposals. Here two examples of such proposals will be examined: on the social problem and on the problem of the nation-state.

The connection between the intellectuals' general concept of man and their judgment upon the present condition of European society lies in their conviction that the present situation represents an epitome in the process of man's self-alienation. There is widespread preoccupation with the problem of the technical civilization in all its ramifications:

mechanization of labor, of the state, of public opinion, of war, and even of thought—the last in the form usually of a critique of the older Cartesian basis of scientific thinking. This concern is hardly new, and it must be owned that the solutions proffered are hardly much of a novelty either. They are in agreement on the necessity of what in general seems to be a liberal socialism. What is surprising is, first, the enthusiastic propounding of such a solution, second, the general theoretical agreement on the subject, and, third, the basis of their position. For the basic motif is neither democratic nor socialistic, but rather individualistic. And this in two senses: first, that ultimately the highest values to be served are values of the individual, and second, that the only possible means of social salvation are these same values of the individual.

What are these values? The names given them are familiar: humanism, liberty, moral spirit. Only these forces, coming from the inherent creative power of individuals—and particularly intellectuals—can create a society in which these forces will be safeguarded. Where then does the socialism come in? Socialism is simply a required condition of engagement and partakes of the dual nature of engagement. It is considered both as an inevitable aspect of the hostile social world in which the spirit must work and as a portion of the transcendent goal to which the spirit must commit itself if man is to recover control over this destiny. This kind of thinking scarcely constitutes a rigorous political system and actually within its framework there is at least one important distinction. For those who fill the labels humanism, liberty, moral spirit, with a traditional content, the emphasis is upon the individual, upon the liberal in liberal socialism.

This tendency is particularly true for men like Karl Jaspers, whose acceptance of the necessity of socialism is reluctant indeed, and finds its extreme expression in the Moral Rearmament group, now active on the continent as well as in England. For the Catholic personalists, who seek to infuse traditional Christian values with a radically new interpretation, individualism and socialism are in delicate balance—and tension. For those thinkers, finally, who consider the common labels simply as forms which provide the necessary conditions of social action but which require a new content that cannot be defined in advance, the emphasis tends to be upon the socialism, in the faith that experience will create a new and genuine relationship between the individual and society and will thereby also create a new ethic. Thus when Sartre helped found his political organization in 1948, he defined its program simply to be revolutionary democratic socialism as a transcendent goal arising from the projection of man's freedom in his actual social situation, but at the same time he admitted that a theory which would bridge the gap between the conditions and the goal could be established only through discussion based upon the experience of the association itself. It can be said that this pattern, in which the initial reality is firmly comprehended, the final goal generally envisaged, and the connecting social means entirely confused, is a quality bequeathed to political thinking by the general character of contemporary thought.

The absence of a clear line capable of resolving in action the dual conception of engagement leaves the impression that the European intellectuals feel the need both to take account of and yet carefully to skirt every vital force in European society. The repeated injunction that men remain "open" to all possible experience, the conviction that all systems contain partial truths, the emphasis upon attitude as opposed to doctrine, with the concomitant striving to penetrate all groups and parties rather than to form parties themselves (hence the recent emphasis on the "Rally" and the "Movement" as against the "Party")—all these ideas testify to the eclecticism of contemporary political thought.

At the same time, however, it must be said that the vagueness of the social thinking by European intellectuals today is at least in part attributable to the conviction that the social problem is not, as such, the ultimate one in the current political scene. This consideration brings us to our second illustration of the results of the intellectuals' engagement— their proposals concerning the nation-state; for what does seem to be ultimate, for them, is the general problem of transcending the old nation-state and of achieving a new level from which European society may take a new start and on which the old formulas may assume new meanings. The prevalent concern with European unity is, for the intellectuals, not so much an issue in itself as a possible wedge into the solution of this general problem. Silone has written that the old distinction between Right and Left, as measured in political or social terms, is an anachronism, and must give way to what is today the essential distinction—prounion and antiunion of Europe—on the grounds that the social problem cannot be resolved within the traditional framework given by the national state.

As far as the international relations of the intellectuals themselves are concerned, the problem of European integration seems to present no great obstacles. Writers of different nationalities meet together in discussion, write in one another's journals, and study one another's output. Again, although no system of thought exists to which intellectuals of various nationalities can subscribe—save possibly Catholic personalism, and this has obvious limitations for unity—the break-up into various schools has not followed national lines. It is true that the empirical tradition remains strongly dominant in England—and this must be accounted an element in the general position of England vis-à-vis Europe—but on the continent the influential role of existentialism in France and Germany, and of Crocean idealism in Italy, is hardly exclusive. In any case, the day has long passed when adherence to a philosophy implied a definite political position or vice versa, and the general presuppositions behind contemporary thought are sufficiently uniform and sufficiently flexible to permit the kind of agreement on general social and political principles such as those discussed above.

Consequently, the intellectuals agree that there is such a thing as a particular European spirit and that it should have its counterpart in a European political union. The basis of the agreement follows the general pattern of contemporary European thinking: it begins from a recognition of the evils of the national state, which is seen as simply another aspect of contemporary society alien to the human spirit, and it postulates a European union as a goal which will do away with the evil by establishing a new political environment. But on this basis the goal is not defined precisely enough to permit a clear view of the means to it. For, if the European union must not become another national state, a danger against which most intellectuals warn, and if the European spirit is defined in terms of a universal humanism, as they do define it, then what is the point of a merely European union? And so indeed many European intellectuals, including the French existentialists, the French personalists, and the Protestants influenced by Karl Barth, refuse to consider Europe in ultimate political terms; rejecting the whole notion of power blocs, rejecting alliance with the national states of both East and West, they invest Europe with the task of working out, in freedom, universal problems common to all humanity. Neutralism, then, is justified for such intellectuals, to apply the terms used previously, by a dualistic conception of engagement which views the existing states as its arena and absolute goals as its transcendent.

This idea was clearly formulated in an open letter signed by a large group of French intellectuals under the aegis of *Esprit* to the United Nations in 1949: referring equally to the Warsaw Congress and statements of American atomic scientists, the intellectuals petitioned for a radical peace policy in order that liberty might be secured and socialism achieved in the European nations. Consequently, neither the French existentialists nor the personalists are particularly enthusiastic about the movement to European Union. The existentialists pass over it in silence, while the personalists see the project not as a creative enterprise but rather as a collection of countries pooling the dishonor and the humiliation which they feel vis-à-vis the United States. Many of the German intellectuals, excluding the social democrats and the Protestants under Barth's and Niemoller's influence but including the German personalists, are, on the other hand, emphatically in favor of European union and opposed to neutralism. British writers like Bertrand Russell and Richard Crossman tend to gloss over European union in favor of the Atlantic community, while the nonsocialist Barbara Ward gives equal emphasis to both. For the Germans the motivations seems clear. For them the European union is an arena of freedom in three respects: it frees them from the dangers of a German state and from foreign occupation while still granting protection from Soviet invasion. The British, who talk in terms of what Crossman calls "democratic realism," tend to associate their values with the existing state-system; Russell's insistence that only a philosophy of empiricism can support liberal politics would seem to be relevant to this line of thinking. Thus, for those who are prounion and antineutralism the arena and goal of engagement meet at the intermediate level of Europe, while for those who are both antiunion and antineutralism transcendence is subordinated to the existing arena or power politics.

This general disparity of the views of the European intellectuals on the question of Europe within a common, vague acceptance of the need for some kind of European collaboration is another expression of the familiar pattern: they are aware of the difficulties of the existing situation and have some idea of a goal which should overcome them, but no clear idea of the path from one to the other. Indeed, we may conclude further: much of the confusion seems to come from the fact that when they say that they want European unity, it is often a cover-name for something else that they really do want. Actually, it is any of the possible permutations afforded by the combined problems of peace or war and of greater or less social change that determines their respective conceptions of European cooperation, and since there is no agreement on how these problems are to be handled it is hardly surprising that the views on the question of Europe are various and that the concern with realizing unity is not urgent.

VI

What, then, can we conclude from this analysis of the European intellectuals?

First, they are convinced that they can understand the reality of our world and our society and that this reality, by reason of its very discontinuity, can be acted upon, within limits, by man.

Second, as their difficult concept of engagement attests, they are making the effort themselves to come to grips with political and social reality while avoiding submergence in it. In this respect they are trying to steer a difficult course in order to arrive at a position approximating the one held in the eighteenth century.

Third, they differ markedly from the eighteenth-century intellectuals in that their political and social ideas do not lead society but rather seem to lag behind it. Despite the new context which they bring to values like humanism, the person, liberty, progress, they do not have sufficient content to distinguish them from the same hackneyed terms which are used in the official language of every-day politics and which are no longer whole-heartedly believed in.

Fourth, one of the reasons for the lack of new content is the incomplete status of contemporary thought—incomplete particularly in the absence of an effective social theory.

Fifth, the absence of new social and political theory is in part the consequence of the fact that the intellectuals do not know to what particular social forces they can engage themselves in order to concretize their general ideas. Sartre's withdrawal from the organization on which he depended to develop a social theory, on the grounds that he felt there was no place for it in the contemporary world of politics, is a case in point.

Finally, then, the intellectuals seem to have completed the circle started in the eighteenth century. Once more, they are the middle-class liberals par excellence. But now their prominence seems to be that, not of the vanguard, but of the stragglers. It is hardly surprising, then, that the theme of political and social engagement has already been labeled the theme of the 1940s and that other intellectual developments, suitable to the new decade, are anticipated.

5 History and Existentialism in Sartre

Existentialism poses both subjective and objective problems for history. As subjects, existentialists espouse positions that are often antithetical to the historical dimension; as objects, they have exhibited ideas and activities that are often opaque to historical knowledge. In Sartre both kinds of problems are joined, and, in what follows, through him a joint solution will be essayed.

The figure of Sartre—philosopher, novelist, playwright, essayist— raises the objective question first: how is a mere historian, as an historian, to set about understanding him? Clearly, this is not much of a problem for an historian who happens to have a special genius for philosophy, the novel, the drama, or the belles-lettres in general, but when we posit, as we do here, an historian without such distinctive character and with only the common method of his craft—such as it is—what then? There are three things that he is equipped to do—things that perhaps only he can do and that may therefore not only perform the service function of making Sartre accessible to historians but even contribute a new dimension to the general comprehension of him.

First, obviously, we can look for the history that is in his work and thought. Who better than the historian can understand and interpret another man's treatment of history and who better than an historian can exploit this treatment for the light it sheds upon the work and thought as a whole? The methodological principle here is: it takes one to know one.

A simple principle. Would that its application were as simple. But it is not. Sartre has written in many fields, but the one field in which he has not written is—unfortunately—history. Even when he has written *about* history, he has tended to disguise it, enveloping it initially in facticity and latterly in dialectic. As its guises have changed, moreover, so have the quality and the quantity of its function. To recognize history in Sartre, the historian must don some cloaks of his own. And so his simple principle acquires a corollary: to wit, it takes one to catch one.

First published in *The Critical Spirit: Essays in Honor of Herbert Marcuse,* ed. Kurt H. Wolff and Barrington Moore, Jr. (Boston: Beacon Press, 1967), 239–66. This paper was originally delivered before the European Seminar of Columbia University's European Institute in March 1951.

The apparent simplicity of the second prescription—the explanation of Sartre by his historical context—is again deceptive. For if we proceed to ask, "what historical context?" we find ourselves confronted with a situation constituted by two radically different dimensions of history. First, there is the philosophical tradition to which Sartre has attached himself and in which the idea of history forms part of the general structure of thought. Secondly, there is the reality of contemporary history, vital, actual, eventful, factual, extra-philosophical. To understand Sartre, we must first give each of these dimensions its separate substantive identity in order to project the distinctive demands which his logic and his experience made upon him.

Our final and most crucial task is to understand how Sartre put these two dimensions together—that is, how he opened his philosophical system to ingest immediate experience—and it is to this end that the historian can employ a third characteristic device, the historisation of Sartre himself. Whatever the logic of his final synthesis may be, we can at least trace the chronology of the stages in the development of his thought at which his idea of history invoked the fruitful appropriation of the reality of history.

Our prospectus, then, is this: first to set up the problem of history in the general existentialist mentality; then—and this will engross the bulk of our attention—to illuminate the problem through Sartre's specification of it and to follow his successive attempts to resolve it under the dual influences of the logical dynamics within his existentialist philosophy and the impact of events outside it; and finally to indicate the bearing of his developing solution upon the role of history in western culture.

Most of the intellectual movements with which we are familiar have developed in two stages, which we may denominate formally as adjectival and substantive. There were conservative, liberal, idealist, historicist individuals and groups before there was conservatism, liberalism, idealism, or historicism. The distinction is not a mere matter of nomenclature, or of self-consciousness, or of stylistic degeneration. It is a matter of distinguishing between the stage in which a tendency develops as part and in the shelter of an already established set of ideas and the stage in which it sets itself up as an independent doctrine or philosophy of its own. At least some of the ambiguities in existentialism stem from the indiscriminate application of the term to both stages of its development and may be clarified by distinguishing them. In its adjectival stage it goes back at least to Hegel's *Phenomenology* and it contributes subordinately to such 19th century stalwarts, in addition to Hegel, as Marx and Nietzsche. In its substantive stage it became an autonomous and characteristic 20th century philosophy, with Husserl its main forbear and Jaspers, Heidegger, and Sartre its primary exponents.[1] On the basis of this pattern we may attempt to define, in general terms, the problematical relationship between existentialism and history.

The nub of this relationship consists in the paradoxical combination of congruity and indifference—at times, indeed, even repulsion—in the existentialist posture toward history. The paradox is visible in both the external and internal relations of these two approaches to reality.

Externally, the relationship between existentialism and historical mindedness is one of rival siblings, spawned in the same cultural matrix and developing through separate but homologous cycles of growth. Both came first to the fore as parallel responses to the demand of early 19th century Europeans for the intellectual recognition and cultivation of the heterogeneous, particularized facts of natural and social reality. Both tendencies, the existentialist and the historical, initially attended to this level of reality within one variant or another of the traditional philosophical systems to which they succeeded in attaching themselves before participating with equal filial impiety in the decomposition of those systems. When both, finally, undertook, around the turn of the century, to make their related view of reality the ultimate reality, they did it by developing the mutually exclusive philosophies of existentialism and historicism.

The internal relations between the two intellectual movements, as evinced in the attitude of existentially-minded thinkers toward history, yields a more definite formulation of the problem. In the 19th century, during the adjectival phase of existentialism, its thinkers simply split on their orientation toward history. One group, led by Hegel and Marx, integrated history and existence into a single temporal process. It seemed a logical enough division of labor between the two collateral categories: history was simply the past of existence and revealed its direction. But another group, equally representative—their outstanding exemplar is Nietzsche—found history indifferent or hostile to the free act that creates existence. The best-known of the judgments in this genre are those of Nietzsche, who condemned as "excess of history," "unrestrained historical sense," and as "the tyranny of the actual," every-

---

1. Kierkegaard, as the one 19th century substantive existentialist, occupies a special place in this roster. Appropriately, the life of his ideas belongs rather to the 20ᵗʰ century than to his own.

thing that was objective and influential in history and who admitted it in the derivative and emasculated form of "a knowledge of the past desired only for the service of the future and the present." For his own time, he would cure "the malady of history" by frank resort to the "unhistorical" and the "super-historical": "The unhistorical and the super-historical are the natural antidotes against the overpowering of life by history; they are the cures for the historical disease."[2] But for both 19th century groups, the relationship between existence and history, whether of the positive or negative type, was not a necessary one, since existence and history were equally subordinate to an overriding metaphysical, ethical, religious, aesthetic, or social principle which permitted flexibility and variation in their respective assignments. With the derogation of this kind of principle from an absolute to a relational status during our own century, however, and with the concomitant rise of existence and history to the status of independent categories of reality, as signalized in the parallel growths of existential*ism* and historic*ism*, the relationship between these two categories became necessary and the problem of it critical.

It is for insight into this problem that we turn to Sartre, with the knowledge that the ambiguities of the relationship that we find in him are not idiosyncratic but reflective of a fundamental dilemma in a characteristic intellectual movement of our age. Sartre is a uniquely qualified subject for two reasons. First, as a first-rate philosopher and simultaneously as a participant in a 20th century French intellectual class which, like the German intellectuals of the 19th century and the French of the 18th, has been particularly open to the broadest range of social influences, he combines a rigor of thought with a responsiveness to the world in a way that makes his performance at once cogent and representative. Secondly, in his development he has traversed the whole spectrum of possibilities from the anti- to the pro-historical postures of existentialism. Consequently, he holds out to us not only the advantages of a bargain rate—the understanding of two types at the cost of only one study—but, if we can discover an historical logic in his development, the prospect of uncovering the function of history in contemporary thinking. For Sartre's development involves a philosophical shift that is larger than the change in his evaluation of history, and the growing centrality of history is the key to it. We may view this development in terms of two main phases, joined by the cataclysmic experience of the

2. Friedrich Nietzsche, *Use and Abuse of History* (tr. by A. Collins, New York, 1957), pp. 12, 22, 42, 69–70.

war. Consonant with the historical approach, we shall consider his second main phase—since it occupies the approximate present—as the given which needs to be explained, and we shall concentrate upon the early Sartre and the subsequent break which serve as the explanation.

Our starting-point must be Sartre's pre-war novel, *La Nausée*, for it is the vehicle of as dramatic and as categorical a rejection of history as was ever penned. A philosophical novel cast in the form of a journal, its diarist is an amateur historian who seeks to escape the sporadic onslaughts of an undiagnosed nausea by writing the life of a Marquis de Rollebon, vicious attendant at the court of Louis XVI and murderous conspirator at the court of Paul I. Unable to establish any meaningful connection with the world about him, including his historical documents—"I understand nothing more about his conduct. . . . Slow, lazy, sulky, the facts adapt themselves to the rigor or the order I wish to give them; but it remains outside of them"[3]–the protagonist suddenly discovers, at the climax of the book, the meaning—that is, the meaninglessness—of all existence, including his own, and at that very moment throws history from him as antithetical to his existence and indeed to existence in general.

M. de Rollebon was my partner; he needed me in order to exist and I needed him so as not to feel my existence. I furnished the raw material, the material I had to resell, which I didn't know what to do with: existence, *my* existence. His part was to have an imposing appearance. . . . I no longer existed in myself, but in him.[4]

Only M. de Rollebon has just died for the second time. . . . Nothing existed but a bundle of yellow pages which I clasped in my hands. . . . Rollebon was no more. No more at all. . . . The great Rollebon affair was over, like a great passion. I must find something else. . . . The thing which was waiting was on the alert, it has pounced on me, it flows through me, I am filled with it. . . . Existence, liberated, detached, floods over me. I exist.[5]

Why this antithesis? Because of the two primary qualities of existence impressed upon the fictionized Sartre in these moments of revelation. First, its absolute contingency. Existent things are simply here, with no ground for their being and no connection among them save friction—"things exist one against the other."[6] "Existence everywhere, infinitely, in excess, for ever and everywhere; existence—which is

3. Jean-Paul Sartre, *Nausea* (tr. by Lloyd Alexander, Norfolk, Conn., 1949), pp. 2–3.
4. *Ibid.*, p. 133.
5. *Ibid.*, pp. 131–4.
6. *Ibid.*, p. 137.

limited only by existence. . . . Every existing thing is born without reason, prolongs itself out of weakness and dies by change."[7] Nausea, super-
fluity, absurdity: these notorious Sartrean terms are simply responses to
this incomprehensible and groundless plethora of unmeaning existence.
Obviously, such qualities undercut any relationship between an historian
and his object, and Sartre explicitly makes the point. Even in the denouement of *La Nausée,* when the protagonist spies a glimmer of hope, he
projects the writing of a book, "but not a history book," because "history
talks about what has existed" and "an existant [sic] can never justify the
existence of another existant."[8]

But the second quality of Sartre's existence cuts even deeper, for it
goes beyond history to destroy the larger dimension of reality which it
inhabits—the past. Existence has no dimensions: it is "the very paste of
things," composed of "soft, monstrous masses, all in disorder," and the
apparent individuality of things in only "a veneer."[9] "Without memory," "existence . . . falls from one present to another, without a past,
without a future."[10] "All that was not present did not exist. Not at all.
Not in things, not even in my thoughts. . . . For me the past (had been)
only a pensioning off: . . . another way of existing, a state of vacation
and inaction."[11] And once again Sartre did not hesitate to associate a
fundamental ontological position with a negative judgment upon history: "How can I, who have not the strength to hold to my own past,
hope to save the past of someone else?"[12]

From this initial exposé of brute existence as the ubiquitous condition of what Sartre will later call "human reality" we may then derive
three propositions about the initial status of history for him. First, even
in the sense of its raw material, of historical objects, history is no part
of original existence. Secondly, in the sense both of historical events and
of historical knowledge the denial of history is associated with the denial of meaning, and by implication we must look for its subsequent affirmation, if such there be, in conjunction with the general affirmation
of meaning. Thirdly, in his denial of meaning Sartre lumps together
three levels of historicity which are usually distinguished: individual
memory or past, which we do not call historical; actions in the past
taken by individuals in reference to other individuals, which we do call
historical; and the knowledge the historian has of such actions. As we

7. *Ibid.,* pp. 178–80.
8. *Ibid.,* p. 237.
9. *Ibid.,* pp. 171–2.
10. *Ibid.,* pp. 178, 234–5.
11. *Ibid.,* pp. 130–1.
12. *Ibid.,* p. 130.

follow Sartre's reconstruction of meaning in the world, we shall, accordingly, have both to look for the internal relationship and even interpenetration which Sartre deliberately maintains across these levels and to distinguish, as he does not explicitly, among these levels as separate stages, each with its distinct problems, in the tortuous reconstruction of meaning out of nothingness.

Sartre's reconstruction of meaning must be viewed as the obverse side of its destruction, and he began it in the initial phase of his development, simultaneously with the doctrine of existence which cleared the ground for it. In form—although not in content—the lines along which Sartre undertook the exposition of meaning during his first phase served as a model for his second as well. In each case, an insight into contemporary existence spurred him to transcend it immediately in the form of artistic creation and then gradually, through the slow and painful accumulation of ideas, in the form of a fundamental philosophical application of meaning to reality which closed out the phase. The aesthetic dimension of the first phase is traceable in *La Nausée* itself as well as in *L'Imaginaire*, its philosophy in *L'Être et le néant*. The hallmarks of this phase are the elemental character of the reconstruction, its individualistic basis and limit, its seeming indifference to history, its provision of what we may call "cognate history," and its provisional failure.

Sartre's immediate response to the opacity of existence was aesthetic. The note of hope on which *La Nausée* ends holds forth the prospect of escaping "the sin of existence" not by penetrating it but by going "behind" it and "above" it to create an intangible something to which existence refers but which itself has being, duration, meaning, and therefore no existence.[13] This something, exemplified in *La Nausée* by a tune and a novel, is generalized in *L'Imaginaire* into any work of art. Sartre here revealed the function of art through the less dramatic but more authentic analysis—at once philosophical and psychological—of the mental process that produces it; by making art the most notable activity of the imagination, he cast a fundamental vehicle of human meaning into the form of a basic unreality. For imagination is an activity of consciousness which creates "unreal" objects out of "analogues" or "substitutes" intentionally directed to that purpose.[14] Imagination and

---

13. *Ibid.*, pp. 234–8.

14. Jean-Paul Sartre, *The Psychology of Imagination* (New York, 1948), pp. 20, 117, 200. This is a translation of *L'Imaginaire: Psychologie phénoménologique de l'imagination* (Paris, 1940), which should be distinguished from Sartre's *L'Imagination* (Paris, 1936), recently translated by Forrest Williams as *Imagination: a Psychological Critique* (Ann Arbor, 1962). The latter work has not been used in this essay.

knowledge of the real are indeed mutually exclusive modes of consciousness: "For the real and the imaginary cannot co-exist by their very nature. It is a matter of two types of objects, of feelings and actions that are completely irreducible. . . . The work of art is an unreality. . . . It is outside of the real, outside of existence. . . . The real is never beautiful. Beauty is a value applicable only to the imaginary. . . . "15 Although alienated from reality, the imagination—and the work of art that is its fullest product—has a crucial function in reference to reality. By denying the real in order to create the unreal, not only is the imagination "the whole of consciousness as it realizes its freedom . . . and the necessary condition for the freedom of empirical man in the midst of the world" but, because imagination must "hold the real at a distance, . . . to deny it," the imaginary consciousness makes man able "to posit reality as a synthetic whole . . . from a certain point of view."16 Simone de Beauvoir recognized the central position of art for Sartre in the 30's but misread its function when she wrote that "the work of art or literature was, in his view, an absolute end in itself; . . . a law unto itself, and its creator . . . a law unto himself."17 Actually, it was not, even then, for Sartre, an end in itself, for it had an essential, if as yet unexamined, relation to the real. "The imaginary thus represents at each moment the implicit meaning of the real," that is, the way in which consciousness grasps reality as a whole in order to surpass it.18

Thus Sartre initiated his fundamental doctrine of a split at the very heart of being, and at this stage he assigned its dynamic mode to the imaginary and the aesthetic. In *La Nausée* he dramatized the inception of this mode; in *L'Imaginaire* he analyzed its operation after inception. The role of history in this syndrome is merely derivative and incidental. Like the general category of the past under which it is subsumed, history, as *La Nausée* has shown us, has no existence before the activation of the aesthetic imagination, and, as *L'Imaginaire* shows us, the existence that it acquires by exercise of the activated imagination is only as a dimension of inert, passive reality. Memory, the past, is "one mode of real existence among others"; as such, it has nothing in common with the time of the imagination, which is arbitrary, reversible, unreal.19

The dichotomy seems decisive enough, and yet there are, even at this

15. Sartre, *Psychology of Imagination*, pp. 210, 274, 280–1.
16. *Ibid.*, pp. 267–71.
17. Simone de Beauvoir, *Memoirs of a Dutiful Daughter* (tr. by James Kirkup, Cleveland, 1959), p. 334.
18. Sartre, *Psychology of Imagination*, p. 272.
19. *Ibid.*, pp. 184–8, 263–4.

stage, signs that Sartre was reaching for a more positive valuation of the past and of history, and these signs betrayed the general needs of his thinking that the more positive valuation was to help fill. In *La Nausée* Sartre's alter ego gropes toward a union of imagination and history in the inchoate notion that his proper genre is the historical novel. "I have the feeling," he wrote anent his incapacity to find any rationale in the historical facts, "of doing a work of pure imagination. . . . I could imagine him so well if I let myself go. . . . But if this is where it all leads me, I'd be better off writing a novel on the Marquis de Rollebon."[20] And in the denouement, after his definitive discover of art, he supplemented this premonition that art could penetrate the past with the hope that, thus penetrated, the past could provide a ground for, could justify, the present. After the projected novel has written, he wrote at the end, "I think that a little of its clarity might fall over my past. . . . And I might succeed—in the past, nothing but the past—in accepting myself."[21] And, as a matter of fact, the closest thing to history which Sartre has written was the series of contemporary historical novels published as *Les Chemins de la liberté*, of which more anon.

In *L'Imaginaire*, similarly, the explicit relegation of the past to a reality which serves as a mere foil to the free play of the imagination does not ban the nagging recognition that, whatever Sartre said or failed to say, his description of the imaginary act as the construction of unreal objects out of real analogues is suspiciously close to what an historian does with his documents. Nor must we content ourselves with mere suspicion, for in *L'Imaginaire* itself Sartre, without recognizing the principle of it, applies valid acts of the imagination to historical reconstruction. Works of art become *de facto* historical sources. The imagination is capable of making Michelangelo's David a "symbolic scheme . . . of the historical period known as the Renaissance," in terms of which we can define it and "consider the Renaissance itself as present in person."[22] But we may glimpse the reason why Sartre could not rise from the illustration to the principle, nor from the historical novel to history proper, when we understand the problem that he has even with this historical illustration, a problem that opens out into the fundamental irresolution of this stage of his thought. For Sartre admits that the symbolic apprehension of *David* requires two progressive acts of imagination, since the image is first formed for its own sake "as the first gropings

20. Sartre, *Nausea*, pp. 23, 82.
21. *Ibid.*, p. 238.
22. Sartre, *Psychology of Imagination*, pp. 155–9.

of a lower thought" and only by "a further creative effort" represents the larger scheme of the Renaissance.[23] But Sartre did not, at this stage, indicate what was ingredient in this further effort. His inability to demonstrate the movement from historical perception to historical synthesis, moreover, was irremediable so long as he associated historical knowledge with the aesthetic imagination. For he generalized this incompatibility between what the real analogue is and what it represents into an "inherent contradiction" and "ambiguity" of all images.[24]

The problem which thus invaded the very core of the imagination, and incidentally attracted Sartre toward but not into history, was twofold. First, his approach to being and meaning through art and imagination, which surrounded and surpassed reality but did not penetrate it, raised the problem of the relations between existence and consciousness in general—that is, consciousness of the real as well as of the image. His aesthetic emphasis upon the image postulated the necessary complementarity of reality, which helped dialectically to define the image and shared both consciousness and existence with it. Indeed, Sartre's reading and thinking along the lines of the complement accompanied his aesthetic approach throughout the 30's. What crystallized this parallel activity into a comprehensive formal work was, externally, his awareness of political and social reality and, internally, the ungrounded connections which he made, willy-nilly, between reality and the aesthetic imagination.[25] For since the imaginative consciousness must grasp reality in order to deny it, we are left with the apparent paradox that what Sartre calls "human reality" is constituted by the faculty that constitutes the unreal. Since, moreover, the imaginary is for Sartre "a fact" and he confers on it the status of existence—"unreal existence"—an unstated generic notion of being underlies this two-dimensional existence.[26] It was this tendency of Sartre's art and imagination to slide over into reality that explains his tenuous attraction to the history he denied. It was to resolve the general problem of relating reality and creation that he rounded out his first stage with the writing of L'Être et le néant, in which he articulated the doctrine of history appropriate to this first stage.

The second problem adumbrated in his early work on art and imagination was, if anything, even more fundamental to Sartre: it went

23. *Ibid.*, pp. 158–9.
24. *Ibid.*, pp. 169–71.
25. On Sartre's early political interests, see Simone de Beauvoir, *Memoirs*, p. 344.
26. Sartre, *Psychology of Imagination*, pp. 200, 271–2.

straight through *L'Être et le néant* to dominate his second stage. This problem was the problem of synthesis and integration—of what Sartre calls "totality." Objects of the imagination, works of art, are themselves "indivisible wholes," but each one is "independent, isolated," without relations to one another or to their milieu: they form no organized world.[27] It is true, as we have seen, that the imaginative consciousness posits reality as a world, but it is always from the point of view of the particular image, and this real totality is always collapsed by the imagination which transcends it toward a particular end dominated by that point of view. For art and the imagination, in short, the world is always being dissolved into what is discontinuous and individual. Simone de Beauvoir's judgment that Sartre was, at this stage, something of an "anarchist" has a more profound reference than she perhaps intended.[28] His persistent dedication to art and psychology, so pronounced during this first phase, was the consistent expression of his individualizing mentality. And yet, as *L'Être et le néant* reveals, this dedication was balanced, and ultimately overbalanced, by the compensatory passion for totality. He overcame, in *L'Être et le néant,* the problem of discontinuity and, in the service of this measure of integration, established the elemental basis for history. But he remained, in this work, within the framework of individuality. It was the internal drive to overcome this limitation upon unity that pushed him finally into the second stage of his thought in search of a supra-individual totality, and it was in the process of this search that history became central to him.

And so *L'Être et le néant* becomes, for us, the pivotal work. Not that there is much in it about what we would recognize as history: there is, indeed, very little. It concludes, as I have indicated, the phase of Sartre's thought in which his existentialism ranges only from the hostile to the indifferent in its orientation toward history. Yet, as the most profound, systematic, and coherent exposition of Sartre's philosophy it is crucial for the revelation of the inescapable limits and problems of that thought—limits and problems which created intellectual needs that history was later brought in to fill. Moreover, since Sartre has never departed from the main foundations of his thought, *L'Être et le néant* also set forth the assumptions which molded the subsequent form of his historical doctrine.

Published in 1943, the work has been interpreted in terms of the impact of war and occupation. But Sartre himself has denied the relevance

---

27. *Ibid.,* pp. 188, 193.
28. Simone de Beauvoir, *Memoirs,* p. 344.

of these conditions, indicating the slow gestation of the work through the whole decade of the 30's and its virtual completion, in the sense of its "method and principal conclusions," by the winter of '39–'40.[29] We have, then, empirical confirmation of what should be clear from the substance of the book—it is the philosophical foundation of the ideas and attitudes that we have been reviewing, the ideas and attitudes of Sartre's first stage. The work is long, the terminology special and precise, the structure tightly joined. I propose here to hack it up, to appropriate only what is pertinent to our purpose, and to translate it into the grosser terms of general usage. Let us simply look for the general theme of *L'Être et le néant* and then list, as select propositions frankly torn from context, the discrete positions which have a coherence in their common reference to the problem of history.

The theme is the relationship of existence and consciousness for the particular kind of being which Sartre calls "human reality." These two sub-types of being manifest a radical rift in the heart of human being as such. This rift manifests itself in the striving of consciousness to create a ground, a reason for being, and to rejoin existence in a unitary, or, in Sartre's term, "totalized" being whose contingency would now be replaced by meaning. The pattern for the action of this consciousness of the real is analogous to the previously developed consciousness of the image—the spontaneous withdrawal from and denial of the existent, the simultaneous organization of the existent into a world to be transcended, and the surpassing of it by the individual consciousness' projection of itself toward its freely chosen end. But the changes of scene entail a process quite different from that of the imaginary arena, for now consciousness is engaged continuously in and with real existence and its vehicle is moral action rather than art. Since this consciousness emerges from existence and seeks to return to synthesis with existence, its primary function is not imagining nor even knowing—but doing.

Sartre's theme was thus the immanent unity of being, and he articulated it by turning existence into a process. He showed consciousness surging out of existence, planting a ladder made of recalcitrant existent materials firmly upon nothing, attaching it to a hand-made star, and climbing with the whole weight of existence upon its back toward that blessed landing where the existence would be justified and the consciousness realized. In the course of the trip Sartre had to bring consciousness to terms with all dimensions of human reality. Yet the

29. Jean-Paul Sartre, *Critique de la raison dialectique* (vol. I, Paris, 1960), p. 34.

historical dimension of this reality, obvious as it is, gets short shrift, and Sartre's orientation of his theme against detached knowledge as an activity and detached particulars as objects—both the stock-in-trade of historians—makes it clear that this was no mere oversight. But his position was more intricate than the specific neglect implied. If we arrange six of his pre-historical propositions—that is, propositions on time and society, the two main constituents of the historical dimension—in the form of a cumulative argument, the bases of both the actual indifference toward and the potential usefulness of history for the pre-war Sartre should stand revealed:

1. Neither consciousness nor existence are *in* time. Time is created by consciousness as the medium through which consciousness transforms existence into a world for which it can take responsibility. All the dimensions of time, consequently, including the past, are derivatives of the "original synthesis" of time and are internally related to one another through it.[30]

2. The three dimensions of time correspond to the three facets of the creative act of consciousness. The present is the free consciousness' withdrawal from and negation of existence; the future is the freely chosen end toward which consciousness projects itself; the past is existence itself, as it exists for consciousness. The past, then, is the "facticity," "the given," the "contingent," the "essence" and "substance" of what we are. It is the unalterable, irremediable, factual necessity that "haunts" consciousness; it is the world that consciousness determines itself to transcend.[31]

3. The role of the past in the constitution of "human reality" is admittedly "a paradox."[32] Consciousness must be *both* its own past—since the past is by definition the substance of what anything is—*and* at the same time it must deny, negate, "nihilate" this very past, for this is consciousness' very reason for being. The past must be *both* continuous with the present—"the origin and springboard of all my actions"—*and* ruptured from it. The past must *both* supply *to* the future the terms in which possibilities are projected and choices made *and* be "illuminated"—that is, offered its "meaning"—*by* the future, since it is in the light of its possibilities and choices that consciousness determines what the past is. In Sartre's trenchant expression of the paradox: "All my past

---

30. Jean-Paul Sartre, *Being and Nothingness* (tr. by Hazel E. Barnes, New York, 1956), p. 107.

31. *Ibid.*, pp. 35, 83–4, 118–9, 140–1.

32. *Ibid.*, pp. 489, 496. For this paragraph see also pp. 141, 436, 453, 465–7, 478.

is there, pressing urgent, imperious, but its meanings and the orders which it gives me I choose by the very project of my end."

As a matter of fact, if not of logic, Sartre did break through the paradox, but he did it now by deciding for the present and future over the past. The past includes both "unchangeable" and "variable" elements—that is, facts and meanings—but "the meaning of the past fact penetrates it through and through," with the effect that unchangeable fact cannot be distinguished as such but must lie "beyond reach" within its layers of variable meaning. The priority of meaning over fact *in* the past entails the priority of present and future over past, "for the meaning of the past is strictly dependent upon my present project" for the future.[33] Consciousness decides now, in accord with its projected ends, what parts of the past it will maintain in continuity with the present and what parts of the past it will in varying degrees break off from the present and leave for dead or in varying degrees of death throes. The past, then, becomes irremediable and effective only in the form that consciousness decides to make it so. The past becomes "the actually revealed materialization of the end which we are." Thus Sartre resolved the paradox at the cost of the past, but he paid for it in ambiguity. "We choose our past in the light of a certain end, but from then on it imposes itself upon us and devours us."[34]

4. The past, as a dimension of temporality, is the basis of history but it does not by itself constitute history. For the past, as such, is a structure of the individual consciousness—it is "my past," of "my consciousness"—whereas history begins only with a social past. The "event" that is "a condition of all history"—that has the effect of "making history possible"—is the "fact," absolute, contingent, inexplicable, of the birth of social consciousness out of individual consciousness—Sartre's terms, "the upsurge" of "being-for-others" out of "being-for-itself."[35] The time dimension which history inhabits is, accordingly, an addition upon original time: it is "universal time," composed by the succession of simultaneous intersections of "my" time and "the Other's."[36] But—and this is the crucial fourth proposition, although it is an interpretation of Sartre rather than Sartre's own interpretation—history is in fact reduced to the individual past, is indeed a mere function of it, and the entire third proposition on the past, with all its ambiguities, applies equally to history. For the Sartre of *L'Être et le néant,* history has no

33. *Ibid.,* pp. 497–8.
34. *Ibid.,* p. 503.
35. *Ibid.,* p. 282.
36. *Ibid.,* pp. 267, 282.

autonomous status whatsoever; what small status it does have derives from its existence as a special case of the individual past. Although he did not bother to define it, he identified as "history" those sections of the past and of the knowledge of the past that had a social reference, but his approach to history in both these senses was such as to make these sections minuscule subsets within the generic past created by individual consciousness. Sartre's quantitative neglect of history—in *L'Être et le néant*'s six hundred pages the two brief excursions into history comprise some six pages devoted to actual history and a mere five sentences to the historian—thus reflected a parenthetical view of history, and this view was, in turn, faithfully reflected in what he did with it on the few occasions he troubled to discuss it.[37]

Sartre could conceive of history in the terms and on the pattern of the individual and his past because he refused to make either of the two distinctions that usually define history. He would not distinguish in principle either between the two senses of history—history as the reality of the past and history as the knowledge of the past—or between history as such and the past. This deliberate ambiguity, moreover, had a tendency, for Sartre used the confusion between real history and known history to make the agents of history act like historians and he used the confusion between history and the generic past to make historians act like any past-creating individuals. Thus when Sartre recalled historical situations it was to adduce in each case an "historical agent," assessing his own past in the manner of an historian, as an example in a larger analysis of individual choice. On the one occasion when Sartre raised history beyond the level of a convenient illustrative individual who happened to live in the past, he simply assumed societies to obey precisely the same rules in the relationship to their past as individuals do. Thus the pattern which he had worked out for individual consciousness whereby its present project decides "the value, the order, and the nature of our past" "is simply the historical choice in general."[38] It applies therefore to societies in the same way as to individuals. "If human societies are historical, this does not stem simply from the fact that they have a past but from the fact that they reassume the past by making it a memorial."[39]

Obviously, if historical agents become indistinguishable from individuals in general by becoming their own historians, then the pattern

37. *Ibid.*, pp. 446–9, 500–3.
38. *Ibid.*, p. 500.
39. *Ibid.*

applies *a fortiori* to historians as such. ". . . The historian is himself historical; . . . he historicizes himself by illuminating 'history' in the light of his projects and those of his society."[40] Neither the society nor the historian has any more right to claim a definitive status for their historical pasts than the individual does for his temporal past: for all these agents alike the meaning of the past will change in the tow of their changing projects.[41] And if there be any lingering doubt about Sartre's reduction of history, it may be removed by his inconsistent but revealing use of the term to characterize the individual's view of his own past, apart from any social consciousness, when he reflects upon it.[42]

5. Behind Sartre's inability to people the historical arena which he defined was his more fundamental—and this time admitted—failure to go beyond the individual and to constitute the society that was to inhabit it. For Sartre, always "the question is of *my* freedom," of "only *my* particular consciousness."[43] This did not mean solipsism but rather the inherent impossibility of discovering or establishing any kind of relationships among individuals that would be reasonable or meaningful and hence that could constitute any kind of group. "Human reality remains alone because the Other's existence has the nature of a contingent and irreducible fact. . . . It is therefore useless for human reality to seek to get out of his dilemma: one must either transcend the Other or be transcended by him. The essence of the relations between consciousness is not the *Mitsein;* it is conflict."[44] This is because individuals apply their isolated temporal processes to a common world: each consciousness knows other individuals as objects in its world to be used and transcended; it experiences the fact of other individuals as consciousnesses—that is, as free beings—only by feeling itself demeaned to an object for them, to be used and transcended. Thus there are only "us objects," that is, common objects for a third party, but this is no union, for each individual here "feels trapped among an infinity of strange existences . . . and alienated radically."[45]

But this insulated, individualized kind of existence was not, for Sartre, simply a fact; it was a failure. Our awareness of others, our development of a social consciousness, tells us not only that a plurality of consciousnesses exist but that this plurality "is a totality." And yet, so

40. *Ibid.,* p. 501.
41. *Ibid.,* pp. 501–2.
42. *Ibid.,* pp. 158–9.
43. *Ibid.,* p. 438. Sartre's emphasis.
44. *Ibid.,* pp. 250, 429.
45. *Ibid.,* p. 419.

imprisoned is each within himself that we can neither know nor do anything about it. "The multiplicity of consciousness appears to us as a synthesis and not as a collection, but it is a synthesis whose totality is inconceivable."[46]

6. Here we have the key to the final and summary proposition of *L'Être et le néant*. It is a philosophy of "perpetual failure."[47] This proposition, be it noted, is not a judgment upon Sartre; it is Sartre's explicit thesis. Repeatedly, at the critical points of his analysis, Sartre affirms failure, not on the part of Sartre but on the part of being, of "human reality." As we have seen above, the individual consciousness cannot realize any union with a community of consciousnesses. Again, the individual consciousness, which, it should be recalled, is in its primary structure an active rather than a knowing consciousness, fails when it tries to unite itself with existence through knowledge, which the active consciousness produces as a secondary mode of its being. For knowledge, operated through "reflection," literally reflects the original disjunction between existence and consciousness in the duality of the known and the knower.[48] Consciousness as such, finally, whatever its structure, fails in its practical effort to rejoin existence by attaining for "the real . . . the dignity of the self-cause."[49]

All these failures are aspects of one generic failure inherent in reality: the failure of its parts to achieve a unity that is actually impossible but is just as actually a target, indicated by reality itself, for their striving. A paradox? Of course. But also an intolerable torment. "The being of human reality is suffering because it rises in being as perpetually haunted by a totality which it is without being able to be it. . . . Human reality therefore is by nature an unhappy consciousness with no possibility of surpassing its unhappy state. . . . Everything happens as if the world, man, and man-in-the-world succeeded in realizing only a missing God. Everything happens therefore as if existence and consciousness were presented in a state of disintegration in relation to an ideal synthesis."[50]

These six propositions are, of course, related, and their connection epitomizes Sartre's position at the conclusion of his first stage. Everywhere he looked he saw isolation and frustration, and, as a corollary, the desired unity and fulfillment of which the frustration was a function. Between the two, nothing. The most tangible block was man's inability

46. *Ibid.*, pp. 252, 301.
47. *Ibid.*, p. 623.
48. *Ibid.*, pp. 218, 624.
49. *Ibid.*, p. 623.
50. *Ibid.*, pp. 90, 623.

to relate to other men and thereby to direct common action to a total human goal. The corollary of *this* inability was the absence of any effective history beyond the type of past that lived and died with each individual or social cognate of individuals and contributed nothing but transient matter to the transcendent goal.[51] And yet, though the denigration of history was a consequence of the inviability of the group, the same philosophy implied history's potential as a power for synthesis. The deprecation of history was a function both of the dependent status of the past and the unreality of the group. But the past and the group were the only possible forces that could form a continuum. If history could be recognized, it could exercise a reverse effect as the medium for the realization of both past and society by internally relating them. Here was the need and here was the possibility that cradled Sartre's growth.

Since Sartre had reached the limits of his own resources in *L'Être et le néant* he obviously could not grow from within. But he was philosophically prepared to absorb actively what came to him from without. What came was the war, the occupation, the resistance—and the effect upon him was cataclysmic. But what, precisely, was the effect? What filtered through the fine mesh, so carefully manufactured, of his thought? According to Simone de Beauvoir, the effect was dual. First, "we discovered the reality of history and its weight.[52] Secondly, the experience taught Sartre "solidarity": whereas he had thought to attain the absolute through art, he now "discovered, with his historicity, his dependence; . . . the universality to which, as a bourgeois intellectual, he aspired, only those men who embodied it on earth could give him"— that is, the proletariat, "the universal class."[53] Now this has the ring of authenticity. As we have seen, history and social solidarity were precisely what the pre-war Sartre needed. But the question is not only *what* were added. It is also *how* they were added, since, as we have seen, Sartre seemed closed to both history and society by necessary paradoxes of his thought. The "how" really involves two questions. In what forms did he perceive the cataclysm of his times? And how did he translate the experience into concepts at least coherent to if not entirely consistent with his philosophy?

For the first question we have the evidence from the trilogy of

51. E.g., *ibid.*, pp. 502, 623.
52. Simone de Beauvoir, *La Force des choses* (Paris, 1963), p. 47.
53. *Ibid.*, pp. 15–7.

novels—*Les Chemins de la liberté*—which embody the contemporary expression of his attitudes for the critical war-time interval spanning the break between the two stages of his thought. For the second question we have Sartre's own direct retrospective testimony.

The trilogy—which is not strictly a trilogy since there is a projected fourth volume that has not appeared—may be viewed as the incomplete representation of Sartre's progressive grasp of the inevitable participation by originally isolated individuals in the life and time of larger complexes of individuals. *L'Age de raison*—the first volume—represents the point of departure, the fictional equivalent of *L'Être et le néant*, but told now from the point of view, not of existence, as in *La Nausée*, but of consciousness. It is, indeed, an account of "unhappy consciousness."

The actors are a set of individuals in Paris, revolving loosely in various confrontations around Mathieu, a teacher of philosophy, but each in his or her own orbit—what Sartre calls "an unbarred cage"—seeking in vain for a meaning in it.[54] The time is presumably during the 30's, but there is no reference to the larger society to date it. Each has his own life and, though these lives "interlace and intersect," they "remain as vigorously personal as a toothbrush"; each has his own past, which offers no support because it "was in continual process of retouching by the present."[55] The want of meaning within each life is internally associated with the incapacity to break out of it toward others. Mathieu, the reflective consciousness who incorporates the age of reason, is "empty," "a negation" because he thinks rather than acts and can find no reason for acting. He feeds upon himself, but sporadically he breaks through to a momentary vision of "above his life a pure consciousness, . . . without ego, . . . unlinked to any person."[56] Concretely, his vision of a meaning is embodied in the Communist, Brunet, whose life has "meaning," is "a destiny" because he has "a whole world in common" with his comrades. "His age, his class, his time—he had deliberately assumed them all. . . . He had joined up, he had renounced his freedom. . . . And everything had been rendered to him, even his freedom. 'He is freer than I: he is in harmony with himself and with the party.'"[57] Mathieu yearns for this kind of solidarity, but his sympathy remains "abstract."[58] He cannot make the leap from his individuality to

54. Jean-Paul Sartre, *The Age of Reason* (tr. by Eric Sutton, New York, 1947), p. 146.
55. *Ibid.*, pp. 242, 272.
56. *Ibid.*, pp. 64, 245, 395.
57. *Ibid.*, pp. 155, 159.
58. *Ibid.*, p. 137.

this extreme pole of solidarity; in the light of this standard his reason can only demonstrate to him, at the end, "the failure of a life."[59] But we must remember Brunet, for the trilogy will end with him as a central character and a real figure. In a sense his passage—the passage of the solidarity that he stands for—from abstraction to reality is the theme of the work.

The passage leads through the second volume—*Sursis*—for our purposes the most important of the three. Ostensibly it is a sequel which follows the experiences of these characters, plus a few new ones, during the week of the Munich crisis and the partial mobilization that accompanied it. Actually, it signified a radical change in point of view, reflected in the dramatically changed technique of the novel. Gone was the mechanical unity of place and of middle class. The familiar individuals are scattered through France, the newer ones extend the scene from north Africa to Czechoslovakia and the types from Neville Chamberlain to an illiterate shepherd. Not only are the encounters between these individuals now fortuitous—most of them never meet—but even their individual orbits are broken, discontinuous.

And yet there is a strong coherence in the work, a coherence now constituted by time, by what we may call social time. The chapters are capped by the calendar days of the Munich crisis, but it is not this device that registers the full impact of the innovation. The scenes shift, from situation to situation, from individual to individual, within the chapter, within the paragraph, within the sentence, led by the logic of a common time which is the measure of the social crisis. Through the medium of time the world, in the form of the imminent war, invaded individuality and smashed it. "The sum" of all individual futures "is peace."[60] But "now the war is there; my life is dead. . . . I own nothing any more, not even my past. It was indeed a spurious past, and I don't regret it. . . . They have rid me of my life."[61] The events of Mathieu's past "belonged to the world's past, together with the peace; his life had been put away in the archives of the Third Republic. . . . This man had shaped a future to his measure: the war had thundered down upon it and crushed it to powder."[62] Thus, through participation in the invisible time of a war that was not yet, the circuit of self-hood was broken. The individual was opened to the world, but still only negatively, recognizing his existence as a thing in a world made by the war

59. *Ibid.*, p. 395.
60. Jean-Paul Sartre, *The Reprieve* (tr. by Eric Sutton, New York, 1947), pp. 47–8.
61. *Ibid.*, pp. 86–7.
62. *Ibid.*, pp. 341, 352.

into an organization of things. "Myself a nondescript entity beneath that vast indifferent arc: that's war. . . . A new world was coming into being: the austere and practical world of functional objects. . . . Outside. Everything is outside: . . . solid objects, all of them. Inside, nothing. . . . Myself, nothing. . . . Inseparable from the world as light, and yet exiled, gliding like light over the surface of stones and water: freedom is exile. . . . "[63] Individuality had lost its substance, its integrity. In a grim climax Sartre makes his point by describing the reluctant submission of the virgin Ivich to an anonymity in precise synchronization with the rape of Czechoslovakia.

Thus opened forcibly, cataclysmically, to the world through membership in the world's time, Sartre initiated his characters to the humanizing of the relationship in *La Mort dans l'âme*. It was the story now of the real war, of the experience of his characters under the impact of the French military defeat in 1940. As the title indicates, the theme once again was of the violation of the individual, but this time by reality and in a more positive sense. The continuity was still supplied by social time, the temporal pattern of the defeat, but no longer were the individual destinies simply chopped up by it: once again they pursued their projects through solid blocks of life. The attenuation of their individuality now served their membership in an inchoate, homogenized, faceless association, for they lived in its time and were unified by its historian. "I can break the shell that separates us only if I wish for myself no other future than his, . . . share his time and his minutes."[64] The association, a society of defeat, was passive, an object rather than a subject, and yet even in this spiritless form it was born into history as a group. "'We're being looked at.' A crowd growing more and more dense was watching them swallow this bitter pill of history. . . . There they stood, guilty forever in the eyes of their sons, of their grandsons, and of their great-grandsons, they, the conquered of 1940 to all eternity. . . . He looked at his comrades, and his mortal eyes met the timeless, petrified eyes of history."[65]

And yet there were also something more than the mere "us object" of *L'Être et le néant*. "At one and the same time they were less than human and more than human."[66] For they had participated in the creation of this general destiny whose embodiment was this defeated army. The war was "each and every one of us, war made in the image of all of

63. *Ibid.*, pp. 348–9, 362–3.
64. Jean-Paul Sartre, *Troubled Sleep* (tr. by Gerard Hopkins, New York, 1951), p. 200.
65. *Ibid.*, pp. 85–6.
66. *Ibid.*, p. 87.

us."[67] Thus the community in which individuals lose their individuality is nonetheless one which they have made and which reflects them all. "At once . . . part of the general whole yet rejected by each individual, perfectly lucid yet utterly deceived, enslaved yet sovereign, I'm just like everybody else."[68] Mathieu, standing for those who cannot accept the immersion of their individuality chooses to die (and when we leave him, he is about to). He has finally made the decision that fulfills his own destiny, but it means "firing on his fellow men, on Virtue, the whole world: Liberty is Terror."[69] Sartre's focus then becomes the group, defined now by the common status of prisoners of war, and personified by Brunet, the Communist organizer, the group man, and Schneider, a socialized Mathieu and clearly the surrogate of Sartre himself. By the standards of the dissatisfied and uncomprehending Brunet we feel the inertia of the group. In Schneider's understanding of the death in the group soul and his collaboration with Brunet simply to give "the boys . . . something to live for" we feel the first glimmerings of the group as an agency for meaning.[70]

If we project the direction of the fourth volume which Sartre has been as yet unable to finish from the angle of the trilogy we may anticipate the growth of an active group consciousness in the Resistance. But, as we shall soon see, it is characteristic of Sartre's second stage that he has as yet not been able to clinch the synthesis of the individual and the group. Involving as it does not only the coherence of an idea but the capstone of a system, this synthesis is itself a becoming, a movement along the dimension of time.

And so the answer to our first question—in what form did Sartre perceive the cataclysm?—is simply this: he absorbed the contemporary experience in the form of contemporary history. That is, he took the break-through of social cataclysm into individual lives and the response of individuals in the form of joint action as proof of a collective reality that was created and knowable through the synthesizing force of a common temporal process upon the activities of individuals participating in it. And because he saw history—which is composed precisely of the relationships which individuals create with one another through time—because he saw history being made, he came to understand how history was made. Because he saw in their possession of a common time the basis of meaningful relations among individuals, he came to see in the

67. *Ibid.*, p. 196.
68. *Ibid.*, p. 193.
69. *Ibid.*, pp. 255–6.
70. *Ibid.*, p. 339.

succession of these relations a meaning not only within but through history.

This illumination lies behind Sartre's own retrospective testimony that the cataclysm marked the decisive turn not only in his life but in his philosophy. According to this testimony, "the war, the occupation, the resistance, the years that followed," "exploded the former framework of our thought. We now desired to fight at the side of the working class, we understood finally that the concrete is history and dialectical action. We denied pluralist realism by recognizing it in the fascists and we discovered the world."[71] This "pluralist realism" of his first stage he now characterized as "a confusion of the individual and the total, . . . a description of artificially isolated essences and types" appropriate to the critical revelation of "the contradictions of reality" but not to its deeper unity. The "reality" that "the whole bloody history of this half-century" suddenly revealed to him, initiating his second stage, he called "the reality of Marxism," but he meant Marxism in the sense of "the only valid interpretation of history," "the conception of concrete syntheses . . . within a moving and dialectical totalization which is nothing else but history"—"the historical process in its totality."[72] In short, what replaced the individualistic temporal paradoxes and failures of his first stage was the conviction, mediated by contemporary history, that individuals could join with their fellows in an *historical* process in which they could recover their integrity. He subscribed to Marxism because Marxism provided both the historical schema and, in the proletariat, the social group to realize it.

This second stage of Sartre's, philosophically grounded in his massive *Critique de la raison dialectique* of 1960, is thus not so much Marxist as historicist, and the work might well have been titled the Critique of Historical Reason that so many philosophers since Kant have been tempted to write. He set as his aim: "to test, criticize, and ground . . . the instruments of thought by which history is thought in so far as they are also the practical instruments by which it is made."[73] Marxism, for Sartre, does indeed reveal the general process through which men make a unity out of human reality through history, but for him, too, Marxists do not know how the process works and, more important, contemporary Marxists have lost the sense of the movement, the dialectic, the real history in the process. The role of existentialism within Marxism

71. Sartre, *Critique de la raison dialectique*, p. 24.
72. *Ibid.*, pp. 24–9.
73. *Ibid.*, p. 135.

then, according to Sartre, is precisely to restore authentic history to it as the only means of knowing and ultimately realizing the "totalization" that is history.[74] Existentialism contributes the appreciation of the individual—the event—views history as the succession of creative moments, and commands the dialectical method that consists in the internal relation of individuality and totality through time. Thereby Sartre means to resolve his own paradoxes through history: practice gets integrated into knowledge as intelligibility, the historical agent into the historian as "the historical man," the individual into society as "the group."[75]

Of this synthetic labor, Sartre has thus far performed half (the *Critique* is labeled volume one). He has integrated, to his own satisfaction, individuals, groups, and the historian into an "intelligible totalization" through the unity of "synchronous" time—that is, the lateral unity at any particular moment of historical time. What he has still to do but has not yet done—and perhaps will never do—is to complete the synthesis by demonstrating the intelligible, "progressive" movement toward human integrity through time.[76] For so tight a system the reach may well exceed the grasp. Nonetheless, the philosophy of perpetual failure has become the philosophy of continuous success.

If we grant to Sartre any kind of representative status in contemporary thought, the implications of his conversion to history are profound.

Because the material of history is the specific, the concrete, and the unique, its function in the cosmos of knowledge is usually characterized or assumed to be the provision of particular information or, at most, particular truths, on a level as close as possible to the original variety of human existence. Our forbears warn us to align particular events with as much indifference as we can muster to any order of general truths. Our social scientific friends adjure us to supply the test of particular information for *their* general truths. Our revisionist colleagues are having great sport using the heterogeneity of grass-roots history to dismantle every general truth in sight.

All these positions deny a synthetic role for history, either by assuming a pre-existing structure of general truths to be merely particularized in history or by rejecting the relevance of general truths to the historical enterprise. But, if Sartre is an even approximately faithful expression of contemporary culture, then these relationships and, with them, our familiar notion of history's function, are anachronisms. If neither logic, nor science, nor art any longer furnish general truths pertinent to human conduct, if their meanings are also utterly fragmented, then history must use the patterns of synchronization and succession of human actions in the common medium of time to link *their* particular fragments and to construct whatever general truths about man we must have. If we do not apply our history to this end we fail both as the historians and as the historical agents of our age.

6 The Historical Hannah Arendt

I write under a title of intentional ambiguity, for I mean to write of the historical Hannah Arendt in both the objective and the subject senses of "history." I shall consider her both as a figure who made history and as an author who wrote history—of history's attitude toward her and of her attitude toward history. The time has undoubtedly come to view Arendt in historical perspective, no longer to judge her performance as a contemporary colleague's or a political rival's, but to understand her work as the expression of a prominent personage in a definite age. The time has come not so much because she has passed physically from among us, leaving the corpus of her writing complete and enabling the historian to apply his approach to the finished temporal process where it works best. The time for historical understanding has come rather because reflection on the totality of her publications makes it clear that she has achieved the status of an individual for history—an individual, that is, who was open to the influences of her own and of past times, who reworked these impressions into products at once original and memorable, and who diffused them in their inimitable and yet communicable form through the community of humankind. She was, then, both a phenomenon in her own right and an articulator of society's more indeterminate culture, and this combination has always made up the kind of personality to which historians have paid attention.

How Arendt would have enjoyed her membership in the company of the great individuals whom she recognized to be the main historical concern of her beloved classical Greeks! And I think that she would have approved, too, of a historian's using her own approach to history as a congenial way of gaining access to what she was and what she stands for. If, then, we use history, both as a measure of her status and as a dimension of her work, we do it neither to eulogize nor to assess but to illuminate from one perspective that which may still be problematic in her achievement. A final introductory point: As a historical thinker, she will figure here only as she appeared in her published works.

First published in the *Journal of Modern History* 48 (December, 1976), 672–87. In a slightly different form, this paper was delivered at a memorial colloquium on the work of Hannah Arendt, held at Bard College, April 26, 1976.

Let us first, then, place Arendt in her age, for proof by association, however dubious in law, is standard procedure in history. Certainly she was an original. She belonged to no identifiable school of thought, and although she was vaguely labeled a philosopher, she adhered to no specialized compartment of learning. Yet she had company, for what she tried to do in her own way, others in the eventful half century since the disillusioned twenties and the dismal thirties have tried to do in theirs; and from the parallelism we can infer a general characterization which may help us to define her. She was, obviously, one of the myriad analysts of cultural crisis. Her cultural criticism was not usually of the Nietzschean and Kafkaesque chronic or recurrent type, whose target she once identified as the "dark times" that "are no rarity in history."[1] Rather, it was radical, of the existentialist and aesthetic avant-gardist type, which sees precisely in the contemporary period an unprecedented destruction of value, of meaning, of human capacity. It is hardly surprising that she perceived such an extent of crisis in the lasting effects of totalitarianism, since she defined totalitarianism in terms of its linkage with the fundamentally anomic nature of mass society. She could write in the immediate posttotalitarian era that "we" still

watch the development of the same phenomena—homelessness on an unprecedented scale, rootlessness to an unprecedented depth. . . . We can no longer afford to take that which was good in the past and simply call it our heritage, to discard the bad and simply think of it as a dead load which by itself time will bury in oblivion. The subterranean stream of Western history has finally come to the surface and usurped the dignity of our tradition. This is the reality in which we live. And this is why all efforts to escape from the grimness of the present into nostalgia for a still intact past or into the anticipated oblivion of a better future, are vain.

For totalitarianism is based on the "organized loneliness of contemporary man" which will outlive it and which "threatens to ravage the world as we know it—a world which everywhere seems to have come to an end—before a new beginning rising from this end has had time to assert itself."[2]

What characterizes Arendt more essentially and more precisely as a philosopher of cultural crisis than even this insight into the implications of totalitarianism was the broadening and deepening of her criticism as the passage of postwar years attenuated the totalitarian occasion and

---

1. Hannah Arendt, *Men in Dark Times* (New York, 1968), pp. viii–ix. All works cited in this paper are by Hannah Arendt.

2. *The Origins of Totalitarianism* (New York, 1958), pp. vii, ix, 478.

riveted her anxiety directly on the primary universal features of contemporary life itself. She became a radical critic who affirmed modern man's entire alienation from the world, along with the concomitant dissolution of coherence in the life of the species, the abolition of identity in the life of the individual, and the attrition of man's basic ability to think, an ability which is the very fulcrum of his nature. "The modern age," she wrote summarily, "with its growing world-alienation, had led to a situation where man, wherever he goes, encounters only himself. . . . In this situation of radical world-alienation, neither history nor nature is at all conceivable. This twofold loss of a world . . . has left behind it a society of men who, without a common world which would at once relate and separate them, either live in desperate lonely separation or are pressed together into a mass." This crisis in mass society means a "crisis in culture" as well, for "mass culture comes into being when mass society seizes upon cultural objects, and its danger is that the life process of society . . . will literally consume the cultural objects, eat them up and destroy them. . . . This does not mean that culture spreads to the masses, but that culture is being destroyed in order to yield entertainment." Where the human capacity for overcoming these conditions should reside, moreover—in the seam between the past which determines men by "things that are no longer" and the future which equally determines them by "things that are not yet"—there is currently only a "gap" that has become "a tangible reality and perplexity for all," for "we seem to be neither equipped nor prepared for this activity of thinking."[3]

This assignment of Arendt to the ranks of the categorical cultural critics only begins to locate her historically. Two substantive qualities of her criticism crystallize her role more definitely and illuminate her thinking more brightly. First, she is one of those critics who exhibited an explicit continuum between the politico-social and the ethico-ontological levels of human culture. For her, the tendencies affecting political structure, social organization, natural science, religion, and philosophy in the human community were joined in a single direction, at once provoking and expressing the basic truths of human and physical nature. This is not the same point as the centrality of politics in her own thinking, of which more later. The point is, rather, her alignment with such intellectual figures as Ortega y Gasset, Croce, and Marcuse, from whom she differed so dramatically in the content of her thought, but for whom, too, there was and is a continuous and explanatory interaction among social criticism, cultural analysis, and philosophical

3. *Between Past and Future* (New York, 1968), pp. 9, 13–14, 89, 207.

principle in society itself and who prove that Arendt was not eccentric in her integrated vision.

The second defining characteristic of her critical posture was its emphatic constructive quality. Here she joins such critics and philosophers as Karl Mannheim, Albert Camus, and her friend Karl Jaspers in a group whose negations can only be understood in terms of the lost positivities which they lament and the potential positivities toward which they strive. In Arendt's case this constructive approach was literally explicit in her derivation of the contemporary crisis of the society and the culture alike from "the decline of the Roman trinity of religion, tradition, and authority" because they "gave the world the permanence and durability which human beings need precisely because they are mortals" and because their "loss is tantamount to the loss of the groundwork of the world." Her constructive approach was equally explicit in her insistence that the disappearance of the trinity "does not entail, at least not necessarily, the loss of the human capacity for building, preserving, and caring for a world that can survive us and remain a place fit to live in for those who come after us" and in her determination to contribute, through the provision of "exercises" and "experience in how to think," to the "new beginning" which "every end in history necessarily contains," which is "the supreme capacity of man" and which must establish "a new law on earth," "a new guarantee" of human dignity "which can be found only in a new political principle."[4] The two sets of constants—the constant principles, now anachronistic, which dominated the past and the constant principles, not yet formulated, which ought to dominate the future—were intimately connected in Arendt's mind, for she defined "the chief aim" of her critical interpretation of the past "to discover the real origins of traditional concepts in order to distill from them anew their original spirit which has so sadly evaporated from the very key words of political language . . . leaving behind empty shells with which to settle almost all accounts, regardless of their underlying phenomenal reality."[5] We must keep this bidimensional constructionist—or, more precisely, reconstructionist—orientation of her cultural and political criticism in mind, for its past dimension led her to history, and what was common to its constructive principles provided the framework within which this history was viewed.

We are led, then, from the consideration of Arendt's historical location to the consideration of her historical perspective. Here we must

4. *Ibid.*, pp. 94–95, 128; *Origins of Totalitarianism*, pp. ix, 478–79.
5. *Between Past and Future*, p. 15.

distinguish between her theory and her practice of history, not for the usual pedantic purpose of checking what someone says by what he or she does, but in Arendt's case because her variant attitudes toward history on the two levels obviously refer to two different kinds of history and differentiate the kind of history she did not espouse from the kind of history that she did. The kind of history that she theorized about was what we might call pure history—the autonomous history that has been a characteristic expression of our culture since the late eighteenth century and is practiced by professional historians—and about this her attitude was largely negative. The kind of history that she practiced and, by implication, of course, approved, was her own hybrid brand of history, and much of what she wrote can be understood as products of her distinctive approach to history and in terms of the demands it made upon her analysis.

Arendt's theoretical attitude toward what she called "the concept of history" was dominated by her view of it as one of the persistent organizing ideas of Western culture, which had their vital origins in the classical ages of ancient Greece and Rome and which not only have themselves decayed in modern times, but, in their decadent version, have actively contributed to the demise of their affiliated organizing concepts—much in the way, say, that the degeneration of power into violence signifies both the decline of the concept of power and the attack on the concept of authority. The modern concept of history in this sense not only is noxious but, even worse, has become anachronistic for the contemporary age—worse in that no role can be assigned to it in the preparation of a new beginning. The modern concept of history, according to Arendt, was a characteristic expression of the modern scientific culture which arose in the sixteenth and seventeenth centuries and became dominant in the nineteenth. Like the modern concept of nature, with which it coincided and shared features, the modern concept of history absorbed "the world-alienation of man" and thus helped to undermine faith in an objective external reality. Therewith, fatefully, it dissolved the classical union of "the concrete and the general, the single thing or event and the universal meaning," which was the condition of the "self-evident" meaning and hence of the "objectivity" and "impartiality" in the ancient concept of history. It replaced this union with the concept of man-made process, which enthrones the principle of mindless action and does away with the validity of universal meaning and the intelligibility of particular events equally.

She rejected the notion of a Christian conception of history in order to deny any mediation of the radical disjunction between the stable, viable ancient concept of history and the arbitrary, meaningless modern concept of history. The modern concept of history is meaningless because in it a particular occurrence is supposed to "derive" its meaning only from "the process as a whole" in which it is "supposedly embedded," but this historical process can never have a meaning because it is subject to the ultimate randomness which, in the Arendt lexicon, is the primary ingredient of mental and moral chaos.

The question for us is no longer whether this or that particular formula is correct. In all such attempts what is considered to be a meaning is in fact no more than a pattern. . . . We can take almost any hypothesis and *act* upon it, with a sequence of results in reality which not only make sense but *work*. This means quite literally that everything is possible not only in the realm of ideas but in the field of reality itself. . . . Any order, any necessity, any meaning you wish to impose will do. This is the clearest possible demonstration that under these conditions there is neither necessity nor meaning. It is as though "the melancholy haphazardness" of the particular had now caught up with us and were pursuing us into the very region where the generations before us had fled in order to escape it.

Small wonder that she herself noted the similarity between this arbitrariness of modern history and the arbitrariness of totalitarianism, which too "is based in the last analysis on the conviction that everything is possible," and that she finally inferred history's self-destruction as a contemporary autonomous principle from its subsumption under technology, which transfers man's processes of acting into history to the new ground of acting into nature. Small wonder, too, that when she pronounced her strictures on "the historian" in general, as she so often did, it was because she lamented his tendency to violate what she considered to be particular truths in the service of random general patterns, or, as she herself put it, because "he is liable to overlook what actually happened in his attempt to discern some objective trend."[6]

But despite her grave reservations about society's approach to history, with which, she felt, "the modern age" futilely "hoped to replace the concepts of traditional metaphysics," there was in Arendt's philosophical position that which drove her to her own history. It impelled her to give historical point to at least the first half of her existential, and bilateral, prescription for understanding: "comprehension . . . means the unpremeditated, attentive facing up to, and resisting of, reality—whatever it may be."[7]

6. *Ibid.*, pp. 52–53, 58–70, 80–89.
7. *Ibid.*, p. 15; *Origins of Totalitarianism*, p. viii.

Three such prohistorical features can be remarked here. First, there was her persistent tendency to analyze the fundamental concepts of Western man—such as authority, freedom, power, tradition, religion, revolution—in terms of what has happened to them through time, that is, in terms of their history. Apart from the historical sketches of these concepts which fill her works, her specific association of "criticism" with the "interpretation of the past" is a specific case in point. Her admission at the start of her essay entitled "What Is Authority?" that "it might have been wiser to ask in the title: What was—not what is—authority?" is another. Still another specific instance is the philosophical statement of purpose that prefaces her *Origins of Totalitarianism*, the work for which she is best known among historians and the most indubitably historical of her writings: "to discover the hidden mechanics by which all traditional elements of our political and spiritual world were dissolved into a conglomeration where everything seems to have lost specific value, and has become unrecognizable for human comprehension, unusable for human purpose."[8]

A second prohistorical factor in her philosophical stance was her decided orientation toward beginnings, origins, foundations. Functionally, the prominence of classical thought in Arendt's work has to do, in some measure, with the origins of the crucial concepts making up the Western cultural tradition in the experience of ancient Greece and Rome. She made this reference literal in her analysis of authority, surely a central concept in her view of Western culture, for she traced its primary meaning back to the Romans' veneration of foundations. When she turned to revolution, along with war one of the "two central political issues" of the twentieth century, she defined it in terms of "a new experience which revealed man's capacity for novelty." She explicitly justified it by "the relevance of the problem of beginning to the phenomenon of revolution," thus making revolution the modern heir to the ancient idea of authority with which it shared a common stake in foundations, and she discussed it characteristically in terms of its specific historical origins in the American experience of 1776 and the French of 1789.[9] It is indicative of her historical emphasis, moreover, that she chose the title "The Origins of Totalitarianism" for a work which devoted almost half of its bulk to a static analysis of the achieved totalitarian structure.

8. *Between Past and Future*, pp. 14–15, 91; *Origins of Totalitarianism*, p. viii.
9. *On Revolution* (New York, 1963), pp. 1, 10, 21–22, 27; *Between Past and Future*, pp. 120, 136–41.

But it is the third of Arendt's prohistorical orientations which, albeit perhaps most latent, was also the most forceful of all: She was convinced that the conditions for all decisive change in human affairs, whether constructive or destructive, whether past or future, lay not in the projection of any continuous development but only in the actual onset of events, unforeseen and unforeseeable. She was careful to emphasize that for each of the main stages that have led to our present predicament the decisive steps in the destiny of the relevant concepts were the results, in each case, of "the break in our history" that was caused by absolutely contingent occurrences. Thus, she scorned the attempt to make "an unbroken continuity" of the change from the religious culture of the Middle Ages to "the secular world we live in" by showing "the gradual transformation of religious categories into secular concepts" to be no more than a facile and invalid connection of ideas. Such an attempt, for her, "bypasses, rather than solves, the great riddle of the sudden undeniable rise of the secular," which she preferred to think of as "an event that can be dated in historical time rather than a change of ideas." She reduced it no further than to the statement of "the fact . . . that the separation of church and state occurred, eliminating religion from public life." Revolution, similarly, can be connected with no prior tendency—"the movement which led to revolution was not revolutionary except by inadvertence"—and, indeed, was conducted in its initial stages by men who aimed, rather, at restoration. Revolution in the authentic sense of a new foundation of liberty was born, in both the American and the French cases, during the actual course of the revolutions themselves. Hence the subsequent association of "historical necessity" with the idea of revolution "owes it existence not to theoretical speculation but to political experience and the course of real events." More recently, finally, "the break in our tradition" that has involved the break in "the continuity of Occidental history" is not the result of the precedent intellectual rebellion against tradition, or of the twentieth-century "silence of the tradition," or indeed "of anyone's deliberate choice." Rather, it is the result of "totalitarian domination as an established fact, which in its unprecedentedness cannot be comprehended through the usual categories of political thought. . . . Neither the silence of the tradition nor the reaction of thinkers against it in the 19th century can ever explain what actually happened. The nondeliberate character of the break gives it an irrevocability which only events, never thoughts, can have." In confirmation of such defenses of specific historicity, Arendt opposed every general interpretation and movement that would trivialize it. She deprecated recourse to theses of "general decline" or "the immanent logic" of an idea as incapable of explaining subsequent events or even "new categories of political thinking," which spring rather from shocking "experiences and political constellations." She scourged all "ideology" and theories that regiment or dismiss "unexpected, unpredicted, and unpredictable happenings" for their "straitjacket of logic" and their "speculative or pseudo-scientific refuge from reality."[10]

Not, of course, that she considered intellectual trends irrelevant to individuals, events, and situations. The view of these discrete individuals, events, and situations from the perspective of general trends was indeed precisely what was characteristic of her approach to history. The relationship was stylistically transparent in her reiterated use of the phrase, "the point of the matter is . . . , " and its several cognates to single out the aspect of a multiple-faceted occurrence which was categorically relevant. Substantively, anyone who argued as determinedly as she did for Hobbes as the philosopher of the nineteenth-century bourgeoisie; for the understanding of presumably antitraditional modern thinkers like Marx in terms of the tradition itself, which both was the reference of their rebellion and continued to supply an old "conceptual framework" to their new material; for the triumphant nation-state that was born in the French Revolution as the carrier of sovereignty bequeathed by the precedent absolute monarchy; and for the bearing of nineteenth-century racial and class thinking upon, as well as its distinction from, the racist and bolshevik ideologies of the twentieth century obviously sought to blend, as the best historians do, general constellations and particular crystallization in ways that do justice to the autonomy of both. For Arendt, precedent generalities, whether of ideas in social time or of social and political institutions in social space, established the environment or "atmosphere" in which innovative events and movements independently arose and provided ideas among which innovative men chose and which they selectively perpetuated.[11]

Part of the blending of general and particular truths was thus Arendt's recognition of the bipolarity that is in Western history itself and is borne by its agents. But part, too, was of her own imposition. For the insight into the general ideas and the generic social relations which preceded the eruption of contingent events and movements triggered her philosophical analyses of the concepts and the categories they

10. *On Revolution,* pp. 37–38, 48–40; *Between Past and Future,* pp. 26, 69–70; *Origins of Totalitarianism,* pp. 5, 183, 267, 347; *Crises of the Republic* (New York, 1972), pp. 109–10, 130.
11. *Origins of Totalitarianism,* pp. 139–47; *Between Past and Future,* pp. 18–25.

embodied, and these excursions into the nature of men and things gave her the key to the interpretation of the novel, arbitrary, and apparently a-rational phenomena that followed. The consideration of Rousseau, for example, induced her to expatiate on the nature of compassion, and the nature of compassion, in turn, helped her to explain Robespierre and therewith the unpredictably abortive course of the French Revolution. Again, the diffused anti-Semitism of nineteenth-century Europe furnished the occasion and materials for the scintillating and abstract discussion of vice and crime which then accompanied her analysis of the role of Germans and Jews in Nazi anti-Semitism.[12] This two-directional blending of what was general with what was contingent within Western history, this equal commitment to both the general validity of ideas and to the concrete surprises of their sources and their applications, made a scarcely differentiated continuum of Arendt's philosophy and her history.

It remains to ask: What does this composite approach of Arendt's explain of what was remarkable in her history and of what was distinctive in her philosophizing? Since she habitually merged both, what, in other words, does her philosophizing explain about her history, and what does her history explain about her philosophizing? On the first count, it obviously helps to explain the areas of history on which she elected to concentrate. She wrote most intensively about totalitarianism and about revolution. Whatever part autobiographical and political considerations may have played in this choice, it is clear that the role of what she called "totalitarian domination" in destroying the last remnants of the intellectual and social order inherent in the Western tradition and the role of revolution in generating the foundation of a new tradition in the form, at once congenial to the old tradition and responsive to the unprecedented conditions of human life, of a new "constitution of freedom," gave to those large historical events a central function in the realization and the visualization of her favored concepts. Her more noteworthy interpretations within each of these historical fields can be analogously illuminated, from above as it were.

Her distinction between an American political revolution and a French social revolution is familiar enough, but her further distinction between the stages of negative liberation, which was applicable to both, and of a positive constitution of freedom, which separated the success of the American Revolution from the distortion of the French Revolution and the revolutionary tradition it spawned, is not. Certainly we

---

12. *On Revolution*, pp. 74–94; *Origins of Totalitarianism*, pp. 79–88.

must not disregard her own explanations for this separation of the American and French experiences—explanations in terms of the respective differentiation and confusion of power and law, the respective irrelevance and incorporation of social misery, the respective conciliar articulation of participant democracy and the atomization of a sporadically violent citizenry. But when we go beyond these overt explanations to inquiry into their assumptions, we are brought up against the implicit internal structure of her history. It may well be that her preference for the moderate American over the radical French revolution owes something to a merely political assumption—to the social conservatism of a Germanic philosophical training which has long subordinated the private social realm, as the sphere of self-interest and fragmentation, to the public political realm, as the sphere of organic community. But whatever the relevance of this problematic heritage, it is historiographically indubitable that Arendt's concern to substantiate the logically difficult concept of a freedom at once spontaneous and traditional, individually centered and politically organized, led her to the history of revolutions and dominated her interpretation of them.

In her study on totalitarianism, two of Arendt's historical theses have seemed especially thorny: the insistence that totalitarianism rose as the antithesis rather than the apotheosis of nationalism and the nation-state, and the lumping together of Nazism and Bolshevism as the only two authentically totalitarian regimes in contradistinction to the Fascist countries of southern and eastern Europe which indeed had their precedent totalitarian movements but were only "nontotalitarian dictatorships."[13] Her own explanations of these positions adduce, for the first, the infinite economic expansionism of the preceding imperialism, which presumably strained to the breaking point the political integrity of the nation-state, and the international ambitions of National Socialism as well as Communism. For the second, they adduce the requirement of a sufficiently numerous population to reach what we would call "a critical mass" and the compromises of the Fascist, vis-à-vis both Nazi and Bolshevik, regimes with traditional ideas and institutions. Once more, it behooves us not to challenge these explanations but to go beyond them. Arendt knew very well that the relationship between imperialism and the nation-state was infinitely more balanced and the relationship between National Socialism and Bolshevism recognizably more contrary than her theses postulated, but the structure of her history required her to select precisely the most universalizable tendencies

13. *Ibid.*, pp. 308–9.

for the purpose of hypostatizing them into essences. She wrote history unabashedly on three levels of generality: She analyzed the basic qualities of the human condition, such as property, equality, law, evil; on a slightly more concrete level, she analyzed in fundamental terms that transcended the consciousness of the age the institutions of state and society persistent through an entire period and over a supranational space, such as the elite, the mob, the class, the party, and the mass; and finally, on the most referential level of generality, she described the covering ideas and conscious relationships held by people of the age. To accommodate thinking on all these levels, obviously the most generalizable features of historical life were also the most appropriate features of historical life.

But it would be a mistake to think that the only historical problems to be illuminated by this kind of thinking are those that raise doubts. Extraordinary penetration and superlative performance are also problems that call for illumination, for they should neither be taken for granted nor attributed to some mysterious inspiration of genius. From her study of totalitarianism and its background, two sections especially stand out for the brilliance of their insights and the cogency of their interpretations, and we must conclude that these are instances in which her characteristic approach simply works. The first is her description of nineteenth-century social anti-Semitism and its homologous reflection among the Jews themselves. Her carefully modulated portrait of postliberation Jews, at once admired and suspected because of their scintillation on the periphery of bourgeois societies in which they had lost their old-regime function, is closely tied to her general view of the nineteenth century as an intermediate age of modernity which hollowed out traditional values by rebelling against them while being unable to escape from them and ended, consequently, with their paradoxical application to incongruous material. Thus transcendent philosophy, with its tensions of freedom, turned into immanent philosophy of history, with its developmental determinism. Public freedom became a system of private rights; an individualized and self-interested society tolerated, but did not participate in, the nation state; the social hierarchy of merit became a society organized into an uneasy and dynamic class structure. This setting of legally emancipated Jewry helped convert it into the problematic "Jewishness" which she presented so well.

The other unforgettable achievement in *The Origins of Totalitarianism* is the unqualified exposition of totalitarian domination itself—a powerfully dramatic demonstration that owes its effect to the categorical purity with which the extreme implications of its principles and practices are set forth. For example, "We may say that radical evil has emerged in connection with a system in which all men have become equally superfluous. The manipulators of this system believe in their own superfluousness as much as in that of all others, and the totalitarian murderers are all the more dangerous because they do not care if they themselves are alive or dead, if they ever lived or never were born. . . . Political, social, and economic events everywhere are in a silent conspiracy with totalitarian instruments devised for making men superfluous." And again,

Totalitarianism's central assumption that everything is possible thus leads through consistent elimination of all factual restraints to the absurd and terrible consequence that every crime the rulers can conceive of must be punished, regardless of whether or not it has been committed. . . . Only in its last and fully totalitarian stage are the concepts of the objective enemy and the logically possible crime abandoned, the victims chosen completely at random and, even without being accused, declared unfit to live. . . . Total domination, which strives to organize the infinite plurality and differentiation of human beings as if all of humanity were just one individual, is possible only if each and every person can be reduced to a never-changing identity of reactions, so that each of these bundles of reactions can be exchanged at random for any other. . . . [The] atmosphere of madness and unreality, created by an apparent lack of purpose, is the real iron curtain which hides all forms of concentration camps from the eyes of the world. . . . Concentration camps can very aptly be divided into three types corresponding to three basic Western conceptions of a life after death: Hades, Purgatory, and Hell. . . . All three types have one thing in common: the human masses sealed off in them are treated as if they no longer existed, as if what happened to them were no longer of any interest to anybody. . . . It is not so much the barbed wire as the skillfully manufactured unreality of those whom it fences in that provokes such enormous cruelties and ultimately makes extermination look like a perfectly normal measure. . . . The difficult thing to understand is that . . . these gruesome crimes took place in a phantom world, which, however, has materialized, as it were, into a world which is complete with all sensual data of reality but lacks that structure of consequence and responsibility without which reality remains for us a mass of incomprehensible data.[14]

Clearly, Arendt's depiction of totalitarianism was a visible version of her conception of the plight to which the being of contemporary man has been brought.

If her philosophy thus obviously contributed to her history, what can we, finally, say of the reverse relationship? How does her history illuminate her philosophy? Here we may single out two key issues, where such illumination is at least needed.

14. *Ibid.*, pp. 427, 438, 445, 459.

First, there is the centrality of politics in her thinking. Now let us be clear about the nature of the question thus raised. The point is not the biographical or psychological one of why she chose the political side of philosophy and the culture to work on—for her choice on this score was variable—but the substantive one of why, in her published view, politics was the most important part of the culture. That such was her view is beyond cavil. She wrote explicitly, in reference to the Roman paradigm of Western values, that "the notion of a spiritual tradition and of authority in matters of thought and ideas is here derived from the political realm and therefore essentially derivative," and she concluded accordingly that "the crisis of the present world is primarily political." Anti-Semitism, she found, became culturally significant only when it changed from a social into a political movement: "The deciding forces in the Jews' fateful journey to the storm center of events were without doubt political." When she considered "the crisis in culture" she thought of it in terms of the relationship between culture and art, on the one hand, and politics on the other; she addressed herself to establishing their connection for the resolution of the crisis. She suggested that cultural taste might well belong "among the political faculties" and that the faculty of judgment, which is geared to all the "phenomena of the public world," could become "the common element connecting art and politics." She identified, indeed, the hope of the future with the definitely political order typified by the American Revolution, and, in this context, she could equate "the spaces" which she deemed essential to human freedom "with the political realm itself."[15]

Over and above these specific references, moreover, it is clear that the whole tendency of Arendt's writing was to regard the withdrawal from politics, whether under social or privatistic auspices, as the main feature of humanistic degeneration and to regard the construction of a politics of freedom, along both philosophical and revolutionary lines, as the only viable path to human recovery. One need only recall the prominence she gave to "statelessness," the deprivation of the right to belong to a polity, as the violation of *the* indispensable human right, to realize the primacy of the political realm to her. "Man . . . can lose all so-called Rights of Man without losing his essential quality as a man, his human dignity. Only the loss of a polity itself expels him from humanity."[16]

The most satisfying explanation of this political focus undoubtedly lies in a philosophical sphere that is beyond my purview. That is, Arendt's philosophical definition of politics, in a sense conformable to

---

15. *Between Past and Future*, pp. 124, 140, 215, 218; *On Revolution*, pp. 87, 279.
16. *Origins of Totalitarianism*, p. 297.

the meaning and range of the ancient Greek polis which she used as a model, goes far to show in itself how political activity, as she conceived it, was the cement of human culture, supplying the fundamental community which linked together its variegated interests and realms and which fulfilled her requirement of an order compatible with human freedom. The modern polity modeled on the polis can provide at once the limited space which endows the actions of the individual with both liberty and form and the fundamental rules of public communication which constitute the ground of all public—that is, cultural, moral, intellectual, economic, and social—activity.[17]

But there was a difficulty for Arendt in this philosophical conception of the polity, to wit, that the Western tradition of political philosophy based on it came to a "definite end" with the theories of Karl Marx in the nineteenth century. For the tradition shows that the polity is not self-sustaining but must be directed from the outside by a transcendent philosophy. Thus at the very beginning of the political tradition Plato and Aristotle set its mold by "turning away from politics and then returning in order to impose [their standards] on human affairs."[18] But the immersion of philosophy in the polity by the middle of the nineteenth century meant that thenceforward the destiny of the culture must be traced in political history itself, since this kind of history has always been the record of the most collective and thus, in its effect, the most uniform facet of the human community, and it has been the favored record, too, of change in the human community. So Arendt was driven by her philosophy to follow the modern changes of human culture in the history of its collective politics, and the requirements of this history, in turn, intensified the centrality of politics both in her vision of this culture's crisis and in the direction of her own philosophizing whereby she would overcome it.

The other of the philosophical problems on which Arendt's approach to history may throw light is the much-discussed "banality of evil," which arose in connection with her coverage of the Eichmann trial. The problem arises from the criticism that was mounted against her on two related grounds: first, her contention that Eichmann, and indeed "so many" Nazi officials like him, "were, and still are, terribly and terrifyingly normal," and her acceptance of the position recognizing "circumstances that make it well-nigh impossible for him to know or to feel

17. *The Human Condition* (Chicago, 1958), pp. 198–99; *On Revolution*, pp. 279–285.
18. *Between Past and Future*, pp. 17–18.

that he is doing wrong" along with the implication that this absence of "intent to do wrong" invalidates conviction for the crime of murder. Second was her contention that the Jews cooperated, "to a truly extraordinary degree," in their own destruction. The two positions were connected, for it was precisely the lack of overt opposition on the part of the Jews, as well as of the other sectors of German society, according to Arendt, that helped to persuade Eichmann about the normality of what he was doing.[19]

The perspective from which she adopted these positions was clear enough, for she identified it herself. Her assertion of Eichmann's innocence on contemporary legal grounds she derived from both the fragmentation and the traditional anachronism of these legal grounds, based as they were on the intent of individuals toward individuals. But she espoused conviction of Eichmann on grounds that would be at once universal and "'ideal.'"[20] Genocide, in this perspective, is "more than a crime against the Jewish or the Polish or the Gypsy people"—rather, it is a crime against "the international order, and mankind in its entirety," and she endorsed the justification that "'evil' violates a natural harmony which only retribution can restore; that a wronged collectivity owes a duty to the moral order to punish the criminal." Her insistence on the complicity of the Jews was based on similarly explicit grounds of moral universality: "I have dwelt on this chapter of the story . . . because it offers the most striking insight into the totality of the moral collapse which the Nazis caused in respectable European society—not only in Germany but in almost all countries, not only among the persecutors but also among the victims."[21]

These grounds, which seemed formal and even rhetorical in their overt, ad hoc expression, acquire substance and authenticity when they are elaborated in the light of the history that Arendt wrote. In this history she ever sought in events and movements that which was universalizable, and she especially sought and found this dimension in the history of totalitarianism. If we recall that, to her, totalitarian domination betokened the final crisis of tradition and order for the whole of humanity and the entrance of "radical evil" into its history, with its policy toward Jews only the entering wedge for its approach to all mankind, we shall better understand her stipulation that Nazi crimes were

19. *Eichmann in Jerusalem: A Report on the Banality of Evil* (New York, 1965), pp. 117, 276–77.
20. *Ibid.*, p. 273.
21. *Ibid.*, pp. 125–26, 275–77.

unprecedented in kind and in scope and that they require responses equally unprecedented and equally universal. And if we recall that in her depiction of anti-Semitism during the whole of the modern age she was always careful to show the parallelism between the image and the self-image of the Jews as modernity brought the comprehension of non-Jews and Jews alike in a single polity, then her homogenization of Jewish and non-Jewish activity, even in the climactic Nazi years, should come as no surprise.

Arendt wrote definitive history no more than she wrote definitive political philosophy. Such, obviously, was not her intention. Thinking, for her, had the task of opening men's minds and preparing them for creative action. It should be provocative rather than conclusive. Certainly, her perspectival history has had its desired effect, for to view the passing stream of history *sub specie aeternitatis* these days is to shed an unaccustomed light upon it indeed. To leave men more aware and more curious than you found them: What more and what better can be expected of a life?

3 INTELLECTUAL HISTORY

The historian's substitution of a definite approach to an indefinite reality for his older indefinite ways of encompassing a definite past has become not only a modern improvement but a practical necessity.

From "Culture, Cataclysm, and Contingency"

There is, then, a distinctive kind of historical logic which is geared to the actual rather than to the possibles or probables of other logics.

From *Ranke: The Meaning of History*

7 The Horizons of History

The most familiar distinction in the meaning of history has become its most fundamental problem. History refers both to what has happened in the past and to the historian's account of it. Now in itself this ambiguity need not—and for centuries did not—raise any momentous difficulties, for the prevalent attitude toward history has been embodied in a third definition which has operated as an effective synthesis of the first two. By this third definition history is the organized past, with events constituting the subject matter and the historian contributing the organization of them, whether narrative or analytical. In our times, however, this synthesis has been shredded. What was once a solution has now become our foremost problem, for the polar constituents of history as the organized past—that is, history as the past on the one hand and history as the historian's organization of it on the other—stand forth in their separate identities.

Behind this dissolution of the historical unit are two different kinds of development. The first is the philosophical tendency which questions both the knowability of the past and the integrity of the historian's organizing faculty. This is the tendency which has stimulated the far-flung debate on historical relativism and has activated the large literature upon epistemology and upon values in history. But at the same time there has been a second, more practical, development at work to undermine the unity of history and historian. Essentially, this has consisted in the burgeoning of history as past events beyond the capacity of the historian to organize it. This growing misproportion is not simply a physical matter of the crushing accumulation of evidence. More profoundly, it involves the addition of different kinds of evidence, with which the historian is only marginally or fortuitously equipped to deal. The very horizons of history are expanding, and as they do, the geography of history changes. The traditional field of history becomes one of many fields, and the traditional implements of the historian become correspondingly limited in their efficacy. It is primarily this development, and

First published in the *American Historical Review* 63:1 (October 1957), 62–74. This essay is a revised version of a paper originally delivered before the Pacific Coast branch of the American Historical Association at Eugene, Oregon, on December 27, 1956.

only derivatively the philosophy of history, that is our concern, for the philosophers of history will juggle anachronisms until we make it quite clear what history is—or more precisely, what it has become. The questions to which we must address ourselves, then, are: What are the new fields of history, and what is their relation to the old unified field of historical cultivation?

What are the new fields of history? A clue to the answer, but not the answer itself, is afforded by the more exotic spatial and substantive divisions within the discipline of history—like African history and intellectual history—which have been receiving increasing emphasis in our repertory. These divisions indicate an awareness of a historical world outside the familiar sphere of the politics of western civilization, but what they do not indicate is that this world has become different in kind from the old. The traditional world of history was made up of discrete events, temporally ordered, and its characteristic form was the chronicle or narrative. Western politics, as the most eventful of historical areas, was the most appropriate but never the exclusive subject of traditional history, and hence the excursions of historians beyond this area often simply extend traditional history in its wonted forms by slicing off those aspects of nonwestern and nonpolitical life which are also in obvious and continuous change. But the definition of the past in terms of chronologically connected events does not account for the entire past. It accounts only for that in it which has proved organizable under certain definite assumptions. The primary assumptions under which traditional history developed were: first, that the ultimate organizing principles of the past were themselves beyond history; and second, that what was essential in these principles articulated itself in the series of distinctive events that was history. The teleological and the pragmatic modes which dominated historiography down into the nineteenth century obviously shared both assumptions. Even the subsequent advocates of historical empiricism have been traditional in the sense of the second assumption, since their skepticism about ultimate principles has gone along with their agreement that specific events embody the motive force of human history. It is by reason of this assumption that traditional history has evolved its characteristic approach whereby description, whether of actions or of background situations, can itself constitute explanation.

The new fields of history arise, then, not from the renewed application of the discipline to the same kind of subject matter in other areas; they arise rather from a revolution of the subject matter itself in all areas. The effect of this revolution has been to obliterate the old line of distinction between those elements of the past that are history and those that are not. What used to be outside of history either as absolute, unchanging realities or as anonymous, uncrystallized, mass activities are now included in the historical past, and these are the areas that make up the new fields of history. The distinctive feature about these new fields is that they still require, for their understanding, canons of validity, methods of analysis, and techniques of research which look well beyond particular events and are alien to the traditional historian. Hence the rise of these new fields has brought an incursion of all the specialized branches of the knowledge of man into the historical context. With this incursion the distinction between the changing and the stable in the career of man no longer signifies a distinction between a historical and a nonhistorical reality; it signifies, rather, distinctive approaches to man within an expanded historical reality. And it raises the problem of the relationship between history, taken in this enlarged sense of the total past, and the historian, taken in the traditional sense of the describer of particular kinds of events within the past.

The revolution in the subject matter of history can be clarified if we break it down into the two stages of its development. The first stage consisted in the tendency to historize all aspects of man's life and activity. Progressively, various areas of human reality which had previously been deemed either above or beneath the vicissitudes of change were brought into the process of time and becoming. This tendency brought confusion into the field of history. On the one hand it confronted the historian proper with the intellectual necessity of explaining everything. On the other hand it confronted him with competitors in the field of history. For the older disciplines grew their own historical schools, and new disciplines—chiefly behavioral, such as sociology, anthropology, and political science—were founded precisely to develop the previously neglected areas of history. All these disciplines were substantive in a way that history was not. Each of them disposed over a definite kind of human activity, and when they projected these activities back into time their claims parceled out the various spheres of human life among them, to the exclusion of a historical discipline whose only dimension was time. Actually, of course, the claims were far from confirmed by actual possession of the field, and historians could develop their own brands of intellectual, economic, social, etc., history in the same areas. But what the line of demarcation should be was never clarified, and the relationship became chaotic between history as an integral discipline and history as a number of heterogeneous fields of life occupied by as many disciplines as there are generic activities of man.

This confusion was crystallized into the present form which the problem of history takes by the second stage in the revolution of knowledge. On top of the historization which broke all extratemporal laws and principles there has followed the tendency to find constant relations within and among limited segments of reality which exist in time. This may be seen as the attempt to found new points of stable and general validity in reaction against the historizing trend, and as such it is a process which reaches from the humanities to the social sciences. Thus the "contextual" approach in literature isolates poetry from the circumstances of its production and seeks immanent rules of criticism. In philosophy, phenomenology "brackets" the flow of existence away from objects and searches through rational analysis for the "transcendental" criteria with which to construct the essence of the objects, while logical positivism balances its critical rejection of all but empirical knowledge with the attempt at a constructive extension of the logic of the scientific method. The newer emphases in the behavioral sciences afford analogous illustrations of the tendency to make analysis subserve the building of valid general concepts. In psychology, "learning theory" is moving from simple conditioning to an analysis of the organism which mediates between the stimulus and the response, and therewith toward theories of value, motivation, and meaning. The cross-cultural approach in anthropology attempts to synthesize constant correlations out of its well-documented insights into cultural heterogeneity. In sociology, the statistical and sampling techniques which once undercut the generalizations of a less scientific age now begin to support a returning concern with the generic problems of social organization, mobility, and stratification. Even in political science, where the historical and descriptive attitudes have persisted longest, the surveying and functional approaches which have grown out of them are now turning to general theories of political behavior.

The hallmark of these tendencies is a revolution of method in which, through a process of aesthetic, symbolic, quantitative, or functional analysis, essential uniformities are abstracted out of a body of data and then cautiously projected into other data with similar qualities. But however much of a reaction against historicism, this method constitutes no rejection of history, taken in the large. The eschewing of universals, the accounting for the observer in each particular act of knowledge, and the intensive working of limited areas and problems with different kinds of logics and methods that are appropriate and in a sense internal to them—such aspects of the analytical approach are consonant with a historical framework. Particularly revealing of this consonance are the two devices, taken from mathematics, which have become the characteristic instruments of the new tendencies in logic and the social sciences—the theory of probability and the making of "models." The notion of probability permits generalizations which are not universal but which are applicable to definite broad classes of situations. A "model" is a symbolic or analogical representation which is intermediate between the statement of such a generalization and its specific application to an empirical situation; it shows how a theory operates in reference to a class of situations. The prevalent inclination to implement and at times even to replace theory with "models" is an indication of the tendency to accommodate rather than to subjugate the diversities of a historically conceived reality. Consequently, behavioral scientists have been developing, with the help of these concepts, such historically pertinent themes as the "theory of action" and the social application of "information theory," which analyzes communication into temporal sequences of events and establishes standards for measuring the relations between such events. Indeed, some of the behavioral sciences are beginning to move once more toward genuine historical themes from the vantage point of their new insights and techniques. Their contemporary interest in economic growth, social change and mobility, and the anthropology of history indicates the historical relevance of these disciplines. What they are doing, in essence, is interpreting historical change on the basis of the stable relationships which they have tried to establish by comparative method and structural analysis within the flow of history itself.

Now what are the implications of this revolution in the subject matter of history for the historian proper? The primary result has been to render inescapable the loss of his exclusive competence over the "facts" of the past. To be sure, certain kinds of past "facts" have long been surrendered to the more specialized analysis of philosophy, philology, aesthetic criticism, classical studies, archaeology, and paleography, but these could well be regarded as peripheral areas which could be divested without undue restriction of the professional historian. What is new is the added encroachment upon the residual areas by the claims of other technical disciplines to the point where the historian must reexamine his jurisdiction over past events as such. Since a historical "fact" usually proves to be a network of relations extending from the outer shell of its external appearance to the inner core of its meaning, such a "fact" may well be more critically ascertained and more certainly interpreted by the substantive discipline which specializes in the internal relations within the fact than by a historical discipline which specializes in the temporal relations between facts. For example, the "facts" about a piece of philosophy or art are indissoluble combinations of occurrences and meanings, and when such works are anonymous or undated the determination of the empirical events of authorship and timing often depend entirely upon the inner structure of meaning which is the province of the philosopher or the critic. Again, the "facts" of an economic situation, like the existence of an inflationary condition, frequently require a grasp of statistics and functional relationships, which are tools of the expert economist.

But even more important than this impact of specialization upon history is the necessity which is hereby imposed upon the historian to fit into the ebb and flow of the past canons which have a general kind of validity and techniques which bracket situations away from ebb and flow. Now the historian cannot avoid doing this, for these canons and these techniques are constituents of our notion of truth; they provide the frame for the truth we seek in the past as in the present. But it does raise the problem of precisely where and how the historian is to affix such molds upon his moving target.

The kind of intensive analysis which has been developed by the other disciplines provides means of doing the three things the unspecialized historian is ill-equipped to do. First, it opens the way to the understanding of the immanent, self-developing tendencies of a particular kind of activity against which the collateral conditions of a historical age must be set. In all kinds of intellectual history, to take the most obvious case, the explanation of any period must have as its prerequisite the knowledge of the technical problems, tendencies, and traditions of the philosophy, literature, art, or science concerned before it can distinguish between what occurs as an insulated response to such technical issues and what occurs as an open response to the more general influences of the era. Secondly, the analytical approach can be applied to the slow-moving, or even unmoving, structural aspects of an age, which are expressed in relationships rather than actions. For example, where the social structure is static throughout a period, this social background is probably tendered better by sociological methods of analyzing the constant relations among definite social types than by the traditional historical method of describing the significant activity of specific individuals and groups. Thirdly, the analytical approach provides the historian with an entering wedge into the difficult problem of freezing the moving process of history at a particular point in time so that he may grasp the total situation of men at that time.

Insofar as the historian works within the framework set up by such types of analysis he synthesizes the specialized disciplines for definite human situations at definite periods. This is an important function, because it calls forth the characteristic universality of the historian's interests, his compulsion to give particular life to general abstractions, and his capacity for avoiding anachronism by aligning the elements of a situation in their precise contemporaneity. Such works of synthesis are essential, but here we come to the crucial point that they are impossible for the historian unless he also adds something of his own. For the historian has no criteria for the selection or the organization of such a synthesis unless he takes them from his traditional approach to the world—unless, that is, his synthesis of a past situation is determined by the relevance of its relationships to concrete *movements* of men through time. The historian derives the hierarchy of meanings in an age—however analytically he may arrive at the definition of those meanings—from the specific sequence of actions which men undertook in that age. Given an optimum set of philosophical, aesthetic, political, sociological, and economic analyses of an era, the historian cannot apply them unless he first goes to the temporal march of events. Only then can he either measure the relative importance of each category in men's overt actions or understand that dimension of meaning which arises during the very process of growth. And so we are led back to the traditional field of history. What is distinctive about this?

Certainly the distinction can no longer be posed in terms of the old Germanic differentiation between the unique events which were the presumed objects of the humanistic disciplines, including history, and the repeatable classes of facts which were the presumed objects of the natural sciences. Beyond the obvious consideration that this differentiation leaves unresolved the relationship of history with the other humanities and particularly with philosophy, which transcends such a distinction, it now fails to meet the challenge created by the recent developments in science. The rise of the behavioral sciences between the humanistic and physical disciplines and the increasing attention which is being paid by sciences of all kinds to "the single case"—that is, the unique event—tend equally to frustrate this formulation. Since the humanities and the social sciences now often deal with the same events (e.g., the sociology of literature and the psychology of creativity), it cannot be said that events are unique or not unique but only that they are more or less unique according to the way in which they are handled. An event that is more unique for the historian than for the social scientist is less unique for the historian than for the art critic or for the biographer, whatever his guild. The historian does not so much treat of unique events as treat uniquely of events.

What distinguishes the historical from the other disciplines, humanistic and behavioral alike, is not the interest in different kinds of events but the different attitude toward the same kinds of events. For if the circumstance that a fact belongs to the past does not now suffice to bring it into the exclusive possession of the historian, it is clear that history differs from the other disciplines in having an approach and not an area of its own. The peculiarity of the historical approach vis-à-vis the humanities and the behavioral sciences is two-fold: the inimitable form which it gives to knowledge and its consuming interest in change.

The arts plumb particular productions, or events, and seek to make their particularity communicable by applying to or deriving from them general principles of composition and criticism. Philosophy and the behavioral sciences, in their respective ways, develop general categories and hypotheses and seek to validate them through application to particular events. Despite the fundamental differences between these fields, and despite the analogous conflicts within each of them on the roles to be played by the particular and general factors of knowledge, they hold in common an approach which confronts the particular fact with the general canon overtly and directly and which frankly orders events by means of general principle, whether this be mathematical, inductive, or organic in substance. The historian, on the other hand, treats neither of events nor of categories as such but rather of something in between which relativizes both. For the historian deals in time, and this means that he treats of events only in their chronological relations and of categories only in their temporal identifications. When viewed historically an event is less particular than it is in itself, and when used historically a principle is less general than it is in itself. The gap between fact and generalization is narrower for the historian than for other scholars because the time axis permits him to conceive of each in terms of the other. Where the scholarship of the humanities treats each of its events as an independent whole to be investigated in its essence, historical scholarship slices it into its chronological stages and treats it for its temporal dependencies. Where the scholarship of the behavioral sciences abstracts from events the uniform qualities which enable them to support general hypotheses projected beyond the events, historical scholarship frames its hypotheses not for why the events occurred but for why they occurred at this time, so that historical hypotheses cannot be projected beyond the connections of the events in a specific time series.

The historian, however, does not concern himself with every sequence of events through time but only with those sequences which either betoken a change from or produce a change in the previous pattern of activity, and this overriding preoccupation with change is the second distinguishing mark of the historical discipline. The notion of change, formerly only implicit in traditional history, has been raised to the status of an explicit primary principle for the historian by the shrinkage of his jurisdiction over events and by the historization of the constant substantive principles which provided the continuity behind and between them. An "event" for him now usually means an event that manifests change. Paradoxical as it may sound, change itself has come to supply the historian with his continuity; for insofar as there has been no change there is no past, and it is through change that the past is connected with the present. Change can fulfill such a function only if it is given a particular definition, since in its broadest sense every action denotes a change of some kind, and this is hardly a criterion for distinguishing among actions. The historian works rather with a special social definition which enables him to trace change as a thread of continuity through time. According to it, change consists in those human actions which refer beyond the time, place, and agency of their commission by realizing implicit developments within old situations or by creating new situations for the take-off of future actions. Excluded from change, by this definition, are both routine actions whose physical motion contributes nothing new to the relationships making up men's situations and maverick actions whose local novelty does not enter into these relationships. Included in change are all actions which register or produce mutations, rearrangements, or shifts of emphasis in the familiar elements of men's relationships and which yet retain sufficient meaning to the inhabitants of these relationships for such actions to leave a permanent deposit upon the conditions of men's living. Where actions that are mere functions of or aberrations from existing relationships are absorbed or dissipated in these relationships, actions that manifest or effect change transcend existing relationships, form new ones, and are immortalized therein. It is precisely this circulation of human actions through human relations that sets up the pulse beat of history, and change is its tracer.

It is true that humanists and behavioral scientists also concern themselves with change in this sense, but for them it is only one of a number of interests, taking its place beside the assessment of beauty or validity by a constant standard, whereas for the historian it constitutes the primary interest. Now this difference is not simply a matter of degree; it is the expression of fundamentally variant attitudes toward change. For one thing, obviously, both humanists and behavioral scientists, because of the limits of their particular disciplines, are apt to restrict themselves to changes within a particular field of human action, while the touchstone of historical change is that it has impact upon several fields of human action. Indeed, one of the great and distinctive contributions which historians make to the knowledge of human nature is their depiction of how changes on one level of man's interests—say, in his ideas—affect his actions on other levels—say, in his political and social activity.

Even more important than this consideration, however, is the historian's distinctive assumption about the fundamental role of change in human affairs, for it is this assumption that validates the historical study of change through time as an independent discipline. It is a commonplace that time has two dimensions. In one sense it is a regular sequence, reducible to quantitative measure, and in this reduced form it has been usable by science. In another sense, however, it is an irregular process, defined by the events which occur arbitrarily within it. In the latter sense, time becomes a primary, irreducible category, change becomes its measure, and the historian becomes its knower. The historian assumes that where men are static—and under this assumption they are static when considered in their constant postures, their repetitive activity, or their finished creations—they are generalizable and can be comprehended by the means which the behavioral sciences and the humanities have predicated for stable or recurrent objects and have applied to situations and completed events. But he assumes too that when men act to change their situation or to create something new, they move through specific, unpredictable, evanescent crystallizations of actions and reactions which can be served only by a discipline working under the sovereign aegis of time. For the humanities and the behavioral sciences alike, the essence of change consists in the fixed relationship between the termini of the change: for the humanities, men's actions are related to the beginning and end products of human creation; for the behavioral sciences, men's actions are converted into situations through the analysis of the stable factors in action, and the situations are then connected by laws or theories of change. The historian is interested neither in the end products of change nor in the laws of change but in the movement that works the change, in and for itself. This is why the historian is inevitably condemned to an indefinite, plural notion of change. The humanities orient themselves toward change as a new creation, to be understood in itself. The behavioral sciences orient themselves toward change as the specific working out of prior general tendencies.

The historian must take the change as he finds it, and he must be prepared to deal equally with prepared and spontaneous innovation.

The absolutely distinctive element in the historian's operation consists precisely in this effort to describe and explain movements of men
through time which are unanalyzable by any system of fixed methods
and general hypotheses. Like other men, the historian fixes his points of
references within a development. This, however, is not for the purpose
of analyzing the generally valid relationships between these points but
rather for the purpose of projecting a vision of what happened between
these points. His analysis of the points of reference is governed not by
the desire to establish the total situation but by the necessity of establishing jumping-off and landing places for the flight of men's minds and
deeds between them. The historian, then, deals with precisely those intangible motions of men which cannot be captured in stable concepts,
for these are the motions by which men undertake actions of their own
and receive those of others.

If there are no generally applicable, or "scientific," rules of method
for such an elusive subject matter, what in the historian's *modus
operandi*—apart from his techniques for discovering the mere occurrence of events—enables his work to have any cognitive validity at all?
First, he surrounds the intangible as closely as possible through the
depiction of intermediate, transitional, and peripheral events and situations. These are data which frequently are valueless to the other disciplines, when they are evanescent or when they simply mix capriciously
what is pristine elsewhere. But they are crucial to the historian, since
they betray the forms in which the relationships of an age affected men
practically.

Secondly, the historian has developed a faculty for moving both
backward and forward through time. If he moves forward in time
together with his historical agents in order to recreate relative
knowledge—that is, the conditions as these agents came to see and feel
them—he also moves backward in time to his historical agents from the
conclusion of their action in order to create absolute knowledge—that
is, knowledge of the conditions which must have prevailed upon and
within the agents unbeknownst to them. The subject matter of history
may indeed be defined as any movement which has developed to a point
of completion in time, for the historian requires such a point for his
retrospection, and the advantage of retrospection is something that he
cannot do without and remain a historian. It is the methodological necessity of moving in both directions along the time axis, and not mere
antiquarian interest, that refers the historian to the past as his essential

medium. To be sure, this is so flexible a method as to hardly warrant the name by the scientific standard, for the legitimate proportions of empathy and retrospection vary widely for every particular case, depending on the availability of the material and the commitments of the historian. The balance that is struck is a matter for decision in terms of art and conscience rather than of explicit rule. Yet this balance is essential to what the historian has of method in a way that is not, for example, to the behavioral scientist. For where the scientist aims at constants or at constant relations among variables which can be projected into typical situations of the future, the historian can only play the possible against the actual for situations that were in fact actuated. From this point of view, Ranke's famous dictum to recreate the past as it really was takes on a new meaning that resolves some of the problems usually associated with it. For it does not mean that the historian must simply remove himself into the past and think in the terms of the men of the past but rather that he must describe and explain the past in the light of the larger knowledge of reality conferred by the future of that past and by our own greater experience of human conduct. By its very nature, history is not the mere memory of humanity but the reformation of its memory.

Now let us, in conclusion, bring together the desiderata of the historian. Two kinds of activity are equally necessary for him. He must educate himself in the new fields of history in order to keep abreast of the most advanced insights into the structure of human situations, and he must retain his feeling for the old field of history in order to explain the movement from one situation to another. If he neglects the first of these activities, the historian loses his body; if he surrenders the second, he loses his soul. Insofar as he does adopt the techniques and results of the specialized disciplines in fixing and analyzing past situations he becomes a hyphenated historian, and the hyphen may refer him to the humanities as well as to the behavioral sciences—that is, he may have to become a philosopher-historian as well as a sociologist-historian. Insofar as he works along the familiar lines of tracing the specific trajectory of movement between fixed situations he is a pure or autonomous historian.

This distinction is not intended as a classification of historians, for inevitability each historian performs both activities. It simply indicates that since the historian does perform two different kinds of functions he should be aware of when he is performing either of them and adapt his methods to it. If, for example, these notions are applied to the crucial historiographical issue which ranges the representative instance against

the unique event as the appropriate mode of depicting a historical subject, then a possible solution would be to use both, assigning each to its
proper place in the historical spectrum. The representative instance, together with whatever general categories or sampling techniques are required for its ascertainment, is appropriate to the description of
situations. The succession of unique events, together with the traditional historical methods for ascertaining it, is appropriate to the portrayal of the process of change.

But if both hyphenated and autonomous history are necessary, yet
they cannot be merely juxtaposed. They must be integrated, and this integration cannot be on the basis of parity. The hyphenated activity must
be integrated into the autonomous activity of the historian. The theories, criteria, and methods borrowed from disciplines which seek to
transcend the limitations of time must become questions to be asked
and not formulae to be applied by the historian to his period in time.
This procedure avoids the necessity of omniscience, for the historian
need follow the path of analysis only in the direction and in the depth
required for his particular change. This procedure, moreover, gives him
a criterion for selecting the elements in past situations, for his organization of the stabilized elements in these situations will be governed by
their relevance to the changes which ensued or preceded.

In the final analysis, such an integration is hardly different in kind
from what the historian has ever done. He has always worked from general concepts which he has found outside the field of history, and his peculiar function has been to identify particular men, events, and
situations by means of these concepts and to follow their concrete interaction, conflict, frustration and/or clarification in the due course of
time. Where these concepts were formerly theological, philosophical,
and ethical in species, we must now broaden them to include the
categories of specialized scientific and aesthetic analysis and then proceed to our history as before, applying our methods, our insights, and
our intuitions to the crucial gap between the stability of discrete general
ideas and the moving complex of particular actions.

If this formulation has any validity, then the ultimate problems of
history—the problems of value, of human nature, of the possibilities
and methods of knowledge—get separated out from the daily labor of
the historian. These are basic issues of the philosophy of history, but
they are not historical issues alone. Since the arts treat preeminently of
the values in truth and the sciences treat preeminently of the reality in
truth, history—like philosophy—enters prominently into the field held
in common with all the arts and sciences. The historian can indeed par-

ticipate in the common discussion on the essences of the human situation, but at the same time he must treat the provisional resolutions of these problems as hypothetical assumptions and go on to his own independent work of testing them on the vagaries of humanity. In this way the historian will not only recount man's deeds but understand how man goes from his being to his doing and back again. From such a central furrow all the fields of history can be laid out in form and unity.

8 *The Autonomy of Intellectual History*

Intellectual historians have become cuckoos in the historical nest. To the consternation of their colleagues they like to think and to talk about method—and thereby hangs our tale. For the problem of intellectual history is not that, like political and institutional history, it has a method too long unexamined or that, like social history, it has a method modeled on more methodical disciplines and requiring adaptation. The problem of intellectual history, epitomized in the current disputes about the social relations of ideas, is that it has too many methods, that this plurality reflects the diversity of its objects, and that this diversity has raised serious doubts about its integrity as a distinct and autonomous field of history.

Indeed, the very propensity of intellectual historians for discussions of method is a symptom rather than a treatment of their problem. For the discussions are not about more or less valid ways of processing a commonly acknowledged material; they are about the appropriate way of processing more or less valid materials. The respective claims of works, propositions, ideas, styles, attitudes, and mentalities to be the authentic objects of intellectual history furnish the primary issue of controversy, and the dubiety of one or another class of this material has evoked the presentation of one or another plausible method to validate it. The hope, then, is that the means will justify the end. In any case, if the plurality of its current species defines the leading problem of intellectual history to be its generic identity, then method would certainly seem to be a derivative dimension of the problem. It is not in the infinite variety of its specific methods that a genus of intellectual history—if there is such a thing—can be found.

Nor can we deduce the integrity of intellectual history from some principle, whether from the principle of special history, abstracted from the seamless web of the past by analogy with other established special fields of history, or from the general principle of intellectual history itself considered in its universal sense of the history of man thinking as

First published in the *Journal of the History of Ideas* 34 (October–December 1973), 499–516. This paper was originally delivered in a shortened version at the session on Methodology in the History of Ideas during the December 1971 meeting of the American Historical Association.

distinct from man doing. Neither principle quite holds because, as it is actually practiced, intellectual history is more general than the special histories and more specific than any categorical definition of it.

Unlike the specific fields of literary history, history of philosophy, economic history, or even history of science, intellectual history has had no special complementary discipline outside the general field of history to supply the internal analysis of its objects and thereby to define the special historical field essentially in terms of external and temporal relations. As for the generic principle of intellectual history, men have deduced from it positions as contradictory as the proposition that all history is intellectual history, that is, the history of thought, and that no history is intellectual history, since the very definition of history as *res gestae,* as past acts and events, requires that what men have thought should always be subsumed under one or another special form of what men have done. However influential these principles may have been on the actual varieties of intellectual history they do not explain these varieties, which have in fact tended to define the realm of ideas for historical purposes to consist of something less than everything man has thought, something more than the separate compartments into which the products of thought have been traditionally divided, and something different from—albeit conditioned by and contributory to—the realm of deeds. Since the understanding of such intermediate enterprises is usually more susceptible to the historical than the principled approach, let us look beyond the principles to the history of intellectual history, with the expectation that even if we do not find there a valid ground for the autonomy of intellectual history upon which we can agree, we ought at least to discover why intellectual historians act as if they had one. This history goes back a long way and demonstrates that the current distinction of intellectual history as an historiographical field has grown out of the distinct role which has been attributed to ideas in the historical process.

The terminological discrimination between intellectual history and the history of ideas is recent,[1] but the differentiation to which it refers is ages old and has roots in the separate origin of each genre. The history of ideas refers to a category of literature in which articulate concepts have themselves been the primary historical agents, with their personal bearers and external relations adduced as conditions of them. Until re-

---

1. Esp. Maurice Mandelbaum, "The History of Ideas, Intellectual History, and the History of Philosophy," *History and Theory,* 5 (1965), 33–66; and Franklin L. Baumer, "Intellectual History and Its Problems," *Journal of Modern History,* 21 (1949), 191–203.

cently the history of ideas in this sense has not been a discrete field; it has been closely associated with the special departments of thought and has its early model in Aristotle's metaphysical history of first principles. Intellectual history refers to an overlapping category of literature that has been more comprehensive than history of ideas in two dimensions: it has included inarticulate beliefs, amorphous opinions, and unspoken assumptions as well as formal ideas; and its primary unit of historical concern has not been the set of these notions as such but rather their external relations with the larger life of the people who have borne them. By its very orientation intellectual history has tended to go beyond the formal contours of the special disciplines and to identify the distinctive role of ideas and attitudes vis-à-vis the other historical activities of men. As such an identifiable and distinctive arena, intellectual history had its earliest model in the accounting for the role of revealed religion in our culture during the early-Christian era. The model of the two cities was articulated into the categorically separate processes of sacred and worldly history, the first subsuming men's actions and institutions under the sequential stages in the incarnation of the true doctrine, the second subsuming earthly ideas as well as earthly desires under the category of the flesh and its aimless cycles of mundane events. This scheme initiated the pattern, which would be so long-lived, of vesting the unifying threads of history in the mind, the spirit, the ideas of men. Whether such a distinctive level of intellectual history would be thought to require a distinctive method was to vary from period to period, but certainly in its early phase it did require one. The method appropriate to Christian sacred history was exegesis, usually biblical and patristic, and it was a method distinctive enough for Bodin and Vico to exclude sacred history explicitly from consideration when they were experimenting with their new methods of organizing worldly laws and cultures into some kind of loose political order.

The exclusion was symptomatic, for whatever their contributions to general history the secular historians of the early-modern period contributed little to the specific enterprise of intellectual history—a judgment, surprisingly enough, as applicable to the historian-intellectuals of the Enlightenment as to their predecessors. What contribution was made continued to be made by historians of religion, whether clerical or anti-clerical, Christian or unChristian. For through both their positive and their negative approaches confessional Christians, unorthodox Christians, and anti-Christians all alike perpetuated the traditional version of a segregated sacred intellectual history into the nineteenth century, even honing upon it the advanced techniques of authentication

and criticism that were diffused through all kinds of historical research
by the end of the eighteenth century, and constituted a benefaction of
intellectual history for the discipline at large. But in the secular historiography of the early-modern centuries worldly attitudes, motives, and
ideas were acknowledged for their historical relevance rather than for
their historical autonomy. The political focus of the secular historians
was too intense, or their impetus toward extended historical coherence
too weak, or their feeling for the legal, cultural, and anthropological interpenetration of ideas and acts within an integral humanity too strong,
or their faith in the timeless source of universal historical patterns too
classical for the developments in their historiography to have any dis-
criminatory effect upon the historical status of ideas as such. In this
early-modern period we can see ideas as inseparable ingredients of ecclesiastical, constitutional, legal, and political history; ideas as one of several sets of events comprising the history of culture, of languages, and
of the arts; and ideas as supra-historical abstractions epitomizing the anthropological history of the species. But what we do not see is a distinctly intellectual history, for if early-modern historiography accustomed
men to think of secular ideas as part of their history it was only insofar
as those ideas were tied to and defined by the rest of men's earthly existence. At the end of the Enlightenment as at its beginning, the only
ideas with an independent historical role were the ideas inhabiting a
separate spiritual space.

The crucial modulation in the history of intellectual history was from
the spatial model prototyped in the spiritual city of the Middle Ages
into the functional model authoritative in modern times, and its mechanics are most accessible in the historicized systems of the nineteenth
century. Comte and Mill, Marx and Engels, integrated the realms of
universal and particular history by expelling transcendent absolute principles from universal history and positing a single social world with a
single history constituted by general laws of development. These laws,
in turn, followed continuously as scientific generalizations from the particular facts of history. The pattern is, of course, familiar to us all, but
what may not be so familiar is the role of ideas in it. Historically relevant ideas were now considered to be functions of society rather than a
distinct level of history leading from God, the recesses of the individual
soul, or the eternal principles of human nature, but their function for
society was distinctive, autonomous, and even, by dint of the fashionable tie of society with nature and the linguistic fashion of patterning
social on natural science, still spatialized. Comte's and Mill's investment
of intellectual history in "social dynamics," Marx's and Engels' in "su-

perstructure" betray the continuing tendency to think of autonomous function in terms of spatial distinctions. For all these thinkers the distinctive function of ideas, the function in which they were autonomous, was their primacy in providing structural unity to history.

But if all agreed in the formal, unifying function of ideas there was a fundamental divergence in the kind of unity that ideas were deemed to provide, and this divergence is important not only for the understanding of nineteenth-century attitudes toward intellectual history but for its origination of the division within intellectual history which would last down to the present. In the view pioneered by Comte and given a mantle of respectability in Mill's *System of Logic,* "the order of progression in all respects will mainly depend on the order of progression in the intellectual convictions of mankind, that is, on the law of the successive transformations of human options." For ideas, operating through the intellectual elite in which they predominate, constitute "the prime agent of the social movement," the "central chain" to "each successive link of which the corresponding links of all other progressions" are "appended" and which confer "a kind of spontaneous order" upon "the succession of facts."[2] In this view, then, ideas are the determining agents in the universal laws of *progress* and they function especially as the laws of the movement *between* static epochs. Spencer characterized Comte's whole purpose as the description of "the necessary, and the actual, filiation of *ideas*" in contrast to his own purpose of describing "the necessary, and the actual, filiation of *things*." It may count as a negative proof of intellectual history's integrative function, moreover, that this same Spencer, who professed to think in terms of things rather than ideas, was contemptuous not only of most historians but of history as such, because it could not by its very nature be anything other than "heaps of stones and bricks," "material for a Comparative Sociology."[3] Here was a striking, albeit admittedly negative, testimonial to the association of intellectual autonomy with lawful history in the nineteenth-century school of progressive sociology.

In Marx and Engels the one indisputable function of autonomous ideas in history was the provision of a unity of a different kind and along another temporal axis: it was a *regressive* unity for the historical facts of the same period. The role of ideas in the progressive movement of history from stage to stage was ambiguous enough in Marx and

2. John Stuart Mill, *A System of Logic Ratiocinative and Inductive* (8th ed., New York, 1881; reprinted New York, 1952), 604–06.

3. *The Evolution of Society: Selections from Herbert Spencer's Principles of Sociology,* ed. R. L. Carneiro (Chicago, 1967), xxii, xxv. Italics in the original.

Engels to provoke the discussions we have had in twentieth-century Marxism on the role of consciousness in revolution and on the differences between Marx and Engels in this respect. Without entering into this intricate discussion of Marxian consciousness in the *general* process of history, we must stress the undeniable attribution of autonomy to the superstructure, at first operational and then explicit, in consequence of its comparative rigidity and growing unresponsiveness to economic change *within each period* before its revolutionary progression to the next. Marx's growing concern with "fetishism" and other modes of "capitalistic false consciousness" definitely implied such autonomy. Engels' actual engagement with intellectual history—in his works on Feuerbach and Dühring—his later notice of the reciprocal "influence" exerted by the superstructure "on the whole development of society, even its economic development," and his frank admission of Marx's and his early neglect of the way in which "ideological notions" were formed—these were express formulations of the same point, of the breaking action of the superstructure, for they were made at the very time—around 1890—that Engels was also stressing the connection between the dynamic movement of nature and the ineluctable development of society's economic base.[4] The distinctive role of ideology within the regressive superstructure, moreover, was its unifying function: it spread a conservative consensus over the fruitful conflicts of the society. As Ernest Labrousse, a later link between Marxism and social history, has phrased it: "movement is *par excellence* . . . economic. . . . The social retards the economic when the social has the initiative itself. . . . But above the social the mental retards in its turn, and the restraints of the mental are the strongest of all. . . . The resistance of static mentality is one of the great factors of regressive history." It is the factor, moreover, which transcends historical fragmentation: ". . . Our goal remains the restitution of global mentality."[5]

Nor was the modified perpetuation of the distinctive unifying role of ideas in western history embodied only in the abstract historical systems of the nineteenth century. In the unquestionably historical works of William Lecky, Leslie Stephens, William Draper, Andrew White, and even of Leopold Ranke himself in his *History of the Popes* (1834–36), ideas of religion and of scientific or utilitarian reason summarized the historical forces of regression and progression whose conflict made western history a comprehensible whole.

4. Karl Marx, *Selected Works* (London, 1942), I, 380–94, 452–62; and Engels, *Correspondence, 1846–1895* (New York, 1933), 510–11.
5. *L'Histoire Sociale: Sources et Methodes* (Paris, 1967), 5.

Thus when, around the beginning of our century, the awareness of historical ideas in general, the self-conscious attribution of the term "intellectual history" and its foreign cognates to their sphere, and the application of the recently sanctified historical methods to them, initiated the discipline of intellectual history in the forms familiar to us,[6] this foundation was itself a sequel to a long tradition certifying the independent role of ideas in our culture. The five easily identifiable schools of modern intellectual history which dominated the first half of our century and remain the bases of current developments in the field are, indeed, reducible for purposes of analysis to two main directions, and the relevance of the tradition to them will become readily apparent. The five schools are: first, the German-Italian historicist school featuring a mix of historical philosophers and philosophical historians running from Dilthey and Croce to Cassirer, Meinecke, and Carlo Antoni; second, the group of socio-intellectual historians centering on Marc Bloch, Lucien Febvre, and the periodical *Annales;* third and fourth, the two schools which can be regarded as American counterparts of these two European tendencies, the *History of Ideas* group of Arthur O. Lovejoy and George Boas, and the New History of Robinson, Becker, and Beard; and fifth, the historians of assorted philosophical, literary, artistic, and politico-scientific theories and theorists—Bury, Barker, Randall, Sabine, Auerbach, Mornet, Hauser, Laski, and their ilk—who accommodated their special subjects to the new standard of historical research. This last group too is divisible for our purpose between the historicists and the socio-intellectuals, since its works were written within its respective special disciplines, and its historical dimension was more purely represented by one of the two main-line historical groups—the philosophers and aestheticians by the historicists, social scientists and social literateurs, like Laski and Mornet, by the historians of the *Annales.*

If we ask, then, just what it was that our immediate ancestors originated and what they carried over from *their* past, we shall look for our answers to the two main directions just indicated. Let us first limit the field of the answer and indicate what the new awareness of intellectual history was not yet, for otherwise we shall not understand what we ourselves are doing in the field. The new intellectual history was not yet a separate field of history, with its own method. Certainly there was a novel concern with method and certainly ideas were identified as distinctive objects in history, but the new methods came from outside of

6. Felix Gilbert, "Intellectual History: Its Aims and Methods," *Daedalus* (Winter 1971), 80–82.

history—from neo-idealism and phenomenology in philosophy and especially from sociology among the newly specialized social sciences—
and they were designed for integration in the method of all of history,
to import principles of coherence into that method, and the awareness
of the intellectual dimension of history was a function of these imported
general principles. Thus while the *Annales* group and the New Historians wrote deliberate intellectual history they did not regard themselves as primarily or distinctively intellectual historians: they stressed
the historical relevance of the methods and concepts of the social sciences, and they arrived at an appreciation of ideas in history by virtue of
their function in retarding or advancing—but in either way in
linking—the centrifugal facts on an increasingly specialized society subject to incessant change. Marc Bloch's subjects were primarily social,
those of his friend and associate, Lucien Febvre, were primarily intellectual, but the essential interest of both was in the mental attitudes most
closely engaged in social relations as their preservatives. Robinson,
Beard, and Becker were similarly socio-intellectual historians in varying
proportions, with an interest in ideas as the comprehensible measure of
the relations between atavism and reform in society.

The other early schools of modern intellectual history—notably historicism and the History of Ideas—drew their methods from philosophy and used them in intellectual history to circumvent the uniqueness
of every individual cultural product and every particular event which
had been established for the methods both of the humanities and of
general history as a humanistic discipline. Both schools revealed their
philosophical origins by segregating, albeit in varying degrees, the
realm of ideas from the realm of social action which had been the traditional focus of history, and if they ultimately drifted into social sche-
matizing it was, as Antoni has shown, in betrayal of their historicist
principles.[7] Further, each of these schools defined the history of ideas
by a different principle of selection, according to the dimension
wherein the continuity was sought. The historicist school, highlighted
by Cassirer and Meinecke, looked to the configuration of ideas and
found relevant, therefore, ideas that were configurable, whether they
were in the form of Cassirer's attempt at what he called the "phenomenology" of the spirit of an age—that is, the essential pattern dis-
tillable from the internal relations among its ideas—or Meinecke's

7. Carlo Antoni, *Dallo storicismo alla sociologia* (Florence, 1940); Eng. trans. by Hayden V. White, *From History to Sociology:The Transition in German Historical Thinking* (De-
troit, 1959), *passim*.

attempt to show the complete reflection of political conflicts in the conceptual relations of a dramatized world of interactive ideas. In Lovejoy's *History of Ideas,* on the contrary, the "unit-ideas" which were the objects of his concern were components analyzed out of the systems and combinations in which they were originally invested and followed for their continuity and development through time and discipline. Although Lovejoy seemed to provide a porosity and extensibility for his unit-ideas by admitting "implicit or incompletely explicit assumptions, or more or less unconscious mental habits" among them, his associate George Boas' recent categorical pronouncement that "ideas, after all, exist on the conscious level and their history has to stay on that level" would seem far more faithful to the logic and to the actual performance of the school.[8] To fulfill their function both within and between periods the ideas in the history of ideas must be articulate and recognizable.

It should be clear by now what was common to the men who earlier in this century identified a kind of history which they labeled variously as intellectual history or history of ideas, which applied to different levels of ideas, and which was worked by methods applying to more or less than the category of all ideas in history—by methods, that is, applying to all of the social past or to only certain kinds of ideas. What was common to them and new for historiography was the loss of faith in the underlying lawfulness either of the principles of human nature or the pattern of social development. What was common to them and old for historiography was their persistent faith in the immanent continuity of history itself, and it was to this continuity that they geared their methods. The connections which could be formerly assumed *for* history had now to be demonstrated *in* history.

What is distinctive about our own generation's approaches to intellectual history? A caveat is required before attempting an answer. Earlier schools and tendencies continue to be influentially represented, by those like Labrousse and Braudel who look directly to the original social and anthropological inspirations of the *Annales* school,[9] by those like Jean Hyppolite, Raymond Polin, and Ernst Nolte who still pros-

---

8. Maurice Mandelbaum, "The History of Ideas, Intellectual History, and the History of Philosophy," *loc. cit.,* 35; George Boas, *The History of Ideas: An Introduction* (New York, 1969), 19.

9. Thus for Labrousse "the history of ideas" still is a history of "collective mentality"—that is, "of judgments, sentiments, and attitudes"—and "a concrete study of collective mentality can only be a study of social mentality"—that is, of the mental in its specific reference to the concrete experience of particular social groups or classes. *L'Histoire sociale,* 5.

ecute genetic and phenomenological studies of individual systems and collective ideologies in depth; and by those like Isaiah Berlin, Passarin d'Entrèves, and Heinz Gollwitzer who actively pursue the history of unit-ideas across the disciplines. Obviously, current protagonists of vintage approaches need be neither epigones nor anachronisms, and the long-lived historiographical fertility of Marxist "consciousness" together with the recent large-scale enterprise of the *Dictionary of the History of Ideas*[9a] offer impersonal confirmation of the truth that in intellectual history anteriority is not equivalent to inferiority.

What is most distinctive albeit not necessarily most distinguished, then, about the contemporary approaches to intellectual history can best be understood as counter-balancing developments from these earlier forms of it. On the one hand, we have separated intellectual history out as a discrete historical field, not only in the mechanical terms of so classifying the historians who profess it and the courses which they teach, but in the constructive terms of detaching ideas and attitudes in history both from their origins in other kinds of disciplines and from their involvement with other kinds of history and collecting them in their own field, defined by their substantive function in the historical process or by the peculiar methods required to know them or by both. On the other hand, the new autonomy thus granted to intellectual history has brought the various forms and levels of man's mental life within the same universe of discourse, has evoked critical discussions over the definition of the field in terms of the relationships among its various intellectual objects, and has eventuated either in an academic struggle for domination or in a permissiveness perilous to the integrity of the field itself. Behind these current developments, helping to explain them and posing new challenges to the longevity of the older schools of intellectual history, have been two contextual developments in our own intellectual and cultural life which have set off the third quarter from the first half of the century and carry a step further the disenchantment with the orderliness of things—a disenchantment which, as we have seen, has ever been the spur in shifting our perspective on the role of ideas in history. The first of these altered cultural conditions, with a constructive effect upon the new intellectual history, has been the dramatic shrinkage in the historical branches of the substantive disciplines traditionally bordering on and overlapping intellectual history—

9a. Published by Scribner's, 4 vols. (New York, 1973), edited by G. Boas, S. Bochner, F. Gilbert, E. Nagel, R. Wellek; H. Cherniss, W. K. Ferguson, E. H. Gombrich, P. O. Kristeller, P. Medawar, M. Schapiro, H. A. Wolfson, and P. P. Wiener.

notably of philosophy, of literature, and of the arts—with the consequence that their specific historical effluence has passed into the general pool of intellectual history.[10] The second of the altered cultural circumstances, with caustic effect on intellectual history, has been the eruption of the belief in discontinuity as a necessary condition of all human affairs. Since the earlier schools of modern intellectual history had strenuously substituted a belief in a man-made continuity *within* human affairs for the older belief in the natural continuity *behind* them, our latest cultural innovation would seem to mark an even sharper break with traditional assumptions about the role of ideas in history.

Because the various current tendencies in intellectual history have responded to both of these contemporary cultural conditions these tendencies evince common features which cut across their original variety. First, they all legitimate the field of intellectual history both by distinguishing the role of ideas from the other functions of society, unlike the older socio-intellectual history, and by building a social relevance into the ideas themselves, unlike the older philosophical history. Secondly, they all adapt the traditional function of intellectual history to the present requirements of our culture by describing "continuities in the mode of discontinuity," to generalize Francois Furet's telling characterization of contemporary "serial history."[11] Because of these common features we can arrange the current approaches to intellectual history in a single spectrum composed by the various combinations of social relevance with distinct ideas, and we can hope to find in the alignment of these combinations, however different the kinds of ideas and of methods in them, a relationship among them which may help us to define their common field, or, at the least, their complementary functions.

We may distinguish three main groupings of current approaches—if we permit ourselves to distinguish for analysis what overlaps in practice—as we move from the more explicitly social to the more explicitly cultural and philosophical ends of the spectrum. The first grouping is composed of new directions in socio-intellectual history. It continues to focus on the popular levels of ideation in society and to deny special methods for ideas as such, but now it identifies ideas and

---

10. An obvious illustration is the very topic of a recent symposium of literary scholars—"Is Literary History Obsolete?"—published, ironically, under the auspices of *The New Literary History.* Characteristically, the concluding attempt at synthesizing the fragmented answers was made by the historian, Hayden V. White, essentially through the translation of literary into intellectual history. *New Literary History,* 2 (1970), esp. 173–85.

11. Furet, "Quantitative History," *Daedalus* (Winter, 1971), 161.

attitudes as the products of a distinct function of society and takes their special requirements into account by drawing new distinctions between the method of social history, which necessarily includes intellectual history, and the method of the other social sciences. What is autonomous about intellectual history here, then, is acknowledgment of an autonomous facet in the historical role of ideas and, because of the quality that ideas contribute to history, it now insists on the autonomy of the specifically historical vis-à-vis the generic social scientific methods. The most prominent of these tendencies is represented in the current merger of the *Annales'* type of approach to socio-intellectual history with Daniel Mornet's type of the sociology of literature that appears in the work of the sixth section of the École Pratique des Hautes Études and that has been labeled by Robert Darnton, its most articulate reviewer in this country, "socio-cultural history."[12] The aspect of its work most germane to the category we are now discussing is its inquiry into the notions and attitudes of the non-intellectual classes, and the novel feature in its inquiry is its interest in the reception of articulate ideas as an autonomous component of these notions and attitudes. Obviously the most responsive tendency within intellectual history to the general democratic movement for the inclusion of the anonymous and inarticulate masses in the historical suffrage, socio-cultural history has especially developed methods of quantification and correlation of gross attitudes which are most appropriate to the measurement of mass mentality, but this obvious feature should not obscure its recognition of the qualitative and autonomous factor in ideas that is entailed in both the diffusion of published ideas and in the variation of ideological level with the social stratification of their recipients. Furet, who works in this field of intellectual diffusion and in other dimensions of social history as well, has reformulated the *Annales'* methodology to meet the new equivalence of his interests. He categorically distinguishes the quantifying methods appropriate to the other social sciences and to homologously quantifiable kinds of history, e.g., econometric history, from the quantifying methods appropriate to "serial history," which takes definite time series as the basic realities of the past, constituted by the measurable relations of comparable homogeneous units in that series. Fed too by the extension of Namierian collective biography to include ideas and principles as independent variables and by the sophisticated Marxist stress of an E. P. Thompson on attitudes and beliefs in constituting the "logic" of

12. Darnton, "Reading, Writing, and Publishing in Eighteenth-Century France: A Case Study in the Sociology of Literature," *ibid.*, 226.

the social relations which define a class,[13] the new socio-cultural history both registers the distinctive role of ideas in the social past and responds to the current demand for historical discontinuity. Furet's emphasis on the series rather than the fact and Thompson's on class as a relation rather than a thing show that it is still a connection that ideas are involved in, and their stress on persistence and cohesion within a single period serves to define both the outer limits and the inner homogeneity of each of their plural series and relations.

Clustered around the middle of the spectrum which runs from mass attitudes to theoretical systems are those tendencies in intellectual history which have become most characteristic of the field—the tendencies which posit ideas and behavioral circumstances as two autonomous levels of history and apply characteristically hybrid methods to relating them. In the form of mere juxtaposition or of the provision of a social context which *ipso facto* makes ideas historical or which somehow socializes them by an invisible osmosis, the approach is scarcely new. What is new is the acknowledgment of formulated ideas and circumstantial conditions as different kinds of historical realities whose mutual relations must be conceived as an historical problem rather than an historiographical assumption, and the innovations in the methods which have been devised to discover actual relations between them. One such method—the use of psychology—is hardly new in itself, recent as Erikson's popularization of the term "psychohistory" may be. We may not go back with Frank Manuel as far as Vico for a precedent psychological history, but we must certainly agree that both Dilthey and Febvre have been our predecessors in focusing upon psychic configurations and structures as the kind of intellectual history which was the matrix of men's past behavior.[14] We can go beyond these particular forbears, moreover, to note that in general the centuries-old association between psychology and philosophy in the common enterprise of investigating the origins and validity of ideas—an association persistent to the present through phenomenological psychology—continues to support the long-standing affinity between psychology and intellectual history. What is new in the current vogue of psychohistory is the prominent role of psychoanalysis, which brings two distinctive qualities to the intellectual history it features. First, because psychoanalysis organizes mental life into a process with clearly delineated temporal dimensions,

---

13. E. P. Thompson, *The Making of the English Working Class* (New York, 1964), 10.

14. Frank E. Manuel, "The Use and Abuse of Psychology in History," *Daedalus* (Winter, 1971), 188–96.

it has underlined the historicity of men's ideas, the multiform vitality of the mental realm, and hence the centrality of intellectual history. Secondly, the obvious stress on the unconscious which psychoanalysis brings to the understanding of mental life has had the effect, in applications like Marcuse's, Erikson's, and Norman Brown's to intellectual history, of grounding the traditional individuality of consciously articulated ideas in the common subterranean impulses of the group or the species.

In addition to the implicit social function of the new historical psychology, there are two other methods which explicitly relate the realms of ideas and social behavior. These methods focus on the specifically intellectual classes—that is, on groups whose precise function, as groups, has been to produce or disseminate ideas. One device, at the social end of this cluster, close to the other work of the sixth section but distinct in principle, has been the expansion of inquiry from the intellectual elite to all intellectual producers, whether personally identifiable or not, with the purpose not of explaining the origin of individual ideas, but of establishing typical correlations among the ideas of intellectuals numerous enough to be considered a social group or active enough to be socially linked by an intellectual institution, such as a journal or an academy. A second socio-ideological device of this kind is the selection, for study, of those intellectual groups which have also been collectively active in those societies which have organized intellectual activities into corporate functions. In these groups there are manifested, as matters of historical fact, connections between ideas and social status, between principles and social action, between the autonomy of ideas and the imperiousness of social circumstances. Patently encouraged by Mannheim's sociological notion of the free-floating intellectual but using it rather as an historical pointer than as a general truth, this device has been especially appropriate to the histories of the German and Russian intelligentsia, a term which connotes precisely the separate social existence and distinct social function of an idea-bearing class and transfers the problem of relating idea and social action from the assumptions of the historian to the process of history.

Because this middle cluster of approaches to intellectual history is geared to register the diachronic development of the individual or group as well as the synchronic relations between ideas and their context within the individual or group, as well as the synchronic relations between ideas and their context within the individual or group, it functions not only as a structural link for the life of a society at any one time but also as a thread through changes in limited time—that is, a thread which lasts as long as the lives of the individual or the group whose personality is the mold for the change.

The final set of contemporary approaches to intellectual history is composed of those which seek within the intellectual sphere itself the larger context—preferably some linkage to society—through which alone ideas become historically knowable and historically respectable. The ideas which have evoked these approaches are still the highly individuated and articulated concepts associated with one or a few definitely identifiable historical personages that have been the stock-in-trade of the older philosophical schools of intellectual history. But new methods have been devised in response to the new emphasis upon historical discontinuity and to the growing historical indifference of the substantive humanistic disciplines, with the consequent devolvement upon intellectual historians of the responsibility to vest their philosophical, aesthetic, and doctrinal ideas with the internal dimension that was formerly supplied by the special histories of the respective disciplines. The consequence of the shift has been to dislocate the older tacit arrangement which assigned to the special historian of philosophy or the arts the internal relations of ideas and to the intellectual historian their external relations. At the same time as the intellectual historian must thus bring a new specialization and a new internality to his perception of his intellectual historical object, thereby attenuating the older connections between externally classified ideas and the respectable historical activities of men, his isolation is intensified by the contemporary cultural movement which underlines the discontinuity, both within history and between history and the historian, above all of those formal ideas, doctrines, and world-views whose historical function had traditionally been deemed to inhere precisely in their built-in continuity. The sins of continuity, whether in the form of the belief in universal truths or the belief in trans-epochal influence, loom large, for example, in the depressing syllabus of errors compiled against the historiography of such "classic texts" by the contemporary analyst, Quentin Skinner.[15]

The intra-mural methods recently put forth for this level of intellectual history, however responsive they may be to these limiting conditions, merely take them as their point of departure, and within their limits construct new continuities and especially new bridges to the social experience of man which remains the central reference point of history as a discipline. The new movement toward the specialized, internal

---

15. Quentin Skinner, "Meaning and Understanding in the History of Ideas," *History and Theory* (1969), 3–53, *passim*.

understanding of the art or -ology laying claim to the idea in historical question has not replaced the old awareness of temporal relations as the essence of the historical discipline. What the new movement has done is simply to displace the old awareness in the direction of stressing simultaneous rather than successive relations and of attenuating the distinction between the internal and the external relations of ideas. Again, historians now do stress the disconnectedness of their intellectual objects both from any long-range developments of ideas and from any community of constant values through or above time; and yet the traditional proclivity of intellectual historians to establish continuity persists, for they treat each disassociated idea or thinker as a microcosm that internalizes the macro-currents of past and present through its own medium, and the junctures which the historian no longer permits *between* ideas are permissibly relocated in the combinations entering into the structure *of* any particular historical idea. The methical innovations in the service of adjusting the old role to the new conditions seem infinite in their variety, so powerful is the urge to retain the temporal axis of historical relations and to reconstitute connections. Four such innovations, representing both the diversity of practice and the community of purpose which marks this kind of intellectual history, may be mentioned here.

First, the application of linguistics, with its quantitative, analytical, and structural varieties and its range from language games to sociolinguistics, itself recapitulates the whole spectrum of intellectual history in the large. This variegated linguistic approach serves to reconstruct the socialized modes of communication which link the individual idea or syndrome of ideas, meaningless and unknowable in itself, with the contemporaries who gave it meaning and with the historian who can know it only with such mediation.[16]

Second, and most akin to the traditional methods of the historian, is the selection of social theory and theorists as the objects of intellectual history. Highlighted by H. Stuart Hughes' attention to the consciousness of society, by Frank Manuel's social prophets, and Jacob Talmon's social messiahs, this method of internal intellectual history is automatically socially relevant by virtue of its content and authentically historical when it treats its theorists as historical sources, contemporary witnesses of their society, subject to the same critical processing as any other historical source or witness.

A third method seeks to resolve the problem of the historian's new

16. John Pocock, *Politics, Language, and Time* (New York, 1971), 3–41.

responsibility for the specialized internal relations of ideas by locating these internal relations in the historical process itself and thus converting their challenge for the historian from a problem of historiography to a question of history. The inquiry here is into the impact of a thinker's social experience upon the formation of his ideas, and the method comes into play when direct evidence fails and the pattern of his ideas affords the only extant traces of the impact.[17] The discontinuities in thought furnish the opportunities of ingress for the thinker's contemporary social experience, which becomes visible in his thought and optimally functions as a kind of bypass connecting the logically discontinuous elements of his thought—that is, precisely as a "continuity in the mode of discontinuity."

A fourth method of this internal intellectual history, finally, expands the field of ideas to include the arts in a new way. It goes beyond the older method of treating artistic works as expositions whose discursive ideas are to be abstracted from the whole composition, and it also goes beyond the older treatment of finished artistic products as intellectual events, to be aligned with other such events in the contours of an age's general style or spirit. Predicated on the insight into the implicit connection between the narrower and broader senses of culture, the new method is designed to perceive aesthetic modes of expression as autonomous kinds of thinking—as acts of thought immediate to experience, irreducible to discursive ideas or to the orthodox criticisms of their final products, and more open than either formal ideas or finished works of art are to the social matrix which cradles them all. The arts are here regarded as comprising a distinct medium of social communication, connected with other channels of ideas through the social community that sponsors them all as so many articulations of its joint existence.[18]

This set of internalized approaches thus testifies as much as the variable socialization of intellectual history to the current substantive plurality and methodic specialization in the field—but it testifies even more to the unbroken drive of intellectual historians, from the dawn of our culture until the present, to hypostatize ideas as the bridges of our history.

What answers does our survey of past and present approaches to intellectual history yield to our initial questions about the relationship of its varieties and its integrity as an autonomous field of history?

17. Leonard Krieger, "Culture, Cataclysm, and Contingency," *Journal of Modern History* 40 (Dec. 1968), 447–73.

18. Carl E. Schorske's presentation in a symposium on "New Trends in History," *Daedalus* (Fall, 1969), 930–33.

First, if intellectual history is conceived as a field in spatial terms, requiring products more akin to one another than to products outside the field and requiring common methods of appropriate cultivation in some measure independent of methods outside the field, then it must be owned that intellectual history is not now an integral or autonomous field of history. At its social end, it studies mass attitudes with extensive methods common to other social history; at its philosophical and aesthetic end, it studies formalized terms and ideas with intensive methods common to other disciplines that are not historical.

But, secondly, intellectual historians, whatever their variety, share the attribution of a common function to ideas in history, whatever the form and level of the ideas—namely, to serve as connections, both among historical agents and between the historical agents and the historian.

Thirdly, the varieties of intellectual history may be aligned as complementary functions of their common service to continuity. The more social varieties have demonstrated their virtuosity in establishing the literal continuity of persistent attitudes; the more philosophical and aesthetic varieties have been addressed to establishing the gossamer continuity through change.

But finally—and here we pass from summary to conclusion—our survey has itself raised a further question which threatens to undercut these general answers. Socio-intellectual history and socio-linguistic history have shown themselves to be especially appropriate to the current conditions affecting the discipline of history at large: they are in tune with the democratization of the scope of history, and they have responded with special sensitivity to the requirement of discontinuity that each temporal series be known and understood in its own terms. Despite the usual fragmentation of their results yielded by the masses of their relevant agents for dimensions of ideas other than persistent attitudes and meanings, in principle the socially oriented varieties of intellectual history are surely on the side of the angels. But how can the more insulated varieties of intellectual history still be justified when to the old charge of social indifference there are now added the charges of elitism and anachronism, since the historical validity of the universal ideas on which they have traditionally depended for the long-range continuity both within history and between history and the historian is now so widely denied?

An answer to this question too can be given if we adduce a second set of functions which overlap the functions of understanding persistence and change in ideas and serve them similarly as complements to the varieties of intellectual history. It is a truism that historical knowledge is a compound of sympathy and criticisms, and if we translate sympathy into truth seen from the point of view of the historical agent and criticism into truth seen from the point of view of the historian, it is clear that in principle our standard operating procedure is a combination of opposites, and that in practice there has always been a valid range of varying proportions in which historians have employed them. The diversity of these principles roughly overlaps the diversity between the more social and the more philosophical species of intellectual history—but in an unexpected way. Earlier in the century, under the aegis of continuity, historical sympathy was deemed particularly appropriate to individual change and historical criticism to social stasis. But now, under the aegis of discontinuity, the qualities are reversed: socially oriented intellectual history stresses sympathy with the past in its own terms, and philosophically oriented intellectual history assumes a critical connection between the historian and the past. For those who believe that history is the past restored, society is undoubtedly the only possible framework for its restoration. But for those who believe that history is the answer which the past gives to the questions of its successive futures, the common ground afforded by the rational forms of articulated ideas provides a communication through time that offsets their isolation from their contemporary society. And for those who believe that both reconstruction and restoration are required by the historical enterprise, conversation with the great dead joins the resurrection of the souls of the mute in common perspective upon the autonomous role of ideas in our history.

9 Historicism's Revenge

"Historicism" is one of those words, like Renaissance, Baroque, and Romanticism, that has so many diverse meanings that historians have been tempted not to use it at all. But let us look at the positive side of such situations. When terms have multiple meanings, then they can mean whatever the user decides that they mean. In such situations the historian has the rare chance to overcome the limitations usually imposed on him by the language which he inherits; and I for one intend to take full advantage of this chance. Let us say, then, that historicism refers to the position in the philosophy of history that dissolves all reality into the stream of historical becoming, eventuating ultimately in the blameworthy position of historical relativism and in the admittedly modern problem of the "anarchy of values"; and, because philosophy of history has such a bad name outside of Germany, let us say also that historicism refers to the position of practicing historians who simply ignore realities outside of history and write as if everything were history, whether they believe it or not. The negative attitude toward all things German which is evinced in the Italian, French, British, and American contempt for philosophy of history is, of course, related to the political noxiousness of Germany during this century, but the noxiousness has served rather to confirm a pre-existing cultural attitude than to ground it, and the matter is more fundamental than reference to Nazism and German war guilt would assume. Like the reprobation of all things French outside of France in the late eighteenth century, the opposition to things German is a matter of style and form as much as political and cultural nationalism. The discussion of this prejudice would take too long a time; it will not be pursued further here.

For in our view of historicist, it is hard to think of anyone save Arnold Toynbee who is not a historicist. It includes the great philosophical nay-sayers like Croce, Collingwood, and Mannheim; the philosophers and sociologists who accepted the historical dissolution of stability, started from it, and tried to overcome it, like Dilthey, Troeltsch, Weber, and Durkheim; and historians like Berr, Febvre, and Braudel in France, like Meinecke and Wehler in Germany, like Stone

First published in *Annals of Scholarship* 1:2 (Spring, 1980), 15–30.

and Plumb in Britain, and like Becker, Gay, Hexter and Aydelotte in the United States who, whatever their other differences, agree that history has to adapt itself to the changing cultural attitudes of the age. They stipulate in common that these attitudes have dissolved or exalted beyond time and space the older certainties which stabilized reality outside of history, whether this reality was conceived philosophically or scientifically, and which used to anchor the historical point of view. As this lineup indicates, historicism, which had such a bad press because of its relativistic implications and which gave history such an evil reputation because of its imperialistic implications, has taken a double revenge which cuts across the philosophical and historiographical divide that the anti-German animus has drilled into American audiences and which has the ambiguous result of separating the substantively anti-philosophical American social historians from their pro-philosophical French confrères of the *Annaliste* and Foucaultian stripe. The double revenge consists in the two kinds of attempt to overcome the radical dissolution promulgated by the historicism of early twentieth-century vintage: later historicists have either invoked temporal structures from outside of history, such as Marxism, to give some stability to history, or they have obscurely constructed forms or relationships or institutions from within history itself to provide a stability which history can get from no other source.

In other words, both versions of historicism—both the philosophical and the historiographical—have had the effect of undermining the coherence that gave some stability to history by denying the validity or the applicability of the constant values which philosophers of history and historians like Hegel, Comte, and Ranke had drawn from outside of history to give a foundation to the connections which they acknowledged in the historical process itself. The historiographical establishment has continued to write history as if such values were still in their unchallenged place, without examining them or their role in history, but for the rest of us the individualizing and the caustic posture of historicism has had the vengeful result either of invoking deliberate coherences whose validity outside of history has been demonstrated and whose applicability to history has been argued, or of building coherences from the individualizing posture of historicism itself, in difficult procedures that have proved hard to follow.

In short, to modify a proposition that deserves a better fate, in this double sense we are all historicists now, either expressly or figuratively. When we categorize philosophers of history and historians within the rubric of historicism, we follow the honorable historical precedent that equates classification with explanation. And when we so classify them, we follow the precedent first made current in literary criticism and assign the figures concerned by our convenience rather than by their own testimony. Never, in short, ask an intellectual figure to classify himself, for we must assume that he knows not what he does. Consequently, we must own that some of these figures will abhor the classmates we choose for them. These figures would not be found, living or dead, alongside the mates we make them live or sleep with.

Historicism was the dominant cultural tendency in the western world during the inter-war period, in the first, express sense represented by the Germans Troeltsch, Meinecke, and Mannheim during the 1920s and in the second, figurative sense represented largely by Lucien Febvre and the early *Annales* during the 1930s. Historicism, in short, has been a dominant cultural tendency that has ensconced itself securely in our current consciousness, and as such historicism has been thoroughly pervasive. It is high time that we accounted historically for it. In the United States the continuity of a self-proclaimed "new history" from the pre-World War I generation of a Robinson, Becker, and Beard to the present generation of social historians manifests the persistence of historicism, since for both generations the similarity of their linguistic appeals to novelty, their common addiction to the social history of the common man, and their joint address to the neighboring behavioral sciences for help and inspiration evinces the shared heritage of historicism which was overt in the credits granted by Beard to Croce, Meinecke, and Mannheim and in the longevity of some of the "new historians." After all, the influential essays in Carl Becker's relativistic *Everyman His Own Historian* dated from as late as 1935 and those in *The Declaration of Independence* from 1942, while a whole breed of still active historians were brought up on the Beard Committee's iconoclastic report of 1946 to the Social Science Research Council. Nor should it be forgotten that Lucien Febvre's insistence upon the alignment of the historical approach with the novel assumptions of Einstein and quantum physics shared substantively the anti-absolutistic posture of contemporary philosophical historicism even when he specifically denied this title or indeed any imprimatur of the "philosophy of history."[1]

We have, then, two kinds of responses to historicism: one which accepts its relativistic implications and looks outside of history for the stability that would counter them, and the other which refuses to accept

1. Lucien Febvre, *Combats pour l'histoire* (Paris, 1953), pp 26–29, 56–58, 123–24.

these relativistic implications and looks within history for the relation-ships and structures that run counter to historical relativism. In the first camp we include not only all those who, like Croce, Collingwood, Mannheim, and Meinecke, are frankly labelled "relativists"—for ex-ample, by analysts like Maurice Mandelbaum—and seek the connec-tions that span the irreducible individuality of historical phenomena in the constancy of logic, sociology, or political theory, but also those like Dilthey, Simmel, Troeltsch, and Max Weber who accepted the caustic process of "disenchantment" characterized by historicism, but who re-fused to accept the relativism implied by historicism and saw in history an embodiment of values whose over-arching validity lay rooted in a transcendent realm outside of history.

This kind of classification makes for strange bedfellows, for it lumps together such mutually antagonistic philosophical schools as idealism, positivism and neo-Marxism; obvious enemies like Lévi-Strauss and Jean-Paul Sartre; and putatively opposed historical schools like that of Meinecke—all alike in their concentration on history as essentially indi-vidualizing and heterogeneous, and in their dependence upon realms outside of history for the source of coherent pattern in history.

Idealist philosophers like Croce, Collingwood, Dilthey, and Troeltsch were obviously historicists (despite Croce's early rejection of *istorismo* as Germanic in favor of *storicismo* as universally valid), since they insisted upon the dissolution of all reality in the stream of becoming and ini-tially postulated the identity of philosophy and history.[2] Whether they and their sociological allies, like Simmel, Weber and Mannheim, simply accepted the historical relativism of values and argued for a temporal perspectivism as the most of stability to be hoped for, or fought against such relativism in the names of logic or the cultural values that linked the historian to the historical agents and the agents to one another, the philosophical idealists at the start of this century modified their nineteenth-century forebears enough to incur the label of historicists without the obvious ontological transcendence which predecessors like Kant, Hegel, and Comte took for granted.

For the positivists of recent vintage, the propositions of the philo-sophical idealists are literally nonsense, but the covering-law model

---

2. Georg C. Iggers, "Historicism," in *Dictionary of the History of Ideas* (1972); 2:457; Benedetto Croce, *Ectetica* (2d ed., Milan, 1904), p. 35. But by 1938, when he published his *La Storia come pensiero e come azione*, Croce gave up the distinction in favor of a com-plete and incomplete rendition of *storicismo*. The latter smacked of invalid Germanic phi-losophy of history. *La Storia come pensiero e come azione* (2nd ed., Bari, 1938), pp. 51–55.

which positivism has devised for history and which maintains that all historians resort to uniformities expressed by general laws as explanations of specific historical facts which are so many instances of them, represents an attempt similar to that of the idealists to establish outside of history a valid source for the universal principles which must be operative within history. The positivists, indeed, have asserted unequivocally one principle that is shared by all self-consciously scientific historians— there is no distinctively historical method; all method worthy of the name is generically common to all the disciplines. In the words of Carl Hempel, a positivist who ranks as one of the founders of the covering-law model, "the nature of understanding . . . is basically the same in all areas of scientific inquiry. . . . Our schemata exhibit . . . one important aspect of the methodological unity of all empirical science."[3] Karl Popper, moreover, the positivist whose tendentious definition of historicism in terms of necessary developmental law has done more to muddy the idea of this much-maligned tendency than any other single position and whose equally tendentious definition of the covering-law model to exclude inductive generalization for scientific as well as historical procedures has also muddied the characteristic attitude of positivists, in *The Poverty of Historicism*, the same work in which he pejoratively distorted historicism, has also argued for the indiscriminate nature of all scientific methodology in the context of the applicability of the covering-law to history as to nature. "The thesis of the unity of scientific method . . . can be extended, with certain limitations, even to the field of historical sciences. . . . A singular event is the cause of another singular event— which is its effect—only relative to some universal laws."[4] Thus Popper, like Hempel, has affirmed the applicability of scientific method to history, despite its recalcitrant subject matter and the comparative indifference of its practitioners, and has thus affirmed, like all positivists, the extra-historical legacy of historicism.

Although neither idealists nor positivists would have anything to do with the neo-Marxism of the twentieth century, at least one group of the neo-Marxists, the Frankfurt school, has shared the orientation of idealists and positivists toward the ultimate individuality of history and toward the search outside of history for the roots of its patterns. The philosophers and aestheticians Theodore Adorno and Walter Benjamin

3. Carl G. Hempel, "Explanation in Science and History," in William H. Dray, ed., *Philosophical Analysis and History* (New York, 1966), pp. 123–24.

4. Karl R. Popper, *The Poverty of Historicism* (New York, 1964), pp. 143–45.

agreed that the human past is disjointed and meaningless until the interjection of philosophy, music, and literature between the moments of history give it integrity and meaning. As Adorno said repeatedly: "History is in the truth; the truth is not in history."[5]

The common experience of the neo-Marxists was the failure of modern empirical history—and particularly of the proletarian agents of it—to converge with the putatively rational and integrated process of objective history in the Marxian format—that is, the failure of the proletarian agents actually to make the revolution that the integral Marxian process called for—and the conclusion of at least Adorno and Benjamin was to deny the validity of rational and integrated process in history. Horkheimer, the leader of the school, shared with Adorno and Benjamin the general anti-Hegelian principle that "history has no reason," but he did not share their confidence in philosophy and aesthetics as the source of actionable faith, and he tended rather to see "a number of explanatory connections" in history and to judge them negatively as so many instances of sociological rationalization—that is, of alienation—in the past.[6] Thus he partially manifested the extra-historical emphasis which characterized both Adorno and Benjamin; he partially manifested the intra-historical emphasis which has characterized Herbert Marcuse, about whom more anon.

Lévi-Strauss's polemic at the end of *The Savage Mind* against the kind of individualizing history associated with Jean-Paul Sartre, as well as the general indifference of structuralism to history—an indifference stressed especially by Jean Piaget in his diatribe against the dominant emphasis of the structuralists on constancy rather than on change and development—has given to structuralism in general and to Lévi-Strauss in particular an anti-historical reputation that can be revised with the help of our categories. It—and he—tend rather to belong to the extra-historical camp spawned by historicism. For it is clear that what the structuralists and Lévi-Strauss have against history is the overweening individualizing tendency which was exalted by historicism and the weakness of patterning activities both by historical agents and by historians—the weakness, that is, of the "derivative" doctrine of an "analytic, abstract continuity" which, according to the structuralists, the historicists imposed upon history from philosophy in order to lend

---

5. Susan Buck-Morss, *The Origin of Negative Dialectics: Theodore W. Adorno, Walter Benjamin, and the Frankfurt Institute* (New York, 1977), pp xii-xiii, 46, 50–51.
6. *Ibid.*, pp. 47–48, 66–67.

coherence to the facts of history. From this point of view, the historical realm is commonly used only "as the point of departure."[7] But around the same time—that is, around 1960—Lévi-Strauss was delivering a lecture in which he not only justified "the historical dimension" of anthropology but openly admitted that "this declaration in favor of history may come as a surprise, since we have sometimes been reproached for being closed to history."[8] It is clear from this and other lectures that Lévi-Strauss looked with approval on "the idea of a structural history" and on "the existence of this historical tradition" which was superimposed on "a critical tradition proceeding essentially from historicism," and that he thus believed in narrowing the gap between the order of individual events and of coherent structures from the side of the coherent structures.[9] His reciprocated regard for the structuralist historian, Fernand Braudel, may stand as a symbol for this convergence of structuralism and history, as may the participation, for two years (1968 and 1969), of Roland Barthes in the historically dominated sixth section of the *École pratique des hautes études*, after a career devoted to a-historical structuralist literary criticism.[10]

Sartre may be Lévi-Strauss's *bête noire* but the antipathy is rather because of Sartre's substance than because of his form. For both men believe in the external derivation of what is intelligible and coherent in history; Sartre's philosophical commitment to the progressive pattern of Marxism parallels the persistent attitudes discernible in primitive man. The difference between the two may be seen in Lévi-Strauss's stress upon the anthropological base of his history vis-à-vis Sartre's countervailing emphasis upon the individualizing "regression" of his existentialism as the indispensable complement of the gross Marxist structures.[11]

Let us leave aside until later mention, the other, internalized, historical dimension of the post-structuralist school that is represented, above all, by Herbert Marcuse. More familiar to us than either the philosophi-

7. Claude Lévi-Strauss, *The Savage Mind* (Chicago, 1966), pp. 261–63; Marc Gaboriau, "Structural Anthropology and History," in Michael Lane, ed., *Introduction to Structuralism* (New York, 1970), pp. 156–69.
8. Claude Lévi-Strauss, *Structural Anthropology*. Trans. Monique Layton (New York, 1976), pp. 12–15.
9. *Ibid.*, pp. 16–18, 276.
10. The a-historicity was interrupted only by Barthes' publication of a literary analysis of Michelet under the title *Michelet par lui-même* around 1954 and his deprecatory essay "On Historical Discourse" in 1967.
11. Jean-Paul Sartre, *Search for a Method*. Trans. Hazel E. Barnes (New York, 1968), pp. 85–155.

cal or the anthropological versions of the external facet of historicism's revenge is the historiographical variant, not only because it is obviously closer to us as historians but also because both the *Annales* school from France and the Meinecke school from Germany have cut a much wider swath in American scholarship than have their non-historical counterparts. What we must realize, first, is that we are here speaking of the *Annales* during its initial period, between 1929 and 1939, the period of the *Annales* associated with the names of its editors Marc Bloch and Lucien Febvre, an initial period distinct, by common consent, in the history of the still ongoing *Annales*.[12] This was a period characterized by the French ambiguity between history as *an* applied field of a generic scientific method and history as *the* distinctive core of a social-scientific method, with the emphasis on the first element of this ambiguity, and the equally French association of this ambiguity with the primary criterion of synthesis in history. This ambiguity was especially connected with the work of Lucien Febvre's honored predecessor, Henri Berr, and through Febvre himself, with the subsequent studies of American social historians.

Thus the American social historians of recent vintage, like Bloch and Febvre of *Annales* fame, stress the generic scientific method, the cooperation of history with the neighboring social sciences, and the preeminence of synthesis or totality in the human past as the prime historical embodiment of social scientific concepts and methods. In the words of one American primer in social history, "the social science approach . . . assumes that there are uniformities of human behavior that transcend time and place . . . ; and the historian as social scientist chooses his problems with a view to discovering, verifying, or illuminating such uniformities."[13] And to this another spokesman adds: "From the historian's point of view, the value of technical research consists in and is determined by the light it can cast on general problems of historical interpretation."[14]

Such American formulations echo the association of synthetic history with the ambiguous external derivation of historical patterns, an association made by such French academic father-an-son combinations as Lucien Febvre and Fernand Braudel, when Febvre wrote that "the sciences are solidary," when he favored "historical synthesis" over "anal-

12. Thus in Fernand Braudel, *Ecrits sur l'histoire* (Paris, 1969), p. 109.
13. David S. Landes and Charles Tilly, eds., *History as Social Science* (Englewood Cliffs, N.J., 1971), p. 9.
14. William O. Aydelotte, Allan G. Bogue, and Robert William Fogel, eds., *The Dimensions of Quantitative Research in History* (Princeton, 1972), p. 7.

ysis" as part of "scientific synthesis, . . . the endeavor to generalize, to disentangle a complex causality in order to discover general factors,"[15] and when Braudel wrote repeatedly of "total history" and of "the unity of history that is the unity of life."[16] The French *Annalistes*, as well as the later social historians of all nationalities, did write of the individual as the primary object of history, but they emphasized even more the historical limitations on the individual, "the regular or repeated factors that cohabit" with the singular and that "enable us to transcend the individual."[17] If the French, moreover, have been more explicit in their defence of the individual in history and in their espousal broadly of "the human sciences" rather than merely the "social sciences" as auxiliaries of history than their American confrères, they also, particularly in the person of Lucien Febvre, have been more open in their redefinition of the particular facts on which historians long have doted and they have stressed more explicitly that these are new kinds of facts because they are functions of the interpretive theories which they putatively ground.[18] We should remember this priority when we are told the facts about the masses for which current quantitative theories presumably account. It is more to the point to say that these theories fill the void left by the historicist abomination of theory and that the theories have the facts they deserve.

At first glance the Meinecke school in Germany and in its American counterparts is as different from the *Annaliste* school of French historians and from the American school of social historians as the latter two groups say it is, since Meinecke not only made himself spokesman for ideas connected to historical reality through the state rather than through the society, but he also is primarily associated with the historicism whose late eighteenth- and early nineteenth-century origins he charted. He is also identified with its individualistic historical bias. It is precisely against these particularistic implications of historicism that the French and American schools have reacted so strongly. But actually, if one connects the philosophical interests of a Meinecke with the scien-

15. Lucien Febvre, *Combats pour l'histoire*, pp. 15–16, 29–33; Lucien Febvre and Henri Berr, "History," in *Encyclopedia of the Social Sciences*, 7:361.

16. Fernand Braudel, *Ecrits sur l'histoire*, pp. 6–7, 24–30; J. H. Hexter, "Fernand Braudel and the Monde Braudelienne," *Journal of Modern History*, 44 (1972):511.

17. Braudel, *Ecrits sur l'histoire*, pp. 20–21; Febvre, *Combats pour l'histoire*, pp. 13–14; Joachim Radkau and Orlinde Radkau, *Praxis der Geschichtswissenschaft: Die Desorientierheit des historischen Interesses* (Dusseldorf, 1972), pp. 30–45; Hans-Ulrich Wehler, "Geschichtswissenschaft und Psycholhistorie," *Innsbrucker Historische Studien*, I (1978):201–6.

18. Febvre, *Combats pour l'histoire*, pp. 21–23.

tific preoccupations of the *Annales*, then from our point of view the two approaches are affiliated by their common tendency to derive the patterning in history from outside of history. Both Meinecke and the *Annales* are ambiguous about this derivation, since they all have the urge "to overcome history through history," as Meinecke's compatriot and fellow historicist, the philosopher and theologian Ernst Troeltsch once wrote, but the two traditions are as one also in their preeminent inclination to break the ambiguity by invoking aid in the patterning of history from outside history. Where the *Annalistes* looked to auxiliary disciplines for the source of outside assistance, Meinecke and his disciples looked to a *Weltanschauung* that elevated individuality into a principle and thus let it be coupled with the realm of ideas to connect them in "the unity of human-spiritual life" which for Meinecke was at once the goal and the starting point of the historical process.[19] In any case, behind Meinecke's protestations that his philosophy came from his history, as behind Febvre's and Braudel's protestations that history was the central discipline of a unified science of human life, lay a conviction, a *Weltanschauung*, arguing that the world was so disposed. Both Meinecke and the *Annalistes* found their views of life to be the sources of their views of the patterns in life's past.[20]

But there has also been a second kind of response to historicism, one that takes seriously its caustic effect of individualizing reality both inside and outside of history and seeks therefore, in full recognition of its difficulties, to execute the task of constructing the coherence of history from the individualities of history themselves. The result is some of the obscurest writing in the history of the philosophy of history and in the history of historiography, an obscurity that truly amounts to one of the keenest vengeances that historicism can take. By and large, current tendencies are classifiable under this second kind of inner historical response, whereas the other, outer kind of historical response characterized the inter-war and immediate post-World War II eras and is more familiar to the older generations among us. Certainly some of the influences leading from one kind of response to the other have a special impact upon historians, such as come from the change in cultural circumstance ending the post-war mentality, a change which favors a more extensive habit of navel contemplation on the part of those con-

19. Friedrich Meinecke, "Ein Wort über geschichtliche Entwicklung," in Friedrich Meinecke, *Aphorismen und Skizzen zur Geschichte* (Leipzig, 1942) pp. 102–9.

20. Walter Hofer, *Geschichtschreibung und Weltanschauung: Betrachtungen zur Werk Friedrich Meineckes* (Munich, 1950), pp. 471–74, 519–39; Febvre, *Combats pour l'histoire*, pp. 16–17, 31–32; Braudel, *Ecrits sur l'histoire*, pp. 6, 106–7.

cerned with history than ever before. Other influences leading from the one kind of response to the other are more indirect in their bearing upon history, such as those which have to do with the recent anti-historical developments in philosophy and the other neighboring disciplines, arts as well as social sciences, developments which make the dependence of historians upon the neighboring disciplines inappropriate. With the shift of philosophy and literature to an emphasis on logic, analysis, and structure which has no place for an interest in history—the well-noted decline of literary history is one case in point[21]—and with the rise of an equally non-historical behaviorism in the social sciences, the invocation of ideas and concepts from these fields has ceased to have point and, for the most advanced historians, has in fact ceased.[22]

And as this invocation from fields of study outside history has ceased it has been replaced by three sub-types of response from those who would construct the patterns of history out of its individual components. Let us concentrate on the three sub-types of constructive response to historicism and the extra-historical challenge to it, leaving aside traditionalists like Jacques Barzun who repeat the individualism, the plurality, and the narrative scheme of the historiographical past, enshrined in historicism, and mavericks like Hayden White, who deny the capacity of history to establish meaningful patterns at all.[23]

The first sub-type of internal response to the problem of coherent stability in history posed by historicism has been the revision of movements standing outside of history so as to make them stand unrevised inside of history. The two chief exemplars of this sub-type have been Patrick Gardiner, the analytical philosopher who has justified the covering-law model in the name of what he takes to be the historian's emphasis on psychological disposition, and Herbert Marcuse, who has represented the rationality of history in the Frankfurt school. Marcuse blended Marx and Freud by historizing both; he used Freud to make Marxism an authentic historical structure, expressive of man's real potentiality.

The second sub-type of this kind of response has been the promulga-

---

21. Rene Wellek, "The Fall of Literary History," in Reinhart Koselleck and Wolf-Dieter Sempel, eds., *Geschichte—Ereignis und Erzählung* (Munich, 1973), pp. 428, 439–40.

22. Lawrence Stone, "History and the Social Sciences in the Twentieth Century," in Charles F. Delzell, ed., *The Future of History* (Nashville, 1977), pp. 8–12.

23. Jacques Barzun, *Clio and the Doctors* (Chicago, 1974), pp. 93–95, 98, 102–2, 123–24, 136; Hayden White, *Metahistory: The Historical Imagination in Nineteenth-Century Europe* (Baltimore, 1973), pp. 428–34.

tion of novel positions that established the autonomy of historical patterns and redefined historical facts to fit them. Two examples of this sub-type may be mentioned here, both of current French vintage. This vintage is hardly accidental, for most of the interesting historical thinking these days is done in France. Partly, this is a result of Fernand Braudel's longevity, since he was a faithful disciple of Lucien Febvre and he is the mentor of several current French historians whom he no longer completely understands. Partly too, the French vintage of interesting historical thought has to do with the French tradition of socio-cultural history, enshrined in the *Annales,* and with recent French vogues of existentialism and structuralism. For the present post-existentialist and post-structuralist tendencies have produced a generation of *Annalistes* and of intellectuals who have sought to historize patterns so as to make them thus internally authentic.

The first example is that of "serial history," a concept coined by Pierre Chaunu for economic history and generalized into an historical approach by others like Francois Furet. The point, for us, of serial history is, as Furet has put it, its "conclusive advantage of substituting for an elusive 'event' of positivist history the regular repetition of data selected or constructed by reason of their comparability"—in other words, it grants first priority to the series or the temporal totality as an authentic, fundamentally historical pattern, and it derives the factual components from "the consistency" of the series itself.[24] Thus "serial history . . . describes continuities in the mode of discontinuity"; it "reveals a time which is . . . an evolutionary rhythm," based on "a series of data both particular and homogenous." "General history" in short, must sit "at the feet of serial history."[25] Be it noted that Fernand Braudel, the survivor of the *Annales'* early phase, exhibited an air of wondering surprise in his review of Chaunu's exercise in "serial history."[26] Be it noted too, in estimating the gap between the early and the later *Annales,* how the tone celebrating the cooperativeness of history has given way to a tone celebrating the distinctiveness of history as a discipline.

Another example of this current second sub-type that preaches the autonomy of historical patterns and their priority over their constituent phenomena is associated with the familiar name of Michel Foucault.

24. Francois Furet, "Quantitative History," *Daedalus,* 100 (1971):153–65. See also Pierre Chaunu, *Histoire quantitative ou histoire sérielle* (Geneva, 1968).
25. Furet, "Quantitative History," pp. 155, 161, 166.
26. Braudel, "Pour une histoire sérielle: *Seville et l'Atlantique (1504–1650),* in Fernand Braudel, *Ecrits sur l'histoire,* pp. 135–161.

Now Foucault himself is a phenomenon who would have to be invented if he did not already exist, since a whole industry has grown up around the various interpretations of his obscure message. A philosopher by trade who writes impressionistic social history by choice, he has become a cynosure for historians especially, since he seems to provide access to social history for those who are not social historians and access to structural history for those who are not structuralists. Foucault, in short, has become the poor man's cultural historian.

Foucault raises again the age-old and probably insoluble problem first brought to the fore in our time by the appearance of an abridged Arnold Toynbee on the best-seller lists: how does one acquire the reputation of being provocative and socially indispensable rather than opaque and socially dispensable? At any rate, for our purposes Foucault is quite simple, for he obviously provides a current illustration of the historical internality we are now talking about. The archaeology he favors is really a new, internalized kind of history, and the "history" he rejects is really the traditional history whose pattern is grounded in what he considers to be unities of person, work, genre, or other non-temporal realities. What he tries to do, instead, is to reconstruct unities on the basis of the discontinuity that results from aborting all extra-historical assumptions from non-temporal unities. In his own words, "the essential task was to free the history of thought from its subjection to transcendence. . . . By freeing [the facts of discourse] of all the groupings that purport to be natural, immediate, universal unities, one is able to describe other unities . . . I have undertaken, then, to describe the relations between statements."[27] Where Foucault takes leave of the structuralists—as he claims to have done—is in the emphasis which his concrete historical works have given to the changes which have taken place in the "classical period" from the sixteenth and through the eighteenth century. He has recognized change by showing how modern institutions have been organized for the bourgeois control of cultural mavericks during the nineteenth century—the asylum, the clinic, the prison—in contrast to the characteristic structuralist stress on the constancy of human things. In his stress on confinement in the clinic or the prison, Foucault has tried to square the historical circle: to show how a new coherent order, compatible with the particularities of individual freedom, has replaced the older imposed order of external universals.

Finally, as a third sub-type of response to the problem posed by his-

---

27. Michel Foucault, *The Archaeology of Knowledge*. Trans. A.M. Sheridan Smith (New York, 1972), pp. 29–31.

toricism to the ground of patterns in history and to their compatibility with the individual facts of history has been the application of the critical approach which has already proved valuable for establishing the individual facts of history to the patterns of history. German, English, and American historians have traveled this route, which involves the historisation of external realities and the consequent revising, loosening, complication, and limitation of coherences which have been applied to history.[28]

But I can supply an answer to the contemporary status of historical reason in terms that will be less parochial than the social historians' and therefore accessible to more kinds of historical practitioners, and I can embody the answer in four brief principles:

First, the touchstone of historical reason is the insertion of any event in a larger context of events, whether this context be synchronic or diachronic. Be it noted that by this principle reason in the sense of explanation is identical with reason in the sense of coherent pattern. A fact is explained by the series of facts in which it is enmeshed, and the series of facts that is focused on the fact to be thereby explained constitutes a relevant rational pattern.

But this principle raises the further question of how the rational context, or series of facts, is to be constructed, and the remaining principles are addressed to this question:

Second, then, when the historical agent acts in the light of a continuity, then that continuity establishes the relevant facts in the series. This continuity again may be diachronic, as in the case of so many theorists who think in the terms set forth by past theorists, or it may be synchronic, as in the case of a political agency that seeks to extend its sway.

Third, for those cases where the series is not in the mind of the historical agent but has to be constructed by the historian, the criterion of this construction is purely temporal—that is, the relationship of succession or of simultaneity among events establishes a connection among them that is stronger than juxtaposition even when none other than the temporal relationship can be adduced. The implication here is that although history, as traditionally conceived, is a social discipline and has

28. E.g., Reinhart Koselleck, "Über die Theoriebedürftigkeit der Geschichtswissenschaft," in Werner Conze, ed., *Theorie der Geschichtswissenschaft und Praxis der Geschichtsunterrichts* (Stuttgart, 1972), pp. 13–17; J. H. Plumb, *The Death of the Past* (Boston, 1970); Geoffrey Elton, *The Practice of History* (New York, 1967); J. H. Hexter, *Reappraisals in History: New Views in Science History and Society in Early Modern Europe* (New York, 1963).

assumed a distinction between historicity and temporality, it is not necessarily social and does not necessarily entail such a distinction. Indeed,
here is one dimension in which this proposal of what history should be
involves a departure from what history has been. The proposal is that
history transcend the usual socialized connotation of what is historical,
and that this temporalized dimension, whether social or not, should be
redefined to be congruent with that which is historical, however un-
traditional such a juncture between temporality and historicity might
be. All biography, for example, should be deemed historical, for the distinction should be drawn between the conditions of a person's thinking
and writing which go into his work and are inevitably social, and the
meanings which come out of his work, and may be social or not, as the
case may be. But these meanings are necessarily historical insofar as they
are temporal, whether individual or social; they do not involve the distinctions between individual and social temporality as such.

Fourth and finally, the prior principles are addressed to the pure historians when there is no such animal as a pure historian alive. We are
political persons, economic persons, moral persons, philosophical persons, or religious persons as well as historians, and we need a principle
that locates time's reasons for this hybrid reality. The principle is this:
the extra-historical dimension should be invoked for the facts of history
rather than for the relations among the facts. We need our extra-
historical knowledge and insights to understand the facts of the past internally, but as long as we are historians we should leave the relations
among the facts to time's reasons. I realize that this categorical distinction between facts and relations is old-fashioned and flies in the face of
recent analyses that would collapse them. But such collapsing brings
chaos in its train, and a more coherent historical view is obtained from
their persistent separation.

Historicism, in sum, has stressed the particular and individualistic aspects of the historical enterprise and it has left a vacuum concerning the
coherent principles of connection among the particulars and the individuals which has ever been the other definitive part of the historical enterprise. In the former instance it has had the direct result of enshrining
the sense of variety and of multiplicity which has been emphasized by
historians ever since. In the latter instance it has evoked the compulsion
of the western mind to find rest in some kind of coherent pattern which
gives rational meaning to the particular events and individual persons
and groups who are connected by it, with all the anachronism, divisiveness, and opacity that has accompanied the assertion of such patterns
when the confidence in the supporting order of things has passed. This

anachronism, divisiveness, and above all opacity, has accompanied the move from the compatibility of the other sciences with history, symbolized in the linguistic structuralism of a Lévi-Strauss and a Roland Barthes, to the historical indifference or even anti-historical hostility of science in its present posture, as symbolized by the tendencies toward post-structuralism in France represented by a Lacan or a Derrida. If revenge is sweet, then the historicists continue to find pleasure in what historians have done both in confirmation of and in response to the relativism that is inherent in the historicist position.

The response of this historian is designed to escape the parochialism, divisiveness and the opacity of other attempts which enthrone philosophy, politics, or aesthetics as their basis of unity. But if the charge is one of anachronism, then I plead guilty with extenuating circumstances. The proposal tries both to justify the history writing of the remoter past and to reform the history writing of the present in the light of the challenge and the response which historicism has presented to it.

10 Culture, Cataclysm, and Contingency

Men have been writing history for well over two millennia, even if we count only by our cultural time, but they have continued, throughout this whole long stretch, to ask themselves what they were writing it for. The one constant answer upon which historians of all vintages have agreed is that history is written for entertainment—presumably of their readers—because it simply adds the extra fillip of reality to men's natural liking for a good story, a lively description, and a temporally or spatially exotic setting. It may well be that this consensus rests on a fundamental truth—that amusement is indeed the only valid purpose of historical writing—but in fact, whether because of the frequent gap between intent and effect in this respect or because of some additional dimension within history itself, its practitioners have not been content with the hedonism that would long ago have laid to rest their anxiety about the contribution of their genre. They have gone beyond the pleasure principle to seek a usefulness for history in its edifying role, and it is in the definition of its instruction that they have found discord, frustration, and—consequently—a perpetual problem.

The problem has, to be sure, been raised somewhat less of late, but this letup has to do less with despair about the issue or with agreement on traditional responses than with the historical discipline's sharing in the general assumption, current in the past century or so, that all knowledge is intrinsically worthy and bestows tangible benefactions via an invisible hand so long as these practical benefits are not directly intended. If, then, to inquire into the usefulness of historical study has become improper at worst and vulgar at best, this deprecation means not the end of the question but the end of this form of the question. In our intellectually affluent society, where knowledge is assumed to command wealth and power, what is asked of any kind of knowledge is not its use value for wealth and power but its exchange value with other kinds of knowledge. We are justified, then, in considering the currently respectable query about the relations of history to the other social sciences or

First published in the *Journal of Modern History* 40:4 (December, 1968), 447–73.

194

the other humanities to be the new, euphemistic version of the older question about the uses of history.

The persistence of the substance and the change in the form of the question explain its longevity. The concern for utility has always been especially insistent for historians, first because they deal in a discipline that does not deliver general truths and that therefore makes relevant the question about the destination of the particular truths it does deliver; and second because they deal in a dimension that applies knowledge to a no-longer-existing reality and therefore raises doubts about the usefulness of this knowledge even over and above its particularity. If this special nature of history helps to explain why the question of its use or purpose has been so appropriate and urgent a motif in the history of history, the alterations in the form of the question indicate why its resolutions have been temporary. For the question of history's usefulness has been asked differently as the idea of history has changed. Formerly respectable answers about the uses of history are not so much inadequate as anachronistic vis-à-vis a new idea of the history whose purpose or use is in question. It is precisely because the answers have themselves been historical that the question has been recurrent.

What we are concerned with here, then, is a use of history that is geared to the contemporary notion of what history is. To define this use, let us distinguish it from the older and more familiar uses which are appropriate to an older and more familiar notion of history. What history teaches, we have been accustomed to think, is either something very specific or the support for something very general. Thus those of us who insist upon the contingency of history's events and the speciality of its lessons have held that we learn what to do—or more often, what not to do—in particular kinds of situations from analogous past situations, or that we learn about definite institutions, ideas, people, or situations that interest us through the historical knowledge of how they started and how they have grown. Those of us who insist upon history's necessary connection with the general truths common to all reality have held that whether it be providence or philosophy teaching by historical example we learn from the past the practical consequences of preformed general principles or that we learn from the past the "cases" or "instances" which become the inductive premises of general laws, whether of human nature or political behavior. The alternatives in the two sets of historical lessons are obviously parallel, and in fact the study of history for its supply of examples, whether of specific situations or universal principles, has long been covered with the single label of "pragmatic history," while the study of history for its empirical contribution to the formulation and verification of a present truth, whether of a genetic or inductive kind, has had a similarly collective career under the rubric of "scientific history."

These applications, given by the specific and the general versions of pragmatic and scientific history, comprise the traditionally accepted uses of history. The successive combinations brought on by their mutual conflicts and their sundry juxtapositions have made up, until comparatively recently, the history of the extrinsic justification of history.

Of late, however, each of the main traditional uses of history has been countered, not by another use, but by what we may call an anti-use. Thus history is no longer considered to have a *specific pragmatic* use because each historical event is held to be too essentially singular for any relevance to a putative analogue to be possible. History is no longer considered to have a *general pragmatic* use on the ground that there are no generally accepted, pre-established universal principles for history to exemplify. History is no longer considered to have a *specific scientific* use because the crucial roles of chance and discretion at every stage of development minimize the genetic role of the past in the explanation of anything. And history, finally, is no longer considered to have a *general scientific* use because the heterogeneity of historical events frustrates any alignment into an inductive series.

The counterpart of these anti-uses has been the prevalent commitment, sometimes avowed and more often tacit, to the intrinsic value of every historical event as the expression of a humanity whose every expression is inherently valuable. Since the value of each piece of history, according to this view, lies in itself as an expression of infinite human variety—or in its connection with another piece of history which is a clearer expression of the infinite human variety—the value of history has no external reference, and we are left with little more than the tautology that the history of human life is written simply to reveal the historical side of human life. This romantic affirmation of life is no more satisfactory than its more utilitarian and technological alternatives, and we usually accompany it with assurances of an unspecifiable function for this history. We are left in the contradictory position of denying both the uses and the uselessness of history.

For our own period, the anomaly of a useful history with no specifiable uses is primarily explicable by the anachronism of applying to the contemporary idea of history notions of use or value appropriate to older ideas of it. For the definition of history has undergone a significant change whose origins and even existence have been masked by the conservative, practical, and unselfconscious mentality of the historical guild. The essence of the change consists in the shift from the conception of history as an *area* of reality—that is, the area inhabited by its past—to a conception of history as an *axis* of reality—that is, the axis determined by its movement through time. The difference between these two definitions does not sound like much for the same reason that the consciousness of it has been obscured—because our terminology and our habits of thought are still molded by the spatial analogy that has furnished the symbols for our traditional ideas of history. But for the actual study of history the distinction between the knowledge of a set of definite objects in time and the establishment of a set of relationships through time is crucial and categorical. Thus the whole of the human past is no longer thought to be a historical past, which comprises only those aspects of it whose temporal arrangement, whether in terms of simultaneity or succession, or of inertia or change, has meaning. Again, the human past is no longer accounted to comprise the whole of history, since the present is also historical insofar as it is studied for its temporal alignments. To footnote the development of this approach to history is a purpose of this essay which we shall come to later, but we may clarify it here in a brief reference to the contemporary cultural tendency of which it is a part. With the secularization of objects formerly outside of time and space and with the conversion of stable spatial objects into discontinuous sets of space-time coordinates, the world of history has suffered an intellectual population explosion of such magnitude and cultural variety that the historian's substitution of a definite approach to an indefinite reality for his older indefinite ways of encompassing a definite past has become not only a modern improvement but a practical necessity.

The familiar pragmatic and scientific uses of history were framed in terms of a history which was conceived as a segment of reality, and it is hardly surprising that they seem invalid at worst and confusing at best when they are applied to a history that is now conceived along a very different plane as a cross-section of reality. Clearly, the question of whether history has uses beyond its revelation of still more human varieties and vagaries than we already see around us is a question that must be reconsidered in terms of the current perspectival—if we may coin a new word for a new view—approach to history.

In its most general and obvious form the question has become simply this: what does the historical perspective on reality contribute to other perspectives on reality? To answer this question as a historian rather than as a philosopher of history, I shall pose it here in a more definite and a more congenial form: what, in fact, has the sense of history contributed to intellectual systems in thinkers who have possessed both? But since, in our civilization, the sense of history has always covered both the feel for the raw material of history and the idea of its meaningfulness, the question really entails a threefold rather than a twofold relationship of its terms and requires a prior definition of them. To give these terms their most fundamental labels, the issue may be restated as the relationship which has been exhibited in our intellectual history between culture, cataclysm, and contingency.

The issue is cultural in that it is a problem arising out of a pattern of thinking reiterated in so many manifestations of Western culture that we may justifiably consider both the pattern and the problem characteristic not of this or that special field but of the culture itself. Expressed in its barest form, the pattern consists in the fruitful blend that Western men have made of systematic thinking that has its own logic and its own momentum with new experience that comes from outside the system, is alien to their thinking and its expectations, and yet gets absorbed into it and changes its course; the problem consists in the mystery of how and when a tightly organized and inclosed structure of ideas gets opened up to ingest a radically different kind of material from an axis of existence transverse to its own.

How, in other words, do we assess, for any one cultural field, the respective roles assignable to the development of rules, concepts, and problems within that field on the one hand and the external conditions produced by activities in quite different fields on the other? The issue is clearest for the fields of culture in the narrow sense of the term—that is, for the arts, plastic and literary, and the philosophies, formal and social. In these fields the problem takes the familiar form of the dilemma which so often impends when a new aesthetic or theoretical development seems equally explicable either as a logical solution of the technical problems in the field or as an effect of political and social environment, but somewhat schizoid when conceived as a resultant of both lines of force. Thus, Giotto's art can be seen as the product of a new use of space or of a new city-state environment; Hegel's *Phenomenology* can be seen as an answer to Kant or an answer to the French Revolution. But the problem is: how can either be seen as both?

Other fields of culture—taken now in its broad, anthropological sense—manifest the same problem, albeit more obscurely, corresponding to the less articulated structure of their ideas, a difference which we often take into account by speaking of "attitudes" rather than ideas for these fields. Thus if economic systems are viewed as a network of long-range relationships which is operated by a stable set of attitudes toward the basic factors of production and exchange, then we find ourselves confronted with a problem analogous to the arts and the philosophies whenever we tried to assess the respective roles of purely economic growth and of extra-economic conditions in the onset of economic change. The example of the Industrial Revolution and the problem it has raised of integrating the relentless demand for cotton yarn with the effects of the English Glorious Revolution or the continental European Revolution of 1848 should suffice to make the point that we have to do here not with a limited aesthetic or abstract problem but with the general problem of how the logicality and the porosity which have equally qualified our culture have combined to make it move.

The historian's usual devices are, more than not, quite unsatisfactory when brought to bear upon this problem. The historian looks for direct contemporary testimony of the effect of circumstances upon the structure of ideas, but the problem must still be solved when such testimony does not exist—as it frequently does not—and contemporary insights into the relationship are often limited even when such testimony does exist. Again, the historian's device of adding causes and calling the juxtaposition an explanation begs the question by assuming the connection he purports to demonstrate. Finally, the historian's predilection for intermediate figures and hybrid concepts—for diffusers of culture, educated politicians, social theories, "public opinion," and similar loose mixtures of ideas and circumstances—excludes the intellectual pioneers whose rigorous systems have molded our culture and evades the problem by postulating a continuous osmosis where a dramatic confrontation is called for.

What is required, then, is a device that, independently of direct testimony, more fundamentally than the juxtaposition of thought- and art-form with social condition, and more definitely than the murky intermediary, permits us to assess the influence of circumstance *upon* thought by pursuing the role of identifiable circumstance *in* thought. For this device, I propose the use of cataclysm as a circumstantial tracer. As a circumstance, a cataclysmic event is not simply more sudden and more disruptive—in a word, larger—than other circumstances, but it possesses three qualities that make it most appropriate to our purpose. First, a cataclysm is intrusive: however absent-minded or ethereal a man may be, if his thought processes are influenceable by circumstances at all they will be influenced by a cataclysm. Second, a cataclysm is inherently and utterly circumstantial, both in the sense that it is by definition a unique and unpredictable event and in the sense that it is by connotation external to the individual, conditioning his destiny but indifferent or noxious to his ideas. Third, a cataclysm is permanently identifiable as a circumstance: it is irreducible, unabsorbable, and consequently always recognizable, whatever the contexts in which men think about it, for the ultimate circumstance it is. We focus on war and revolution rather than on the flood, the earthquake, the volcano, and the conflagration, because, impressive as the spectacle of natural cataclysms has been to thoughtful and sensitive men, its effect has dwindled under the growing sense of nature's orderliness, until the autonomy of these circumstances has become much less credible than the growing mystery of the arbitrary convulsions brought on by collective human agency. As a matter of actual record, moreover, social and political cataclysm has been infinitely more provocative to thinkers, in part for reasons of frequency and propinquity but more fundamentally because its human provenance has underlined both the possibility and the urgency of finding a place for it in human ideas.

But the tracing of political and social cataclysms as ingredients of thought is only the first part of our task. If cataclysm guarantees the permanent *substance* of circumstance for our inquiry, we still need to identify the *form* it must take to have an ideational or logical function if we are going to understand what it is doing in that function. The logical form or mode of circumstance is contingency, which stands in this context for any subject of thought considered purely as a matter of fact, with no logical or rational connection to any predicate or any other subject of thought. Contingency thus gives circumstance a place in thought as the active limit of logic, and through contingency we can ascertain the function of circumstance in thought by following the intellectual process through which it affixes the frontiers of rational thinking.

Our formula, then, is this: choose an activity of the culture especially prolific in self-inclosed systems of ideas; use social and political cataclysm as indelible circumstance; and investigate the logical role of contingency ("logical," since the negation of logic is an important category of logic) in relating culture and cataclysm to each other. To apply this formula, we shall choose here the philosophies rather than the arts for our cultural field. For our cataclysms, we shall use the wars and revolutions whose impress is traceable in the thinking of philosophers. So to trace, under the aegis of time, the course of thought and the perception of cataclysm to the moment of their intersection is a historical enterprise, and since the figures are the historical actors in this intellectual drama, we may call it "history for us."

For our category of contingency through which to follow the subsequent intellectual role of the cataclysm, we shall look to these philosophers' own ideas of history, since contingency is *the* logical principle underlying the historical approach. The converse, to be sure, is not true: there are other approaches to contingency besides the historical, as the current vogue of individualized "things" and unconnected "happenings" in literature and the arts makes abundantly clear. But the historian's distinctive contribution to contingency makes the idea of history particularly appropriate to our problem of considering contingent events in their relationship to rational and coherent truths. The historian, like others similarly disposed toward the restoration of the sovereign "thereness" of happenings, strips his events of their rational dependencies and reconstructs their integrity out of the lifeless components into which they have been analyzed. But peculiar to the historian is the logical function of his logical disservice: he frees contingent events from the bonds of logic for the purpose of submitting then to a chronologic. By thinking contingent truths according to an order in time, history creates the possibility of relating them to the rational truths that are thought according to their parallel order in logic. Hence through their ideas of history, the philosophers have organized circumstances into non-logical series that have proven negotiable with their logical systems of ideas. Since in this context our philosophers are not so much historical agents as model historians, we may call their ideas of history "history for them."

Our inquiry into the problem thus posed will involve us with two kinds of philosophical thinkers. The first kind consists of those whom we may call "the contributors": they registered the effects either of intellectual tensions *or* of cataclysmic events—but not of both—upon the idea of history and thereby contributed the continuity between the landmark achievements of the second kind of thinker—"the synthesizers"—who reinforced contingency through their experience of cataclysm and rebuilt intellectual systems to include it, thereby creating new stages in the history of the idea of history.

The "contributors" are legion, for our culture abounds in systematic thinkers who have produced philosophies of history alongside schematic philosophies of nature, mind, morals, and art, and in unsystematic thinkers who have been open to the massive political and social events of their time. But the "synthesizers" who developed rigorous intellectual systems, lived amid cataclysm, and internalized it, are so few that the conjuncture in them may seem capricious and their prominent role in our project misproportioned. And yet, few as they are, they remain the nodal figures for our problem, which becomes distorted without their occupation of a central role in it. The unsystematic thinkers whose susceptibility to contemporary experience has influenced their idea of history raise the question of historical anachronism or presentism, but however valid this problem of the direct influence of one vintage of circumstance upon another vintage of circumstance may be, it is obviously different, in itself, from our problem of relating the axis of circumstance to the axis of logical thinking.

The other category of "contributors"—the unsusceptible philosophers of history—likewise displaces the terms of the problem unless they are considered in relation to the synthesizers of culture and cataclysm. Between a thinker's system of ideas and his theory of history, an immediate experience of the independent force of circumstance must intervene, whether through cataclysm or any other traceable form, if history itself is to be guaranteed a hearing in his system. Without this intervention, a philosophy of history often has no independent function in thought, for it has served merely to provide circumstantial evidence for systems of ideas by identifying the temporal sequence of events with the logical sequence of concepts. There is, indeed, a whole tradition of thought in which temporal circumstances are subsumed under extra-temporal nets of ideas, and there is a special meaning of contingency— the sense of dependence upon something prior—which applies to it. But the philosophy of history in this function and contingency in this sense make up a question in the philosophy of history that is only a part of our problem of history itself. The philosophical question assumes the logicality of history and asks how the special material of history can be turned into propositions. Our historical problem assumes the non-logicality of history and asks how the autonomous material of history affects propositions.

For the full treatment of our problem, then, we must align both contributors and synthesizers in an order of historical development. Only so can we show how contemporary circumstances and intellectual systems created separately the sense for history and the idea of history that the cataclysmic philosophers combined into the function of history, and how, consequently, the function has changed with the changing circumstances and ideas of history.

But before we embark upon the historical account of our cultural issue, let us anticipate to the extent of characterizing the general framework within which the functional idea of history develops, for it is a framework that is common to all its stages and that is surprising enough to require this advance announcement if we are to be properly oriented.

We are used to thinking of history in terms of fragmentation, discontinuity, and evanescence, and although it has often enough been considered only in terms of these qualities, in the context of our problem—the relationship of history to intellectual system—the main line of Western thought has in fact assigned to history a constructive and unifying function. If we examine the thinkers who were both theorists of history and historians, whether as seismographers of cataclysmic contemporary history or as chroniclers of the remoter past, then we find that in case after case history becomes intellectually fruitful for them when the logic of their ideas has brought them to an impasse that opens up their systems to impulses from outside the systems. Only those whose systems have reached such a stage have been intellectually sensitive to circumstances, whether in the form of contemporary cataclysm or older history, for they have required a unifying force from a completely different axis of reality to repair the rent in their ideas caused by logic alone. Hence they have fed into their theory of history the nonlogical ordering of reality from actual history, and they have thereby equipped their idea of history with the power to supply a new kind of unifying principle to their system of ideas. Each thinker has, to be sure, worked this alchemy in his own way, but a common formal pattern can be ascertained: each man started with an idea of history that was a function of his systematic thought; and when the consistency of this thought cracked under the pressure of its internal tensions, a new experience of circumstantial reality, in part evoked by intellectual need and in part pressing in from without, altered the idea of history from a derivative to an independent contingent order and assigned it an active role in re-unifying the logically divided system.

What has changed, along with the development of the idea of history, has been not the general synthetic function of history but the way in which history does its synthesizing—a change that falls into two main stages. This function, this development, and this change are now our business.

Our story begins with the very opening of the modern period of our culture, for the "revolution in history" which scholars have assigned to the sixteenth century refers in good measure to the conjunction of a new role for human history with the new emphasis upon nature, man, and morals which we still associate with modernity. Leo Strauss has brilliantly described the intellectual tendency of the age to turn from philosophy to history, spurred by its novel bent toward the practical application of ideas and registered in such influential figures as Bodin, Lipsius, Bacon, and the early Hobbes. Men of this period turned to history first to find a better source than mere precept for effecting the practice of valid philosophical norms and then, increasingly, to find a source for the replacement of those philosophical norms whose validity was being undermined by internal doubt.[1] What we may now add is the notice of the political and social cataclysms which punctuated this same era, through figures like Machiavelli, Guicciardini, Bodin, Grotius, Hobbes, and Pufendorf, and which turned men's attention to the original power of circumstance in history, joining with the practical development of the intellectual system to create a new role for history.

From this angle of vision, the modern idea of history and the modern problem of history begin with a miniature cataclysm. Because the "barbarian" invasion of 1494 disrupted and finally engulfed a whole small but self-inclosed culture of Italian city-states, it was experienced as a cataclysm whose effects were felt all the way from the actualities of politics to the ideas of human destiny. It awakened Niccolò Machiavelli and Francesco Guicciardini, the first of the recognizably modern thinkers, to set the pattern for posterity by indicating the constructive role of history in a rational dilemma that would become typical. Both Machiavelli and Guicciardini tried to work out the maxims of human behavior in the civic context of a city-state culture. They shared originally in the contemporary humanistic idea of history which would mine the Roman past for confirmation of the principles of civic life, but they shared too, each in his own way, in the moral dilemma that had been developing within Renaissance thought between the implications of the civic ideal as an ethical principle and the implications of the civic idea as a category of political reality. The fascinating and unresolved interplay of both in Machiavelli's *Discourses on Livy* and the equally fascinating dialectic on the potential and the actual principles of human nature in Guicciardini's *Ricordi* furnish striking evidence of the internal debate which, however unsystematically, manifested the strains in the logic of late Renaissance ideas. Into this intellectual tension burst the perception of the cataclysm, transformed by both men into contemporary history—by Machiavelli in *The Prince* of 1513 and Guicciardini in his unfinished *History of Florence* of 1508–9. This perception exploded their intellectual tensions into an open break in their ideas as the massive proportions of the change severely limited the validity of the traditional humanist principles of human behavior that could not account for them. The last enterprises which Machiavelli and Guicciardini un-

---

1. Leo Strauss, *The Political Philosophy of Thomas Hobbes: Its Basis and Genesis* (Chicago, 1963), pp. 82–98.

dertook were histories of their native Florence and Italy, Machiavelli between 1520 and 1525 and Guicciardini between 1538 and 1540, and both juxtapose historical events with civic philosophy in the attempt to make the actual unit of historical fact the common source of the surprising divergence of real and moral principles at work in the fading world around them.[2]

The extension of the historical revolution to the rest of Europe during the sixteenth and seventeenth centuries, however much prepared by the intellectual tensions arising from the blends of the new humanism with a far greater persistence of medieval elements in the "barbaric" north, had its own cataclysmic trigger. It was not the religious reform itself that was so experienced but, rather, the political and social convulsions that accompanied it. The civil wars in France and the Netherlands, the Thirty Years' War in Europe, and the Puritan revolution in England were so many local variants of the cataclysm that influenced the idea of history and therewith the relations between historical and rational truth in such representative theorists as Bodin and Grotius and in the rigorous system of Thomas Hobbes, where it assumed a fixed form paradigmatic of the "age of reason."

Grotius represents but one side of our syndrome, for, although he was a historian, he developed no clearly defined idea of history which aligned his historical work with his general thought. But he is historically notable for us because he absorbed both the domestic and the international convulsions of religious politics in the early seventeenth century. The difference between the formal statement of his juristic principles in the limited context of his work on the *Law of Prizes* in 1604 and the classic development of them, in his *Law of War and Peace* of 1625, into principles of universal law which organize the diverse practices of all mankind can be in good part explained by his intervening experience of contemporary history. From the fact of pervasive conflict, he elicited a notion of the general connection among men which his ill-assorted combination of rational and empirical principles in the law could not in itself afford him.

But it was with Bodin and Hobbes that the massive conflict which introduced the modern age found its typical embodiment in the function of history, for with them the receptivity to the circumstances of contemporary history was combined with both a striving for intellectual system and a theory of history appropriate to it. The pattern for

---

2. Felix Gilbert, *Machiavelli and Guicciardini: Politics and History in Sixteenth-Century Florence* (Princeton, N. J., 1965), pp. 267–70, 280–82, 291–97.

this functioning of history in the early modern period was drawn first loosely by Bodin and then made definite and memorable in the rigorous structure of Hobbes. Early in his career, Bodin aspired to the construction of what he himself called a "system" of universal law which would go beyond the bewildering amalgam of concepts from Aristotle and principles from the Roman law that he had inherited. For this construction he enlisted the aid of history, outlining in his *Method for the Easy Comprehension of History* of 1566 the alternation of juristic analysis in the logical style of Ramus and historical interpretation in an unprecedented comparative mode to achieve the empirically tested logical sequence of general outline, forms, postulates, definitions, and rules that would comprise his universal jurisprudence.[3] There followed for him a decade of practical activity in strife-torn France, as a royal legist, as party member of the *Politiques,* and as representative in the Estates General, ever pressing for the unification of the country and ever more susceptible to the internal rift in his thinking between the general logic of the law and the particular diversity of the legal practices by which it was tested. The impact of his experience upon the tenuous structure of his thinking produced Bodin's monumental *Six Books of the Republic* in 1576, in which the function of history shifts from its vague status as the empirical support of *legal* reasoning to its definite incorporation into a *political* system as the organic principle in the complex structure of power.[4] Bodin's experience of contemporary history thus helped to jell the loosely connected principles of a universal jurisprudence into the tightly articulated principle of political sovereignty, and with this development the role of history changed from inductive support of legal propositions to constructive mediation between the diversity of legal practices and the unity of political principle. In this context, Bodin used history to show how the various kinds of states and the various kinds of administration within each kind of state were historically devised to execute, under differing circumstances, the same principle of a supreme and undivided sovereignty.

The point of Bodin's performance was the use of history to create a system of politics within which history then becomes unrecognizable, and in Hobbes—as his antihistorical reputation attests—this synthesizing function of history was carried through to its logical conclusion.

    3. John Bodin, *Method for the Easy Comprehension of History,* English trans. Beatrice Reynolds (New York, 1945), pp. 2–3; Jean Moreau-Reibel, *Jean Bodin et le droit public comparé dans ses rapports avec la philosophie de l'histoire* (Paris, 1933), pp. 52–57.
    4. Julian H. Franklin, *Jean Bodin and the Sixteenth-Century Revolution in the Methodology of Law and History* (New York, 1963), p. 73.

The early Hobbesian idea of history, evidenced in the Preface of his Thucydides translation of 1628, helped to replace Hobbes's initial unsatisfactory Aristotelianism by the concern for the actual laws of motion and the practical direction of human action that produced his relentless system of political philosophy. This pragmatic idea of history can be recognized as an integral component of his system in the form of the hypothetical development of man from the state of nature into political society and the possible development from the past imperfect into a future perfect tense of this society—developments which can be viewed as steps of a rational logic cast in the form of a historical sequence for the sake of its verisimilitude.[5]

But to this internal evolution of Hobbes's idea of history, powered by the successive intellectual impulses of Hobbes's humanism and his scientific rationalism, must be added the external effects of his actual involvement in the English civil war. We may leave aside, as inessential, the rearrangement it persuaded him to make in the execution of this system whereby he worked out his political theory first, with brief prefaces on the nature of man, rather than as the concluding work of the tripartite deductive sequence in which he originally planned to descend to politics from prior analyses of nature and man. We may leave aside too, on the principle of Occam's razor, the confirmation which the rebellion brought to his theoretical deduction of the intolerable alternatives to undivided sovereignty. But what was essential in his extended experience of the cataclysm, and what perhaps can be seen only from the point of view of this experience, was the awareness it opened in him of the distinctively contingent—that is, logically independent—character of history.

The argument has been made, with some justice, that Hobbes came to deprecate explicit history as he developed from the *Elements of Law* in 1640 to the *Leviathan* of 1651 and replaced the practical ethical function of history with the political philosophy in which it was submerged.[6] But still, in the *Leviathan* as in the *Elements of Law*, Hobbes persisted in classifying history as one of the two main branches of knowledge: history registers the knowledge of facts alongside philosophy, which registers the rational (or "scientific," as he called it) knowledge of propositions and their necessary connections.[7] While the

5. Strauss, *Hobbes,* pp. 95–105; Raymond Polin, *Politique et philosophie chez Thomas Hobbes* (Paris, 1953), p. 98.

6. Strauss, *Hobbes,* pp. 96–98.

7. Thomas Hobbes, *Leviathan* (Oxford, 1909), Part I, chap. ix; Hobbes, *The Elements of Law, Natural and Politic,* ed. Ferdinand Tönnies (Cambridge, 1927), Part I, chap. vi.

logical proceedings of reason deliver the more certain knowledge, still the autonomy and indispensability of history is preserved in his distinction between historical knowledge as "absolute" and logical knowledge as "conditional," since a fact either is or is not, while reasoning is conditional upon the existence of the subject reasoned about. In his subsequent division of the fields of knowledge, he assigned political philosophy to the realm of logic, and it was only from the partial point of view of his rational system that he either derogated the arbitrary quality of historical contingency or turned it into a hypothetical function of his logic.

But history did remain for Hobbes a sphere of knowledge necessarily independent of his use of it as an existential postulate of his political reasoning; it was through his experiencing of his contemporary circumstances in the form of contemporary history that he maintained his feel for the independent function of history beyond the mere epistemological assertion of it. Around 1668, toward the end of his long life, Hobbes wrote his *Behemoth*, subtitled *The History of the Causes of the Civil War*—a work in which he invoked cataclysm to make history perform its inimitable task of filling with fact the gap between the multiplicity of individual passions and the singularity of rational authority in his political logic. The title itself indicates history's status, in the reference of history to the biblical land-monster, *Behemoth*, representing the persistence of chaos, as the complement of philosophy's analysis of the sea-monster, *Leviathan*, representing the mastery over chaos. The content of the work indicates the function of history, which is to explain what philosophy cannot explain—disorder within the state as the link between the original natural chaos and the ultimate political order. History supplies to reason not simply the materials from which it must abstract its propositions but, more fundamentally, the real parties and issues which provide the actual meeting ground and resolution for oppositions that cannot be resolved by reason alone.

Behemoth is historical in content rather than in form: it is a dialogue that reads more like the analysis of a negative case according to the principles of Hobbesian political science than either a description of a historical situation or a narrative of historical events. Even in this final resort to history, Hobbes thus dressed it in the logical forms that were to become standard for much of history in the seventeenth- and eighteenth-century ages of reason and confusing to historiographers thereafter.

The ambiguous position of history in the eighteenth-century Enlightenment, mainly derivative from rational principles but also provocative of independent interest and creative thought, was schematically projected in the reciprocal but unbalanced relationship which Hobbes set up between the system of scientific and moral reason and the history of human actuality. For the standard-bearers of Enlightenment, as for Hobbes, the rational network of meaning was primary, and to this extent history was primarily a function of it, supplying the materials of its mesh, the proofs of its reality, and the stages of its development. But however subordinate this intellectual function of history may have continued to be in its ends, it also continued to predicate what we have already seen in Hobbes—an independent origin of history in a kind of truth different from reason and necessary to it. Indeed, this autonomous dimension in the role of history was far more overt for the eighteenth-century philosophers than for their more rationalistic forbears by virtue of the scions' far greater appreciation of act, variety, and movement in the world and their far lesser commitment to unbroken chains of logic. More prominently than in Hobbes, then, did history come to be invoked not only to illustrate ideas that were firmly held but to contribute a unifying impetus to ideas that were otherwise paralyzed in logical dilemma.

Of logical dilemmas, the Enlightenment, as recent studies have stressed, suffered aplenty, and while these dilemmas encouraged the autonomous function of history which was their beneficiary, it also roused skepticism about the idea of history as a function of the rational principles which were themselves being thrown into doubt. But in part because of the comparatively unsystematic character of eighteenth-century thinking and in part because of the comparative placidity of its social and political circumstances, the questioning of the rational coherence behind Enlightenment ideas, including the exemplary function of history in it, did not achieve fundamental formulation and memorable status until the conjunction of Kant and the French Revolution.

Prior to this conjunction, the only human events to register a cataclysmic effect were those produced by Louis XIV's blend of domestic despotism and international aggression, and the only historical thinkers who clearly experienced it as such, Bayle and Leibniz, did not, for different reasons, clarify the relationship between autonomous and derivative history whose ambiguity was the essence of Enlightenment historiography. Stimulated by the tyrannical obscurantism that drove him into exile, Bayle applied historical criticism to doctrine and rational criticism to history, but his bent was so skeptical and the logic of his own beliefs so unarticulated that he did not work out any constructive function for history. Leibniz' was a more complicated case and a much

nearer miss, for through the ecumenical program with which he responded to the European crisis, his perception of that crisis conditioned
both the systematic philosophy and the narrative history that came
from his pen. And yet Leibniz himself remained too faithful a protagonist of the Enlightenment to do more than repeat its formulas for
history and remain apparently oblivious to the way in which his
metaphysics and his experience were covertly pushing him beyond
them. He made a fundamental principle of the Enlightenment's distinction between the necessary truths of logic and the contingent truths of
historical fact. He adumbrated the Enlightenment too by combining an
addiction to the writing of history with the assignment to history of a
merely illustrative function for general principles and with the deprecation of its merely contingent truths aside from that function.[8] Actually,
Leibniz's monadology injected a dynamic and individualizing force into
the logical development of eternal truths that may well have been influenced by the agitated conditions of his age and that had its own influence upon later historical thinking. But for Leibniz himself, the
circumstantial impact of his contemporary history upon his metaphysics
has not been traced, and the function of history in it, given the complete
absence of historical residue in his logical movement, may well be un-
traceable.

The culture of the Enlightenment surmounted the crisis of war and
conscience that ushered in the eighteenth century by cynically accepting
the one as a running sore and shrewdly avoiding the ultimate assumptions of the other behind its typically loose combination of reason and
reality. The intellectual tension between the actualities of life that
eighteenth-century men appreciated and the rational connections that
gave them meaning yielded two notable kinds of challenge to the dominant notion of history as a distinct kind of knowledge whose primary,
albeit not exclusive, function was to furnish a real ground for rational
principle. No more than the earlier notions of Bayle and Leibniz did
these challenges raise the understanding of history's function to a new
level, but they did presage the direction this understanding would take.

The first of these challenges, embodied in the line of writers from
Vico to Herder who led what Carlo Antoni has called "the fight against
reason," need not detain us. However important their historism may
have been for later developments in the idea of history, it did little to
clarify the intellectual use of history: it applied history as the principle

---

8. Lewis W. Spitz, "The Significance of Leibniz for Historiography," *Journal of the
History of Ideas*, XIII (1952), 333–48.

of variety against reason as the principle of uniformity, but accompanied it with no alternative structure of cogent thinking in which historical knowledge found a valid role. Such, indeed, was the emphasis of a Vico or a Herder upon plurality and discontinuity as fundamental principles that scholars are still puzzling over the connections they did not articulate.

The second kind of challenge to the idea of history dominant in the Enlightenment was a challenge that grew from within and was represented in David Hume. More than the historists' attack from outside the citadel did the distinctive emphasis which Hume placed upon history within the general scheme of the Enlightenment lay bare the covert function that history was playing in it. A respected crony of the *philosophes*, Hume shared in the fundamental tenets and values of the Enlightenment—its skepticism, its attraction to the concrete, its practicality, its belief in the constancy of nature—but he quietly dissented from the way in which the standard-bearers of the Enlightenment put them together. It was not, indeed, his theory of history that was remarkable, for he did not much address himself to its theory, and when he did his assertion of history's pragmatic uses and the alternation of cycles and progress in his patterning of it were hardly unusual for his age.[9] What was unusual and suggestive was the relationship which history bore to the rest of his thought, for this relationship, in conjunction with Hume's critique of the Enlightenment's standard version of rational coherence, emphasized the autonomous side of history's unifying function in such a way as to raise doubts about its derivative function under reason.

The indisputable fact of the matter is Hume's deliberate turn, in the decade of the 1750's, from philosophy to history as the main field of his intellectual endeavor. The reason behind this fact remains highly disputable. The personal cataclysm that he experienced of a complete public unresponsiveness to his *Treatise of Human Nature*, the personal cataclysm that he feared from his further prosecution of skeptical attacks on religious tradition, the philosophical dilemma into which he fell when he denied all coherence save that which he tried in vain to find among the vagaries of human nature—these factors have all been adduced, and none has been generally accepted. But whatever the cause, the fact of Hume's distinctive focus on history, combined with his undistinctive idea of history, shifted the locus of coherence from the rela-

9. John B. Stewart, *The Moral and Political Philosophy of David Hume* (New York, 1963), pp. 288–301.

tions of ideas to the relations of facts and showed that history could serve as the same kind of ordering medium as the logic of abstract reason. For if Hume subscribed neither to a necessary connection between ideas nor to the primacy of reason among the human faculties, he did subscribe to general principles in human nature; and, in his attempt to elicit them and their non-logical relations, he stumbled on history as a vehicle for organizing the varieties of human reality.

But it was only in the half-century from the French Revolution to the European revolutions of the mid-nineteenth century that the function of history as the empirical source of and test for general principles whose validity lay outside of history was isolated, subjected to rigorous analysis, mined for its paradoxes, and reconstructed into the final formulation of the synthesizing usefulness of history considered as the field of past human reality. Frankly recognizing diversity and unity as fundamental logical antitheses and remorselessly driven by the generalizing passion of reason to overcome them, Kant, Hegel, and Marx absorbed the experience of their contemporary revolutions and under their influence developed the idea of history into the process conducting the principle of diversity toward the principle of unity—Kant through a factual emergency detour, Hegel through the reciprocal historization of logic and logicization of history, and Marx, finally, through the total historization of logic.

Kant dovetailed rational antinomy and circumstantial cataclysm in his intellectual development and emerged with a new consciousness of the importance—and the problem—of actual history in the hypothetical union of reason and history. In the decades before the revolution, Kant had worked out his critical philosophy in terms of the categorical distinction between the realms he variously labeled knowledge and action, nature and freedom, particularity and universality. During this period, he assigned history—in his essays of 1784 on *What is Enlightenment?* and an *Idea for a Universal History from a Cosmopolitan Point of View*—to the realm of nature, with the variety of individual human actions becoming comprehensible only if they were organized under a hypothetical, collective principle of progress based on a natural analogy with the moral unity in the sphere of freedom. The French Revolution broke in upon him just as he was striving to bridge the gulf between his two realms by means of the teleological mediation attempted in the second part of his *Critique of Judgment*. He could not here get beyond the provision of a logical foundation for the regulative, or hypothetical, use of the teleological principle in nature on the analogy from moral ends, and in this situation the French Revolution appeared to him a massive moral act, entering and convulsing the world of nature.

Hence it was more than a mere figure of speech when Marx called Kant the German version of the French Revolution. Because the revolution meant to Kant the creation of political and social circumstances as an effect of a unified moral will, he henceforward looked to the state and society as the arena and to history as the process by which moral freedom would be realized and humanity led from a natural aggregate into an ethical community. History could thus be read as the record of the events through which the mechanical ordering of circumstances external to and compelling upon man gradually yields to the organic coherence of circumstances rationally produced by men acting together in the world of experience under the moral law.

Both in its achievements and in its limitations, Kant's position on history epitomized the Enlightenment of which he was at once paragon and critic. His achievements were to demonstrate the fundamental polarity in the structure of thought which opened it to effects from contingent events and, by raising particularity in circumstance and individuality in action to the status of basic principles rather than mere functions of the universal, to make the historical realm the arena for the interaction of fundamental ideas.

But Kant's position on history also threw into the limelight the two limitations which would require its reconstruction. First, his revised idea of history still was more hypothetical than actual, and now was more implicit than explicit. The validity of history remained for him as conditional upon its capacity to make the contradictions of politics make sense as it had been on its capacity to make the antinomies of human nature make sense, but the same hypothesis of a specifically historical development from natural compulsion toward moral freedom became much less identifiable as such when he made it a tendency of a politics that he already conceived as an intermediate realm between nature and freedom than when he had imposed it upon the mechanism of human nature. Second—and this was the substantive limitation obviously connected with the first—the function which Kant now attributed to history was indeed crucial and unique, but only as a central arena for the relationship of supra-historical principles that could relate in no other way. Human circumstance was either a phenomenon of nature or the product of a moral act. History generated no principle of its own; it was essential as the residual mode of reality for a human nature that could not realize its ends directly and immediately, and it was essential as the hybrid mode of knowledge for measuring the relations of a nature and a morality subject to two categorically different forms of reason. However essential the facts of history were for bringing the different modes of reality and of knowledge into conjunction, for Kant the process of history remained the function of extra-historical principles.

Hegel's contribution to the utility of history was, for our purpose, transitional: he developed the logic of the Kantian ideas into categories appropriate for the reception of historical circumstance, but he merely juxtaposed the compatible categories of logic and history that Marx then blended. As an object of history for us, moreover, Hegel is not centered on our problem of assessing the impact of circumstance upon established thought systems. However well founded the familiar judgment of his continuity attention to contemporary social and political conditions may be, the only traceable impact upon the main structure of his thought is the cataclysmic perception of the French Revolution which is apparent in his *Phenomenology*. But this perception contributed to the formation of, rather than a confrontation with, his system.[10] Impelled both by his own drive to overcome Kant's limits and by his experience of the overwhelmingly dynamic character of human existence, Hegel performed for history the service of integrating the cognate principles of particularity, individuality, and mobility into a continuously unifying process of logic itself. Thereby he enabled the knowledge of history to illuminate logical categories which seemed tailored for it. This was service indeed, but it must not be overstated, as it sometimes is. Whatever the role of history in the original construction of Hegel's system—in the early and flexible *Phenomenology* analysis and history are ingeniously if problematically conjoined—the *mature* structure so thoroughly absorbed the principles of individuation, alienation, and activity into a purely logical and metaphysical process that it no longer needed history either for its movement or for proof of its reality. The movement of the mind along the categories of logic and the movement of human action along the medium of time are parallel movements of spirit. Not only the pattern of Hegel's system but the difficulties which he encountered in attuning the actual record of the past to the logical requirements of spirit in his *Philosophy of History* make obvious the ultimately supra-historical nexus which was to become submerged in the historical realism of Karl Marx.

Marx represents the climax of the tradition of Western thought that would find in the *facts* of human history a unitary basis for the discursive or polar diffraction of ideas. His original idea of history, developed during the 1840's in the intellectual context of the Young Hegelian human-

10. Z. A. Pelczynski, "Introductory Essay," in *Hegel's Political Writings* (Oxford, 1964), p. 5; G. W. F. Hegel, *The Phenomenology of Mind*, English trans. J. B. Baillie (New York, 1931), pp. 75, 599–610.

ization of Hegel's categories and the social context of uncrystallized movements toward reform, historized the Hegelian logic so thoroughly that he abolished in principle any distinction between logic and history, between essential and contingent truths. The dialectical form of reality was produced by the specific actions of actual men who sought continuously to recover the integrity they had themselves alienated. The process of human circumstances and the process of human ideas were not two different processes relating to two different kinds of reality but only two stages of human activity, measurable by history: circumstances were deposits of past human action, ideas the concomitants of present human action.

But when the catastrophe of 1848 broke upon this system, its carefully hidden seams began to show, and what seemed like a unitary rational historical process separated, under the impact of events in which no one acted as he should, into three strata: the development of underlying "forces" embodying the logic of society, the empirical record of contemporary events occurring under the influence of circumstances now regarded as alien, and the intermediate level of history whose function was to relate the two other levels of human reality. Henceforward, Marx and Engels were to stress such logical tools as economic analysis and the theory of evolution to buttress the "natural laws" of a system in which history served to mark the stage that had in fact been attained. Thus, Marx carried to its logical conclusion the traditional idea of a history whose intellectual usefulness consisted in the positive grounding supplied by historical fact to a rational process that was itself independent of history.

Since the middle of the nineteenth century, the star of history has risen as the belief in rational systems has waned. The two movements are obviously related, and the increasingly pervasive solvent use of history against the stability of ideas and ideals can be viewed as the crowning success of a skeptical function that goes back at least to Lorenzo Valla in the fifteenth century. But there is another, countervailing use of history in our modern period. It continues in another form the constructive tradition that we have been describing, and it becomes visible if we approach it with our double vision of cataclysm and contingency. For as the scope of the rational systems that supplied the coherence both outside and inside history has shrunk, the size and the range of the political and social cataclysms that make up our contemporary history have magnified until they are no longer simple events but networks of internal relations that are themselves connected with the effects they produce. Under the combined influence, then, of an intellectual tendency which has progressed from the dissolution of stable systems to the dissolution of stable facts, and of a cataclysmic experience which has called increasingly for the internal logic of the fact, history has resumed its synthesizing function, but now not so much through its positive factuality as through the non-logical ordering of its temporal sequences and simultaneities. In other words, where history once provided facts to serve as the positive grounding of extra-historical coherences, it now provides a coherence to serve as a chronological ordering of any kind of facts.

The intellectual assumptions behind this function of history are visible negatively in the apparently antihistorical tirades of a Nietzsche and positively in the historiocentric philosophy of the young Croce. In the light of his friend Burckhardt's explicit endorsement of the "sudden devaluation of all mere 'events' of the past," we may see in Nietzsche's castigation of the "historical disease," directed against the burden of the dead past upon the life of the present and future, an attack upon the traditional usage of historical fact, both because the fact itself was dead—"lumber," as Burckhardt called it—and because Nietzsche, like Burckhardt, disbelieved in the extra-temporal systems it was wont to serve. Unlike Burckhardt, who found "continuity" as well as "mutability" within history, the history that Nietzsche did believe in had no coherence of its own but drew its sustenance from the present aesthetic and religious needs of the living individual. It was, indeed, precisely in the negation that took him beyond Burckhardt that Nietzsche adumbrated a new and fruitful function for history: where Burckhardt still sought to capture the "immorality" of "the spirit" through "the recurrent, constant, and typical" in history and thus internalized the old quest for stability within history, Nietzsche recognized in history the principle of mutation and would use it as such to convert discrete aims into unified process.[11] It may not be too much to read into his later idea of "eternal recurrence"—a recurrence bereft of either the cyclical regularity of tradition or the spiritual continuity of Burckhardt—Nietzsche's attempt to define for human history the principle most appropriate to its ultimate contingent quality.

But it was only with the generation of historicism around the turn of our century that the unease with "scientific," or "positivistic," or "objective," or "empirical" history—as the target of the same rejection is vari-

11. Jacob Burckhardt, *Force and Freedom: Reflections on History,* ed. James Hastings Nichols (Boston, 1964), pp. 52, 82–85; Friedrich Nietzsche, *The Use and Abuse of History,* English trans. Adrian Collins (New York, 1957), pp. 38–39, 69–73.

ously labeled—revealed the fundamental reorientation toward history that underlay the aesthetic distaste and polemical quibbles of the critics. What was denied was not simply the historical school under attack but the whole traditional approach to history as the record of past facts, and it was denied not so much on the ostensible grounds of the death, the externality, and the unknowability of such facts as on their essential incapacity, under contemporary intellectual assumptions, to carry on the synthetic function which had always been history's primary contribution to Western thought and was now more than ever required of it. The general intellectual revolution that accompanied the dawn of the new century dismantled the old stable absolutes and therewith the mediating function of the particular historical events in which they engaged one another. In its stead the revolutionaries developed their own idea of history, which preserved its mediating function by transforming it from the recording of past events to the perspective on temporal process. Where history had provided a factual realm for the meeting of universal principles it would now provide a unifying process for the coherence of relative principles. The intellectual systematizers of the pre–World War I era sketched only the general forms of the new history their systems called for; it took the successive cataclysms of our century to give the historical perspective an independent direction and a constructive place in contemporary thought.

Croce was the pivotal figure in the reorientation, for he first gave the most rigorous and categorical definition of the historical perspective in response to the intellectual requirements of prewar thought, and he then showed how a content for it could be developed in response to the social cataclysms of this century. In the essays of 1912 and 1913 that he later assembled into the well-known *Theory and History of Historiography,* Croce rejected the traditional notion that history was concerned with "the factual truth" of the past precisely because he deemed "brute facts" to be "disconnected" from one another and "extrinsic" to the rational notions of cause-and-effect or of final ends that had to be imposed on the facts in order to connect them. The distinction of the historical from the non-historical is a matter not of "the quality of the facts" but of "two different spiritual attitudes," for history consists essentially in "inseparable syntheses of individual and universal," and, since there are no "universal and permanent 'facts'" to be found in history, only the universal perspective of the historian can produce the true synthesis that is history.[12] For the prewar Croce, indeed, the historical perspective had

12. Benedetto Croce, *History: Theory and Practise* (New York, 1960), pp. 18–82.

become *the* synthetic mode of consciousness indispensable to the unity
of his general thought. He designed the *Theory and History of Historiography* as the final volume of his systematic *Philosophy of the Spirit,* to
supply the continuity for the aesthetic, logical, and practical moments
of the mind that could not otherwise be internally related.

But if this view of life as an essentially historical process promoted
history over both art and logic as the primary medium for the organization of human reality, it did not thereby close out systematic thought or
the tensions attendant thereto. For Croce and his fellow-historicists of
prewar vintage, the reversal of roles that now vested the unity of knowledge in the flow of history and its discontinuous structures in discrete
values and principles finessed indeed the old tensions between primary
values or principles, but these were replaced by a new tension between
the two termini of the historical perspective which rendered doubtful
the derivation of any value or principle whatsoever. The two termini
were, of course, the life that was to be known historically and the mind
of the historian who was to know it, and since the primary relation between them was now deemed to be precisely the characteristic historical
relationship of change, the projected unity of the historical process
seemed limited to the purely formal unity of time and decomposed, for
the rest, into a contradictory welter of variety in transit.

With this intellectual impasse, the way was once more open for the
invasion of circumstance, and the successive cataclysms of two total
wars connected by peace-time totalitarianism expanded the experience
of circumstance into a massive intellectual force. Croce himself revealed
its power, for despite his well-known "Jovian" separation of direct political influences, the transmuted evidence of cataclysm is traceable in his
work. Both his *History of Europe in the 19th Century* and his *History of
Italy,* written under fascism between the wars, stop with 1915, in recognition of the fundamental turn given by the war and its aftermath to the
liberalism whose principle was interwoven in his early philosophy.[13]
And when he came, in the Italy of 1938, to publish his *History as
Thought and as Action* (the literal title, translated under *History as the
Story of Liberty*), he admitted that he was resuming the subject of his earlier *Theory and History of Historiography* but was augmenting it with
"new considerations . . . stimulated by new experiences of life."[14] The
tendency of the additions revealed the lesson of the cataclysmic experi-

13. Hayden V. White, "The Abiding Relevance of Croce's Idea of History," *Journal of
Modern History* XXXV (1963), 122–23.
14. Benedetto Croce, *La storia come pensiero e come azione* (2d ed.; Bari, 1938), p. vii.

ence: the sense of the basic human needs that furnish common bonds of principle and of direction across the historical process. So Croce ended by converting historical variety into the principle of freedom, directing the open-ended historical process toward the cumulative progress in the range of choices open to every historically conscious actor, and skewing the balance of art, thought, and action toward its meaning for the freedom of the historian as an aesthetically and thoughtfully prepared actor in history.

But more impressive, both in the cogency of its definition and in the dramatic reversal of its former position, has been the existentialists' development of a coherent function for the historical process. Starting from the Nietzschean rejection of history as the most superfluous part of meaningless existence, the existentialists of our century, led by Jean-Paul Sartre, have developed, in the temporal dimensions of historicity, means of communications among individual existences otherwise isolated. Sartre has himself recapitulated the stages of the existentialist approach to history and in the course of this intellectual career becomes a model for the crystallizing effect of cataclysm upon thought. Sartre's early deprecation of history as the facticity of absurd existence and his consequent idea of history as the derivative function of the individual who uses the past only as the existential springboard into the present and future led to the philosophical disjunctions of *Being and Nothingness*, between the individualized existence that was the condition of human reality and the totalized goal that alone could give it meaning. From this dilemma he was jolted by World War II and its attendant resistance movement in France, an experience of contemporary history which led to the positive revaluation of history in his postwar *Critique de la raison dialectique*. Here he has developed a crucial role for the patterns of historical synchronization and sequence as the matrixes which bind the otherwise discrete and static groupings and categories of Marxist sociology together in a vital unity. However much or little we may subscribe to Sartre's existentialism or to his qualified Marxism, we should recognize in his initiation of a special historical logic to associate real groups and to connect transcendent ideas the culmination in our age of the long history of useful history.

If we consider the record of constructive history that we have just sampled, we can probably understand well enough how men used to find in historical fact a kind of reality in which there coexisted effects of ideas whose connection was otherwise doubtful or diffuse, but a question may be—nay, should be—raised about the more recent synthetic use of history, to wit: how can the historical perspective, which is predicated on individuality, variety, and change, be used in a synthesizing function that is predicated on generality, unity, and constancy? Or, in other terms: how can the occurrence of an event or the emergence of a situation before, after, or at the same time as another event or situation supply an intellectually satisfying connection of the ideas which these events and situations are taken to embody?

The later models in our story, to whom this question particularly applies, offer both a negative and a positive answer.

Negatively, no competing scheme of coherence now seems any more satisfactory than the temporal. Most of us indeed still try to live in accordance with a logical pattern of ideas that transcends local time, but however indispensable the logical *form* of our ideas remains, the *substantive* truth of the ideas that inhabit these forms has no dependably firmer basis than the historical process that brings them about.

Positively, the use of temporal relations as a system of coherence makes sense in terms of the special context for which this use has been developed: that is, the use of the historical perspective as a principle of action rather than of knowledge. Even in its most traditional usage as the edifying factual example of a higher law, to be sure, history was oriented toward action; but whatever the conflicts on the sources or effectiveness of knowledge, no fundamental distinction was yet drawn between the principles of knowledge and of action and therefore between the knowledge and the practical use of history. But, gradually, ever since Kant, we have been working out precisely such a distinction, and from the middle of the last century the positive side of this distinction—the unifying function of history itself in the realm of action—has become one of our more pervasive assumptions. However ambiguously, Comte initiated this redefinition of history in terms of action when, late in his career, he came increasingly to define his historical law of the three progressive states of human knowledge to be cumulative stages in the moral unification of consciousness for the purpose of social action. A generation later, Bergson supplied the unambiguous philosophical basis for this redefinition when he associated "pure knowledge" with spatial dispersion and "action" with the unity of consciousness to be found only in temporal duration.[15]

With the subterranean spread of such attitudes, the temporal relations which are contingent and non-logical from the point of view of

15. Frank E. Manuel, *The Prophets of Paris* (New York, 1965), pp. 287–92; Henri Bergson, *Matter and Memory*, English trans. N. M. Paul and W. S. Palmer (London, 1911), pp. 302–3.

knowledge can now be used as a logical kind of coherence in the categorically different realm of action. The two realms intersect, of course, and the confusion of the overlap is compounded by the inevitable carry-over of terms like reason, idea, and logic, which are native to the world of knowledge, into the qualitatively altered universe of action. But this, at least, is clear: however much the realities of action may repeat the truths of knowledge, the arrangement of them diverges radically for the two realms. The contemporary use of history for a logic of action presumes every producer and consumer of history to be a historical actor who must learn to synchronize the momentum from the past and the impact from the present in the unitary decision that precedes action. And this he learns both from the historical perspective that gives him a judgment of the temporal momentum coming to him out of the past and from the model of other historical actors who have registered precisely such syntheses of the temporal dimensions in the decisive deeds that have made past history.

So let us now, in conclusion, turn the lesson offered by our own models to the original problem of accommodating changing circumstance to the consistency and integrity of the ideas that make each of us a person. The lesson which they offer on the use of history would seem to be this: when the inner turmoil of our ideas and the force of social circumstance join to make the conditions in which we think and live both inexplicable and unmanageable, we may still save ourselves if we subject these conditions to a historical scrutiny. For we may thereby turn these conditions into a coherent series of events from which we may either abstract a general principle or project a probable future and, in either case, grasp a new reality intelligible enough to enter into the marrow of our thought. Around this new reality we must then organize our ideas into the desperate, forced unity required by the necessity of action upon the circumstances which paralyze our thinking. Under such conditions we must act to master cataclysm and make of circumstance our own creation, thereby to repair our fabric and equip ourselves for the next contingency. For it is through the alternation of reason and existence—not their mingling—that we grow.

4 HISTORY AND NATURAL LAW IN EARLY MODERN EUROPE

The primary importance of the XVIIth century for historiography . . . has less to do with the study of history itself than
with developments in the reigning non-historical dimension. . . .

In [seventeenth-century] politics, the dominant tendencies in both
external and domestic relations favored the exposition of law in
historical forms.

From "History and Law in the Seventeenth Century: Pufendorf"

11 History and Law in the Seventeenth Century: Pufendorf

There seems to be a connection between the social growth of a profession and its intellectual ambitions. Before its practitioners achieve autonomy, its field is ancillary to other kinds of knowledge. After the profession is absolutely secure, intellectual autonomy aspires to intellectual sovereignty. Certainly for many historians today the independence of their calling has as its intellectual counterpart an historical attitude toward life in general which mobilizes principles only recently well established. The relationship between historical experience and extra-historical presupposition has become a crucial problem in determining the principles of knowledge and of conduct. It may be worthwhile to refresh ourselves with the recollection of the original function of history at a time when its devotees were separating it out from other kinds of knowledge and in the person of an early professional caught in the process of parturition.

The time is the XVIIth century. For historiography this age was an interlude, its framework inherited and its efforts within that framework a store for the future. The great political history of the Renaissance statesmen, Machiavelli and Guicciardini, lay in the past; the great cultural history of the Enlightenment men of letters—Voltaire, Gibbon, Herder—was still to come. Certainly, as the historiographical manuals attest,[1] there was progress during the XVIIth century, but it was progress not so much in the products as in the materials of historical writing—the collections of sources, the criticism of documents, and the auxiliary sciences. The failure of the historical works that were raised upon this improved foundation to achieve new insights or interpretations of the historical process can be attributed to the continued prevalence of extra-historical occupations among the historians and of extra-historical preoccupations in their writings. The historians were politicians or officials, classicists, clergymen, and jurists. Where their vocational attach-

---

1. E.g., Eduard Fueter, *Geschichte der neuren Historiographie* (3rd ed., Munich, 1936), 307–310.

First published in the *Journal of the History of Ideas* 221:2 (April–June, 1960), 198–210. In a slightly different form, this paper was delivered at a session of the American Historical Association on December 28, 1958.

ment was not to the state or the church it was to universities in which they occupied chairs of theology, law, or of combined humanistic and historical studies—History and Poetry, History and Rhetoric, History and Philology, and the like. They were concerned, correspondingly, with clarifying ecclesiastical or legal tradition, with revising the traditional academic chronicles of universal history, and with refining the humanist tradition of history as exemplary past politics in its application to classical, national, or territorial materials.

The primary importance of the XVIIth century for historiography, then, has less to do with the study of history itself than with developments in the reigning non-historical conceptions which favored the growth within them of an historical dimension. These developments went beyond the much-remarked external connection between the critical empiricism of the new science and the progress in historical techniques, for they affected the very substance of the authoritative political and philosophical values. The most pertinent of these developments, for our purposes, were those which heightened the centrality of law.[2]

In politics, the dominant tendencies in both external and domestic relations favored the exposition of law in historical forms. Public attention was increasingly diverted from static ideals of the Christian community of rulers on the international stage and of the Christian hierarchy of authorities at home to the aggressive claims of independent territorial states against one another and of their sovereigns against their privileged subjects. Since this shift was an expansion rather than a rejection of the accepted standards of political conduct it called forth the enunciation of uniform legal principles in forms that would harmonize the old order with the new facts. Hence when princes or councils desired the justification of their foreign policies to the rulers, officials, and scholars of other powers in the new unstable system of states it was to the jurists that they turned for the historical validation of their acts. When governments or parties desired to justify their roles in recent in-

---

2. It should be emphasized here that the relations of law and history made up but one strand in the historiographical development of the XVIIth century. The relations of religion and history, which provided the framework simultaneously for the growth of pragmatic church history and for the improvement in the critical techniques of historical research, constitute the other main line in the emergence of history as an autonomous discipline. Despite the parallels that can be established for the growth of historical dimensions in legal and in religious doctrines, the problem of religion and history in the XVIIth century had its own process and will be considered towards the end of this paper only at the point where Pufendorf had contact with it.

ternal convulsions, commissioned scholars or advocates wrote national or contemporary history to show the constitutional and moral lawfulness of their actions. And when the wonted framework of universal history which had integrated politics into the religious scheme of the four empires was undermined during the XVIIth century by the growing secularism of political interests, it was to jurisprudence that the benefits of theological retrenchment accrued. The extension of its influence over the field of the political present entailed its predominant responsibility for reordering the political past, for the purpose both of explaining present politics and of setting examples for recommended policies. Thus the limited consciousness of the historical requirements of jurisprudence, which had emerged during the XVIth century in the 'French mode' of commentary upon Roman Law, grew by the end of the century into the more general coincidence of law and history in politics. If we take only the most prominent figures in the annals of political history and political theory between the late XVIth and the end of the XVIIth century this coincidence of law and history is striking indeed. The best-known political historians were probably de Thou, Bacon, Clarendon, and Pufendorf—all were jurists. Of the political philosophers, Bodin wrote on the philosophy of history, while both Grotius and Pufendorf were practicing historians. Hobbes, Spinoza, and Locke wrote no history,[3] but none of them was a lawyer either, whether by education or profession. Leibniz, the only one of the great metaphysicians

---

3. That is, they wrote no independent history works. This is not to deny Hobbes' and Spinoza's interest in history. Hobbes translated Thucydides' *Peloponnesian War* into English in 1629, and his *Behemoth: or an Epitome of the Civil War in England from 1640–1660*, published in 1679, can be considered a species of contemporary history, while his *Historical Narration concerning Heresie and the punishment thereof*, of 1680, falls overtly into the genre of religious history. But the Thucydides' translation was a humanist exercise undertaken before Hobbes turned either to philosophy or politics; the *Behemoth* is a moralistic dialogue; and the history of heresies was a brief pamphlet in defense of the *Leviathan*. It is generally agreed that for Hobbes historical knowledge occupied a distinctly derivative and merely rhetorical place. See Leo Strauss, *Political Philosophy of Hobbes: its Basis and Genesis* (Oxford, 1936), 80–107, and Raymond Polin, *Politique et philosophie chez Thomas Hobbes* (Paris, 1953), 81–86. As for Spinoza, his introduction of historical criticism of the Bible in the *Theologico-Political Treatise* of 1670 had little that was specifically historical about it. He admitted that his "method of interpreting scripture does not differ widely from the method of interpreting nature—in fact, it is almost the same," since it consists in "inferring the intentions of its authors as a legitimate conclusion from its fundamental principles" just as the definitions of natural phenomena are deduced from fixed axioms. See Ernst Cassirer, *The Philosophy of the Enlightenment* (Boston, 1955), 184–186.

of the century who applied himself to history, was trained in law at the University of Jena, and the juristic stamp was patent in his historical writing.

The juristic met the philosophical dimension of law in the secularized doctrines of natural law, which came to dominate XVIIth-century thought in the fields of ethics and politics. The impact of natural law upon history worked in two opposite directions at once. It established rules of behavior that were universally applicable to all times and places, and it assigned to human reason and human will, operating in *particular* times and places, the function of recognizing and of applying them. The problem posed for general history by these two facets of natural law during the XVIIIth century provided Friedrich Meinecke with the starting-point of his study on historicism.[4] But it was a problem that characterized the XVIIth-century proponents of natural law as well. Since, in the earlier century, the framework of absolutes was more inclusive and the sphere of history less inclusive, the issue was not yet the combination of general ethical and concrete historical factors into a system. Rather it was the dawning relationship of history to a system maintained as valid without it. It is true that for the XVIIth century as for the XVIIIth the relation of rational to empirical truth was the primary problem of knowledge, but empirical facts were themselves so much less homogeneous for the XVIIth century than they were to be for the XVIIIth century that the distinction between the empirical and the historical was a far more pressing problem for the earlier period than for the later. So we find that in the natural-law jurists of the XVIIth century the problem of history took two forms: it involved first the integration of empirical facts, in the form of legal precedent and custom, into the framework of rational principles; but it also involved the role of historical facts, in the form of separate works of political narration, *vis-à-vis* this empirico-rational legal system as a whole.

So much for the age. Now what about the man? Samuel Pufendorf was unique for the balance of law and history which characterized his professional life and influence. He was a jurist and an historian not by virtue of having simultaneous interests but by successive and exclusive profession. Between 1661 and 1677 Pufendorf was a professor of law, at Heidelberg until 1670 and thereafter at the Swedish University of Lund. His professional commitment to law during this period worked as a powerful personal drive within him; it bulked large in his decision

4. F. Meinecke, *Die Entstehung des Historismus* (2 vols., Munich, 1936).

to move from his native Germany to Sweden, for his irregular position as law teacher in Heidelberg's philosophical faculty rankled as much as the prospect of the post as topranking professor in Lund's law faculty gratified.[5] His subsequent dedication to history was hardly less complete. When Charles XI of Sweden appointed him to the joint post of court historian and secretary of state, Pufendorf abandoned both university and law, never to return. His function as secretary of state, moreover, was honorary rather than active;[6] the only extant evidence of activity in this capacity, a report in 1680 on the Franco-Swedish alliance, was largely historical in approach,[7] and what there is of his correspondence, silent as it is on any political or administrative business and full as it is of his historical concerns, reveals how unreservedly he held his duty to be that of state historian.[8] Nor did Pufendorf's move to Berlin in 1688 change the professional tenor of his life. He went as court historian and privy counsellor to Brandenburg's Great Elector, and his final years were absorbed in writing the history of the two Electors under whom he served.

The pattern of Pufendorf's publications confirms this clear-cut division of his career, for his writings as well as his functions were concentrated first on law and then on history.[9] During his historical phase he

5. Erik Wolf, *Grosse Rechtsdenker der deutschen Geistesgeschichte* (3rd ed., Tübingen, 1951), 325.

6. Heinrich von Treitschke, "Samuel Pufendorf," in *Historische und Politische Aufsätze* (Leipzig, 1897), IV, 268–269.

7. This is apparent from its title: *Dissertatio de Occasionibus Foederum inter Sueciam et Galliam*—title given in Paul Meyer, *Samuel Pufendorf: Ein Beitrag zur Geschichte seines Lebens* (Grimma, 1894), which contains the most complete listing extant of Pufendorf's works.

8. For Pufendorf's repeated acknowledgments that his historical labors left him no time for any other pursuits, see letters of Pufendorf to Thomasius, March 24, 1688 and Jan. 7, 1693, in Emil Gigas, ed., *Briefe Samuel Pufendorfs an Christian Thomasius* (Munich, 1897), 19, 71–72; also Pufendorf to Paul von Fuchs, Jan. 19, 1688, and to Ernst von Hessen-Rheinfels, July 8, or 18, 1690, in Konrad Varentrapp, ed., "Briefe von Pufendorf," *Historische Zeitschrift*, LXX (1894), 26–27, 196.

9. His main works on law were all published by 1677: *Elementorum Juris Prudentiae Universalis Libri Duo* (The Hague, 1660), recent English translation by W. A. Oldfather (Oxford, 1931); *De Obligatione erga Patriam* (Heidelberg, 1663); *De Statu Imperii Germanici ad Laelium Fratrem Dominium Trezolani Liber Unus* (Geneva, 1667), published under pseudonym Severinus de Monzambano Veronensis at The Hague, recent edition and German translation under title *Über die Verfassung des deutschen Reiches* (Berlin, 1922) by H. Bresslau; *Dissertatio de Republica Irregulari* (Lund, 1668); *De Jure Naturae et Gentium Libri Octo* (Lund, 1672; expanded ed., Frankfurt, 1684), recent English translation by C. H. Oldfather and W. A. Oldfather (Oxford, 1934); *De Officio Hominis et Civis Mixta*

wrote on law only in the special context of religion,[10] a context, which, as we shall see further on, made this activity consistent with his concern for history. Pufendorf admitted frankly, in his correspondence during the 80's, that his professional responsibilities as historian precluded any further work by him on the system of natural law, despite his acknowledgment of the need for it.[11] In terms of influence, moreover, Pufendorf, alone among his contemporaries, wrote works that were widely used as text-books for both juristic and historical students. Both his study *On the Law of Nature and Nations* of 1672 and his general history of Europe of 1682 were so applied. They were republished frequently down to the middle of the XVIIIth century, and appeared in Latin, German, French, English, and Russian editions.[12]

Legem Naturalem Libri Duo (Lund, 1673), an epitome of the *De Jure Naturae*, English translation by Frank G. Moore (New York, 1927); and assorted brief articles in *Dissertationes Academicae Selectiores* (Upsala, 1677).

Pufendorf's historical works were, with one exception, post-1677: *Einleitung zur Historie der vornehmsten Reiche und Staaten in Europa* (Frankfurt, 1682). Extended sections on the Papacy—the exception, published in 1674—and on Sweden were published separately. *Commentariorum de Rebus Suecicis Libri XXVI ab Expeditione Gustavi Adolphi Regis in Germaniam ad Abdicationem Usque Christinae* (Utrecht, 1686); *De Rebus a Carolo Gustavo Sueciae Rege Gestis Commentariorum Libri Septem* (Nurnberg, 1696); *De Rebus Gestis Friderici Wilhelmi Magni Electoris Brandenburgici Commentariorum Libri XIX* (Berlin, 1695); *De Rebus Gestis Friderici III Electoris Brandenburgici, post Primi Borussiae Regis Libri III Complectentes Annos 1688–1690. Fragmentum Posthumum ex Autographo Auctoris Editum* (Berlin, 1784). The only legal writing which Pufendorf undertook during his historical period was a series of rebuttals to criticisms of his *De Jure Naturae* (most, but not all, of these rebuttals were published in *Eris Scandica qua Adversus Libros de Jure Naturali et Gentium Óbjecta Diluuntur* (Frankfurt, 1686) and a version of his *De Statu Imperii Germanici* (the basis of the new edition published by J. P. Gundling for the Berlin Academy in 1706).

10. His *De Habitu Religionis Christinae ad Rem Publicam* (Bremen, 1687) and his *Jus Feciale Divinum sive de Consensu et Dissensu Protestantium, Exercitatio Posthumus* (Lübeck, 1695).

11. Pufendorf to Thomasius, Mar. 24, 1688, in Gigas, ed., *Briefe Pufendorfs*, 19.

12. The prevalence of piracy in copyrights during the XVIIth and early XVIIIth centuries makes it difficult to establish the precise number of editions which these works went through. I have counted 9 Latin editions of the *De Jure Naturae* by 1759, 7 French editions by 1771, 5 English editions by 1749, and single editions in German, Russian, and Italian; 16 Latin editions of the *De Officio* (a compendium of the *De Jure Naturae* designed specifically for student use) by 1769, 7 French editions by 1756 and single French editions in 1822 and 1830, 4 English editions by 1716, and a German edition in 1691; 5 German editions of the *Einleitung zu der Historie der vornehmsten Reiche . . . in Europa* by 1746, 10 English editions by 1764, 5 French editions by 1759, 3 Latin editions by 1704, and a Russian edition of 1718. For recent acknowledgment of the influence exercised during the XVIIth and XVIIIth centuries by Pufendorf's treatises on natural law, see Robert

But, as this reception indicates, Pufendorf was unique in his combination of law and history rather than in the quality of his work on either. Indeed, one is attracted to the paradox that his uniqueness consisted primarily in his being more representative than anyone else of the professional and intellectual attributes of his age. Neither the cautious courage of his legal doctrines, permitted by the limited autonomy of his position as professor of law, nor the political conformity of his history, dictated by governmental surveillance of his position as professional but official historian, was extraordinary. His application of the revolutionary geometrical method to jurisprudence; his eschewal of the revolutionary implications of natural-law doctrines for positive law and politics; his channeling of documentary sources into the humanist tradition of pragmatic political history; his retention of an orthodox religious faith—in his case Lutheranism—alongside his devotion to natural law and humanist history: these tendencies—and the problems implicit in them—were all characteristic of the times. They held even for Leibniz, creating an intellectual connection with Pufendorf over and above his substantive philosophical differences with and his explicit hostility toward the latter.[13] What distinguished Pufendorf was his articulation of the implicit relations among ideas which were generally shared.

What then, were Pufendorf's solutions for the problems of law and history?

His solution to the problem of working an empirical content into his natural-law doctrine offers few difficulties, for the merger of natural-law principles with traditional positive law and institutions was the most prominent feature of his system. Consequently, the procedure which he adopted toward this end is patent throughout his legal and political writing. Essentially, this procedure consisted in the adoption of a both-and attitude which was a testimony less of logical rigor than of the urge to account for as much of existence as possible. This attitude determined each of the three basic steps of his formal thought. First, the fundamental principles of morality included both rational principles, or

---

Derathé, *Jean-Jacques Rousseau et la science politique de son temps* (Paris, 1950), 78–84. For the use of Pufendorf's general history in German universities, see Emil Clemens Scherer, *Geschichte und Kirchengeschichte an den deutschen Universitäten* (Freiburg, 1927), *passim*, esp. 179.

13. The common influence stemmed from the Cartesian mathematician at Jena, Erhard Weigel, who taught both men. For Leibniz' strictures upon Pufendorf and for the misinterpretations upon which they were in part based, see Gaston Grua, *Jurisprudence universelle et théodicée selon Leibniz* (Paris, 1953), 23, 418, 421–423.

'axioms,' whose truth "flows from reason itself, . . . merely from the bare intuition of the mind," and experimental principles or 'observations,' based upon "the comparison and perception of individual details uniformly corresponding with one another."[14] This juxtaposition of empirical and rational approaches induced Pufendorf to insist upon man's temporal context—that is, to exclude the ideal of a perfect, or pre-lapsarian state of nature entirely from consideration[15]—and still to endow him with a constant character within that context. In the analysis of this character Pufendorf's syncretistic method led him to replace the psychological abstractions of social appetite and self-seeking passions, which Grotius and Hobbes had raised as polar opposites, with the more flexible notions of 'sociability (*socialitas*)' and 'weakness (*imbecillitas*),' which he conceived as complementary permanent attributes of human 'nature,' knowable from both the observation of the human experience and the dictates of moral reason, and interacting in proportions that varied with time, place, and circumstance.[16]

Secondly, in treating the substantive principles of natural law, Pufendorf's inclination was ever to subdivide his principles into propositions of equal validity, one categorical, the other comprehensive and adapted to experience. This natural law was founded both upon the rule of reason and upon the positive command of a superior.[17] It prescribed both duties that were absolute and duties that were conditional.[18] It legitimated both rights that were perfect—that is, valid and enforceable—and rights that were imperfect—that is, valid but unenforceable.[19] Thirdly, the application of natural to civil law was oriented toward the imposition of absolute criteria not so much for discriminating among positive laws and institutions as for recognizing, relating, and rationalizing them. Thus he acknowledged a broad field of discretion in the execution of natural law itself, since many of its precepts were 'indefi-

14. Pufendorf, *Elementorum* (trans. W. A. Oldfather), II, 209. This dual approach characterized his later natural-law work as well. "Now the dictates of sound reason are true principles that are in accordance with the properly observed and examined nature of things, and are deduced by logical sequence from prime and true principles." *De Jure Naturae* (trans. C. H. and W. A. Oldfather), II, 203.

15. *Ibid.*, II, 154–155; Samuelis Pufendorfii, *Eris Scandica, qua Adversus Libros de Jure Naturali et Gentium Objecta Diluuntur* (Frankfurt, 1759), 19, 32–33.

16. Pufendorf, *De Jure Naturae*, II, 205–219; Hans Welzel, *Die Socialitas als oberstes Prinzip der Naturrechtslehre Samuel Pufendorfs* (Heidelberg, 1930), 8–17; Wolf, *Grosse Rechtsdenker*, 319–320, 343–346.

17. Pufendorf, *De Jure Naturae*, II, 217–221.

18. Pufendorf, *Elementorum*, II, 159.

19. Pufendorf, *De Jure Naturae*, II, 118–119; *Elementorum, II, 289*.

nite,' and beyond this he admitted an even broader field of 'permission.' Here, natural law applied only very indirectly, through the derivative and formal criteria of equity and "the particular advantage of individual states."[20] In public law Pufendorf admitted the legitimacy of both absolute and limited sovereignty;[21] in private law he admitted the bulk of Roman law, with an admixture of German.[22]

But what does all this have to do with history? Actually we find no recognizable historical description or narration in Pufendorf's works on natural law. We cannot go beyond the observation that Pufendorf's appreciations of the alternative within the context of men's action in political society opens his system to a place for history. The kind of history which was possible within his natural-law system appeared not in his theoretical works but in his treatise on the German constitution,[23] the only publication of his juristic period which contained narrative history. His historical sketch of German constitutional development was in the context of his emphasis upon the real rather than the formal relationships of the German Empire, but in the final analysis it was not autonomous history, for it served primarily to be measured against Pufendorf's natural-law principle of sovereignty and to be used as evidence for the label of 'monstrous' which he affixed to the constitution.

What, then, was the relationship of Pufendorf's system to the independent historical works which he wrote as a professional historian? Certainly there was some continuity between the two. In terms of vocation, it can be pointed out that Pufendorf's general history of Europe, which received final form and publication while he was court historian in Stockholm, was apparently based upon lectures which he had given as professor of natural law at the University of Lund.[24]

The connection between the law and the history can be made in

20. Pufendorf, *De Officio* (F. G. Moore Eng. tr.), II, 125–126; *De Jure Naturae*, II, 32–33, 1132–1137.

21. *Ibid.*, II, 1063–1079.

22. R. Stintzing and Ernst Landsberg, *Geschichte der deutschen Rechtswissenschaft* (Munich, 1898), III, 15–16. But Pufendorf was no Romanist. He claimed that he had refused an appontment in Roman Law at Heidelberg, and he grounded both his appreciation of it and his deviations from it on the conformity of large parts but not all of the Roman Law with the natural law. Pufendorf to Thomasius, Oct. 16, 1688, in Varentrapp, ed., "Briefe," *Historische Zeitschrift*, LXX, 36–37; Dec. 1, 1688 and Apr. 9, 1692, in Gigas, ed., *Briefe Pufendorfs*, 32, 67; Pufendorf, *Eris Scandica*, 125.

23. Severinus de Monzambano, *De Statu Imperii Germanici ad Laelium Fratrem, Dominum Trezolani, Liber Unus* (Geneva [actually The Hague], 1667). It was written in 1664.

24. Pufendorf, *Einleitung*, preface; H. Treitschke, "Pufendorf," in *Aufsätze*, IV, 274.

terms of ideas as well. In both his general and his archival histories, Pufendorf's concentration on political and contemporary history, his pragmatic dictum that the value of history is, besides pleasure, its usefulness for policy-makers by showing examples of good and bad actions, and his frank espousal of 'the real interest' of states as the canon of such actions,[25] all manifest the mold of lawful politics into which his history was poured. This notion of 'the real interest' of states, in the more familiar designation of *raison d'état*, has been particularly stressed as the point of union between the natural-law system and the history,[26] for Pufendorf had used this idea in his theoretical writing to cover the flexible union of the duty prescribed upon the ruler to govern for the good of the people and his permitted right to interpret this duty variously in varying empirical conditions.

But we can carry the implications of Pufendorf's natural-law system even further, for it is an aid toward understanding the assumptions of Pufendorf's historical methodology. Pufendorf contended that the historian must be at the same time impersonal and partial. On the one hand, he must be no 'advocate,' but he must "report things as they happened, without favor or aversion;" he must reveal "not his own judgment" but "the uncorrupted truth from authentic sources for posterity."[27] On the other hand, however, Pufendorf insisted just as categorically that the historian "expresses with his pen the sentiments of the lord he serves;" "as public interpreter of the acts and motives of the prince or commonwealth whose history he writes he cannot avoid expressing their views."[28] Pufendorf himself never tried to reconcile these two assumptions of his history, but his political notion of the reason of state seems both objective enough and particular enough to cover them. Thus the outstanding characteristics of his archival histories of Sweden and of Brandenburg seem explicable by his use of 'reason of state' as his historical criterion: on its objective side, the focus on the contemporary

25. Pufendorf to Thomasius, Nov. 26, 1692, in Gigas, ed., *Briefe Pufendorfs*, 69; Pufendorf, *Einleitung*, preface.

26. Thus Ernst Salzer, *Der Übertritt des Grossen Kurfürsten von der schwedischen auf die polnische Seite während des ersten nordischen Krieges* in Pufendorfs 'Carl Gustav' und 'Friedrich Wilhelm' (Heidelberg, 1904), 13–19; F. Meinecke, *Die Idee der Staatsräson in der neueren Geschichte* (Munich, 1924), 279–303; Wolf, *Grosse Rechtsdenker*, 357–358.

27. Pufendorf to J. F. von Seilern, Mar. 5, 1690, in Varentrapp, ed., "Briefe," *Historische Zeitschrift*, LXX, 43–44; Pufendorf, *De Rebus Gestis Friderici Wilhelmi Magni*, preface and 445; Salzer, *Der Übertritt des grossen Kurfürsten*, 5, 8.

28. Pufendorf to Paul von Fuchs, Jan. 19, 1688 and Pufendorf to J. F. von Seilern, Mar. 5, 1690, in Varentrapp, ed., "Briefe," *Historische Zeitschrift*, LXX, 27–28, 43–44.

history of foreign policy, the concentration on the discussions and ne-
gotiations leading to decisions rather than on causes or events, the
treatment of individuals as spokesmen of policies rather than as personalities, and the long verbatim excerpts from the documents; on the subjective side, the approach in each history from the position of the state
for which he wrote, the deliberate restriction to sources from the archives of that state, the manufacture of discussions to fill in particular
gaps of validly established policies, the occasional suppression of material still deemed confidential, and the abstention from general interpretations.[29] Politics, in short, was for Pufendorf the meeting-ground of
law and history, for his politics had its base in his natural-law system and
it projected the framework for his historical work. Through politics the
'moral science' of law was sufficiently loosened for history to have a
place in the nature of human things.

This kind of interpretation has, in varying forms, been applied to
Pufendorf by his commentators, from Droysen to Wolf. It is clear and it
is valid. It is also inadequate. It leaves unaccounted something that was
absolutely essential for Pufendorf. Meinecke caught a glimpse of this
something in a negative way when he complained of the gap between
Pufendorf's announcement of 'reason of state' as an historical principle
and the absence of any general principle in his actual history-writing.[30]
Meinecke attributed this gap to a flaw which ran all through Pufendorf
and the XVIIth century—the want of a conceptual capacity to integrate
the rational and the empirical. But what was a flaw and a want for
Meinecke was something quite positive for Pufendorf. Pufendorf did
not attempt such an integration for the simple reason that for him the
truth of law and the truth of historical existence belonged to two different orders of knowledge, each equipped with its own validity, its own
authority, it own methods, its own empiricism. From the very beginning of his writing on natural law Pufendorf distinguished between the
necessary truth of the *relations* among particulars, which was perceived
by reason as a natural law, and the *contingent* truth of the particular facts
themselves, which depends on probability and faith.[31] In his only refer-

---

29. For analyses of Pufendorf's archival histories, see Salzer, *Der Übertritt des grossen
Kurfürsten*, Johann Gustav Droysen, "Zur Kritik Pufendorfs," in *Abhandlungen zur neueren Geschichte* (Leipzig, 1876), and Hans Roedding, *Pufendorf als Historiker und Politiker
in den 'Commentarii de Rebus Gestis Friderici Tertii'* (Halle, 1912).

30. Particularly in reference to Pufendorf's general history. Meinecke, *Die Idee der
Staatsräson*, 228.

31. Pufendorf, *Elementorum*, II, preface.

ence to 'the historian' in the works on natural law, Pufendorf explicitly assigned historical knowledge to the order of contingent existence.[32] But this division of knowledge did not ever mean, for Pufendorf, the deprecation of the 'contingent' in favor of the 'necessary.' On the contrary, if the truth of moral laws was 'necessary' in a logical sense, it was also 'hypothetical' in a metaphysical sense—that is, its reality was conditional upon the existence of its particular subject, and the proof of this existence lay outside the realm of moral or legal science.[33] The two kinds of existence in which he was particularly interested were revealed religion and history. They could not, of course, be known in the same way, but they shared the quality of positive rather than rational knowledge and they both lay outside the natural-law system, since from the facts which they supplied no propositions could be deduced. It is hardly fortuitous, then, that after his juristic period Pufendorf wrote not only on history but on religion as well, nor is it surprising that the only kind of knowledge which he permitted Scripture to furnish for 'speculative discipline' was historical knowledge.[34] In the correspondence of his historical period Pufendorf himself explicitly connected his religious and historical interests by proposing canons for the writing of ecclesiastical history along impersonal and pragmatic lines avowedly analogous to those of 'civil history.'[35] Here the two main lines of XVIIth-century historiography, the political and the religious, converged in Pufendorf, and their relationship in him reflected the larger connection for the century as a whole—the meeting in history of kinds of facts that were irreducible to science.

In the light of this interpretation Pufendorf's whole enterprise takes on a pattern quite different from the one which would make his history simply a further step in the specification of his moral and legal system. He was not a man who sought to move the facts of existence on the fulcrum of his natural-law principles. He was rather a man who accepted the positive institutions of his time, placed their existence outside his system of reason, and sought to rationalize the ideas about them and the relationships between them. He has been adjudged representative of the bourgeoisie by virtue of the rationality of his principles and the practical common-sense of his application of them,[36] but it

32. Pufendorf, *De Jure Naturae*, II, 37.
33. *Ibid.*, II, 23; *Eris Scandica*, 24–25, 256, 273.
34. *Ibid.*, 276.
35. Pufendorf to Thomasius, Dec. 30, 1688 and Nov. 6, 1692, in Gigas, ed., *Briefe Pufendorfs*, 35–36, 69.
36. Wolf, *Grosse Rechtsdenker*, 330–331.

must be remembered that he was a XVIIth-century burgher too in his recognition of where real authority lay, his acceptance of this authority, and the orientation of his criticism simply to the removal of its obfuscations. The two stages of his intellectual career should be seen as a process of development in which he first sought to weave the reasonable network of law into the institutional world he observed around him, and then moved outside this network to deal directly with the facts of religion and political sovereignty upon whose existence his legal system hinged. The difference between these two stages has little to do with the banal distinction between rationalism and empiricism. The natural-law system of his first phase was, as we have seen, itself both rational and empirical, while the common element of the religious and historical works of his second phase was their concern with facts that were not observable. The difference in his approaches to law and history was epitomized in his distinction between the *relations* among moral actions already committed, which were subject to the universal principles of legal science, and the *process* of bringing such actions into existence, which was a work of moral freedom, flexible in its operation upon different times and circumstances but unknowable by merely applying general law.[37] The distinction here was not between a greater or lesser empiricism but between an order of reality that was susceptible to general reason and an order of reality that was susceptible to particular judgment.

It was not incapacity or neglect on Pufendorf's part to have supplied his history with a pragmatic purpose drawn from his legal system and then to have refrained from drawing the generalities which would have led from his historical facts to it. The restraint was deliberate. "If the moral is to be drawn from history," he declared "the reader must supply what the historian does not venture to write."[38] Between history and moral law, in other words, there was an inevitable gap. His firm conviction that he was serving the cause of historical truth while frankly representing the side of his prince was not simply an anomaly explicable by the flexible principle of *raison d'état*. Pufendorf did not feel the tension

37. "And so long as we deliberate, we are properly called free, while the effects that will follow our actions are properly called, with respect to that liberty, contingent; but when we have determined upon some action, the relation between our sets and all the effects depending thereon, is necessary and quite natural, and therefore capable of demonstration." Pufendorf, *De Jure Naturae*, II, 26.

38. Pufendorf, *Einleitung*, II, preface, quoted in E. Salzer, *Der Übertritt des grossen Kuerfürsten*, 8, note 25. This division of function between the historian and everyman was so essential to Pufendorf that he repeated his statement of it both in his *Commentariorum de Rebus Suecicis*, preface, and in his *De Rebus Gestis Friderici Wilhelmi Magni*, 445.

within this conviction, because he assumed a strict independence between the realm of historical facts and the realm of political reality to which they led.

Two principle conclusions emerge from this early case-study in the growth of a modern historical sense. First, the feeling for historicity did not always grow within the sheltering confines of theological, metaphysical, or moral systems until the dissolution of these systems in the late XVIIIth and the XIXth centuries gave it independence. Even in the most systematic stages of this process there were men like Pufendorf who viewed history as an autonomous realm with an irreducible content that not only moderated but set ultimate limits to the applicability of systems. Secondly, this pattern of knowledge was not merely unstable, transitional, or schizoid. It derived its strength and its persistence from the circumstance that the realms of absolute principle and of historical fact, while not reducible to each other, were related to each other. This relationship consisted of more than the obvious positive connection between principles that were open to historical specification and an experience that required principled guidance for history in the making. At least as potent was the negative connection whereby the spheres of life that were rationally grounded afforded a secure springboard for the adventure into those spheres of life which, like history, were not. For such men as Pufendorf, the distinctiveness of reason's field served both to permit the recognition of different kinds of reality and to instill the confidence that the past and the transcendent can be organized around the firm certainty of the here and now in the cooperative quest for knowledge.

12 The Distortions of Political Theory: The Seventeenth-Century Case

By a curious paradox historians leave the problem of historical knowledge to the philosophers and adopt the problem of contemporary knowledge as their very own. They eschew the philosophy of history which examines the validity of past knowledge, but they elect a *modus operandi* in history which examines the validity of the immediate knowledge which their historical informants have of their environs. Behind such apparently innocuous devices as "the critical use of sources" lurks the demon of philosophy. When historians ask, "how did he know?" rather than "how do I know?" they merely transplant the epistemological question from the method of history, where they can avoid it, to the very substance of history, where they cannot avoid it.

It must be admitted that for the most part such epistemological operations of the historian are on the level of perception and are not very challenging. But there is a kind of history in which the thorny issue of the crucial relationship variously described as between general and particular truths, concepts and experience, or categories and phenomena, is an inescapable part of the historical subject-matter. This kind of history is the history of ideas which the historian, as is his wont, relates to their specific environment as to their object. If historians are indeed so engaged, it seems fair to ask what the historical discipline can characteristically contribute to the resolution of the generic issue, in which philosophers and scientists, both natural and social, are so much more prominently engaged—what, that is, the objectification of general propositions and particular realities into equivalent functions of a common past can do for the understanding of their relations.

A full answer would entail an entire philosophy of history. The beginnings of an answer may be found in the isolation of one typical and distinctive—if not exclusive—activity of the historian: his quest for distortions. The historian is, in fact, a logician of distortions. A distortion may be defined in this context as a significant discrepancy of a representation from the thing represented. Obviously, no representation is per-

First published in the *Journal of the History of Ideas* 25:3 (July–September 1964), 323–32.

239

fect, but inadequacy or error becomes distortion when the deviation harbors a meaning. Where the philosopher and scientist seek truth and account for error, the historian, on the level of distortion, seeks error and accounts for truth. It is not simply that the historian, submerged as he is in the sequence of particular events and the fallible human reactions to them, is inevitably confronted with distortions and forced to deal with them. Rather does he find his *métier* to lie increasingly with them. Thus for him a distortion is not so much an error or a "deviant" as simply a problem, a call to practised action. It has not always been so with historians, but as the regular gaps in history have been more and more diminished by the empirical researches of their own colleagues and the rational analyses of their more generalizing allies they have branched out, more and more, into the "problem approach," which tends to be articulated in the investigation of irregularities or distortions because there is something in their traditional discipline that is adaptable to it. The historian's approach to such problems dovetails into the broader issues of disciplined knowledge when the distortions which he attacks alienate the theory from the practice of an era and so inhibit the unified comprehension of it.

The historian's approach to distortions of this kind may be best identified by observing it in operation. Political theory is particularly suited to the purpose because its works are usable and have been used as historical documents testifying to contemporary generic political realities not otherwise perceptible through the specific political realities of decisions and events, and yet its representations are obviously subject to distortion through the inter-mixture of normative considerations. Again, among the possible exemplars of this suitable field, the XVIIth-century brand of political theory seems especially conducive as one of its types which evince a provocatively even balance between its claims to the realism of a science and its actual adherence to the speculative tradition.

Let us specify the context which our problem requires for the examination of this political theory, since it is not the usual one or even, for the theory, the most valid one. A standard treatment of the theory itself should probably locate it as a level of political opinion, analyze the artificial category of a "XVIIth-century brand" into substantive individuals, schools, or types, and, if a final composition appears possible and desirable, draw up a balance-sheet of these XVIIth-century brands which would register the relationships within formal political thinking characteristic of the age as a whole. But history, as it is currently practised, deals as much with the vertical relations between fields of human activity as with the horizontal relations between actions in the same field of human activity, and it is precisely the vertical relation—between theory and practice—that is involved in the problem of distortion. To set the balance-sheet of the period's whole political opinion against its practice would undoubtedly yield a more faithful reflection than any particular entry, but this would not only obscure the problem of distortion but deprive us of its distinctive intellectual benefits. Let us essay, then, a kind of exercise in phenomenological suspension. Let us isolate, as a characteristic strand of XVIIth-century political theory, its school of natural law, and approach some typical expressions of it as historical documents, stemming from a concrete historical situation and descriptive of it. Let us assume, moreover, our independent knowledge of specific events and institutions in this concrete situation, sufficient to permit the identification of a distortion. Our task, then, will be, first, to estimate the angle of distortion; secondly, to note the devices which may be used to correct for it; and finally, to assess the historiographical fruitfulness of the distortions worked by this kind of political theory.

To assure the transparency of the model, the examples are familiar ones: Grotius on international law, Hobbes on sovereignty, and Locke on toleration. Grotius set forth the existence of a secular law of nations, grounded in the absolute prescriptions of natural law and extended by consensus, which conferred real obligations as well as rights upon the heads of states in the initiation of war and in its conduct, as well as in peace, at a time when the states of Europe were administering a naked *raison d'état* in their bellicose relations, qualified only by the religious passion which was the one modification that Grotius categorically excluded. Hobbes recognized the reality of all states worthy of the name to consist in the exercise of an absolute, indivisible, and inalienable sovereignty resting only on the consent of the governed in exchange for the rendition of a well-defined set of security services to the governed, and this at a time when throughout Europe princes were still being widely regarded as the anointed of God, when they were justifying this regard with their sectarian meddling and their self-image of the Christian patriarch, when aristocracies were still fighting for a divided sovereignty, and when his own England was summarizing these actual confusions of politics in a bloody civil war. Locke argued that, since political power "is bounded and confined to the only care of promoting" the "civil interests" of the community and since a church is "a free and voluntary society" for public worship effectual to the salvation of the souls of its constituents, toleration as a principle is a necessary consequence of the very nature of both state and church.[1] But he argued this at a time when

1. "A Letter concerning Toleration," *The Works of John Locke* (London, 1823), VI, 10–13.

Louis XIV was revoking the permissive Edict of Nantes, the Stuarts were employing toleration as a sectarian instrument, and the grudging concessions of the subsequent revolutionary settlement made toleration smack more of political necessity than of either political or religious principle.

But when these relations are so summarized we seem to have over-shot our mark. Each theorist seems to be not so much distorting political reality as rejecting it. The thesis of rejection would, moreover, appear to be confirmed by the support of empirical evidence. Thus Grotius explicitly announced in 1625 that he wrote his masterwork, *On the Law of War and Peace,* as a protest against the contemporary practice of international relations: "Throughout the Christian world I observed a lack of restraint in relation to war, such as even barbarous nations would be ashamed of."[2] In the same vein Locke expressed, during 1689, the publication year of his famous first *Letter on Toleration,* his dissatisfaction with the concessionary Toleration Act.[3] The implications of this evidence for our problem are serious indeed. It would sustain the obvious thesis that the differential factor between a political theory and a straight description or analysis of political reality is the normative element in the former—that the gap between the distortion and the rejection of political reality is merely a matter of degree and that both may be corrected simply by measuring the strength and deviation of unrealized ideals. Were this so, little more would need to be said and the historian could claim no special function in the business save perhaps to document the discrepancies. But, for XVIIth-century theory at least, this is not quite so.

To counter the outer buttress of specific confirming evidence, first we find that the repulsion of both Grotius and Locke from contemporary practice is germane to their *publication* of the works in question rather than to the ideas which they embody. Grotius had worked out the essence of his principles on international law in his unpublished *Law of Prizes* of 1604, and this on the occasion of confirming rather than repudiating a contemporary practice. Locke wrote his *Letter on Toleration* during 1685 and 1686, before the Revolution, but, more significantly, his basic theory of the subject goes back to his unpublished *Essay on Toleration of 1667,* when, far from the discordance of reality from his ideals, he was just beginning to work out the political theory of those ideals under the stimulus of the practical politics which he found in

2. Hugo Grotius, *De Jure Belli ac Pacis* (Eng. tr., Oxford, 1925), II, 20.
3. H. R. Fox Bourne, *The Life of John Locke* (London, 1876), II, 152–5.

Shaftesbury's household.[4] As for Hobbes, the easy conclusion which might be drawn from the coincidence of his political phase with the revolutionary turmoil that he abhorred should be qualified by his judicious statement in the conclusion of the *Leviathan* that he had shown when and why men were politically obligated to a conqueror because "the civil wars have not yet sufficiently taught men" these truths, and that, although "occasioned by the disorders of the present time," his work had no other design than "without partiality . . . to set before men's eyes the mutual relation between protection and obedience."[5]

So much for the neutralization of the bits and pieces. The main point arguing for the distortion of political reality by the natural-law theorists as something more fundamental and more interesting than its present rejection and future reformation in terms of a norm was the basic conviction, common to the whole school, that, far from being an ideal as yet unrealized, their norm was itself already a reality. It can be maintained, of course, that whatever their conviction they actually put into this reality what they wanted to see it become and that it is still essentially a case of the ideal versus the real. But to argue thus is to commit the genetic fallacy. It is important, certainly, for the understanding of any principle, to identify whatever normative component there may be in it, but when this principle is conceived by its author as a constituent of reality, then its validity and its meaning depend upon its function as a constituent of reality. The tendency of recent scholarship to divest Hobbes and Locke of ethical or epistemological *apriorism* in approaching their political theory reinforces this position. Macpherson starts "by assuming that Hobbes was trying to do what he said he was doing, i.e., deducing political obligation from the supposed or observed facts of man's nature," and he maintains, moreover, that Hobbes' theory of this nature was accurate and adequate "as a reflection of his insight into the behavior of men toward each other" in the society of his time.[6] Laslett insists on the autonomy of Locke's political theory from his philosophy, shows its growth in the context of practical politics, and maintains that for Locke the rational natural law "at all points . . . must be compared with, made to fit into, the observed, the empirical facts about the created world and human behavior."[7] Grotius needs no such secondary

---

4. Printed in *ibid.*, I, 174–94.

5. Thomas Hobbes, *Leviathan* (New York, 1950), 621, 630.

6. C. B. Macpherson, *The Political Theory of Possessive Individualism: Hobbes to Locke* (Oxford, 1962), 13–15.

7. Peter Laslett, ed., *John Locke: Two Treatises of Government* (Cambridge, 1960), 87.

support, for he himself supplemented his well-known dictum divorcing the validity of natural law from the authority of God with the explicit foundation of it upon the actuality of men's "strong bent toward social life."[8]

If, then, we accept the theorists' claim that for them the natural law which was their norm was descriptive of reality and had been discovered by them in reality, the question follows: what kind of reality and how does it square with the unmistakable reality of the contemporary conditions that were antithetical to it? Their answer in essence was: it is a *general* kind of reality, and it is related to contemporary conditions as the universal and unitary is to the particular and diverse. The most rhetorical expression of this position is Hobbes' characterization of his *Leviathan* as a model of self-knowledge in the sense of knowing "not this, or that particular man, but Mankind," since the thoughts and passions of men are similar but their objects vary, and it is in connection with this variation that "the dissembling, lying, counterfeiting, and erroneous doctrines" enter which obscure truth.[9] More common to the school was the philosophical formulation which derived the "existence" of natural law from the universal qualities of man's real nature and made it the norm of human relations in the sense of its representing the dimension of human reality that was unified and therefore meaningful. Thus Grotius equated "the law of nature" with "the nature of man," and he accepted as proofs of this law both the logical consequence of man's "rational and social nature" and the existent general consensus of men on the rules of human relations.[10] For the whole school, the state of nature was a device to demonstrate men's universal qualities, in terms of which the laws of nature were both descriptive and prescriptive, prior to social differentiation. Whether or not the state of nature has ever existed as the integral human condition, the natural-law theorists were agreed that it has always existed and still exists on the level of what is common within and among all men. It underlay Locke's political theory and it underlay too his doctrine of toleration: "The sum of all we drive at is that every man may enjoy the same rights that are granted to others."[11] Toleration was not to Locke a specific concession or a blessing of variety: it was a real universal right to voluntary worship which was obscured by the particular varieties of intolerance.

Let us grant the theorists' version of their own procedure: the gen-

8. Grotius, *De Jure Belli ac Pacis*, II, 12.
9. Hobbes, *Leviathan*, 4–5.
10. Grotius, *De Jure Belli ac Pacis*, II, 13, 42–43.
11. "A Letter concerning Toleration," *Works of John Locke*, VI, 51.

eral qualities of human nature and behavior are known to be real because they are derived from the observation, comparison, and analysis of the particular facts of individuals and societies in history and contemporary life, without which general qualities this history and this life become incomprehensible. The natural laws which make a norm of these general qualities for particular human activities are known to be real because they simply translate the qualities into men's relations with one another: they express, that is, what is common to the various types of human relations; they are what would later be called concrete universals, generalities that have real existence. Thus there are two levels of reality, doubly related; on the one side, the general level is known from the particular level; on the other hand men integrate themselves by approaching what they do in particular to what they are in general.

If we grant that the theorists were indeed doing this, then any distortion between their general theory and the particular political reality around them becomes identifiable: it is that they make general and categorical propositions out of what in particular practice is graded and shaded. Grotius made secular international law out of the actual tendency, hybrid as it was, of the European nations to form a system of states, each a sovereign unit and related to the other by the long-range, intersecting formulation of their interests and by permanent diplomatic institutions for their negotiation. Hobbes' doctrine of sovereignty registered the actual tendency, equally adulterated and obscured by the spectacular division and conflict of religions, of central governments to absorb the authority of churches and nobles not merely through the vacillating fortunes of conflict but more importantly through the increased services to the regional community that the central power was able to render. Locke's notion of toleration, finally, full as it was of the traditional ideas which for a century and a half had been crying in the wilderness for the Christian charity, the fideistic other-worldliness and the non-sectarian practical ethic of the Gospel, developed into a full-blown and memorable theory when he generalized from the increasing actual tendency of governments to define their religious functions by their political needs, thereby providing the basis for Locke's dictum that "whatsoever is lawful in the commonwealth cannot be prohibited by the magistrate in the church."[12]

We may identify the distortion, then, as the degree by which the general propositions of the theory, conditioned as they are by the universal and logical requirements of reason, deviate from the observable sum of

12. *Ibid.*, VI, 34.

actual particulars. What further can we do about it? Can we, that is, correct for it by showing how the general propositions themselves may account for the distortion? We may leave aside, as not quite to the point, the fortunate case in which we can trace a theory creating its own practical truth through its direct influence upon a practical agent. In any case, this is rare for the XVIIth century, where we have no Catherine the Great with her politically bowdlerized Montesquieu.

Historians do habitually employ, however, two devices for relating general theory to particular practice where they are at odds. First, they investigate the primary theorists for undue inconsistencies, qualifications, and complications, not for the purpose of assessing their validity but for the purpose of tracing the intrusion of an alien particular or set of particulars for which the theorist feels he must account and for the purpose of analyzing how the general propositions are used to account for them. Philosophers and political scientists have identified many such theoretical problems in the natural-law school and have worked them to their own ends. These problems are of various kinds and origins, and they are certainly not all reducible to existential influence, but the historian does test them for that dimension. Thus Grotius' well-known addiction to the authority of Scripture, positive law, and its commentators; his cloudy notion of sovereignty; the use of the doctrine of consent to cover the problematic relationship between the rules of international law prescribed by the law of nature and the usually more permissive provisions of the "voluntary" or customary law of nations: all these manifest Grotius' wrestling with particular realities that did not entirely fit into his rational scheme. Hobbes' system is much tighter and consequently less susceptible to this kind of analysis. It is quite definitely not appropriate to such fundamental issues as the relations of his philosophy and his politics or the moral source of his political obligation, but it may well be applicable to his overly protested concern with religion in general and Catholicism in particular. Locke is more systematic in his religious liberalism than in other sections of his theory which have been called into question, but in his inability to decide, by virtue of his principles, the crucial issue of a conflict between the prescription of a sovereign and the conscience of the individual in matters of morals which relate both to civil interest and to salvation, and in his exclusion of atheists, Mohammedans, and implicitly Roman Catholics from the orbit of toleration, there may be seen evidence not only of his own latitudinarian Protestantism but also of an attempt to come to terms with contemporary practice.

The second device which is commonly employed to rationalize distortion and is especially cherished by historians consists in the investigation of secondary theorists—disciples, adapters, popularizers. Often attributed by outsiders to the historian's mysterious passion for the obscure and inconsequential, this device is usually motivated by the desire to trace the transmission or diffusion of ideas from their origins in an individual or a small group of intellectuals to the society at large. It is applicable to our purpose because these second-level figures tend to be less rigorous in their logic and more open to particular influences of the environment than their mentors. Consequently they exhibit a diminished angle of distortion; sometimes, indeed, they make it their avowed business to diminish it. The result is that they show how the general propositions of theory can be modulated or opened up so as to account more precisely for the existing balance of particular movements and institutions. Pufendorf, one of the most-read theorists of the century, may double for Grotius and Hobbes, whom he sought to combine, in this function.[13] He adapted Grotius to contemporary international relations by limiting the binding force of international law to the prescription of rational grounds for starting war and frankly reducing all other aspects of international affairs in war and peace to the will of the sovereign who is bound only by the interests of his own state. He adapted Hobbes to contemporary political practice and operational beliefs by re-introducing God as the necessary if indirect source of political obligation; by applying the concept of sovereignty indiscriminately and without favor to all unmixed forms of the state, including therein by a tortuous argument even the species of "limited sovereignties"; and by accommodating it to the idea of a politically subordinate corporate society, of a kind that did prevail in Europe. For Locke, we may adduce the figure of Christian Thomasius, who crossed Locke with Pufendorf to incubate a doctrine of toleration based upon "common sense" and dependent for its existence ultimately upon the moral purpose of sovereign policy. If we move from Locke to Thomasius to Christian Wolff, who extended the sovereign's rights over the realm of the spirit, to Frederick the Great and his policy of toleration grounded in religious indifference, civic ethics, and political expediency, a full circle is achieved: the general principle which was drawn from particular politics and transcended it is brought back down, with suitable modifications, into it.[14]

13. Samuel Pufendorf, *De Jure Naturae et Gentium* (Lund, 1672).
14. Christian Thomasius, *Fundamenta Juris Naturae et Gentium Sensu Communi Deducta* (Halle, 1705); Christian Wolff, *Jus Naturae Methodo Scientifica Pertractatum* (Frankfurt, 1740–48).

But for the historian distortions are not simply remediable evils. If they make it dangerous to draw literal conclusions from theories about the conditions they purport to account for, they also reveal information that can be acquired in no other way. The revelation is of three kinds:

First, obviously, the assumptions of a theory are much more clearly visible through the deviations of perception that they effect than through a straight reflection of or even a reliable selection from the objects of the theory.

Second, the situation that is distorted is itself illumined by the distortion. Amid the plethora of diverse particular phenomena in any historical situation, the historian is frequently hard put to assess their proportional weights and directions. The qualities and dimensions that theory blows up into general truths thereby receive contemporary testimony of their relative strength *vis-à-vis* what theory neglects. They are, moreover, likely to be precisely those aspects of the total situation that are in the process of change or development, whether in an ascending or declining direction, for it is often movement that attracts the attention of the theorist. And since, for any period, it is what changes that is the prime target of historical consideration and that is most susceptible to comprehension by the distinctively historical approach, theory guides the historian to the proper objects of his labors.

We are brought now to the third and final fruit of distortion, which brings us also back to our starting-point. It provides the historian with a model for deriving valid generalizations out of centrifugal particular or "unique" events. We have never stood so badly in need of such a model. In a generation which has taught us that the American Constitution was *not* invented to protect bondholders, that Victorian England was *not* governed by laissez-faire bourgeois against the opposition of paternalistic landlords, and that revolutions from the XVIIth-century through the XIXth were *not* made by a rising social class—in such a generation we need to learn how to make and accept generalizations that will inevitably conflict with some particulars or even with the apparent sum of particulars. Political theory—or at least its XVIIth-century brand—teaches us that a generalization is of a different order of truth from the particulars from which it is drawn, yet a genuine order of truth nonetheless. The distortions of political theory—in the sense both of the distortions it works and the corrective distortions which we work upon it—should teach us how we may use the shuttling devices that are the stock in trade of the historian to move quickly back and forth between the universal and the unique, each time narrowing the gap between them.

Past distortion thus becomes a path through which historians pass into the common pursuit of coherent knowledge. Suitably corrected, it reveals how men actually undertook to rationalize the apparently irrational. Since this is one of the undertakings that span all the ages of our civilization, we have here a valid lesson of history which may assist in the leveling of a parallel resistance to our own quest for comprehension.

13 Kant and the Crisis of Natural Law

In its outward appearance the doctrine of natural law would seem to be a complex of ideas which, like many another, has served its time and should be allowed to rest in peace. To be sure, as historians we are, inevitably, grave-robbers, but we acknowledge the mortality of human beings and have learned to conduct ourselves with a decent respect for the dead, recognizing that their contribution to the ongoing stock of humanity entered into other forms divergent from the original identity. We tend to treat the natural law accordingly, as a concept of political and moral theory that flourished during the early formative centuries of our culture, sickened with the convulsions of the 16th century, reformed and took on a new lease of life during the 17th and 18th centuries, only to betray during the latter period increasing symptoms of the decrepitude foreshadowing its demise early in the following century. The doctrine which underwent this career was a compound constituted by the juncture of political theorists, who found in nature the seat of constant principles consonant with but superior to the unstable and incomprehensible variety of particular institutions, with philosophers and theologians who found in nature the arena for making *their* constant principles applicable to the various particular activities of men. As Americans we have a special sentimental and utilitarian attachment to the doctrine, since it presided over the foundation of the nation and remains enshrined in the charters that still command our formal allegiance, but as historians we know that before the natural law sanctioned the natural rights of man it validated the authority of rulers, and we realize that the same ineluctable flux once responsible for such a change in emphasis from authority to rights within the natural law has subsequently undermined the bases of our belief in a substantive natural law as such. It is hardly surprising, then, to find this natural law often treated as an historical event, evanescent like any other, and to find Kant aligned with Bentham, Burke, and Rousseau as reflectors and agents of its demise.

First published in the *Journal of the History of Ideas* 26:2 (April–June, 1965), 191–210. This paper was originally delivered at the Spring History Conference of the State University of Iowa in April 1964.

In this sense what we have to deal with is the final phase of an historical process. In another sense, however, we have to do with something more immediate—with a problem that extends the meaning of natural law into our own times. There are three peculiarities about the history of natural law that refer it beyond its explicit terminus.

First, its longevity. The express doctrine of natural law runs as a central and continuous current in western thought from the ancient Greeks well into the modern period. The importance of this long span is the indication not only of its adaptability but of its flexibility—that is, not only has the same doctrine been applied to differing situations but the doctrine has itself been able to undergo change and yet retain a generic identity as natural law. The most striking of these changes refers to the development of what is variously called from the old to the new or from the classical to the modern types of natural law during the 17th century, a development which registered the drastic shift from the transcendent and communitarian to the immanent and individualistic approach and yet managed to perpetuate the category of natural law.[1] A category susceptible of such reincarnations should make us wary of premature conclusions about its final decease. Obviously, it possesses an integrity that is not identifiable with its substantive principles at any particular time and that must be looked for on another level. It would be convenient if we could find this level in the most concrete of all possible evidence—in the literal subscription of a thinker to the natural law—but unfortunately, in intellectual as in other kinds of history, men have acted in response to their own concerns rather than to the questions that historians would later ask of them. Such indubitable subscribers as Descartes, Spinoza, Adam Smith, and Condorcet scarcely mention it by name; such limited subscribers as Bodin, Leibniz, and Montesquieu seem wholehearted in their verbal endorsement; as forceful an opponent as Burke pays it lip-service; such explicit rejecters as Bentham and Hegel betray actual appropriations of it under other forms. Clearly, we must look elsewhere for the identification of natural law.

The second peculiar attribute in the history of natural law that directs us beyond the overt career of its principles is its continuity. Although the break at the end of the 18th century suffices to dislocate it from the main stream of western thought it has persisted, unbroken, in two of the most powerful intellectual movements spanning the 19th

---

1. For the distinction between "classical" and "modern" phases of natural law, see Leo Strauss, *Natural Rights and History* (Chicago, 1953).

and 20th centuries. Its persistence in Catholic ethical and social theory might perhaps be discounted as an expression of parochial traditionalism were not the impact of its modernization under Catholic auspices reinforced by its more unequivocally modern evolution in the form of Marxism. It has become fashionable to distinguish Marx from Engels, but in this case Engels' resort to the natural-law syndrome made explicit what Marx had built into his original system. The Catholic and Marxist examples show that the adaptable and flexible capacities of the natural law did not necessarily atrophy in confrontation with the recent tendencies in our civilization. They provide, indirectly, an intellectual respectability for the popular natural-law assumptions of political programs which have been sustained during the past century and a half by many men who would subscribe to neither extreme but have no theoretical warrant of their own.

The third and final discrepancy of the natural law from its customary portrait consists in its contemporaneity. Our own age is witnessing a revival of natural-law thinking, particularly in the field of jurisprudence. Outside of Germany, where the discussion has been widespread and lively, the movement is of limited dimensions and tends to take the form rather of a prospectus than a full-blown theory.[2] But the recurrence is sufficient at least to raise the question of the permanence of the natural-law category, and, with this question, to raise the possibility that since the 18th century it has been not submerged but camouflaged.

Considerations such as these suggest that neither the meaning nor the fate of the natural-law doctrine should be looked for only in what men have explicitly written about it. They suggest that if, for political theory and philosophy, it must be judged as an integral whole that either is or is not present, for history it is a composite that has been present not only in different ways but in different degrees. Since its substance is so variable, the historian identifies it, like so many other themes which provide a constant focus for men's changing circumstances and aspirations, by its inimitable function. So long as the function is fulfilled, the natural law is present, whatever men call it, and through the change of the function, when it does change, we may trace the destiny of the parts that went into the natural law even after its integrity was dissipated.

The function of the natural law, ascertainable by generalizing from

2. E.g., *ibid.;* Roscoe Pound, *Law and Morals* (Chapel Hill, 1924) and *Contemporary Juristic Theory* (Claremont, 1940); Allessandro Passerin d'Entrèves, *Natural Law: an Introduction to Legal Philosophy* (New York, 1951); Heinrich Mitteis, *Über das Naturrecht* (Berlin, 1948); Hans Welzel, *Naturrecht und materiale Gerechtigkeit* (Göttingen, 1950).

its constant rule in the different doctrines where it was explicitly and indubitably present, has been to provide a universal principle of coherence for the lives of men. "Coherence" here must be taken in its original sense of "connection"; the function of the natural law has been to connect the fundamental principles of reality with the fundamental principles of action—in other words, knowledge with morality—so that men may guide their behavior by an absolute rule and thus may make their actions and their lives meaningful by aligning them with the ultimate nature of things. This coherence has entailed, first, a unitary explanation of reality, so that it may yield general principles; secondly, an absolute basis for ethical precepts, so that the general principles of reality may be relevant to the variety of human conduct; and thirdly, a necessary linkage between these general principles of reality and this absolute basis of ethical precepts—between what is and what ought to be. In short, natural law involved a *description* of reality in terms of laws which became *prescriptive* for men. The one additional attribute posited for such laws was the requirement that they be universal, in the sense both that they be knowable by all men and be binding upon all men. Hence they had to be natural, since nature represented by definition what was common and accessible to all men, as against the supernatural which was by traditional definition accessible only to a selective faith or contemplation; and it had to be rational, since reason represented the generalizing faculty of men as against the particularity of sensations and perceptions.

From the point of view of this function, the rejection of natural law in the 19th century was the dissolution of the total conjunction between the *is* and the *ought,* and its replacement first by increasingly tenuous partial conjunctions and later by a frank disjunction. The substantive symptom of this process was the demotion of nature to the realm of the physical, indifferent or hostile to moral purpose, and the substitution for it of entities like history and society as the media for selecting relevant *sections* of reality as the ground of moral precepts. But by breaking up reality into the natural and the historical or the natural and the societal, those who emphasized history and society as the appropriate real contexts of morality broke up the generality of the real. They dissolved thereby the conjunction between the *is,* as such, and the *ought.* But in their arguments against the uniformity and stability of reality, the proponents of the romanticism, vitalism, and evolutionism that may be subsumed under the shorthand label of "history" seemed to deny any general structure in the non-natural sector of reality germane to human morals and to expound a doctrine of external flux; while, correspondingly, the utilitarians, social theorists, and social scientists who shared in the exaltations of "society" seemed to deny any universal or absolute basis for morality and to expound a doctrine of social relativism. But did the literal rejection of natural law actually entail so categorical a rejection of its function? Or—to put the question in more basic terms—have men given up—as they have seemed to do—the intellectual faith in a universal actionable truth which remains the practical assumption of their free institutions? Let us tackle this question as historians, that is, at its beginning. Let us look at the crisis of natural law at the end of the 18th century, to assess whether this turning-point marked a death-throe or a transformation.

The spotlight will be on Immanuel Kant, not so much because he has been the most influential figure in modern philosophy—although he has been—as because he represented the crisis of natural law in its most categorical terms and developed the crisis to its most explicit denouement. Kant's notorious so-called "dualism" was a classic statement invalidating, among other things, the traditional function of the natural law. This is hardly surprising, since his inspirations were Hume for his theory of knowledge and Rousseau for his ethics—the Hume who had denied the descriptive validity of law in nature and the Rousseau who had rejected the prescriptive validity of any intellectually known law for human action. Kant combined these piecemeal insights into a radical and systematic dialectic opposing knowledge to action and nature to morality, and undermining thereby the very foundations of the natural law as it had been previously conceived. These foundations, common to the classical and modern schools of natural law and common as well to both the authoritarian and liberal branches of the modern school, had included, as their essential feature, a general level of reality, conceivable by reason from the total nature of all things or, alternatively, of all men, which was the absolute sanction for general ethical and legal precepts. In the two critical works which remain the most prominent monuments of his fame—the *Critique of Pure Reason,* published in 1781, and the *Critique of Practical Reason,* published in 1788—Kant destroyed this syndrome by dissolving its crucial middle link, the general principles that functioned simultaneously as truths of nature and of morality. Natural truths, for Kant, were limited to the organization of particular phenomena, and he separated out the faculty of the understanding from the faculty of reason as the only faculty producing valid knowledge of natural reality precisely in order to underline its address to the manifold of particular sensations and perceptions. The faculty of reason which had as its objects general ideas beyond particular phenomena registered no ascertainable existence and produced no valid truths about existing reality. "Nature" is thus, for Kant, confined to "an aggregate of appearances," "the sum of given objects," and such general objects as freedom, God, and immortality are not knowable from it.[3] The realm of morals—in Kant's term, of the practical—which requires precisely such absolute universal principles as its postulates cannot therefore base itself on the knowledge of nature but must have an independent structure completely apart from nature.

And so we have two completely distinct realms—that of nature, inhabited by phenomena or appearances, related to man through knowledge, and characterized by the principle of necessity; and that of morality, inhabited by noumena or the intelligible, general grounds of appearances, related to man through action, and characterized by the principle of freedom. The laws of nature, in this system, belong entirely to the first of these realms: they are produced by the faculty of the understanding operating upon the manifold of particular natural objects through the category of causality, and these laws of nature are precisely what endow nature with the necessity that renders it antithetical to morality.

Consequently, all events are empirically determined in an order of nature. Only in virtue of this law can appearances constitute a nature and become objects of experience. This law is a law of the understanding from which no departure can be permitted, and from which no appearance may be exempted. . . . The understanding can know in nature only what is, what has been, or what will be. We cannot say that anything in nature ought to be other than what in all these time-relations it actually is. When we have the course of nature alone in view, "ought" has no meaning whatsoever.[4]

The moral realm does indeed have its laws, but these are categorically distinct from the laws of nature.

Everyone must admit that a law, if it is to hold morally, i.e. as a ground of obligation, . . . must not be sought in the nature of man or in the circumstances in which he is placed, but sought *a priori* in the concepts of pure reason, and that every other precept which rests on principles of mere experience, even a precept which is in certain respects universal, so far as it leans in the least on empirical grounds . . . may be called a practical rule but never a moral law. . . . Applied to man, [all moral philosophy] borrows nothing from knowledge of him, . . . but gives him, as a rational being, *a priori* laws.[5]

3. Immanuel Kant, *Critique of Pure Reason* (tr. Norman Kemp Smith, London, 1933), 140, 172, 661–662.
4. *Ibid.*, 470–473.
5. *Foundations of the Metaphysics of Morals* in Immanuel Kant, *Critique of Practical Reason and Other Writings in Moral Philosophy* (tr. and ed. Lewis White Beck, Chicago, 1949), 52.

The reason involved here is not theoretical but practical reason, that is, a reason that bestows not knowledge but the rules for action. Behind this opposition of formal attributes and its specialized terminology lay a dramatic insight which we may perhaps clarify by reformulating it. What Kant was saying was that we can know only the outsides of the already formed things that our experience presents to us and beyond that only their external relations to one another. The only inner or essential realities of which we can be certain are those that we produce ourselves through our own actions. The laws which govern our knowledge of externals are natural laws, the laws that govern our creation of internals are moral laws.

In this segregation of natural law for the purpose of making room for moral freedom Kant was seeking an escape for man from the implications of secularized, impersonalized natural science, and his argument became standard for the subsequent rejections of natural law in its integrative function. And yet Kant could not remain content with this disjunction. He spent the rest of his philosophical career in seeking to rejoin what he had put asunder, for, as he himself recognized, the human mind tends toward unity, and only there does it find peace and satisfaction. He set forth the basis for this unification in the very critiques whose main tendency went to produce the duality which we have been discussing. He was careful to frame the division between nature and morality in such a way as to provide for the *possibility* not simply of their co-existence but of their integration, and thereby he laid down the fundamental directives for a revival of the traditional coherent function which had been filled by the natural law. These directives indicate that the celebrated Kantian dualism was in fact an unbalanced dualism, for morality was not simply an equivalent counterpart of nature but was its ultimate foundation; and this transforms morality's apparent division from nature into an organic unity with it. Morality and nature were compatible not only as two separate series concerned with two different orders of reality, but as a relationship of dependence in which the moral noumena functioned as the final causes of the natural series of phenomena. Essentially, this relationship is between the process of creating reality and the reality that has been created. "When we are dealing with what happens there are only two kinds of causality conceivable by us; the causality is either according to nature or arises from freedom. The former is the connection in the sensible world of one state with a preceding state on which it follows according to a rule. Since the causality of appearances rests on conditions of time, . . . it follows . . . that the cause of that which happens or comes into being must itself also have come into being, and that in accordance with the principle of understanding it must in its turn itself require a cause. By freedom, on the other hand, . . . I understand the power of beginning a state spontaneously. Such causality will not, therefore, itself stand under another cause determining it in time, as required by the law of nature," but, "independently of those natural causes, and even contrary to their force and influence, can produce something that is determined in the time-order in accordance with empirical laws and can therefore begin a series of events entirely of itself."[6]

This was Kant's position in the *Critique of Pure Reason*, where he wrote from the point of view of natural knowledge. From this point of view the freedom series is unknowable; it is a "hypothetical" or "regulative" idea of reason which corresponds to no reality but shows that an ultimate unity on the basis of freedom is not logically impossible. Otherwise, it leaves nature and its laws intact in the world of phenomena.

But Kant also began to bridge the gap from the side of morality, in his *Critique of Practical Reason*, and from this point of view the function of nature and nature's laws underwent a significant expansion. For since the realm of moral freedom was so utterly independent of nature that it did not derive even the objects of its action from it and at the same time so exclusively populated by noumena—or fundamental realities—that it constituted the ultimate grounding for nature, Kant's problem was to show how moral law could possibly have natural effects, and to do this he had to add a wing to nature which would accommodate it. He called this wing "supersensuous nature," and he indicated that here the moral law could enter into nature. The moral law

gives to the sensible world, as sensuous nature . . . , the form of an intelligible world, i.e., the form of supersensuous nature, without interfering with the mechanism of the former. Nature, in the widest sense of the word, is the existence of things under laws. The sensuous nature of rational beings in general is their existence under empirically conditioned laws, therefore, it is, from the point of view of reason, heteronomy. The supersensuous nature of the same beings, on the other hand, is their existence according to laws which are independent of all empirical conditions and which therefore belong to the autonomy of pure reason. And since the laws, according to which the existence of things depends on cognition, are practical, supersensuous nature . . . is nothing else than nature under the autonomy of the pure practical reason. The law of this autonomy is the moral law, and it, therefore, is the fundamental law of supersensuous nature and of a pure world of the understanding, whose counterpart must exist in the world of sense without interfering with the laws of the latter.[7]

6. Kant, *Critique of Pure Reason*, 464–465.
7. Kant, *Critique of Practical Reason*, 153–154.

It might seem from this that Kant was restoring a moral law of nature, applicable to men, but his real meaning was quite different. His "supersensuous nature" turns out to be not an actuality but a hypothesis indicating possibility, and it has reality only in the special sense that for morality the possible is the real.

> . . . In actual nature as an object of experience, the free will is not of itself determined to such maxims as could of themselves establish a nature based on universal laws . . . ; rather, they are private inclinations, which form a natural whole according to pathological (physical) laws but not a system of nature which is possible only through our will acting according to pure practical laws. However, through reason we are conscious of a law to which all our maxims are subject as though through our will a natural order must arise. Therefore, this law must be the idea of a supersensuous nature, a nature not empirically given yet possible through freedom . . . ; to this nature we give objective reality, at least in a practical context, because we regard it as the object of our will as pure rational beings.[8]

Basically, then, the status of nature for the moral law is similar to the status of moral freedom for the laws of nature: they indicate *possible* junctures but leave the actual foundations of the moral law rooted as strongly as ever in the internal structure of a reason independent of all possible experience and the internal requirements of a morality independent of all possible connection with natural ends and motives, just as freedom left the natural law actually closed within the circle of descriptive necessity. The difference lay in Kant's conviction that possibilities constitute no reality from the point of view of existence but that they do constitute realities from the point of view of morality, since morality is the process of creating existence and possibilities are the real guidelines of what is coming into existence but does not yet exist.

We have arrived now at a crucial point of our analysis, for when we ask next, as we must—what is the precise role of this nature in a moral law which is fundamentally independent of it?—we are asking, in the particular case of Kant, the general question: precisely what happened to the natural law after modern man rejected it as the universal standard for his conduct? Kant gave two answers which, if we may bring them into a systematic relationship, although he did not, may stand as one essential reply organized into two parts.

First, he distinguished between a "substantive" and a "formal" meaning of nature. Its substantive meaning is the one with which we are familiar—the aggregate of sensory appearances actually connected as

8. *Ibid.*, 154.

cause and effect through physical necessity. Its formal meaning refers to the "inner" general character of any thing, whatever its outer identity and in whatever realm it may be, which connects it with other things through any kind of necessity. "Natural, in the formal sense, means that which necessarily proceeds according to laws of a certain order, whatever order that may be, thus even the moral order."[9]

Thus Kant provided logically for his "supersensuous" nature, and in his second answer to the question of the moral meaning of nature he spelled out a content for it. This content was hinged on the idea of an analogy, which Kant called a "type": substantive nature became formalized and pertinent to morality by virtue of individuals defining the moral law in analogy with the natural law. Thus Kant defined his famous moral categorical imperative originally as: "Act only according to that maxim by which you can at the same time will that it should become a universal law"—but then, in order to make it more than an "empty concept" he added that it "can be expressed as follows: Act as though the maxim of your action were by your will to become a universal law of nature."[10] What this means is that the moral law can be applied to undertaking possible actions and judging actualized actions in the world of sense—that is, of nature—only if it translates itself into a form analogous to the law of nature, since only thus can the natural object become relevant to morality. In Kant's terms:

The moral law has no other cognitive faculty to mediate its applications to objects of nature than the understanding . . . ; and the understanding can supply to an idea of reason . . . a natural law. But this natural law can be used only in its formal aspect . . . ; and it may, therefore, be called the *type* of moral law. . . . Natural law serves only as the type of a law of freedom, for if common sense did not have something to use in actual experience as an example, it could make no use of the law of pure practical reason in applying it to that experience.[11]

But what happens to the natural law when it thus becomes a moral form? How has it changed and how has it remained constant in comparison with its traditional function? It has changed in one essential way: where it had functioned as the *source* of moral rights and obligations it now functions as a means to the *object* or *end* of moral rights and obligations whose source lies outside it. What it retains of its traditional function and contributes to its new moral context are its attributes of

9. "The End of All Things," in *Kant on History* (ed. Lewis White Beck, New York, 1963), 76; Kant, *Critique of Pure Reason*, 392.

10. Kant, *Critique of Practical Reason*, 80.

11. *Ibid.*, 177–178.

necessity and universality. Since the independent moral law is located outside of time and space in the practical reason—that is, the creative capacity—of each individual, it is inherently indifferent to such categories, and yet it needs them if its precepts are to have real objective authority. Consequently, it borrows from the traditional natural law the notions of a moral necessity which subjects all particular actions to the law and of a general scope for the moral law which subjects all individual men equally to it. For Kant, then, if the natural law no longer sponsored morality it might still help to provide it with form and direction.

But what Kant had tried to demonstrate in his two primary works was that it was logically possible to harmonize his separated laws of morals and of nature. What he had not questioned or demonstrated was whether they were actually harmonized. "A system of nature may or may not actually arise according to these maxims of the legislation of a possible nature—all this does not trouble us in this *Critique*."[12] But it did trouble him in all his other intellectual enterprises. Indeed, when we look at him for the analysis of the actual conjunction of morality and nature we find an embarrassment of riches. He tried to join them in his philosophy of history, in aesthetics, in the philosophy of nature itself, in his theory of politics, and finally in the applied ethics that he called anthropology. Clearly the urge was powerful in him to unify his system, and in his efforts to do so he made more concrete the new role of natural law which he had so generally outlined.

Of these various arenas in which Kant saw an interplay between his two primary realms, we shall select the two which were internally related and contributed a third dimension to his attempted solution of the problem. In Kant's view the realms of history and politics were filled with such capricious particular mixtures of nature and morality as to form autonomous media for their interaction. The disorder of historical events and the irrationality of political institutions challenged him to an ever further resolution of the duality between nature and morals. The impact of history and politics on Kant's system can thus be seen as two successive stages in the joining of Kant's two spheres of pure and practical reason with an existential cement, and in the course of his continuing struggle to integrate a world that he had so profoundly divided, the future role of the idea of natural law took tangible shape.

Kant made his approach to history in three sketchy essays published in the mid-1780's, but despite their brevity they stand as the landmark

12. *Ibid.*, 156.

of his first attempt to bridge the worlds of nature and morality.[13] Since he wrote them at the same time as he was working out his moral theory it is tempting to think that in his moral theory he categorically distinguished morality from nature not only on the assumption of the logical possibility of their reconciliation as part of the theory but more securely on the assumption of the actual possibility of their reconciliation which he wrote into his philosophy of history. The common problem of the essays is the condition of chaos and evil that characterizes past and contemporary human history arising from the conflict, within humanity, between the individual and the species, between reason and instinct, between freedom and compulsion—in summary, between morality and nature—and their common theme was the resolution of this conflict by the conversion of the disorderly existential relationships into the orderly progression from nature to morality through historical time. The agency of this progression is nature, viewed teleologically, for man's freedom is "lawless" until nature's laws develop his natural capacities to the point where he can replace them with the free execution of the moral laws.

Whatever concept one may hold, from a metaphysical point of view, concerning the freedom of the will, certainly its appearances, which are human actions, like every other natural event are determined by universal laws. However obscure their causes, history, which is concerned with narrating these appearances, permits us to hope that if we attend to the play of freedom of the human will in the large, we may be able to discern a regular movement in it, and that what seems complex and chaotic in the single individual may be seen from the standpoint of the human race as a whole to be a steady and progressive though slow evolution of its original environment. . . . Individuals and even whole peoples . . . , each, according to his own inclination, follows his own purpose, often in opposition to others; yet each individual and people, as if following some guiding thread, go toward a natural but to each of them unknown goal. . . . Are we not to suppose that Nature . . . follows a lawful course in gradually lifting our race from the lower levels of animality to the highest level of humanity, doing this by her own secret art, and developing in accord with her law all the original gifts of man in this apparently chaotic disorder?"[14]

The ends which nature intends for man are the achievement of a civil constitution granting maximum freedom under the law and of a degree

13. Leonard Krieger, *German Idea of Freedom* (Boston, 1957), 93–95; Beck's Introduction to *Kant on History*, xviii–xvi.

14. Kant, "Idea for a Universal History from a Cosmopolitan Point of View," *loc. cit.*, 11.

of "enlightenment" or "culture" which "will be strong and perfect enough to become a second nature," for these are conditions for the meeting of the natural with the moral capacities of man, and especially of his natural faculty with his moral use of reason.[15] "As nature has uncovered . . . the seed for which she most tenderly cares—the propensity and vocation to free thinking—this gradually works back upon the character of the people, who thereby gradually become capable of managing freedom. . . ."[16]

In this historical context, then, not only does the natural law nurture such moral items as reason and freedom in the service of the natural plan, but there seems to be no essential bar to the gradual transition from the final stage of nature into morality—"the coarse, natural capacity for moral discrimination into definite practical principles, . . . a society of men driven together by their natural feelings into a moral whole."[17] Moreover, as we might expect from this apparent conjunction of nature and morality, Kant hangs upon it the familiar doctrine of natural rights. He speaks of "the rights of mankind" whose infringement is "absolutely null and void," whether perpetrated by monarchs, parliaments, or peoples, since such an infringement would be "a crime against human nature."[18]

Now all this seems too good to be true, and it is. As he himself readily admitted, his history was not actual history but "conjectural history," "to some extent based upon an a priori principle" and written "in accordance with an Idea of how the course of the world must be if it is to lead to certain rational ends"[19] This "Idea" was the regulative principle of teleology, subsequently defined as the problematic and analogical application to nature, which actually has no ascertainable ends, of a purposiveness not only borrowed from but leading to the moral realm.[20]

Thus the morally pregnant nature in Kant's idea of history is not an actual nature at all; it is a possible nature whose moral dimension has been attached to it for heuristic use. The matrix for the junction of nature and morality here was not, as it seemed, the teleological conception of nature, but it was the realm of human history itself, whose essential

15. *Ibid.*, 16–17; "Conjectural Beginning of Human History," *ibid.*, 62–63.

16. "What Is Enlightenment?" *ibid.*, 10.

17. "Idea for a Universal History," *ibid.*, 15.

18. "What is Enlightenment?" *ibid.*, 7.

19. "Conjectural Beginning," *ibid.*, 53; "Idea for a Universal History," *ibid.*, 24–25.

20. Kant, *Critique of Teleological Judgment*, tr. James Creed Meredith (Oxford, 1928), 335, 98–100.

characteristic of development through time now sponsored Kant's first exposition of teleology as a unifying doctrine. History was not, as Kant literally portrayed it, a product of nature, but the idea of nature was rather a product of history. Thus the natural rights of humanity which he upheld were rooted not in any stable realities or values of human nature but in its historical destiny—that is, the "progress in general enlightenment," its "progress . . . towards improvement." Correspondingly, the worst of all offenses against natural rights were offenses against "posterity."[21]

Kant's history, then, cradled his unifying teleology and in this context replaced nature in its traditional function of integrating reality and morality. But within history nature and nature's laws continued to supply a cognate of their former role. Kant deliberately made nature rather than freedom the theme of his history because only from nature could history obtain any lawful structure and universal scope. The replacement of nature by history reflected the attenuation of unity in the western world-view since the palmy days of the natural law, for a time-process was now needed to convoy a communication that had been a matter of logic, but within this narrowed field and on a derivative foundation this law continued its wonted role of leading the authority of reality to the values of men.

History in the Kantian approach left open both a final level of concreteness and a final level of integration, and it is revealing that these two operations, usually so ill-assorted, should here go together. His history obviously was wanting in concreteness, since it was dominated by a regulative idea which rendered it merely hypothetical and possible. That this history was actually rather than logically possible made it indeed more concrete than his ethical theory, but its advantage over actual history in proposing meanings out of "the notorious complexity" of empirical events did not blind Kant to the realization that, as truth, it was "no match for a history which reports the same events as an actually recorded occurrence."[22] The second inadequacy of Kant's history was the imperfect integration resulting from the preponderance of nature over freedom in it. This was not simply a matter of presenting historical freedom exclusively in its natural analogy but, more importantly, of omitting the whole dimension of individual action from history. Kant repeated time and again that his history regarded the species rather than the individual, because the natural law of progress impinged only upon

---

21. "What is Enlightenment?" in *Kant on History*, 7–8.
22. "Idea for a Universal History," *ibid.*, 25; "Conjectural Beginning," *ibid.*, 53.

the species while the individual acted through a freedom that was "law-less" and "identical" with "the rule of blind chance."[23] At this stage of his thought, indeed, Kant was denying that nature sponsors any kind of ordering principle for individuals. He agreed that "the doctrine of obli-gations (*Verbindlichkeiten*) in natural law is superfluous and can often mislead," in its application both to the presumed mutual natural obliga-tions of individuals to respect one another's rights and to the presumed obligation of each individual to enforce his own rights.[24]

Kant's one-sided portrait of history, whatever its advantages, became vulnerable at a crucial point: nature could prepare the conditions for the realization of morality, but the decisive step from one stage to the other would have to be undertaken through an act of freedom, for which, in Kant's conception of history, there was no provision.[25] This act of freedom, capable of producing a more perfect integration, Kant found not in history but in contemporary politics.

The solution to both problems—that is, both the concrete applica-tion of his philosophy and the theoretical resolution of its duality—Kant discovered in a single definite event which broke in upon his phi-losophy from the outside world: the French Revolution. Like many others, he welcomed it enthusiastically, but unlike the others he clung to his advocacy of it until his death in 1804. He was intellectually com-mitted to its defense, because it stimulated and was embodied in the philosophy of politics which, as the long-sought-for actual meeting-ground of nature and morality, became his primary interest during the 1790's. The Revolution registered such a powerful impact upon him be-cause it represented the existential synthesis of all that had remained ra-tionally separated: the creation of a moral reality in nature through an act of *collective* freedom. This union of morality and nature meant for him the actual arrival of the final stage of teleological history, and conse-quently the conversion of historical into political relationships. The Revolution was, for Kant, a "phenomenon," but a phenomenon which awakened "an expansive moral causality" in the minds of observers and which itself uncovered the existence of "a capacity in human nature for the better which nature and freedom alone, however unified in legal principle, could promise only indefinitely and contingently in the

23. *Ibid.*, 60; "Idea for a Universal History," *ibid.*, 20.
24. "Rezension von Gottlieb Hufelands Versuch Über den Grundsatz des Natur-rechts" (1786), in Immanuel Kant, *Sämtliche Werke,* ed. Karl Vorländer, (Leipzig, 1922), VI, 174–175.
25. "Idea for a Universal History," in *Kant on History,* 17–18; "What is Enlighten-ment?" *ibid.*, 3, 4.

course of time."[26] This phenomenon, which exemplified the naturalization of man's moral capacities, Kant identified as the "evolution of a constitution according to natural law"—that is, a constitution both "lawful and morally good in itself" because it embodies the people's right to legislate for itself.[27] Thus once more Kant seems to have recalled the natural law to its wonted function of supplying absolute norms to politics by uniting reality and morality.

But once more the literal impression is illusory. In the formal political theory which Kant constructed to analyze the new political actuality in terms of his philosophy and to develop his philosophy in terms of the new political actuality, the natural law was indeed prominent, but it was enmeshed in problems that betokened an important change of function for it. On the positive side, Kant rooted politics in an autonomous sphere of law whose concern with external freedom and obligation joined nature and morality and, while differentiated from either, was yet itself joined more closely to morality as its predominant component. He assigned it a separate part within the "metaphysics of morals" and identified the statesman as "the moral politician, . . . who so chooses political principles that they are consistent with those of morality" as opposed to "the political moralist," who subordinates morality to "the mere mechanism of nature" and a politics which "is the art of using this mechanism for ruling men."[28] The fundamental principles in this legal sphere are given by natural law, which supplies "the unchanging principles to all positive legislation" and which consists in "the single innate right" of "freedom," "belonging to every man by nature," prescribing liberty under a general law which provides for the mutual compatibility of individual liberties, and including therein by necessary implication innate equality, the presumption of innocence, and the right of free expression.[29] Kant summarized his notion of natural rights in a definition which made transparent its status as the juristic counterpart to the self-legislation of the moral law: "external (or juridical) freedom . . . is the privilege to lend obedience to no external laws except those to which I could have given consent."[30]

Kant signalized the moral function which he now seemed to confer

26. Immanuel Kant, *Der Streit der Fakultäten* (1798), in *Werke*, ed. Ernst Cassirer (Berlin, 1916), VII, 398–401.

27. *Ibid.*

28. Immanuel Kant, *Metaphysische Anfangsgründe der Rechtslehre* (1797), *ibid.*, VII, 14–20; "Perpetual Peace," in *Kant on History*, 119.

29. Kant, *Rechtslehre*, in *Werke*, VII, 39–40.

30. "Perpetual Peace," in *Kant on History*, 93.

upon the natural law by applying a different term to it. In the history of the doctrine, a verbal distinction had often been made in the denotation of "law" which is glossed over in English. The Latin distinction between natural *lex* and *ius* went over into German, as into other continental tongues, and became the distinction between *Naturgesetz* and *Naturrecht. Gesetz,* like *Lex,* is law with the connotation of imposed validity by statutory command of a superior. *Recht,* like *ius,* is law with the connotation of a relationship among independent persons and of a validity derivative from the inherent equity of this relationship. Until this point Kant had used the term "*Gesetz*" for the laws both of nature and of morality, presumably to signify the statutory functions of the understanding and the practical reason respectively but also to imply the imposition of the natural law upon the moral dimension of man and the analogous imposition of the moral law upon the natural inclinations of men. But now, in the political context, Kant picked up the term *Naturrecht,* the standard appellation for natural law in its traditional function, apparently to signify his reversion to its role of legitimizing and relating the rights of man.

On the negative side, however, this abstract subscription to the full course of natural rights produced political conclusions which could hardly have been drawn from them if Kant's natural law actually was as central as it here seemed to be. The most striking of these surprising inferences, in view of Kant's definition of natural law in terms of the natural rights of the individual, was his categorical declaration that "the ruler in the state has, *vis-à-vis* his subjects, only rights and no compulsory duties" and that, whatever the provocation, neither the individual subject, nor a representative assembly, nor the people can raise "justifiable resistance" against him.[31] Kant here denied the rights both of resistance and of revolution because of the violation they would inflict upon the civil constitution that invested the supreme legislative power in the ruler, for "only through subordination to his general legislating will is a condition of law (*Recht*) possible."[32] But what, then, has happened to the natural law which enshrines the freedom of the individual in terms of *his* sacred legislative right? We have the interesting constellation whereby the natural law is superior to the constitutional law, and yet the subject's obligation under the constitutional law is superior to the ruler's obligation under the natural law.

The answer to the puzzle lies in the subordination of the natural law

31. Kant, *Rechtslehre,* in *Werke,* VII, 125–127.
32. *Ibid.,* VII, 126–127.

to political society. Natural law—that is, *Naturrecht*—effectively connects the juridical and the moral freedom of the individual, but in the actuality of civil society this natural right "is only an idea," for it does not suffice to establish an "actual condition of law."[33] Such a condition does not exist in the state of nature, for only the collectivity of men, inevitably using natural force against individual rights in a civil constitution, can establish it.

Certainly the will of each individual to live under a juridical constitution under the principles of freedom (i.e., the distributive unity of the will of all) is not sufficient to this end [i.e., perpetual peace]. That all together should will this condition (i.e., the collective unity of the united will)—the solution to this troublous problem is also required. Thus a whole of civil society is formed. But since a uniting cause must supervene upon the variety of particular volitions in order to produce a common will from them, establishing this whole is something no one individual in the group can perform; hence in the practical execution of the idea we can count on nothing but force to establish the juridical condition, on the compulsion of which public law will be later established.[34]

Kant pursued this crucial emphasis upon the political society by distinguishing categorically between a "natural" natural law and a "civil" natural law—"the primary division of natural law must be into natural and civil law"—and by assigning private law to the former and public law exclusively to the latter.[35] This meant that the natural law which grounded the rights of individuals was limited to personal possessions and conferred only a "provisional" or "presumptive" legal right to them; the natural law which applied to political society directed the sovereign, i.e., "public-legislative power," to the securing of these rights in a "lawful condition," which does not exist in the "lawless" state of nature, but otherwise simply sanctions the monopoly of public law by the sovereign. The step from the state of nature in which each individual has "his own right to do what seems to him right and good" to the state of political society in which he must unite with others "to subordinate himself to public, statutory, external compulsion," is a dictate not of experience but of an "*a priori* in the idea of reason."[36] Hereafter, practical reason validates a notion of law (*Recht*) for the community which absorbs and replaces the notion of natural law (*Naturrecht*) which had validated the rights of individuals independent of the community. The

33. *Ibid.*, VII, 118; Kant, *Streit der Fakultäten, ibid.*, VII, 400.
34. "Perpetual Peace," *Kant on History,* 118.
35. Kant, *Rechtslehre, op. cit.*, VII, 44.
36. *Ibid.*, VII, 58–59, 117–119.

natural right of man to legislate the law which he obeys is absorbed, for the political community, into the standard of a law which the people could have legislated but usually has not.[37]

Thus for Kant the fact of political society became a primary meeting-ground of reason and nature and transformed the status of the natural law that had exercised this function. In the context of this society, natural law is no longer the source of rights and duties, for the law legislated and enforced by the sovereign has replaced it as the union of nature and morality pertinent to the community.

The origin of the sovereign power is, from the practical point of view, inscrutable to the people who are subject to it. . . . The civil law (*Gesetz*), which is so sacred (inviolable) that it is a crime even to doubt it in practice and therewith to suspend its effect for a moment, is so conceived as if it must derive not from men but from a supreme infallible lawgiver. The meaning of the proposition— all authority is from God—expresses not an historical ground of the civil constitution but an idea as a practical principle of reason: the existing legislative power is to be obeyed, whatever its origin.[38]

But if it is no longer a source and sanction, the natural law still does play a role. Both it and the rights of the individuals which it prescribes enter into the structure of the sovereign will as its norm and end. "When a remediable defect is found in the constitution of the state or in its relations to others, the principle of the moral politician will be that it is a duty, especially of the rulers of the state, to inquire how it can be remedied as soon as possible in a way conforming to natural law as a model presented by reason."[39] The political "dependence" and "inequality" of citizens "in no way is opposed to their freedom and equality as men," because the former attributes are necessary conditions for a "people to become a state" and translate the human rights into the requirement that the politically dependent and inferior "be treated by all the others according to laws of natural freedom and equality as *passive* parts of the state."[40] Just as in Kant's history, the natural law has lost its integral function and its independent validity, but it enters into the service of the more particular principle that has replaced it and guides it toward a universal aspiration.

With Kant we have cut into the career of the idea of natural law at its turning point, when it was yielding to historicity and society but when

37. Kant, *Streit der Fakultäten, ibid.*, VII, 400.
38. Kant, *Rechtslehre, ibid.*, VII, 125.
39. "Perpetual Peace," *Kant on History,* 119.
40. Kant, *Rechtslehre, Werke*, VII, 121.

the mechanics of the transformation was still in evidence. On the basis of this case, we may hazard the hypothesis that even after the identifiable Kantian residues of natural law had dropped away their legacy of a universal truth binding upon men's behavior remained built into their successors. From this angle, Marx's insistence that both history and society were nature for men was a radical confession of what was held more moderately and more covertly elsewhere along the intellectual spectrum. In the final analysis, the staying power of the idea of natural law in its various forms reflects the fundamental belief of our culture, that infinite creativity may well be the ideal of the arts and sciences but that our creation of moral acts should conform to the reality of our common humanity.

5 MARX AND ENGELS AND HISTORY

Freedom . . . is the essential condition for the realization of all other values.

From "European and American Liberalism"

. . . the measure of greatness is the illumination of what is fundamental to humanity in all ages."

From "The User of Marx for History"

14 The Uses of Marx for History

I

Discussions of Marx have become invitations to banality. The Machiavellis, the Vicos, the De Toquevilles rise and fall but Marx goes on forever. So ubiquitous has he been in our intellectual experience and so all-encompassing have been the commentaries that it seems at times advisable simply to accept the inevitable and work him into the collection of old maxims which so frequently spare us the trouble of thinking. Thus: Marxism is a fine position to visit but I should hate to stay there. Or: Marx hatched the egg that Hegel laid while standing on his head.

For those whose tastes run rather to the utilitarian, perhaps the time has come to draw up a list of serviceable prescriptions wherein Marx figures. For example: Our views will be generally acceptable if we apply Marx to the analysis of any country but our own; the more hostile the country, the more acceptable the views. And again: We shall find Marx very convenient in explaining any social system about which we know very little; the less we know, the more unqualified and therefore the more brilliant the explanation. This use may be labeled "Marx as a teaching aid."

But we are not interested here in enriching our store either of proverbs or of injunctions. Nor are we interested in Marx merely as an object of study—whether as part of the "Know Your Enemy" series or as a revealing representative of nineteenth-century social and intellectual history. The relevance of the first is obvious, but for this purpose we should patiently follow the criteria of Marx chosen by the "enemy" rather than select our own. The relevance of the second is equally patent, although as historians we should probably prefer someone more obscure who could be rehabilitated. In any case it may be accounted, on this occasion, a parochial concern. What we are really interested in is the question of Marx's longevity, of Marx as a subject, if subject be taken to mean citizenship in that exclusive republic of letters whose collective mind, formed slowly over the centuries through the sifting out of

First published in *Political Science Quarterly* 75 (September, 1960), 355–78. This paper was originally delivered before the Russian Institute of Columbia University.

the transitory, the contingent and the inadequate, bequeaths the quintessential treasure of western culture to us, its novitiate.

When regarded in these fundamental terms, the answer to the question of Marx's permanent value may well be considered to be all or nothing at all. For if we consider many of Marx's particular contributions, we find them double-teamed, and fretted into that worn-out category of the "transitional". We have been assured that they had their origins before Marx, and we know that they have been formulated more truly—or let us say, for the skeptics, more to our taste—since Marx. For the dialectic, Marx is surrounded by Hegel and the existentialists; for the class struggle and the science of society, by Saint-Simon and Max Weber; for social history, by Lorenz von Stein and Marc Bloch, to name but one luminary of the modern approach. But if we then proceed to assert that it is not what he said but the way that he said it—that is, the combination of these particular insights into a more or less compatible system—then we have advanced only from the trivial to the trite. More important, to emphasize the substantive totality of Marx's system, whether in the ambitious form of dialectical materialism or in the more modest dress of the economic interpretation of history, is to emphasize precisely that aspect of Marx which, whatever its popular appeal, has been most wholeheartedly rejected by the academic community. Nor can it be maintained that Marx's total scheme amounts only to a dispensable scaffolding, an early crutch with no valid function in his mature thought. For even a cursory reading of Marx reveals that his characteristic interpretations applied generally to complete historical processes and not to specific events. His analyses of particulars were frequently perceptive but not especially distinctive. Consequently his system stands and falls with his over-all framework. And yet, while Marx's particular insights have generally called forth a "Yes but" response from scholarly posterity, the compound as a whole is typically answered with an "Oh no." In this posture he is aligned with Hegel and Toynbee as the protagonists of absolute historical laws in whose very possibility we no longer believe. Perhaps historians can still make their reputations by proclaiming themselves against determinism and the primacy of economic man—in short, against sin—but I doubt it.

Substantively, then, Marx provides little sustenance for historians today. We proceed on the assumptions of historical discontinuity, plurality of causation, and merely formal absolutes when we admit any at all. Marx's undoubted contributions to the social identification of the undifferentiated "people", or "masses", to the disciplined, or scientific, study of society, to the awareness of the ideological component in ideals and of the relations of material interests to them, to the social analysis of political power, and to the periodization of social history have all been absorbed and refined to such a degree that their classic formulation in Marx functions less as a model than as a straw horse. When even the disciples have had, admittedly or covertly, to revise Marx's analysis as men and times have changed, how much more exception has been taken by those whose assumptions as well as circumstances differ widely from Marx's own.

II

If we turn now from the substance to the form of Marx's thinking we come to the heart of our problem of his current usefulness, for here filial condescension is out of place and we must look to Marx as a master. In three different ways Marx provides approaches that must still be studied for problems that are still vital. For two of these approaches Marx must share our attention with his fellow members of a select company of intellectual pioneers. In the third, he stands alone.

First, Marx is one of those pivotal thinkers in whom—and only in whom—the fundamental antinomies of human life are not only expressed but, in some mysterious way, resolved. The criteria of intellectual greatness in our culture are varied. For some judges, either more impressionable or more partisan than most, they revolve around the function of innovation. For other observers, who can dissolve any putative novelty into its traditional components until there is nothing new any time anywhere under the sun, intellectual performance is measured by the comprehensiveness with which the assumptions, methods and ideas already current in an age are articulated and integrated. But if we take a less historical view of the problem and make our distinction between the primary thinkers from whom we can learn directly and the secondary figures who simply enter somehow into the development which has made us what we are, then we can probably agree on the truism that the measure of greatness is the illumination of what is fundamental to humanity in all ages. The problem, of course, is, whose fundamental?—since one man's necessity is another's contingency. But the problem does get resolved in practice, for there is a surprising consensus on the authoritative figures of our culture, and if we review their ranks the rationale of greatness becomes clear. Almost without exception the immortals are those who, regardless of their partisan solutions and followings, have something to say to everybody because they encompass both sides of eternally vital issues. Moreover, they encompass these oppositions in ways that are not only inimitable but almost incomprehensible. Idea and appearance in Plato, the two cities of Augustine, faith and reason in Ockham, necessity and virtue in Machiavelli, the spirit and the world in Luther, predestination and freedom in Calvin, mind and body in Descartes, reason and reality in Hobbes, transcendence and immanence in Spinoza, reason and nature in Rousseau, imperative and freedom in Kant—these fundamental contrasts, which seem disjunctive to lesser minds and which have even required a rather obvious developmental mediation by an Aristotle, an Aquinas and a Hegel, were not opposites for the masters. Indeed, so persuaded are they of the essential compatibility of these principles that they take it for granted and seem hardly aware of the problems that have beset their progeny. The delicate balance which is so natural in them has struck their successors as an intolerable strain, and so we have had the pattern of the original equilibrium of principles giving way to resolutions on the one side and on the other. Now, despite the Hegelian developmental format of his thought, Marx's place is with the dealers in dualities. "Evolution and revolution" is but the most familiar expression of the underlying balance between necessity and freedom which Marx with such assurance upheld. The vision of human destiny which men of this stamp shared is, I think, still beyond us. When we do catch a glimpse of it we grasp it usually in a particular formulation and then only fleetingly. The distance is too great, and the insight soon drops away or is hollowed into mere verbalism. We must read Marx along with the others—perhaps, since his idiom is familiar to us, even more than the others—to raise ourselves to the comprehension of this most elevated strand of our cultural heritage wherein the diversity of man's fate is recognized and yet composed to unity. For Marx illuminates the crucial insight on this level: that particulars and totalities are subject to very different processes; that we are equally committed as individuals to the freedom and variety of the one and as members of collectivities to the order and determination of the other; and that from this interplay of private spontaneity and public channel comes the final single direction of tomorrow's history.

The second application of Marx affects the general rather than the philosophical historian, for it concerns interpretation within, rather than across, particular periods. There has been much talk—if somewhat less use—of integrated history. With the expansion of the historical process to include the full range of human activities, from the economic and technological to the cultural and religious, the problem of how these varied strains are to be put together has come to the fore. In general, five devices have been adopted to this end. First, the specialized approach: one field of history is chosen and the rest lumped together as "background", to be brought out again in case of emergency when all intra-field explanations have failed. Second, the additive approach: this consists of several chapters on politics and one chapter each on everything else, together with the pious hope that it will all add up to something. Third, the grain-of-sand approach: an issue or theme that cuts across several fields of interest is examined for the play of various kinds of influences upon it, with the pious hope that historical man in this case was more unified than he usually is and was concerned in all his activities with this same issue. Fourth, the atmospheric approach: this is an aesthetic procedure in which variegated movements, events and anecdotes are grouped into a kind of historical portrait which yields a dominant impression. Fifth, the stylistic approach: here a label is selected, usually from the arts—like Renaissance, baroque, classical, romantic—and the qualities associated with it are applied across the board to all kinds of endeavors unto Renaissance tyranny in the name of the Roman republic and romantic economics in the name of infinite profit-seeking. These devices are certainly an improvement as modes of integration over the traditional organic analogy of rise, maturity and decline—which, incidentally, they have not entirely replaced—but their very variety shows that they are not entirely satisfactory.

In any discussion of this urgent problem of coherence Marx is essential; for, whatever our reservations on his substantive notions of base and superstructure, his method of integrating man's historical activities in any one period is the most intellectually satisfying means yet devised. What is unsatisfactory, of course, is Marx's commitment to economic primacy and to political and ideological dependence as absolute principles. Nor does it help much to tinker with this formulation and to claim with the early Marx and the late Engels that the relationships admit of reciprocity. What we must do is something more radical. We must "relativize" Marx's formulation and insist that, as he put it, it holds for some situations and not for others. But even when we deflower Marx's doctrine in this way, we are still left with a model structure of integration. Its essential prescriptions are two: that in every period the kind of activity with which men are most concerned—which they consider the most important—gives tone and color to the rest; and that this kind of activity must be one that concerns not only a capriciously selected few artists, writers or statesmen but the great body of men who are active.

If it be objected that our formulation has departed too far from the original Marx, it should be remembered that in the first large-scale articulation of his system what Marx opposed to the speculative history of consciousness was basically not economic history as such but the history of "real living individuals" and *"their* consciousness".[1] Consequently, history itself became for Marx a "real, positive science", and the coherence within a period is given by "abstractions" or "assumptions", which "have no value in themselves" but which "stem from the study of the real life process and the action of individuals of each epoch" and "serve only to facilitate the ordering of the historical material and to indicate the hierarchy of its particular levels."[2] Marx explicitly assigned to his first classic exposition of the economic interpretation, which followed hard upon this introduction, a place simply as "some of these abstractions which we use vis-à-vis ideology. . . . illustrated by historical examples."[3] Certainly this wider framework was rarely operative in Marx's subsequent writing, and in the *Capital* he was expressly to deny that classical antiquity and the Middle Ages were less dominated by their economic bases than were modern times.[4] Yet the breadth of Marx's ultimate conception of integration did have at least two important results for his work.

It permitted him to acknowledge, not only in historical practice, but in historical principle, that "even within a nation the individuals have entirely different developments, apart from their property relationships," since on the one hand traditional interests may exercise a political and theoretical influence disproportionate to their already "destroyed form of exchange", and on the other hand "particular points [*einzelne Punkte*]" of a society allow certain theorists to form "a more general synthesis" and thus "to appear at times further advanced than the contemporary empirical relations."[5] It was this kind of vague consciousness of a wider context for the economic interpretation that explains the surprising latitude in some of Marx's actual history-writing and helped Marx to account for himself.

The other important consequence of the broader context in which the economic interpretation was imbedded was that it permitted Marx to announce the principle of the particularity of each era and thereby to delimit the dependence of the superstructure upon the economic base for historical interpretation. Marx could castigate Proudhon for having

1. Karl Marx and Friedrich Engels, *Die deutsche Ideologie,* in V. Adoratsky, ed. *Marx/Engels Gesamtausgabe* (Berlin, 1932), I/5, p. 15.

2. *Ibid.,* pp. 16–17.

3. *Ibid.,* p. 17.

4. Karl Marx, *Capital: A Critique of Political Economy* (New York, 1906). p. 94, note.

5. Marx and Engels, *Die deutsche Ideologie, loc. cit.,* I/5, p. 62.

"substituted the means and men of our century for the men and means of previous centuries and misunderstood the historical movement by which successive generations transformed the results acquired from the generations which preceded them."[6] Now obviously Marx himself saw a pattern common to all ages, but since for him this was an admitted abstraction derived by synthetic judgment from experience rather than a necessary law imposed upon experience, it did not abridge the autonomy of each era of humanity. He even asserted, in his usual sweeping fashion, that with "immutable laws, eternal principles, ideal categories . . . there no longer is any history."[7] This insistence had the effect not only of maintaining historicity *between* eras but also of loosening the rigidity of integration *within* eras.

Since economic primacy was no absolute principle, the super structure could not be implied in it, inferred from it, or be considered any kind of logical function of it. For Marx the common substance of history was the activity of men—"men as simultaneously the authors and actors of their own history"[8]—and this activity extended equally to all levels: modes of production, social relations, ideas and categories.[9] Consequently in society "all relationships co-exist simultaneously and are mutually supporting".[10] "Definite individuals" are "the producers" of all these relationships, and the hierarchy of relationships is established simply by the fact that the conditions of physical existence define for every age the general orientation of the individuals whose activity produces the society, the state, and the ideas of that age.[11] If we subtract the substantive assumption prescribing only economic considerations as the conditions which delimit the area of significant activity, then we are left with the fruitful insight that the chief of men's concerns or values in any period form a kind of mold within which their other interests are organized.

But the uses of Marx as a model for the admission of antinomies and for integration within historical periods both lead inexorably to the problem that is at once Marx's most distinctive contribution and his greatest difficulty. For Marx is by professed method and by a body of actual insights as concrete and empirical as we are, and yet he somehow also gets out of this method and puts into his insights a total process, a

6. Marx, *Misère de la philosophie*, in *ibid.*, I/6, p. 187.
7. *Ibid.*, p. 184.
8. *Ibid.*
9. *Ibid.*, pp. 179–180.
10. *Ibid.*, p. 180.
11. Marx and Engels, *Die deutsche Ideologie*, in *ibid.*, I/5, pp. 15–16.

total meaning, such as we should wish to have. It is true that some of Marx's approximate contemporaries, like Comte, Spencer, Buckle and Ranke, evince similar patterns, but they do not touch us so nearly. Either the seams in the pattern are too evident, as in Comte and Ranke, or the scheme is so attuned to the material, whether by the amorality of the scheme or the limitation of the material, that we do not particularly care whether it is true or not. In either case we may endorse or criticize; in neither case can we participate. What intrigues us about Marx is his capacity to find an essentially ethical rationale running within and across the centuries at the very same time that he perceives the diversity and complexity of historical existence. Certainly we may simply shrug our shoulders and call him inconsistent. The trouble is that he is too inconsistent; the contrast is too blatant for us to be able to explain the inconsistency with the patent observations that a moral coloration seeped into the admitted "assumptions" or "abstractions" which constituted the sinews of his system. If this were all, the process would be familiar enough and we should be in a position to teach rather than to learn.

But Marx's thinking is striking in two ways. In the first place, where we cautiously and self-consciously separate our assumptions from the reality that we treat and look to the *validity* of our methods, Marx deliberately threw this caution to the winds, buried his assumptions without residue in the substance of history, and found in the manifold of reality the rational truth that he had placed there. He called his assumptions "actual assumptions" (*wirkliche Voraussetzungen*),[12] and felt that the pattern was as objectively existent as the particular facts of which it was entirely composed. All it required was inclusion of a set of facts—that is, the economic—which historians had not yet "bothered to observe or treated only as inessential, isolated from the historical process."[13] When he dwelt upon the "illusions" of the past, as he so often did, his concern was, not to show their invalidity, but to assess them for the degree of reality which they expressed and to demonstrate the distortion in approaching reality as anything less than a total process. Secondly, Marx's system holds our attention because of the apparent absurdity of the form which he chose for its cohesion. At the very period when Marx lashed the Hegelians for applying the categories of mind to "material" reality, he apparently adopted a developmental dialectic which made sense as a category of mind and applied it to "material" reality, where, by his own lights, it does not make sense. Marx had too acute an intelli-

12. *Ibid.*, p. 10.
13. *Ibid.*, p. 28.

gence to have made such an application baldly without realizing the incongruity of it. Actually, there was an intermediate step between his dialectical scheme and the raw material upon which it was imposed—a step which made the imposition seem congruous. Here we may perhaps glean something about the principles of synthetic judgment which we so sorely need.

III

What this process of mediation was, in Marx, can be specified, for it was not only a logical but a chronological development. It forms a crucial chapter in his intellectual biography, and we can watch it grow. Indeed, we can approach it only genetically, for Marx's situation was not that of a philosopher who held simultaneously to first principles and brute reality and sought a logical connection between them. Rather it was the situation of an intellectual who developed out of his first principles the mediating mold which was to cradle the brute reality from its first apprehension. It was not, then, as might appear from the finished system, the scheme that was applied to the reality, but rather the reality that was fitted to the scheme. Not only did this process signify a kind of prefabrication of Marx's reality which automatically ensured its consonance with the pattern—an obvious and not uncommon procedure—but, what was far more important and distinctive, it signified the development of principles which positively opened the way for Marx to reality. Can it be surprising, therefore, that he saw these principles as part of the reality itself? Let us see how this development worked.

The writings of Marx's pre-communist period, which stretched approximately from 1841 to 1844, are filled with a double effort: to retain the rationality, the meaningfulness, of Hegelian idealism and to reach for its concrete realization through action. Marx himself rang the keynote of his endeavors when he confessed in 1842: "The existence which I love seems truly to me a necessary existence, which I need, without which my being cannot have a full, satisfied, and complete life."[14] In response to this impulse toward realization, his first step, which he took between 1841 and 1843, was to *in*vert Hegel—a half-way stage toward his ultimate *sub*version of the master. Marx complained that Hegel had reversed the proper relationship of subject and predicate, and he insisted upon changing them back into their proper order.[15] Leaving

14. Marx, "Debatten über Pressfreiheit und Publikation der Landständischen Verhandlungen," in Adoratsky, ed., *op. cit.*, I/1a, p. 184.
15. Marx, *Kritik des Hegelschen Staatsrecht*, in *ibid.*, pp. 410, 426–427.

aside the philosophical implications of this formulation, we may say that in substance it amounted to a shift from the Hegelian notion of the determination of reason in phenomena to the notion of the rationalization of existence by phenomena. Thus "Hegel starts from the predicates of general determination instead of starting from real being. . . . Hegel does not [as he should] consider the universal as the idea of the real-finite, that is, of the existent. . . . "[16] "[For Hegel] . . . the philosophical element is not [as it should be] the logic of the thing, but rather it is the thing of logic."[17] Here, incidentally, is the root of Marx's life-long addiction to the rhetorical converse: it was his way of placing what he considered to be false diversions from existence back within the sphere of existence. Marx's rationalizations of existence at this stage made sense in terms of the particular kind of existence to which he was now addressing himself: to rational men in their relationship to the state, an institution which was traditionally deemed an arena of rational construction. A few random quotations will serve to illustrate. "The will of a people can no more than the will of an individual go beyond the laws of reason."[18] "Sovereignty is nothing else but the objectified spirit of the subjects of the State."[19] "The affairs and activities of the State are bound to individuals (the state is active only through the mediation of individuals.)"[20] "In the State it is conscious reason which should rule."[21] Rejecting Hegel's "dualism", as he saw it, which opposed the conscious formal constitution of the state to its unconscious, necessitous actuality, Marx identified the resolution of freedom with the immanent rationality of existence when he asked: "why not recognize the law of the thing, of reason, as the law of the State?"[22] Thus Marx, in this early period—that is, between 1841 and 1843—was essentially a political democrat, calling for the assumption of the rational control of the state by the people through an act of revolution.[23]

But the political world of his age was neither rational nor democratic; hence, his synthesis of reason and existence was marred by a glaring fault. When Marx confronted this issue, he was forced to reveal that he, too, was still operating on two different levels of reality.

16. *Ibid.*, p. 427.
17. *Ibid.*, p. 418.
18. *Ibid.*, p. 468.
19. *Ibid.*, p. 427.
20. *Ibid.*, p. 423.
21. *Ibid.*
22. *Ibid.*, p. 466.
23. *Ibid.*, pp. 467–468.

In modern States, as in Hegel's philosophy of law, conscious reality, the true reality of the general welfare, is only formal. . . . Hegel is not to be blamed because he describes the being of the modern State as it exists, but because he gives for the being of the modern State that which exists. That the rational is real, that is precisely in contradiction with the irrational reality which is everywhere the contrary of what it expresses and expresses the contrary of what it is.[24]

It was in this context, as early as 1842, that Marx adopted the Hegelian notion of "alienation" as the device for relating rational and phenomenal components in a single order of existence.[25] Alienation at this point was for Marx essentially political: it consisted in the separation of civil society away from the state into a purely private status, and in consequence the separation of the individual away from his true social being into "a purely external material being".[26] The remedy is similarly political—participation of all individuals in the constituent legislative power as their "natural right", for "only in his political posture is the member of civil society . . . worthy of the title of *man*."[27] At this stage, then, the integrity of Marx's realism demanded an act of collective political reason. Neither history nor economics entered into the problem.

The analytical point of view which this framework sponsored for Marx emerged in his journalistic activity on the *Rheinische Zeitung* during 1842. Essentially his analysis consisted in the critical measurement of current events by the standards of categorical universal political ideals. What was distinctive about this analysis was that for Marx the ideals were at least as real as the events and that consequently his measurement tended to take the form of assessing events as subordinate parts or divisions of the unities represented by the ideal within the real. Thus his criticism was double-pronged. On the one hand he set his own categorical principles as realities against "mystico-religious" theories of "imagination."[28] Not only did he now oppose "communist theories in their present form" because they had no "theoretical reality," much less any possibility of "practical realization,"[29] but he even deemed the conservative nobility to live, when measured by his standards, "beyond the real world." But even they must, to fight for their social existence, "al-

24. *Ibid.*, p. 476.
25. *Ibid.*, p. 496.
26. *Ibid.*, pp. 497–499.
27. *Ibid.*, pp. 498, 508–510, 525.
28. Marx, "Debatten über die Pressfreiheit," in *ibid.*, pp. 199, 220.
29. Marx, "Der Kommunismus und die Augsburger Allgemeine Zeitung," in *ibid.*, p. 263.

low universal reason and general liberty to enter into their bad sentiments and their chimeras."[30] "Liberty so constitutes the essence of man
that even its adversaries realize it while fighting the reality of it."[31] On
the other hand, he analyzed moderate positions as not merely partial
but even essentially opposed to the general reality. "It is in the opposition to a general liberty that the spirit of the definite sphere, the individual interest of the particular class, the naturally unilateral aspect of
character manifest themselves with . . . most brutality."[32]

It is not a question of knowing if the liberty of the press ought to exist, since it
always exists. It is a question of knowing if the liberty of the press is the privilege of some individuals or the privilege of the human spirit. It is a question of
knowing if the "liberty of the spirit" has more right than "liberties against the
spirit".[33]

Nor did specific forms of the principle fare any better than its limited
application. "We do not like the kind of liberty which appears only in
the plural. England shows us . . . how dangerous the limited horizon
of 'liberties' is for 'liberty'."[34]

We can see here the origins of Marx's ideas of "class". It had meaning
only over against a whole rational principle, of which it was both a part
and an opposite. Class thus started as the alienated phenomenon of real
reason. Marx even formulated a philosophical class conflict: "There is
the intolerance of one species of liberty which will support the others
only if they renounce their special nature and declare themselves its vas-
sals."[35]

The first tentative extension of these categories to social issues came
late in 1842 in Marx's articles on the wood-theft law. For here the general scaffolding was still much in evidence, with law and the state replacing liberty as the concrete universals under discussion, but their
antithesis now was the partial private interest of "property owners",
into which he lumped all the "privileged estates" without discrimination vis-à-vis the "class (*Klasse*) of the poor"—the "unpropertied".[36]
Marx's concern, however, lay not with this class opposition as such. It
lay rather with the illegality and irrationality of the property owners' ef-

30. Marx, "Debatten über die Pressfreiheit," in *ibid.*, pp. 198–199.
31. *Ibid.*, p. 202.
32. *Ibid.*, pp. 184–185.
33. *Ibid.*, p. 202.
34. *Ibid.*, p. 226.
35. *Ibid.*, p. 221.
36. Marx, "Debatten über das Holzdiebstahlsgesetz," in *ibid.*, p. 273–275.

forts to use law and the state as instruments of private interests; the un-propertied class, consequently, was not an active agent but functioned simply as an object upon which the state could vent its humane activity. Marx still gave neither an economic nor a historical basis to these classes; they were simply the palpable expression of the existential challenge to the integrity of human reason. His only approach toward history was his designation of feudalism—and of the customary rights which the privileged estates continued to claim from it—as the product of the "animal" age of man, but this was actually a philosophical rather than a historical reference since Marx's purpose here was to emphasize the freedom and the humanity of the conscious statutory law of the state by its contrast to the bondage and blindness of social custom.[37] "The statute [*Gesetz*] . . . is the universal and authentic judge over the lawful nature of things . . . [and] must conform to the lawful nature of things."[38]

The function of the state, "conformable to its reason, its universality, and its dignity," was to administer the "immortal" law.[39] The classes of the rich and of the poor were equally, although differently, alienated from these rational totalities, the rich because of their commitment to exclusive private property and interests—summed up as "accidental arbitrariness"—and the poor because of their divorce from the organic body of society, their delivery to "need" and "chance".[40] The fervor of Marx's passion for unity as a basic reality and of his deprecation of class as an alienation from it comes out graphically in his elaborate analogy between the class of the poor, cut off from the integral life of society, and dead wood, which has lost all connection with the rich life of living things.[41]

There is no more characteristic feature of Marx's philosophical framework than this categorical reprobation of economic interest as a distortion vis-à-vis the whole moral man.

The small, dry, spiritless, and self-seeking soul of interest sees only one point, the point at which it is violated, like the primitive man, who . . . makes the one point at which a passer-by touches him into the only point at which the essence of this passer-by touches the world. . . . But the State must see in the wood thief more than a stealer of wood. . . . Does not each of its citizens cohere to it through thousands of life-nerves, and should it sever all these nerves because

37. *Ibid.*, p. 272.
38. *Ibid.*, p. 269.
39. *Ibid.*, pp. 282, 298.
40. *Ibid.*, pp. 275–276.
41. *Ibid.*

that citizen has himself severed one? So the State will also see in the wood thief a man, a vital member in which its heart's blood flows, a soldier who defends the fatherland, a witness whose voice counts in court, a member of the community who should exercise public functions, the head of a family whose existence is sanctified, and above all a citizen of the State.[42]

Despite the apparent transvaluation of values which stamped his subsequent development Marx never departed from the fundamental conviction of his philosophical phase that acts of class interest could be neither justified nor understood save by reference to the total structure of reason in man and that the status of rationality in human affairs found its primary expression in the political act, where practice and consciousness joined. Hence in November 1842 it was still the state which had to restore integrity to men, through rationalizing the rights of the poor and generalizing the private interests of the rich. "Particular interests" did not represent matter itself but an "abstraction" from matter, and against "this depraved materialism, this sin against the holy spirit of peoples and humanity," Marx set the "political solution of material problems" —"their connection with the whole wisdom and morality of the State."[43]

It was all very well for Marx to translate Hegel's Reason into the reason of living men, but to burden rational activity with a metaphysical as well as a moral function is to place a great strain upon patience, and Marx was not a patient man. In his correspondence during 1843 Marx is still the political rationalist, calling for the "democratic state" as "the order of free humanity instead of the order of dead things."[44] "To become men means to be spiritual beings; to become free men means to be republicans."[45] But he was now obsessed with the search for "revolution" as the only means of bringing about the desired order. The urgency of revolution stemmed from a moral and political imperative but brought on an intellectual crisis which led Marx to a more practical development of his principles. "We want . . . to act on our contemporaries. . . . How to go about it? That is the question."[46] He acknowledged the disinclination of the Prussian government and the middle-class liberals to initiate political reforms on the one hand and the "anarchy" of intellectual reformers on the desired state of reason on the other.[47]

42. *Ibid.*, I/1a, pp. 277–278.
43. *Ibid.*, p. 304.
44. Marx to Ruge, May 1843, in *ibid.*, pp. 561, 564.
45. *Ibid.*, p. 561.
46. Marx to Ruge, September 1843, in *ibid.*, p. 574.
47. Marx to Ruge, May 1843, in *ibid.*, pp. 561–566, 573.

With this acknowledgment Marx's former acceptance of two juxtaposed existences and his confidence in the triumph of the true rational reality were undermined from both ends. Irrational existence must now be taken seriously; both its relationship to reason and the kind of rational reality which this relationship disclosed must be investigated and defined; in the service of the revolution which existing men would make to establish the rational society, the starting point could no longer be reason and the subsequence the arbitrary declination from reason, but the beginning must be the actual conditioning of men's reason by existence and the actual operation of men's reason in the conditions of existence considered as a single process. Hence, Marx abjured all discussion of rational reality as such and announced his intention of "finding the new world only through criticism of the old world."[48] But what must be emphasized here is Marx's confidence in the essential integrity of the intellectual process: the shape of reason could be discerned only by the inquiry into the conditions of its existence and the conditions of existence could be explicated only by reference to the operations of human reason.

Reason has always existed, but not always in the form of reason. Criticism can start then from any form of theoretical or practical knowledge, and from existing reality's own forms develop the true reality as its goal and final objective. . . . The reform of consciousness consists solely in . . . explaining its own actions [to the world]. . . . It will appear . . . that humanity is not beginning a new task but finishes its old work by taking consciousness of it.[49]

At this point, we can see Marx's system driving him to break out of the circle of philosophy toward history and out of politics toward economics. It is crucial for the understanding of Marx to realize that history and economics entered his system together. In his attempt to merge existence and reason into a single level of reality the interplay of the dialectic was flattened out into a concrete development through time. If reason could be known only through all the conditions of its existence, and if men then used their rational faculty, thus fortified, to create more appropriate conditions, then obviously a historical dimension enters in. By the same token, if reason is now homogenized in the sense of being a conditioned force operating through all spheres of human activity, and if the further rationalization of the political sphere is blocked by the passivity of all politically active classes—Marx lumped

48. Marx to Ruge, September 1843, in *ibid.*, p. 573.
49. *Ibid.*, pp. 574–575.

conservatives and liberals alike under the label "philistine"[50]—then the motive force of progress must be sought outside of politics in a more fluid sphere and among men less susceptible to the prevailing form of conditioned reason. Marx still felt that "the modern forms" of the state "comprise the requirements of reason," but he now saw the contradiction within the modern state between "its theoretical definition and its real hypothesis" as a contradiction within politics rather than as an alienation from politics. Consequently, the resolution of the contradiction had to come from outside, from "the social struggles, the social truth," which the state no longer resolved but "expressed."[51] It had to come from the social group that was alienated from the existing forms of society by the prevailing system of "acquisition and exchange" and enlightened toward political rationality by the intellectuals.[52] Marx was not yet either a philosopher of history or an economist, but his tentative gropings in these directions already indicate the main lesson of his development: that a system of principles, when treated for their reality rather than their validity, far from inhibiting actually stimulates the infinite expansion of empirical investigation. When they are genuinely universal and when faith in their validity is strong enough to require no further buttressing, the inevitably mixed testimony of their realization presses inexorably toward universal research in the effort to reach a final assessment.

The seeds which Marx planted in this published correspondence of 1843 were harvested during the following year. During this last phase of his pre-communist development, which led up to the first classic formulation of the familiar system in the *German Ideology* of 1845, Marx introduced the economic basis of his doctrine and joined it to his older framework through a philosophy of history. The chief products of this phase were the published introduction of the projected *Contribution to the Criticism of Hegel's Philosophy of Law*, assorted unpublished papers brought together and printed in 1932 under the appropriate title of *The Economic-Philosophical Manuscripts,* and the better-known *Holy Family.* The importance of these works for our purposes lies in their revelation of the role of history in Marx at a time when he still was holding explicitly to philosophical and political principles, before they were transmuted into assumptions of primary historical and economic categories. They show that Marx resorted to history for three reasons: first, to

50. Marx to Ruge, May 1843, in *ibid.*, p. 565.
51. Marx to Ruge, September 1843, in *ibid.*, p. 574.
52. Marx to Ruge, May 1843, in *ibid.*, pp. 565–566.

explain in terms of anachronism or anticipation some of the discrepancies between ideas and conditions; secondly, to set the changing forms of men's practical reason against the claims to absolute validity by contemporary theorists; thirdly, and most importantly, to add the necessary dimension to human economic activities which could justify Marx in identifying those activities with the fundamental life-process of humanity.

Under the first head, we have Marx's argument in his essay on Hegel, that "the mission" of history is "to establish the truth of the present life," that this truth consists in the demonstration of the theoretical and practical "alienation of man from himself," that in the case of Germany this alienation consists in the representation of modern times by "ideal history"—that is, by theory—and the adherence of its "real history" to the *ancien régime,* and that the action which establishes integrity in Germany must consequently be the historical action of modernizing existence by "realizing philosophy."[53]

Under the second head, Marx's use of a historical orientation to emphasize his argument against the absolute claims of theory went far beyond the expected reference to history as a "movement" operated by the actions of real men.[54] He denied that history could even yet be the real history of man; it could only be "the history of the origins of man"—that is, the prehistory of man.[55] Obviously, then, history could not yet embody integral forms of reason.

Marx's third argument follows from this. The motive force of this prehistory was the process by which man was producing the material conditions for his life as man, and the connection between this material production and the ultimate rational self-development of human culture could only be a historical one—that is, the movement from prehistory to history. For Marx, industry was the prime vehicle of interaction between nature and man, and it was the historical dimension that even within the realm of prehistory generalized the meaning of economic activity. "Industry is the actual historical relationship of nature . . . to men. . . . The nature which is developing in human history . . . is the real nature of man; therefore, the nature that is developing in industry, even if in alienated form, is the true anthropological nature."[56] Marx

53. Marx, "Zur Kritik der Hegelschen Rechtsphilosophie: Einleitung," in *ibid.,* pp. 608–613.
54. Marx, *Ökonomisch-Philosophische Manuskripte aus dem Jahre 1844,* in *ibid.,* I/3, p. 153.
55. *Ibid.*
56. *Ibid.,* p. 122.

complained that "the history of industry" had hitherto not been "comprehended in its connection with the essence of man,"[57] and he adapted his own historical philosophy to the purpose.

How did he work this? Apparently by a play on the broader and narrower sense of "produce."

This material, directly perceptible private property is the material sensory expression of alienated human life. Its movement—production and consumption—is the sensory revelation of the movement of all previous production—that is, the actualization and actuality of man. Religion, family, state, law, morality, science, art, etc. are only particular forms of production and fall under its general law. . . . Religious alienation as such appears only in the realm of inner human consciousness, but economic alienation is that of real life—the transcendence of it therefore includes both sides.[58]

The role of history, then, is to mediate between both these meanings of production. It becomes for Marx the common denominator for tracing the relationships among the various kinds of human production.

Marx's development toward communism had the effect of divesting philosophy and politics of their former integrity without, however, enthroning economics in their place. All these activities were partial, and Marx's emphasis was always on wholeness, totality, as the only basis for rational freedom. It was to be expected that philosophy as the expression of consciousness only and politics as the organization of "a ruling group in the society" around "an abstract whole"[59] would be insufficient, but more surprising is the fact that for Marx economics was, too. Marx came to economics via the proletariat and not the other way around. In his search for an agency of rationalization he advanced from "suffering humanity" to "the proletariat" by the end of 1843 because he decided that this was the one group that had "the standpoint of the whole," that was alienated from "the human essence" as such, that "has a universal character through its universal sufferings," that "is, in a word, the complete fall of man and that can reconquer itself only by the complete reconquest of man."[60] Hence Marx did not arrive at his economic primacy by expanding the dominion of economic primacy over human nature but rather by emphasizing the totality of human nature against both philosophical man and political man and then by specify-

57. *Ibid.*, p. 121.
58. *Ibid.*, pp. 114–115.
59. Marx in *Vorwärts*, 10 August 1844, in *ibid.*, I/3, p. 22.
60. Marx to Ruge, May 1843, in *ibid.*, I/1a, p. 565; "Zur Kritik der Hegelschen Rechtsphilosophie," in *ibid.*, pp. 619–620; *Vorwärts*, 10 August 1844, in *ibid.*, I/3, pp. 21–22.

ing economics as the least organized, the least determined, and the most generalized field of human activity, and consequently as the one from which impulses for the increase of rationality most freely came. But however primary in sponsoring the primitive forces and establishing the general possibilities of change, the attitude born of economic relations had to be formed and directed by "philosophy, which finds in the proletariat its material arms," toward "political revolution with a social soul."[61] Moreover, man's condition of alienation furnished assurance that none of these activities was deducible from the other. Only history could describe the pattern of their relationships and consequently the changing components of "human nature" for which economics furnished the mold. Surely the professional imperialists among the historians can make good use of Marx here.

What, then, was the character of his history which had such a cardinal role in the formation of the Marxist system? Essentially, it was the story of "the common reason of men active and acting in different centuries,"[62] striving, because it is the nature of rational beings so to strive, to recover its identity from the myriad forms into which it had been split. This process of immanent rationalization informs history with a pattern. The process as a whole moves toward world history as man attempts to recover his universality, and the movement is spurred by man's struggle for the means of existence, as the most general sphere of life which catches up into the process of world history the great bulk of people who are unaffected by anything else. But the pattern is not all. It is but the skeleton of history. Since man has alienated himself on all levels he must recover himself on all levels. Hence every act, every event, every institution, every idea is important in itself, for each contains a part of man and has its place in the whole.

IV

Such was the conception of history that went into the building of Marx's system, and, despite the calcification which it endured in his later years, such are still the assumptions that make it intellectually respectable. It remains to ask: how did this philosophy of history work for him and how can it work for us?

How true was Marx's own writing of contemporary history? Obviously, given Marx's record of political failure and intellectual influence,

---

61. Marx, "Zur Kritik der Hegelschen Rechtsphilosophie," in *ibid.*, I/1a, p. 620; *Vorwärts*, in *ibid.*, I/3, pp. 22–23.
62. Marx, *Misère de la philosophie*, in *ibid.*, I/6, p. 185.

the answer must be the historian's favorite: medium. With the help of our analysis, however, we may perhaps illuminate this a bit. In the period before the revolution of 1848 Marx's pattern was right but his empirical insight was not. The philosophical conception which called for a revolution of reason for the self-government of humanity was a true intuition into the nature of his age, but his scientific inferences on the status of industrial capitalism and its social agents were true neither on the level of consciousness, where he could account for failure, nor on the level of economic reality, where he could not. During the revolutionary period his system reached the height of its fruitfulness for history. The motif of the class struggle, however temporary, did actually arise to mingle with the political revolution of freedom, and the conformity of this situation with the constituents of Marx's philosophy of history produced the best history he ever wrote. After the revolution Marx's vision of contemporary history was again distorted, but this time in the other dimension. The world of man became—and has continued to become—more self-interested, more diffuse, more empirical; if the Marxist social science could be taken up as appropriate, the Marxist philosophy of the integral revolution certainly could not.

If applicability were all, we could simply conclude with a pious reflection on the flexibility of syntheses, which usually continue to be right somewhere even if they are wrong somewhere else. But applicability is not all. The remarkable fact is that Marx's value lies more in the parts of his thinking that were wrong than in those that were right. The contribution of the early Marx to history lay precisely in his perception of an empirical economic and social movement that hardly yet existed. The contribution of the later Marx consisted in his retention, amid a diffused reality, of a rational scheme that did not materialize. These distortions were contributions in two different ways. First, their function was to place historical knowledge in the service of political and moral action, and history used to this end has ever been—and perhaps must ever be—in some measure distorted. For how are historical conditions to be resolved in one of several possible directions unless history is interpreted from the point of view of the desired end? And it must be remembered that Marx always justified himself in the name of reality, that he wrote contemporary history in terms of future reality. Secondly, the Marxian distortions also perform an intellectual function. By expanding the scope of meaningful reality and then clamping his system down tightly over the whole vast area, Marx created a model of the hypothetical unity which enables the historian to make clear sense of those things wherein the historical agents of the past found only confused sense or nonsense. We have come to recognize, with Marx, that a distortion of the past in the direction of unity is a necessary correction for the distortion by the past in the direction of partiality.

Our situation, then, is this: We cannot use the substance of Marx but we can use the form in which he couched it. What does this mean concretely? It means that we must emulate Marx's combination of historical breadth and rational pattern, but only under certain conditions. We must use an approach like Marx's not only because our passion for literal empirical truth threatens to drive the history of man from our grasp but because we must make conscious and deliberate the vagaries of assumptions which in any case determine our judgment even of the empirical fact. But if we are not to pursue the enticing form of reason into that mirrored chamber where, like Marx, we should find only reflections of ourselves wherever we turned, we must observe three conditions in the organization of history.

First, we must employ our categories as questions and not as canons. So variegated is the material of history that our questions must be categorical if we are to penetrate it at all. Thus even the particular substantive categories of Marx, like economic primacy, class struggle, ideology, and so forth, invalid as they usually are in themselves, become valid when they are applied, along with others, as *queries* to the material for the purpose of translating it into some kind of rational process. The question to be asked is always, how does it fit?—and we must ask this in terms of all the categories which, both singly and in combination, bear meaning for us.

The second condition which qualifies our search for historical rationality prescribes that our pattern be recognized as bearing only upon the historical material at hand and never upon situations which have not been fitted for size. Thus our patterns will not disappear into laws, and history will not disappear into social science. The distinction is visible in the development of the cautious Marx of 1845, who distinguished between "estate" and "class," calling the latter "a product of the bourgeoisie,"[63] into the doctrinaire of 1848 who flatly announced that "the history of all previous society is the history of class struggles."[64]

The final condition requires the choice of categories which lie beyond or across, but never coincide with, the explicit issues in our historical material. This is not only a matter of preventing commitment from degenerating into partisanship. It is also a matter of illuminating the ex-

---

63. Marx and Engels, *Die deutsche Ideologie, loc. cit.*, I/5, p. 66.
64. Marx and Engels, *Manifest der Kommunistischen Partei*, in *ibid.*, I/6, p. 525.

ternal relations of historical facts and of finding a common measure for them, in all their diversity and conflict. Marx's fruitful application of philosophical categories to economic processes is a case in point. When he began to think of them as economic categories his development as a historian ceased.

But here a final question arises: if we circumscribe universals with such limitations and if we reject all historical metaphysics like Marx's, what kind of rational pattern is left to apply? Are we doing more than simply renewing the vague appeal for general meanings which historians have raised periodically from Renaissance pragmatism to the "new history" of the last generation? Certain specifications can be made. Marx has little, if anything, to teach us directly about universals in the form that dominates contemporary philosophy of history—the categories of historical knowledge. He assumes an identity between historical agent and historian which begs the whole question. Marx does have something to teach us, as has been indicated above,[65] about the comparatively narrow problem which concerns the coherence of man's activities within a particular age or context. But the crucial question is far more fundamental: can we use, in any shape, a rational pattern that runs between as well as within the different ages and contexts of history and thereby provides a constant measure for human evolution? It is well known that historians of our century have dismissed philosophy of history in the sense of such cosmic schemes—whether of the drama of salvation, the progress toward the heavenly cities of freedom or social justice, or the dour cycle of human destiny. When we talk of universals and of laws, we mean—or more precisely, we say we mean—the universals and the laws of knowing and of method rather than of development. Yet it seems to me that the distinction between an acceptable philosophy of history that is epistemology and an unacceptable philosophy of history that is metaphysics is a false one. A rational pattern extending across the ages is as intellectually necessary for the philosopher of history as is the rational community that makes historical knowledge possible for him. For, between the historical man who is to be known and the historian who is to know, there lies an actual historical process, and the knowing depends upon an assessment of what has developed, in the field of the historical action concerned, between the two terminals of knowledge. Obviously, we do not need, for such patterns, the belief in a single grandiose law of substantive history that assures our future as well as our past, and this facet of Marx we cannot use. We restrict our-

65. *Supra*, pp. 275–281.

selves to a plurality of patterns, appropriate to the discrete problems of our investigation, but within these limits—and, indeed, even more urgently because of these limits—we can use the awareness of that universal dimension of historical action which has united men in shared traditions and common enterprises and which furnishes the connecting links both within and between all the particular historical processes leading across the ages from an event to its historian.

We are, then, more modest than Marx, but we are more ambitious too. For we look into history, as it has been lived, for the integrity of humanity, which, in his view of history, has yet to be created.

15 Marx and Engels as Historians

I

Amid the plethora of paraphrases, studies, exegeses, and criticisms on the subject of the economic interpretation of history, a thoroughgoing analysis of the specific historical works by Marx and Engels has been entirely lacking. Two reasons may be adduced to explain the omission. First, there has been general acceptance of the idea that these works simply embody the consistent imposition of a pre-conceived philosophy of history upon a limited historical subject. Engels himself seems to have furnished the authority for this conception,[1] and commentators in general have been content to follow along this line, dismissing the Marxian historical studies as examples of the theory of historical materialism and proceeding to deal directly with the theory itself, in its more schematic formulations.[2] Secondly, little importance has been attached

---

1. In his introduction to the 1895 edition of the *Class Struggles in France*. V. Adoratsky, ed., *Karl Marx: Selected Works* (New York, 1936), II, 169–170.

2. For example, Paul Barth, *Die Philosophie der Geschichte als Soziologie* (Leipzig, 1915, 2nd ed.), I, 635; Ernst Troeltsch, *Der Historismus und seine Probleme,* in *Gesammelte Schriften* (Tübingen, 1922), III, 330–331; Karl Federn, *The Materialistic Conception of History: A Critical Analysis* (London, 1939), 4; Joseph A. Schumpeter, *Capitalism, Socialism, and Democracy* (New York, 1942), 9–10. A complete bibliography of works on the philosophy of Marx and Engels cannot be given here. The most complete compilation, for the most part still unpublished, has been drawn up by Robert S. Cohen. Sections of this have been published, in the form of critical studies, in *Review of Metaphysics,* IV (December, 1950), 291–311, and *ibid.,* IV (March, 1951), 445–459. The published general bibliographies are Ernst Drahn, *Marx-Bibliographie* (Berlin, 1920) and *Marx-Engels Archiv,* I (1926), 471–527, which together cover works up to 1925. Most useful for this paper, in addition to the above-mentioned studies by Troeltsch and Schumpeter, have been: Georg Lukács, *Geschichte und Klassenbewusstsein* (Berlin, 1923), the best sympathetic analysis, and Herbert Marcuse, *Reason and Revolution* (New York, 1941), the best general analysis; Mandell Morton Bober, *Karl Marx's Interpretation of History* (Cambridge, 1927); Alfred Braunthal, *Karl Marx als Geschichtsphilosoph* (Berlin, 1920); Auguste Cornu, *Karl Marx: l'homme et l'oeuvre* (Paris, 1934), also published as *La jeunesse de Karl Marx* (Paris, 1934); Benedetto Croce, *Historical Materialism and the Economics of Karl Marx* (London, 1931); Hans Rothfels, "Marxismus und auswärtige Politik," in Paul Wentzcke, ed., *Deutscher Staat und deutsche Parteien* (Munich and Berlin, 1922); Henri Sée, *Matérialisme historique et interprétation économique de l'histoire* (Paris, 1927).

First published in the *Journal of the History of Ideas* 14:3 (June, 1953), 381–403.

to the historical works for the development of the Marxist system. In general—and this is particularly true of the older treatments—the system is analyzed as a constant whole, with materials drawn indiscriminately from the earlier writings culminating in the first full presentation of the economic interpretation with the *Poverty of Philosophy* of 1847 and the *Communist Manifesto* of 1848 and from the mature articulations of the theory in the introduction to the *Contribution to the Critique of Political Economy* of 1859 and *Capital* (1867–1894). Interest in the development of Marx and Engels has been focused almost exclusively upon the early shift, completed by 1845, from the philosophical idealism of the Young Hegelians to the first unambiguous expressions of dialectical materialism.[3]

These grounds, however, are not binding, for on each count they raise questions which require more intensive analysis of the historical works for their solution.

First, there is reason to doubt, even on the evidence of the commentators themselves, that the histories written by Marx and Engels should be considered as simple applications of their general theory. For these studies have come in for a positive evaluation by men who do not subscribe to the materialistic conception of history.[4] In more general terms it has been recognized that the passion for the comprehension of facts which drove Marx and Engels from the Hegelian dialectic to dialectical materialism drove them at the same time to a search for a command over historical and social knowledge.[5] The implication is that the historical studies are independent compositions and that their relation to the philosophy of history which lies behind them is a problem rather than an assumption.

Secondly, the presupposition that Marx's and Engels' system remained constant after its formulation in the middle 1840's implies its imperviousness to the cataclysm of 1848 which marked a decisive turn

3. This problem has especially concerned recent scholarship, in part because the definitive edition of the works of Marx and Engels by the Marx-Engels-Lenin Institute in Moscow (1927–1935) includes writings only up to December 1848 (although the Marx-Engels correspondence is published in full).

Thus Cornu, *op. cit.;* Sidney Hook, *From Hegel to Marx* (New York, 1936); Konrad Bekker, *Marx' philosophische Entwicklung: seine Verhältnis zu Hegel* (Zurich and New York, 1940); H. P. Adams, *Karl Marx in His Earlier Writings* (London, 1940).

4. A. J. P. Taylor, *The Course of German History* (New York, 1946), 77; G. Barraclough, *The Origins of Modern Germany* (Oxford, 1947), 416, note 1; Friedrich Meinecke, *1848: eine Sekulärbetrachtung* (Berlin, 1948), *passim;* H. Sée, *op. cit.,* 33; E. Troeltsch, *op. cit.,* III, 330–331.

5. H. Rothfels, in *op. cit., passim;* J. Schumpeter, *op. cit.,* 9–10; H. Sée, *op. cit.,* 50–51; E. Troeltsch, *op. cit.,* III. 342.

in the ideas of so many men of that generation.[6] We know, however, that the immediate post-revolutionary years did witness a transition in the externals, at least, of Marx's intellectual development. Although the neat arrangement of Marx's life into a philosophical phase until 1845, a political phase until 1850, and an economic phase thereafter, is contradicted by his economic investigations of the later 40's and by his political activity in the First International during the 60's and 70's, it does reflect something of the essential direction which Marx's work took during the course of his career. Engels tells of Marx's turn to economic studies during 1850, after the frustration of the hopes he had drawn from his interpretation of contemporary French history in the first three sections of *The Class Struggles in France*.[7] To what extent the shift in the forms of Marx's thinking involved a development in the substance of his ideas thus becomes a valid problem. The historical studies which Marx and Engels wrote in the transitional period from 1850 to 1852 are important for the investigation of this problem, first, because they constitute the major works of this phase, and secondly, because the striking contrast in quality between the history written at this time and the analogous *Civil War in France* of 1870–71 furnishes a clear index, on a single plane, of the change in the emphases within Marx's system.

This paper will attempt to open the analysis of these problems.[8] The writings to which attention will be devoted are those on the revolution of 1848—Marx's *The Class Struggles in France* and *The 18th Brumaire of Louis Bonaparte* and Engels' *Germany: Revolution and Counter-Revolution*.[9] These are the studies most relevant for this complex of problems. They are revolutionary history, and this kind of history was

6. H. Marcuse, *op. cit.*, recognizes the fact of development in this period but does not attempt to trace its features.

7. Engels' introduction to *The Class Struggles in France*, in V. Adoratsky, ed., *op. cit.*, 171–172.

8. It should be emphasized that this paper will not be concerned with Marx's and Engels' philosophy of history as such and that the analysis will not be based upon the philosophical criteria of coherence and validity. It will attempt rather to seek out the peripheral area in which philosophy of history and specific historical material meet and to investigate their reciprocal effects.

9. The articles which compose *Die Klassenkämpfe in Frankreich* were written by Marx for the *Neue Rheinische Zeitung*, which Marx edited in London, between January and October, 1850. The first three sections were originally articles for the January, February, and March issues, and what is now the final chapter was a part of an article on the English commercial crisis published in the final double issue of the journal for the months May to October. The papers were combined into book form and given an important introduction by Engels in 1895. *Der 18. Brumaire des Louis Bonapartes* was written by Marx during January and February, 1852, for *Die Revolution*, a short-lived journal edited by Joseph

most typical of Marx and Engels; they are contemporary history, and in this kind of history the central issue finds its most rewarding formulation; and they are of the vintage 1850–52 years, which are crucial for development within the Marxist system.

II

We must first examine the general features of these historical works. The historiographical issues raised by the revolutions in France and Germany are so different as to require separate treatment. In *The Class Struggles in France* and *The 18th Brumaire of Louis Bonaparte*, Marx was confronted with a historical situation in which economic developments and social groupings were complicated by the continuing role of political traditions and institutions. These traditions and institutions did not easily fit into a simple scheme of economic interpretation. In his effort to comprehend both sets of factors, Marx conceived of the historical process as operative on two distinct, albeit connected, levels, and he utilized two corresponding methods to treat of them: on the one hand, the level of day-to-day history, which included the workings of political institutions and the specific course of social events and could be grasped by the usual empirical means of research; on the other hand, the level of fundamental, rational, long-range history, which was manifested in the basic economic development of society and its presumptive political demands and could be ascertained by the philosophical means of the historical dialectic taken over from Hegel. Marx's task was to find a synthesis of the two lines of approach, using the concept of the class-struggle as the link between them. In this process the dialectical scheme was softened, its bold dicta endowed with nuances and complexities as Marx strove to encompass the ineluctable events of the revolution and the particular conditions of French society which underlay them. The course of the revolution, in his treatment, was minutely divided and subdivided. He saw it as a retrogressive development, of which the

---

Weydemeyer in New York. It was first re-published in book form at Hamburg in 1869. *Germany: Revolution and Counter-Revolution* was written in English and published in the *New York Tribune* as a series of twenty articles from October, 1851, to December, 1852. Although published under Marx's name, the articles were actually written by Engels, and the correspondence between the two makes it clear that while they all passed through Marx's hands he had little if any share in their composition. Cf. V. Adoratsky, ed., *Karl Marx, Friedrich Engels: Historisch-Kritische Gesamtausgabe* (Berlin, 1929), III/I, 229–392, *passim.* For this paper I am using the English versions of the three works in V. Adoratsky, ed., *Karl Marx: Selected Works*, II.

main stages were: the bourgeois republic with social institutions, the pure bourgeois republic in its founding phase, the constituted bourgeois republic, and its dissolution in favor of "the parody of Imperial restoration." The actors in the revolution were similarly subjected to painstaking analysis in order to explain a course of events which was inexplicable by a general interpretation in terms of class struggle. Consequently, the classes were dissected into an involved series of subclasses, which Marx set up with criteria given by their concrete social and political activity.[10]

Thus Marx's theory of the class struggle became infinitely complex as he built the structure of temporal events on the framework of his philosophy. The integration of the two elements was not always successful, and at time the skeleton protruded. On the one hand he was addicted to bare didacticism when the reality derived from the dialectics of social development found no counter-part in the realm of men's conscious action. For instance, after he described the peculiar economic and social structure of France, he exclaimed:

> In France, the petty bourgeois does what normally the industrial bourgeois would have to do; the worker does what normally would be the task of the petty bourgeois; and the task of the worker—who solves that? No one. It is not solved in France; it is proclaimed in France.[11]

On the other hand, the substance of history occasionally seemed to elude the pattern entirely. In his repeated attempts to explain the rise of Louis Bonaparte, Marx not only saw him variously as the expression of

10. Marx divided the ruling bourgeois class into land-owning, financial, and industrial sections, all distinguished from an idealistic republican coterie which had no economic basis in the capitalistic middle class but were bourgeois none the less. These distinctions were employed to give meaning to what otherwise might appear paradoxical facts, viz., the bourgeois opposition to bourgeois domination under the July monarchy, the predominance of the moderate republican group in the early part of the revolution, its replacement by a royalist middle-class majority, the division of this majority into monarchical factions and yet the necessity of their cooperation in a republican form of government. The proletariat was itself subdivided into an advanced section, which appeared late in the revolution under Blanqui, and a mass which demonstrated its immaturity by political adherence to the utopian socialist doctrinaires who preached class harmony. The petty bourgeoisie were simply represented in the democrats of the Mountain, but Marx went to great pains to arrive at an intimate understanding of their position in order to explain their shift from alliance with the *grande bourgeoisie* in the June days to alliance with working-class socialists after the consolidation of bourgeois rule. Finally, the peasants, to whom again Marx devoted intense effort, were portrayed as an independent group which both did and did not constitute a class; Marx wavered between his view of them as a barbarian mass whose political expression was the Napoleonic idea and his conviction that a growing section of them was destined for a revolutionary alliance with the proletariat.

11. Marx, *The Class Struggles in France*, in *op. cit.*, II, 276.

the common opposition of all other classes to bourgeois political rule, as the chief of the *Lumpenproletariat,* and as the representative of the peasants. He also interpreted Bonaparte's role as the embodiment of the monstrous state-machine which had risen like a Frankenstein creation to predominance over bourgeois society, and as the last resort of that bourgeoisie in its quest for social order against its own principles of political liberty.

But beyond these individual cases, Marx's distinction between two levels of history had important consequences for his general interpretation of the revolution in France.

First, it produced two versions of the revolution and two corresponding methods, varying with the time of writing. In the earlier *Class Struggles in France,* the emphasis was on the specific development of events, analyzed, to be sure, in terms of the theory of the class struggle, but earnestly traced as an open process as if Marx were himself uncertain of the specific forms by which his Logos was working itself out in history. In *The 18th Brumaire,* on the other hand, when the same ground was covered it was treated as a closed, determined historical process; the tone was doctrinaire, the analysis not so much developmental as logical. This approach was the product of time and the hindsight it brought. The main sections of *The Class Struggles,* written at the beginning of 1850, were predicated on the assumption that the revolution of 1848 was the realization of the teleological "revolution of the nineteenth century," that it was continuing, and that the proletariat, enlightened by its earlier stages, stood ready to consummate it. When *The 18th Brumaire* was written at the beginning of 1852, Marx realized that the revolution of 1848 was over, and while its educational function was still admitted, its events now appeared to him as a false start, still bound by the illusions of the past and quite distinct from what the dialectic showed to be the true reality of the general revolution of the nineteenth century. Whereas in *The Class Struggles* the levels of empirical and philosophical history appear on a more equal footing, in *The 18th Brumaire* historical events are definitely subordinated to the overriding general process of history.

A second consequence of the twofold interpretation of historical truth indicates some of its implications. Not only the history itself but the agents of the history were endowed with a twofold existence. When Marx emphasized how much "in historical struggles must one distinguish the phrases and fancies of the parties from their real organism and their real interests, their conception of themselves from their reality,"[12]

---

12. Marx, *The 18th Brumaire,* in *op. cit.,* II, 344–345.

he was not, in any historiographical sense, seeking to separate truth from illusion, but rather to order two diverse elements within the field of history along the lines of what amounted to a kind of subject-object relationship. However hierarchical their arrangement, "subjective" ideas and actions on the one hand and "objective" historical law and the situation which it produced on the other were distinct forces by reason of their imperfection and were necessary to each other for the making of history.[13] Fundamentally, this is the familiar idea of the "superstructure," but what makes it significant for our purposes is that in Marx's approach to history it was not simply a device to deprecate ideologies but also a means of accepting into his account actions and ideas which were not in full harmony with the "objective" social process.

The implications become clear when we go on to the third and still more specific application of Marx's historical ambivalence. He intended to identify class with "objective" reality and party with "subjective" existence. Party was the class's conception of itself. Class and party, the social and the political agents in the historical process, fell therefore into two different historical categories, to be approached via two different historical methods. The position of a class was derived from the stage which, in the unrolling of the productive process, the general dialectic had reached; the position of a party could be empirically determined on the basis of its program and policies, and its subsequent analysis in terms of the fundamental social process was necessary only for the final evaluation. Thus Marx called the socialism of 1848 "the theoretical expression of the proletariat only so long as it had not yet developed further into a free historical self-movement,"[14] that is, a political movement consonant with its "objective" social and economic interests.

13. In this formulation men's "conception of themselves" belongs to the "subjective" side of history, which should be understood to include not only men's conscious ideas but the action taken in terms of those ideas. "Real organism" and "real interests" form part of the "objective" side of history; this refers to the actual historical situation, which includes men as un-selfconscious beings, that is, men in the basic groupings and activities immediately necessary for life in a given era. When the situation is accurately perceived in consciousness and is developed by effective practical activity in which "conception" and "real interests" meet, the subject-object distinction is transcended. But until the era of communism is reached, this can never be fully achieved, because of the alienation of men from their conditions of life originating with the institution of private property. The historical process progresses through the interaction between specific conscious acts with specific historical situations which are but imperfectly comprehended by such acts. Despite the role of consciousness in history, consequently, the direction of historical advance is set not so much by it as by a general dialectical law which works through conscious acts from outside them to select what is valid in them for the historical situation.

14. Marx, *The Class Struggles in France*, in *op. cit.*, II, 289.

For Marx the "objective" plane of history remained primary but the validity he did accord to men's conscious actions made it necessary to account for them. His problem can be epitomized as that of harmonizing political action with class position.

A detailed discussion of Engels' *Germany: Revolution and Counter-Revolution* is not necessary here, for he was dealing with a simpler situation whose chief relevance for our problem is to throw into sharper relief the meaning of Marx's approach to the French studies. In Germany the complicated interaction of parties and classes, of political institutions and social interests, such as characterized the France of 1848, had hardly yet begun. Political groups and ideas were comparatively new and had been first developed from philosophical and theological origins by intellectuals who formed almost an independent middle-class estate, since the economic middle classes were still weak and a self-conscious proletariat almost non-existent. Consequently, parties and classes tended to maintain separate orbits during the revolution. Engels recognized this peculiar German background (and indeed departed from the Marxist pattern in a nationalistic sense as well by endorsing the German claim to represent western civilization against the Slavs[15]), but in the main he used this situation to dismiss the parliamentary aspects of the revolution, which he considered as the futile forms of a political development that had little to do with the real life of the society,[16] and to develop a simplified scheme of the revolution on what has become the classic Marxist model. He concentrated not on the parties and politics, which were heterogeneous in the various German states of 1848, but on the putative economic and social groups, which provided him with a homogeneous basis for treating the revolution as a unified process susceptible to a straight Marxist interpretation.

It should be possible now to understand how the combination of theoretical and empirical elements in these writings of Marx and Engels distinguished them from the other historians of their period, and to evaluate their place in the historiography of the nineteenth century.

Certainly the idea of a double reality in historical life was not in itself original with Marx and Engels. Their age was pervaded by such combinations. In Germany not only Hegel's historical panlogism but even the Historical School, which utilized "organology" to balance their em-

15. Engels, *Germany: Revolution and Counter-Revolution*, in *op. cit.*, II, 120–121.
16. He saw the Frankfurt Assembly as "the parliament of an imaginary country," discussing "the imaginary government of its own creation," and passing "imaginary resolutions for which nobody cared." *Ibid.*, II, 85.

phasis on the specificity of historical forms, provided the chief impulse, while in France Comte claimed for his positivistic sociology the status of a philosophy which made history a system subject to the governance of uniform absolute natural laws. Under their aegis the historian used the new tools of critical scholarship with the aim of revealing ideas as the driving forces behind concrete historical events. The Prussian school of political historians identified the history of the state with the development of its idea, while the French historians identified the development of society with the idea of progress. Both drew a sharp distinction between a philosophical and an empirical reality. And even Ranke, who believed ideas to be immanent in the historical process, maintained that the history of states reflected, in an inscrutable manner, a higher spiritual order. But to these historians the philosophical reality made its way in history through political institutions. Meaningful history was for them political history.[17] Thus the first distinguishing feature of Marx and Engels as historians was their introduction of the social instead of the political factor as philosophically meaningful in history.

It must be admitted, however, that Marx and Engels were not alone in their social awareness. Under the influence of figures like Ahrens, Robert von Mohl, and Lorenz von Stein in Germany, and Saint-Simon, Comte, and Michelet in France, an increasing number of historical writers took cognizance of the operation of social forces. If the revolution of 1848 be taken as the basis of comparison with Marx and Engels, we find it frequently characterized as a social revolution in contemporary histories.[18] For many of these historians, however, economic and social forces, though recognized, remained secondary, to be empirically ascertained for their effects upon the political progress which remained basic.[19]

17. Thus the numerous German contemporary histories of the revolution of 1848—like those of Haym, Duncker, and von Raumer—in which the material was parliamentary and the issues exclusively political.

18. Even Ranke, in his private memoranda to the King of Prussia, not only took into account the demands of the French workers for political power in order to raise their economic status but recommended comprehensive social legislation in Prussia to deprive political radicalism of its mass support. Leopold von Ranke, *Sämmtliche Werke* (2nd and 3rd ed., Leipzig, 1887), XLIX-L, 588–589, 597.

19. This meant, in effect, the precise reverse of the Marxist formula. Thus for Louis Blanc, social cleavages were the expression of the idea of individualism, which in the ethical evolution of mankind had to give way to the ideal of humanity, to be realized through the organization of labor by the democratic state. L. Blanc, *Pages d'histoire de la révolution de février 1848* (Brussels, 1850), 8–11. Lamartine recognized the rise of explosive forces

But the three men who, along with Marx, wrote the most important contemporary histories of the French revolution of 1848—Proudhon, Tocqueville, and Lorenz von Stein—went beyond this and approached Marx in their evaluation of the significance of the social element for its interpretation.

At first glance, the similarities between the historical interpretations of Proudhon and Marx are striking indeed. Not only did both men focus their attention upon the revolution of 1848 as a decisive stage in the general "revolution of the nineteenth century,"[20] but for both it was essentially a social revolution, explicable through the fundamental historical movement of society rather than of the "state." Despite these similarities, however, Proudhon's work diverged from Marx's in its adherence to an older scheme of historical interpretation. For Proudhon's social emphasis in history was no transvaluation of values but simply another application of the older historical values. His concentration upon society as the decisive historical unit did not mean a renunciation of the traditional cosmic spiritual framework but rather its embodiment in society, which Proudhon viewed as the vehicle of the absolute moral plan of an "infinite Spirit."[21] Correspondingly, knowledge of the social process could come only through the philosophical understanding of the general laws of history rather than through research into historical facts, "the arbitrary side of history."[22] By concentrating, in his history of the revolution, upon what he interpreted to be the death-bed of the state, Proudhon revealed almost literally the process by which its traditional moral role in historiography was bequeathed to its successor, society.

Tocqueville, who rejected "absolute systems" of history,[23] emerged with a multiple interpretation of the revolution which can be reduced to two essential elements, the social and the moral. On the first count, he forthrightly subscribed to the emphasis on class struggle in the revolu-

---

in society, but he still identified them with the generic "people": "It is a moral idea which produces the explosion in the world. This idea is the people . . . the regular accession of the masses to political affairs." Alphonse M. L. de Lamartine, *Histoire de la révolution de 1848* (Paris, 1849), I, 3–4.

20. Proudhon published three books dealing with the revolution: *Les Confessions d'un Révolutionnaire* (1849); *Idée générale de la Révolution* au XIXe siècle (1851); and *La Révolution sociale démontrée par le coup d'Etat du Deux-Décembre* (1852). Editions used here are from *Oeuvres complètes de P. J. Proudhon,* I, XII, XIII (Paris, 1924–1936).

21. P. J. Proudhon, *La Révolution sociale,* in *ibid.,* XIII, 263.

22. P. J. Proudhon, *Les Confessions d'un Révolutionnaire,* in *ibid.,* XII, 148–149.

23. J. P. Mayer, ed., *The Recollections of Alexis de Tocqueville* (New York, 1949), 64. Translated from new French edition: Luc Monnier, ed., *Souvenirs d'Alexis de Tocqueville* (Paris, 1944).

tion, although in much more general form than Marx's highly articulated analysis.[24] But on the other hand, he saw the revolution also as the
result of the moral deficiencies of the rulers, a degeneration in "the inner spirit of the government."[25] Ultimately Tocqueville, while recognizing the profundity and the permanence of the social problem, tipped
the balance in favor of the ethical and implicitly the political element.
Socialism, "the essential characteristic of the Revolution of February,"
was, he concluded, the action of "false theories" upon the "greed," the
"passions," the "instincts of the crowd,"[26] and was ultimately traceable
to the political analogue of these, "the democratic disease of the
time."[27]

Lorenz von Stein, in his history of the revolution of 1848,[28] approached history from the opposite point of view: eternal and unchangeable laws, similar to the laws which rule material life, rule the
movements of political and social life.[29] He wound up correspondingly
closer to Marx, who had read and praised Stein's work before 1848. For
Stein the basis of society was the class struggle, its principle slavery. The
principle of the state he proclaimed in good Hegelian fashion to be
the principle of freedom. History was the movement resulting from the
conflict of slavery and freedom embodied in society and state, for the
principles were opposed but the institutions were mutually conditioned. Stein's ideal was an equipoise of the two elements, with the state
holding the balance over a society to whose conditions it had perforce
adapted itself; he envisaged a neutral monarchy allied with the ruled
class and thereby maintaining the independence of the state against the
ruling class and its threat to absorb all political institutions. This antinomy of an ideally superior state in conflict with a materially superior
society made Stein's general solution unstable, and in the application to
France he was forced to admit the priority of the social factor.[30] Yet
when in 1850 Stein declared the basic alignment in France to have become socialism and democracy against industrialism and reaction,[31] he

24. *Ibid.*, 150.

25. *Ibid.*, 14.

26. *Ibid.*, 79–80.

27. *Ibid.*, 11.

28. Lorenz Jakob von Stein, *Geschichte der socialen Bewegung in Frankreich von 1788 bis unsere Tage* (Leipzig, 1850), III.

29. *Ibid.*, III, preface iii.

30. "Neither political rights nor social development stand alone, but the order of society conditions and produces the constitution of the state much more than the converse."
Ibid., III, 421–422.

31. *Ibid.*, III, 472–473.

implied that any further historical development must be based upon the re-establishment of parity between autonomous political principles and social forces.

Even for those contemporaries, then, who were closest to the Marxist evaluation, history remained the theater of independent moral and ideal forces, in the traditional pattern of political historiography. The departure from this pattern which Marx and Engels undertook involved two main points. First, by taking over the framework which an idealistic philosophy of history had created in order to bind morals with politics and using it to associate value with the "material" forces of economic and social development, they made man's economic and social activity the central arena of universal history and thereby gave a radical and unforgettable expression to the tendency of their age to include such forces within the scope of historical interpretation. Secondly, by rejecting the autonomy of politics Marx and Engels thought that they were overthrowing the very concept of an *a priori* framework in history, and consequently laying claim to a truly "empirical" interpretation. Clearly enough, there was implicit opposition between what they were doing and what they thought they were doing, between their actual theory of history and their desired mastery of the facts, and this opposition was manifested in the difficulty which they experienced in integrating empirical political fact into established social framework. An analysis of their historical writing shows that they wrote their most satisfactory history when they treated political events and ideas as tributaries, feeding fresh empirical elements into the slow-flowing course of the social dialectic. It remains to be asked, then: what historical situations were at once most appropriate to their economic and social schematism and most conducive to calling forth their sense for the empirical?

Surely it was in treating the process of revolution that Marx and Engels produced their best historical results. Indeed, apart from Engels' *Origin of the Family, State, and Property,* their book-length histories were all concerned with revolutions. Orthodox historians took the institutions into which the diffuse economic and social actions of the masses are ordinarily channeled for the permanent and real essence of society, and assumed that unorganized forces are blind. But in revolutions a rupture of the political and social process takes place; the continuous integration of mass action into institutions is broken. Marx and Engels were specially equipped to understand the revolutions of their time. Their philosophy was a generalization from the fact that in their particular age economic motives were rising to challenge the older political ideals and institutions. Consequently, they could comprehend a mass movement which embodied such motives when it operated outside and against these institutions.

Marx and Engels were themselves conscious of the special demand which revolutions make on historical analysis. In a letter to Marx in February, 1851, Engels wrote:

A revolution is a pure phenomenon of nature, which is led more according to physical laws than according to the rules which in ordinary times determine the development of society. Or rather, these rules take on a much more physical character in revolution; material power emerges much more violently.[32]

It was for this reason that the German revolution, with its clear separation of political from social action, was so much more susceptible to a straight Marxist analysis than was the French revolution, in which traditional political ideas and organizations did not entirely lose their hold over the social movement. Marx's interpretation was most valid where this hold became tenuous, to wit, during February and June, 1848. He faltered at the point where the political and social structure was re-knit: his early error on the prolongation of the revolution and his difficulties with the figure of Louis Bonaparte[33] were indications of the resistance he met outside the field of revolutionary history proper.

Secondly, the strength of Marx and Engels as historians lay in their inclusion of contemporary events in the general historical process. The revolutions of 1848 evoked an unprecedented plethora of publications in which the men of the age sought to account for the divergence between expectation and event, but Marx and Engels stood almost alone in attempting to encompass the whole of the French and German movements.[34] They felt that they held a valid key to an immediate general interpretation. Engels admitted that he could not write a "complete history," but his aim was the discovery of "rational causes based upon undeniable facts, to explain the chief events, the principal vicissitudes of the movement, and to give us a clue as to the direction which the next and perhaps not very distant outbreak will impact to the German people."[35] Marx and Engels were fitted to tackle contemporary history

32. V. Adoratsky, ed., *Marx/Engels: Gesamtausgabe*, III/I, 148–149.

33. See above text between notes 11 and 12.

34. In Germany, authors like Rudolf Haym insisted that it was impossible to write "a true history of the great movement . . . in the midst of this movement," and claimed for their works the mere status of source materials. R. Haym, *Die deutsche Nationalversammlung* (Berlin, 1848), I, 1. In France, the titles were more ambitious, but here too many of the participants wrote extended memoirs or political apologias in the form of contemporary history, *e.g.*, Blanc and Lamartine.

35. Engels, *Germany: Revolution and Counter-Revolution*, in *op. cit.*, II, 42.

on broad lines because the schematism of their system afforded a corrective to the bewilderment imposed by the manifold details of the events around them. At the same time they were peculiarly accessible to such details. The interaction between scheme and contemporary fact was strengthened by their personal situation from 1848 to 1852, when as acting revolutionaries but political lone-wolves they were vitally interested in the general course of events but detached from the heat of specific party tactics.[36] As revolutionaries they subscribed to a certain freedom for contemporary human action, and both *The Class Struggles in France* and *Germany: Revolution and Counter-Revolution* could describe political crises as if the results depended upon a free choice by the participating groups. Moreover, in order to explain the fact of their political isolation and its general implication that contemporary events did not fulfill their expectations, Marx and Engels were forced to recognize that their theory of history was still too broad and general to account for the specific forms of their day. On both counts, then—both to understand undetermined political action and to refine the general framework of the dialectic—they learned, during the revolution, to follow carefully the empirical record of political events and economic fluctuations. But once the nature of the political decision and the momentary condition of the economy were known, these facts were themselves objectified, and became the indices of the specific stage which the dialectic had attained. The plasticity of contemporary history gave way to the determinism of history in perspective. Marx wrote to Engels a week after the *coup d'état* of December 2nd, 1851: "I have let you wait for an answer, for I have been quite bewildered by the tragicomic events in Paris. . . . It is difficult, indeed, impossible, to prognosticate in a drama whose hero is Crapulinski."[37] Yet in *The 18th Brumaire*, written some weeks later, he declared categorically: "If ever an event has, well in advance of its coming, cast its shadow before, it was Bonaparte's *coup d'état*."[38]

III

If Marx and Engels, during the revolutionary period around 1848, recognized the facts of contemporary history and merged them into their theory, the question follows: how did these facts, and the historical

36. Engels to Marx, February 13, 1851, in *Marx/Engels: Gesamtausgabe*, III/I, 148–149.

37. Marx to Engels, December 9, 1851, *ibid.*, III/I, 295. "Crapulinski" was Marx's derogatory name for Louis Bonaparte.

38. Marx, *The 18th Brumaire of Louis Bonaparte*, in *op. cit.*, II, 401.

study which elicited them, affect the theory? It may be argued that in view of the role of the Marxian theory as an interpretative principle of historical facts—particularly after contemporary history had become past history—the historical experience of 1848–51 was simply forced into the mold of theory and had no lasting effect upon it. Certainly in a general sense the fundamentals of the materialistic conception of history remained constant from its first full formulation in *The German Ideology*[39] to its final expression in *Capital:* the manifestations of consciousness, whether in politics, economics, or social affairs, whether as concepts, institutions, or events—in short, those materials which make up the empirical data of history—were always placed in dependence upon the mode of production and the social relations emanating from it. But the possibility of a development within this general framework was not thereby excluded. "Forms of consciousness" and "modes of production" were not ultimate realities: they were social rather than metaphysical categories, and the fact that the basic structure of society, described by the dependence of consciousness upon mode of production, remained unshaken, did not for Marx and Engels bar changes in their ideas of how ultimate forces operated within this structure. Freedom and necessity, for example, were not identifiable with consciousness and mode of production, respectively, but worked on a different plane through both categories: changes in the conviction of what man's freedom could accomplish were not only quite compatible with an unchanged dependence of consciousness upon mode of production but could bring changes in the concrete meaning of the latter relationship. Actually, such changes did take place. The impact which the experience of 1848 had upon the Marxian system can be traced in the changing role of history within that system. The place of history, in turn, underwent development in association with the concept of consciousness, since it was in the category of consciousness that both historical study and much of historical action lay.[40]

The two poles of this development were embodied in the famous letter written by Engels in 1893, when he said of the works written by Marx and himself:

We all laid and were bound to lay the main emphasis at first on the derivation of political, juridical, and other ideological notions, and of the actions arising

39. Published in full only in V. Adoratsky, ed., *Marx/Engels: Gesamtausgabe,* I/V.

40. An exhaustive consideration of this problem would require a general analysis of the changes in the Marxist system which cannot be undertaken here. This section presents a possible line of approach.

through the medium of these notions, from basic economic facts. But in doing so we neglected the formal side—the way in which these notions come about—for the sake of the content.[41]

These notions and actions were produced by what Engels called "a false consciousness," and the neglected "formal side" of this false consciousness Engels indicated to be an understanding of the way in which thinkers take their material and their judgments of validity from the realm of "pure thought," without feeling the necessity of going beyond such thought to the real economic processes which condition it. Engels applied this particularly to "the ideologist who deals with history," and it was in this context of what Marx and Engels had neglected that the latter gave the well-known admonition that the ideological spheres, although not independent, were in an interacting relationship with the basic economic facts and consequently had an effect on history.[42] This confession by Engels of the short shrift which he and Marx had given to the component of consciousness in historical thought and action was actually a reaction rather against their later works than against their works as a whole. For in the 40's, in their analyses of Hegel, the Young Hegelians, and Proudhon, they had worked out the formal as well as the substantive sides of consciousness. Though still too enmeshed in the later development of the Marxist theory to recapture the point of view of the earlier writings, Engels, writing in an atmosphere of intellectual revival during the 90's which in many ways recalled that of the 40's, could yet feel the problem which the theory had slighted in its latter years.

The very structure of *Capital* reveals the target of Engels' criticism, for it is the structure of "derivation," with little regard for "the formal side." Starting with the basic realities of capitalist production, Marx followed in volume one the development of the "perversion" and the "mystification" of these realities in the minds of men through the abstractions associated with simple commodity-exchange, in volume two the complications of the process of circulation, in volume three the reification of the distributional forms as they appeared on the surface of society, to the illusory economic conceptions analyzed in volume four. Certainly Marx had been occupied with the problem of "consciousness" from his Young Hegelian days. But the crucial difference between his attitude before 1848 and this later approach to the problem was that

41. Engels to Mehring, July 14, 1893, in *Karl Marx and Friedrich Engels: Correspondence, 1846–1895* (New York, 1933), 510–511.
42. *Ibid.*, 512.

while in the latter period he was concerned with "false consciousness," in the former he looked to "true consciousness."[43] In September, 1843, at a decisive moment of his turn to communism, he wrote:

Thus our slogan must be: reform of consciousness, not by dogmas, but by analysis of the mystical consciousness, which is unclear to itself, whether it rises in religious or political form. It will then be shown that the world for a long time possesses the dream of a thing, of which it must only possess the consciousness in order really to possess it.[44]

The writings of the later 40's, in which the Marxist system was sketched out, abridged this sovereignty of consciousness by making it derivative from the material conditions of life. But still there remains an essential difference in the treatment of the problem between these earlier writings and the later *Capital*. In the works of the 40's the relation between the material substratum and the conscious superstructure was direct and simple: the latter was an unambiguous reflection of the stage reached by the former.[45] This direct reflection was "true consciousness." In consequence of this simple relation Marx blithely assumed that "for the mass of men, *i.e.*, the proletariat, these theoretical notions do not exist and hence do not require to be dissolved. . . ."[46] In *Capital*, on the other hand, the relation was infinitely more involved, and all the agents of production, including the non-capitalist producer, were entrapped in the illusions arising from the capitalist process of production.[47] Indeed, so strong were the factors making for "false consciousness" (*i.e.*, the distorted reflection of material conditions by the conscious superstructure) in this later period, that it was intimated to be a product of the very nature of things: "So long as the ordinary brain accepts these conceptions, vulgar economy is satisfied. But all science would be superfluous, if the appearance, the form, and the nature of things were wholly identical."[48] What the difference means is that for

43. For a discussion of "consciousness" in the Marxist system, see Georg Lukács, "Klassenbewusstsein," in *Geschichte und Klassenbewusstsein* (Berlin, 1923), especially 62–66.

44. Marx to Ruge, September 1843, in *Marx/Engels: Gesamtausgabe*, I/Ia, 575.

45. "It is self-evident . . . that 'spectres,' 'bonds,' 'the higher being,' 'concept,' 'scruple,' are merely the idealistic, spiritual expression, the conception apparently of the isolated individual, the image of the very empirical fetters and limitations, within which the mode of production of life, and the form of intercourse coupled with it, move." Marx and Engels, *Die deutsche Ideologie, ibid.*, I/V, 21.

46. *Ibid.*, I/V, 30.

47. Karl Marx, *Capital* (Chicago, 1909), III, 52, 952–953.

48. *Ibid.*, III, 951.

the younger Marx "consciousness," as the faithful expression of material development, was always relatively true although it might be absolutely false, *i.e.,* ignorant of the future direction of this development. For the later Marx, the problem was to explain how "consciousness" could be both absolutely and relatively false, *i.e.,* unaware of the real relationships in the ripened capitalist process of production.

A profound change lies behind this distinction. The early Marx was anticipating the imminent rise of revolutionary "consciousness" in response to a developing capitalism; the later Marx was investigating the lack of such "consciousness" despite a developed capitalism. In the early Marx the role of "consciousness" was intimately associated with the emphasis on the creative activity of man in the genesis of the fundamental economic forces and forms which conditioned his conscious social, political, and spiritual life. While keeping carefully within the limits of the dualism which posited the dialectical and mutually conditioning relationship between man and nature, subject and object, social action and historical forms as ultimate realities, Marx gave full weight to the formative "subjective" factor in these relationships.

The first premise of all human history is, of course, the existence of living human individuals. The first fact to be established is thus the corporeal organization of these individuals and their resulting relationship to the rest of nature. . . . All historical writing must start from these natural bases and their modification in the course of history by the action of men. . . . They begin to be distinguished from animals as soon as they begin to *produce* their means of subsistence, a step which is conditioned by their corporeal organization. When men produce their means of subsistence they produce, indirectly, their material life itself. . . . This mode of production is to be considered not merely as the reproduction of the physical existence of the individuals. It is rather a definite form of activity of these individuals, a definite form of expressing their life, a definite mode of life. As individuals express their life, so are they. What they are thus coincides with their production, thus with what they produce and how they produce. Thus what individuals are depends on the material conditions of their production.[49]

Not only are the historical economic forms which condition political and social structures and the abstract manifestations of "consciousness" thus themselves the product of a dialectical relationship involving creative human activity, but these structures and manifestations must themselves be seen as the product of the reciprocal relationship between men's activity and their environment.

49. *Die deutsche Ideologie,* in *Marx/Engels: Gesamtausgabe,* I/V, 10–11.

The social structure and the state emerge continuously from the life-process of definite individuals—but individuals not as they may appear in their own or in others' conceptions, but as they really are, i.e., as they work and produce materially, thus as they are active under definite material limits, assumptions, and conditions which are independent of their will. . . . Men are the producers of their conceptions, ideas, etc.—but real, active men, as they are conditioned by a definite development of their productive forces and the corresponding intercourse unto its broadest formations. Consciousness can never be anything else but conscious being (*Sein*), and the being of men is their real life-process.[50]

History, consequently, is defined in human terms, as "the succession of individual generations, of which each exploits the materials, capital, and productive forces handed over to it by all previous ones, and thus on the one hand continues the traditional activity under completely changed circumstances and on the other hand modifies the old circumstances with a completely changed activity."[51] The culmination of Marx's and Engels' stress, at this stage in their development, upon the "subjective" aspect in history comes with their emphasis on revolution. Although successful revolution is predicated upon the presence of "the material elements of a total transformation," these material elements include, besides the necessary productive forces, "the formation of a revolutionary mass which revolts not only against specific conditions of the existing society but also against the existing 'production of life' itself, against the 'total activity' on which it is based. . . . "[52] The function of the communist, it follows, is stated in general terms as that of "revolutionizing the existing world, of attacking and changing existing things in practice."[53]

Thus the early Marx's positing of "consciousness" as a "derivation" did not imply the futility or passivity of the human, or "subjective," factor in history. Indeed, he made "consciousness" itself liable to change by human action:

All forms and products of consciousness can be dissolved, not by spiritual criticism . . . but only by the practical overturn of the real social relations from which these idealistic frauds came. . . . Not criticism but revolution is the real driving force of history, as of religion, philosophy, and other kinds of theory.[54]

Marx's and Engels' early concern was rather to relate "consciousness" to material processes than to subordinate it to them. What they opposed

50. *Ibid.*, I/V, 15.
51. *Ibid.*, I/V, 34.
52. *Ibid.*, I/V, 28.
53. *Ibid.*, I/V, 32.
54. *Ibid.*, I/V, 27.

was not an historical conception of an active role for "consciousness," but the philosophical conception of its essential independence. They denied "consciousness" in the Young Hegelian form of a prime metaphysical reality, but recognized it in the form of practical activity. In this form "consciousness" could only be "true consciousness," for its efficacy in activity was predicated upon its precise correspondence with the material reality to which it was internally related.[55]

Certainly in the later Marx of *Capital*, the fundamental dualistic structure was still much in evidence, in the shape of the essential "contradiction" of capitalist production. For although this "contradiction" consisted in the economic distinction between the direction and bondage placed upon production by the historically and socially conditioned forms of capital on the one hand and the "tendency to develop the productive forces absolutely" on the other,[56] Marx clearly showed the general implications of this "contradiction" when he explicitly associated the latter tendency with

the productive activities of human beings in general . . . , independent of societies, lifted above all societies, being the common attribute of unsocial man as well as of man with any form of society and a general expression and assertion of life.[57]

In a sense, then, *Capital* may be seen as a mere transfer of the discussion from philosophical to economic terms, as an analysis of the capitalist system on the basis of the general insights gained in the early writings. But while the Marxian "dialectic," with its claims to penetrate "concrete reality," could mold itself to the special forms of capitalist economics and reach special conclusions which as descriptive of a single moment in the movement of history avoided contradiction with the general system, yet these special results had certain general implications and forced a certain shift of emphasis in the theory as a whole.

The basic change lay in the dislocation of the Marxist dualism to favor the "object" over the "subject," alien conditions over human activity, necessity over freedom. Already in his preface to the *Contribution*

---

55. "This conception of history thus depends on the development of the real process of production, starting from the material production of immediate life; the comprehension of the form of intercourse connected with this mode of production and produced by it, and thus of civil society in its various stages, as the basis of all history; its delineation in its action as the state; the explanation of all the various theoretical products and forms of consciousness . . . from it; and the tracing of their process of development, in which naturally the whole thing in its totality (*and consequently also the reciprocal effect of the various sides on one another*) can be shown." *Ibid.*, I/V, 27. Italics mine.

56. Marx, *Capital*, III, 292.

57. *Ibid.*, III, 949.

to the Critique of Political Economy of 1859, which was designed as a
summary statement of his general position, Marx for the first time described his system in wholly "objective" terms, as a movement of impersonal economic forces and social relations in which human activity
received no explicit mention. Along with this shift, the preface revealed
a turn in the related problem of "consciousness": it was no longer a
simple "derivative" from material conditions, but is rather described as
explicable "from the contradictions of material life, from the existing
conflict between the social forces of production and the relations of
production."[58] Just as human activity was dropped out of the characterization of the historical process, so was "consciousness" removed from a
direct relationship with its primary material elements. These ideas, in a
preface devoted to summarizing his system as a whole, testified to the
general effects of the concentration upon political economy.

In *Capital* the pattern sketched out in 1859 was fully elaborated. In
his preface to the first volume of *Capital,* Marx defined his standpoint as
one from which "the evolution of the economic formation of society is
viewed as a process of natural history,"[59] and this point of view he executed radically, with all its implication of the complete subjection of
life to forces and conditions external to it. That workers should be represented as enslaved under capitalism by their own objectified labor is
hardly surprising, but the capitalists are shown to be likewise in bondage. This fact is hammered home time and again. Economic and social
forms are ever "spontaneous" products of development, and humans
are but their "agents." Thus the capitalist is simply "personified capital"; even his passion for wealth is "the effect of the social mechanism,
of which he is but one of the wheels;" he is in general completely at the
mercy of "the immanent laws of capitalist production," which appear to
the capitalist as "external, coercive," or "immutable natural law." The
collapse of capitalism is to be the result, not of revolution but of the
evolution of its contradictions, which are themselves dependent upon
"the immanent laws of capitalist production" and independent of anybody's will. Finally Marx extended the determinism which characterized
capitalist society beyond that society to the sphere of material production in all societies. Thus the very sphere in which during the 40's he
had seen the initial arena for practical human activity, Marx now con-
signed to "the realm of necessity," even under communism; all aspects
of man's struggle with nature for material production "in all forms of

58. In V. Adoratsky, ed., *Karl Marx: Selected Works,* I, 356.
59. Karl Marx, *Capital* (New York, 1906), I, 15.

society and in all possible modes of production," were now included in this realm, and "the realm of freedom" began only beyond it, with "that development of human power which is its own end."[60]

The new concentration on human bondage under capitalism gave meaning to the new emphasis on "false consciousness" which was its corollary. While the existence of an intelligible relationship between consciousness and material reality continued to be posited,[61] stress was now placed on the complexity of the relationship, on its tenuousness for men living in the social process of capitalism, and on their consequent inability to recognize or to act upon that process.

> If it is realized . . . that the analysis of the actual internal inter-connections of the capitalist process of production is a very complicated matter and a very pro-tracted work; if it is a work of science to resolve the visible and external move-ment into the internal actual movement, then it is understood as a matter of course, that the conceptions formed about the laws of production in the heads of the agents of production and circulation will differ widely from these real laws and will be merely the conscious expression of the *apparent* movements.[62]

Thus "consciousness" is now an expression of mere appearance; the "internal connection of things," the "internal essence and internal form of the capitalist process of production" is hidden from it.[63] One of the crucial purposes of *Capital* is clearly evident in Marx's long attempt to understand and to explain the process whereby material reality produces the "perverted" forms of consciousness which have become so alienated from it. Whereas for the early Marx it was the hypostatizing of consciousness that was called into question, now it was the political, economic, and social forms of consciousness themselves which were declared false, even in terms of the limited reality underlying them.

From these indications of salient points in Marx's development, it should be possible to assess the role of historical study. For the study of history cannot do without the study of what Marx called "the super-structure"; it is the study of "consciousness" in its practical political and social as well as its theoretical forms. Marx's development from the early conception of "true consciousness" to the later emphasis on "false con-sciousness" was at the same time a development of a belief in the futility of historical study for the understanding of social processes. In this

---

60. *Ibid.*, III, 954–955.
61. The "imaginary expressions" of bourgeois economics "are categories for the phe-nomenal forms of essential relations." *Ibid.*, I, 588.
62. *Ibid.*, III, 369. Italics mine.
63. *Ibid.*, III, 102, 109.

sense, Marx's shift from the arena of contemporary history to that of economics was something more than an attempt to supplement his former studies; it revealed the growth of the positive conviction that for capitalist society, at least, the "dialectic" in the form of economic analysis could reach the fundamental level of reality where the exploitation of historical research could not. In *The German Ideology* of 1846, where Marx and Engels turned definitively from philosophy to history, the role accorded to the creative activity of man caused them to prize concrete historical research as an avenue to the comprehension of social reality.

The fact, then, is this: definite individuals, who are productively active in a definite way, enter into . . . definite social and political relations. Empirical observation must in each case show empirically and without any mystification and speculation the connection of the social and political structure with production.[64]

This was the method followed in the *Communist Manifesto,* in which the analysis began with the flat assertion that "the history of all hitherto existing society is the history of class struggles,"[65] and went on confidently to develop the economic basis of the historical process from the social and political forms of this struggle. But the later Marx specifically and emphatically rejected this method. In the preface to the *Contribution to the Critique of Political Economy* he wrote:

In considering such transformation [social revolution] a distinction should always be made between the material transformation of the economic conditions of production which can be determined with the precision of natural science, and the legal, political, religious, aesthetic or philosophic—in short, ideological—forms in which men become conscious of this conflict and fight it out. Just as our opinion of an individual is not based on what he thinks of himself, so can we not judge of such a period of transformation by its own consciousness.[66]

In *Capital,* where science in the sense of "the precision of natural science" is exalted to the position of the only possible method for penetrating to the essence of reality, the extent of the divergence from the earlier position becomes clear: one can no longer start with the empirical determination of the historical forms of "consciousness" and work down to "reality"; rather must one begin with a scientific analysis of

---

64. In *Marx/Engels: Gesamtausgabe,* I/V, 15.
65. In *Karl Marx: Selected Works,* I, 204.
66. *Ibid.,* I, 356.

"reality" and then work up to explain the forms of "consciousness." In the course of this development Marxism became a closed system: having already absorbed a philosophical structure and then renounced philosophy, it now showed that it had digested its historical material and was completing the process of insulating itself from further convulsions conveyed by history.

This development away from history seems to have been brought about by historical study itself, by the difficulty which Marx and Engels experienced in digesting the contemporary history of the Revolution of 1848. The complexities of *The Class Struggles in France,* the repeated expressions of bewilderment over the post revolutionary French developments in the correspondence between Marx and Engels,[67] Marx's return to economic studies during 1850 in the attempt to find explanations not vouchsafed by his historical labors, and finally the tremendous effort made in the *Contribution to the Critique of Political Economy* and *Capital* to translate the specific forms of "consciousness" which go to make up history into a malleable mass automatically explicable by his theory—all these factors attest to the impress made upon the authors by the problems and the results of their historical writings on the revolution. Indeed, the turning-point in the development can be traced in these very writings. The differences between *The Class Struggles in France* and *The 18th Brumaire of Louis Bonaparte* are precisely those of the larger development, albeit still in the shape of tendencies rather than completed forms. In *The Class Struggles* the Revolution was a reality which banished illusion,[68] and the activity of its participants became itself the key to the fundamental movement of history. The emphasis in *The 18th Brumaire,* on the other hand, was upon the farcical, illusory quality of the Revolution,[69] and upon its necessary linear movement toward a pre-appointed end. Here, then, began the development which was to lead equally to *Capital* and to the *Civil War in France* (1870–71), to the final elaboration of a system which worked with the efficacy of an absolute principle to subsume the multiplicity of existence in both the theory and the practice of the historical discipline.

The historical studies written by Marx and Engels between 1850 and 1852 served in a special way to define the position of these two thinkers

67. Engels to Marx, October 15, 1851; Engels to Marx, December 3, 1851; Marx to Engels, December 9, 1851; Engels-Marx, January 6, 1852; Engels-Marx, August 21, 1852; in V. Adoratsky, *Marx/Engels: Gesamtausgabe,* III/I, 278–279; 292–293; 294–295; 303; 383–384.

68. V. Adoratsky, ed., *Karl Marx: Selected Works,* II, 192.

69. *Ibid.,* II, 315–316, 384.

in both the historiography and the general intellectual history of the nineteenth century. Because these works dealt with contemporary and revolutionary history, kinds of historical material for which their method was particularly appropriate, Marxism took into itself the experience of Europe at a critical point in its development and to that extent kept pace with the realistic emphasis which characterized the second half of the century. But because the unifying historical principle for which these works bore testimony was a more highly integrated synthesis of concrete existence and rational principle than that of their contemporaries, it escaped the dissolution which overtook the latter, and amidst the flood re-affirmed its own systematic nature. By absorbing the initial characteristic elements of the new age and then repairing to another level, where it held itself impervious to the further onslaught of history, Marxism became one of the few systems of thought to bridge effectively the two halves of the nineteenth century.

16 Detaching Engels from Marx

The team of Marx and Engels is indissolubly linked with the associated concepts of historical materialism and the economic interpretation of history. The first is the philosophical concept which defines ultimate reality as the incessant practical activity through which men engage nature to produce the changing material conditions of their lives. The second is the universal historical concept which explains the overt forms of man's movement through time as functions of the social relations produced by the successive stages of this basic material production. Together, these concepts constitute the most influential philosophy of history ever devised. So overpowering has the theory been that the excursions undertaken by Marx and Engels into history proper have often enough seemed more like the verifications of a scientific hypothesis than like authentic inquiries into the past. No less an authority than Engels himself characterized one of Marx's histories as an occasion for him to have "put his law to the test on these historical events," and he indicated that the limited sequences which were the subjects of their historical works represented an intermediate stage in the theoretical continuum between the abstract statement of universal law and the interpretation of the discrete political events of the present in terms of this law.[1]

From this point of view, the historical works of Marx and Engels have been immortalized as models for the application of Marxist categories to any concrete history whatsoever. They remain models in this way, moreover, to believers and nonbelievers alike. To the devout, they form part of the canon and provide literal lessons for the interpretation of history in terms of class struggles. To the uncommitted historian, their relevance has been archetypal, providing case studies in the use of economic and social structure as the secular rational unity behind

First published as the editor's introduction in Friedrich Engels, *The German Revolutions: The Peasant War in Germany,* ed. Leonard Krieger, Classic European Historians (Chicago: University of Chicago Press, 1967), ix–xlvi.

1. See Engels' introductions to Marx's *The Class Struggles in France 1848–1850* (1895 edition) and *The Eighteenth Brumaire of Louis Bonaparte,* in Karl Marx, *Selected Works* (London, 1942), II, 169–70, 315.

321

the apparently fortuitous series of heterogeneous intellectual and political events.

But this is only one side of the position that the historical works of Marx and Engels hold in the history of history. Over and above the philosophy of history which they exemplify, they remain classics in their own right, landmarks in the interpretation of the specific aspects of the European past that is their subject matter. Without exception, their full-scale historical writings dealt with revolutions.[2] This focus indicates that Marx and Engels wrote history not simply to confirm their principles but to explain particular historical situations in which they were vitally interested. For to them, revolutions were the occasions for men to act directly upon the political and theoretical superstructure of their lives in the light of their economic basis, and they were the only occasions therefore on which political events and ideas were, both individually and in sequence, fundamentally meaningful. More, this historical course of revolutionary events and ideas had an independent rather than a derived meaning: the knowledge of its specific history was necessary to pinpoint the precise point of development reached by an economic process which yielded only general structural relations to direct analysis. Only when the empirical determination of what happened in particular was meshed with the rational analysis of the general situation in which it happened was the Marxist explanation complete. And so it was that Marx and Engels became historians as well as philosophers of history.[3]

Undoubtedly it was the integration of history and the philosophy of history which Marx and Engels achieved by logicizing history and historicizing philosophy that is their ecumenical contribution to historiography. So tight does the integration appear that it is often hard to find where the one leaves off and the other begins. Thus the two fullest statements of the philosophy of history, in the *German Ideology* of 1846 and the *Communist Manifesto* of 1848, have sketches of universal history built into them, while the empirical histories of particular revolutions

2. Marx's *The Class Struggles in France, 1848–1850* (1850), *The Eighteenth Brumaire of Louis Bonaparte* (1852), *The Civil War in France* (1870–71—all reprinted in full English translation in *ibid.*, II, 169–426, 446–527—and Engels' *Germany: Revolution and Counter-Revolution* (1851–52) were contemporary histories of revolutions. Engels' *The Peasant War in Germany* (1850) and *The Origin of the Family, Private Property, and the State* (1884) (English translation; Chicago, 1902) dealt with social revolutions of the remote past.

3. For a discussion of this relationship between history and the philosophy of history in Marx and Engels, considered as *joint* authors, see Leonard Krieger, "Marx and Engels as Historians," in *Journal of the History of Ideas*, XIV (1953), 381–403. [See this volume, chap. 15.]

refer to the philosophy of history continuously as their assumption and sporadically as their explicit explanation. The pattern of authorship, moreover, seems to offer external confirmation of the interpenetration, since Marx and Engels composed the standard works on their philosophy of history jointly and since both followed with specific histories in apparent application of it.

But if the history written by Marx and Engels seemed continuous with their philosophy of history by virtue of the homologous combinations of philosophy and history that they put into both kinds of works, this same history becomes discontinuous from the same philosophy of history by virtue of the problem which Marx and Engels confronted in combining philosophy and history. The intensity and persistence of this problem, which may be identified in Marx and Engels with the problem of relating the general and the particular levels of reality, not only infected both their philosophy of history and their history but, what is more important in this context, infected them in different ways. In their philosophy of history, Marx and Engels sought to relate general and particular reality from the point of view of general reality; in their history, they sought to relate general and particular reality from the point of view of particular reality. When so considered, the movement from the subsumption of historical facts under dialectical law in the philosophy of history to the inference of social evolution from political and ideological events in the histories is not so much a specific application of a closed theory as a succession of equivalent attempts to solve an open problem. Even the external evidence that seems to confirm the general impression that Marx and Engels dovetailed their philosophy of history and their history turns out, upon closer inspection, to belie the appearance of indiscriminate authorship and to imply a differentiation in the respective approaches to the two fields. First, Marx and Engels were the joint authors of the works that developed their philosophy of history, but they wrote their histories separately. Second, Marx was predominant in the philosophical partnership that produced the first category of works, while Engels' own writings were the more genuinely empirical of the histories that composed the second.

Thus, whether we start from the general impressions of the works or from the external evidence of their authorship, the relationship of history and the philosophy of history in Marx and Engels points in two contrary directions: it indicates both their conjunction and their disjunction. But this same evidence also yields two inferences that open a path to the investigation of the problem. It shows, first, that the problematical relationship between the two fields may be profitably studied in terms of the intellectual relationship between the two men. It shows, second, that if the relationship between the fields is to be investigated from the side of history, it is Engels rather than Marx who should be our protagonist. Hence it is Engels' history that in the following essay on its theoretical assumptions we shall attempt the delicate surgery of detaching Engels from Marx.

Friedrich Engels enjoys a unique place among the immortals of our culture. It is a place fixed by two different functions, whose juncture is inherently problematical and yet has been essential to Engels' apotheosis since neither was sufficiently creative by itself to account for it. Engels was both Karl Marx's collaborator in the formulation of the original system that bears their joint imprint and, as executor of that system, the founder of *Marxism* as a doctrine stemming from the original system but assuming forms independent of it. When considered from the point of view of the original achievement—as it usually is—this anomaly is resolved pejoratively: since Engels is generally acknowledged to have been Marx's first disciple and himself freely admitted that the basic idea of the system "belongs solely and exclusively to Marx," the ancillary character of his early collaboration joins the derivative character of his later adaptations to bestow upon him a borrowed glory. But when considered from the point of view of the system's longevity, then Engels' two roles acquire a positive connection: he equipped the original system with the capacity for adaptation which permitted its development from theory into doctrine—that is, from Marx into Marxism. From this angle, Engels can be seen as having inserted at one end the thread that he ultimately drew out at the other.

What was the nature of this thread? What, in other words, did Engels bring into the joint philosophy of history that made it usable for his own brand of history?

Behind the most harmonious intellectual duet in the history of Western culture lay, obviously, a relevant set of fundamental attributes which Marx and Engels shared. The common features of their environment, training, and orientation were direct influences upon the initial convergence and ultimate accord of their ideas. By origin and early rearing, both were middle class, urban, non-Catholic, and Rhenish—circumstances which exposed them to the legally most advanced status and the socially most advanced movements in German life, to an appreciation of political power in the form of Prussian sovereignty, and to the resentments of a minority position vis-à-vis both province and state. Members of the same post-1815 generation, both grew to young manhood during the agitated years that followed on the revolutionary movement of 1830, and ran the usual gamut of the avant-garde from the defiant composition of bad poetry to the definitive appropriation of the radical form of the Hegelian heritage, with its demand for the systematic renovation of the world. Both grew up to be activist by disposition, communist by conviction, and revolutionary by policy. They even began with parallel filial rebellions of a kind that would be later stereotyped by Freud, although with Marx and Engels it seems to have been rather the effect than the cause of their alienation from respectable society.

But harmony is not unison; the importance of the qualities that Marx and Engels did share should not obscure either the existence or the intellectual effect of those they did not. The differences seemed indeed comparatively personal and superficial, and in the context of a basic concord they attracted rather than repelled. But this very attraction indicates the relationship of opposites which these differences could attain within their limited sphere. However superficial in origin, moreover, at least Engels' personal idiosyncracies colored his understanding of the joint Marxist principles and infected his style of applying them to history.

Taken separately, the distinctive features in Engels' background, disposition, and interests seem inessential, but there was a consistency about them that made their cumulative impact highly relevant to his thought. Where Marx came from the liberal administrative city of Trier, Engels came from the more obscure and conservative industrial town of Barmen. Where Marx grew up in the free-wheeling atmosphere of the liberal professions and Enlightment rationalism, Engels grew up in a household dominated by the narrow values of the family enterprise and pietistic Lutheranism—environments which may well have contributed to Marx's taste for abstract ideas and indifference to religion and to Engels' conversion of these sentiments. Where Marx acquired his philosophical tools through six years of university study, emerging with a doctorate and the ambition to teach philosophy, Engels never went past secondary school and completed his self-education in direct communication with the vital groups of whatever community his business apprenticeship, his military service, and his managerial career brought him to. Where Marx tried his fancy on vague romantic poetizing, dedicated to love and disembodied ideals, Engels tried his on pseudo-epics celebrating legendary national—and particularly the German—pasts. Where Marx came to Young Hegelian politics through Hegelian philosophy, Engels came to Hegelian philosophy through liberal politics in an ever widening circle that carried him through the German Student

Union movement and the littérateurs of Young Germany before entering the Hegelian orbit.[4] Where Marx found the circumstantial basis of
his conversion to socialism in the vicarious experience of French revolutionary politics, Engels found his in the firsthand observation of the English working class. And when, in the spring of 1849, the revolution
that was to trigger their writing of history was in its death throes, Marx
and Engels wound up their joint career as active revolutionaries with a
characteristic parting: Marx went to Paris to agitate politically for the
resurrection of the social revolution in France, and Engels went to the
Palatinate to participate in the last-ditch military insurrection for a democratic and united Germany.

The temperaments of the two friends varied directly with these experiences that gave them their definitive form. Where Marx was intense
and sardonic, Engels was expansive and witty. Where Marx was ar-
rogant and mistrusted even within the narrow circle of like-minded socialist intellectuals, Engels was flexible and at ease even in the broad
circle of Manchester society. Where Engels acknowledged Marx to be
the deeper, Marx acknowledged Engels to be the quicker.

Their variant backgrounds and dispositions found intellectual expression in the different channels they chose for the articulation of their
common faith after it had taken definite form with the close of the revolutionary era in 1850. Where Marx focused ever more sharply on the
twin activities of scholarly economic analysis and partisan political organization, Engels spread his beliefs to cover a whole complex of academic and cultural interests which his practical and restless mind found
relevant to the continuing validity of historical materialism or to the
successful issue of the future communist revolution. He cultivated the
natural and life sciences, anthropology, military science, languages of
all shapes and kinds—ancient and modern, Germanic, Slavic, and
Oriental—and history. Marx himself admired the universality and
pliability of Engels' knowledge, a judgment which confirms the impression yielded by the list of his accomplishments. And yet both the judgment and the impression are seriously misleading if they are not
immediately qualified. For Engels' was the more universal mind only if
knowledge is taken in the sense of information rather than understanding. It was not only that his cosmopolitan collection of facts and tools
for getting facts was accompanied by a parochial preference for things

4. For Engels' youthful development, see Auguste Cornu, *Karl Marx et Friedrich Engels: leur vie et leur oeuvre* (Paris, 1955), I, 123–31, and Horst Ullrich, *Der junge Engels*
(Berlin, 1961), *passim*.

German, but more fundamentally that this preference testified to the limited range of the universal principles he used to organize the collection. Marx, whose universality was more authentic, was perhaps dimly aware of this lack in his friend when he complained that Engels spread himself thinly among so many objects "for his own enjoyment."[5] In truth, the distinctive factors in Engels' experience and character illuminate the peculiar distribution of his interests: his intimate affirmation of life in all its concrete manifestations, his passion for all possible facts, his appreciation of the infinite multiplicity of forms that must be practically managed, all led him through and beyond the inverted Hegelianism that Marx had provided to account for a more disciplined vision of actuality. For Engels, historical materialism replaced his original familial Pietism as his absolute principle because it was designed to come more directly to grips with the richly diversified existence which he would appropriate, but in his hands the forms of existence that historical materialism did rationalize supplied an emotional certainty that supported his confident excursions among the forms that it could not rationalize.

The role of historical materialism in Engels offers the clue to the role of Engels in historical materialism. His role in the Marxist philosophy of history thus comprised two related functions: first, he intentionally extended and adapted it to make it account for as many real facts as possible; second, he unintentionally claimed that it accounted for particular circumstances for which it could not logically account. The combination of these two functions made Engels' work a model for the subsequent indiscriminate applications of Marxism as both a revised and an unrevised doctrine. The overt forms of Engels' relationship to the system manifest the first function, his own version of historical materialism the second.

The tangible contributions of Engels to the formation of historical materialism and to the elaboration of the theory after it had taken its definite form are of a piece: they emphasize the empirical and pragmatic bearing of the doctrine. The appearances in this respect—that is, the bare record of publications—are deceptive, for they seem to indicate a development of Engels from economics to philosophy that balances Marx's development from philosophy to economics. Engels' share in the principles of historical materialism that Marx and he worked out together during 1845 and 1846 was indeed to give to materialism a concrete economic substance. He brought to the partnership both the

5. Quoted in Gustav Mayer, *Friedrich Engels: eine Biographie* (The Hague, 1934), II, 528.

socialist critique of classical economic doctrine in terms of capitalistic realities that he had already published in article form during 1844 and the intimate acquaintance with the proletariat under conditions of industrial revolution that he had written up as *The Condition of the Working Class in England.*[6] But the shift in the field of Engels' main publications from economics to philosophy after 1850 did *not* bring, as one might expect it would, a shift from the concrete to the abstract. It is a common error, in the interpretation of Marxism, to identify concretion exclusively with economics and philosophy exclusively with ideology. In Engels' case the same emphasis on the practical and the actual that found an economic expression in his early career was applied to philosophical issues in his later years. This consistency is indicated both by the context of his other intellectual interests in these same years as they appear in his correspondence and his subordinate publications and by the general tendency of the major philosophical works themselves.

On the first count, the massive weight of unspectacular evidence demonstrates his overriding concern with extending Marxism in an empirical direction and adducing its relevance to all kinds of facts and conditions. The historical and anthropological studies that came to the surface in his *Origin of the Family, Private Property, and the State* of 1884, and the numerous prefaces that elaborated Marxism in the light of the changing social, political, and technological conditions of the latter nineteenth century are the best-known cases in point.

On the second count, the graduation of Engels' two late philosophical works into permanent monuments of Marxist philosophy has obscured the practical orientation that sponsored them. *Herr Eugen Dühring's Revolution in Science* of 1878 (better known as *Anti-Dühring* and best known in its abridged form as *Socialism: Utopian and Scientific*) and *Ludwig Feuerbach and the Outcome of Classical German Philosophy* of 1888 share three attributes that reveal a characteristically empirical orientation within the philosophical field they inhabit. First, they were, in their origins, occasional essays, designed like so many of Engels' social and political comments to apply Marxism to the newer circumstances of his day: only in this case the circumstances were the intellectual ones of a fashionable scientific materialism and an equally modish neo-Kantian

---

6. Engels' "Outlines of a Critique of Political Economy" has been recently republished as an appendix in Dirk J. Struik (ed.), *The Economic and Philosophic Manuscripts of 1844 by Karl Marx* (English translation by Martin Milligan; New York, 1964). See too, W. O. Henderson and W. H. Chaloner (eds. and English translators), Engels' *The Condition of the Working Class in England* (Oxford, 1958), for the best translation of the work from the original German edition of 1845.

idealism. Indeed, each volume was a re-edition in book form of what had originally been published in journals as extended review articles. Second, the whole point of Engels' philosophical analysis was to demonstrate the replacement of philosophy by the sciences. Third, the single tendency which runs through Engels' conception of nature—the central theme common to both works—is the emphasis upon its relative, particular, and transitory character, a character that he demonstrated by using Darwin and cognate recent developments in the sciences to historicize nature. Thus Engels extended Marxism into a philosophy of science by elevating the empirical and the historical over the lawful and the logical elements in the dialectic that he found common to both.

Obviously, the empirical emphasis through which Engels exalted science over philosophy and the historical emphasis through which he exalted the development over the absolute laws of nature produced a version of the Marxist philosophy of history that was more appropriate to an independent historical discipline than was the original. But Engels paid a price for this adaptation, for it meant that what in Marx was a problem of the relationship between a logical philosophy of history and an empirical history was carried by Engels into the very heart of the philosophy of history itself. Engels' appreciation of the empirical historical element in Marxism was so strong that it bore him, even in theory, beyond the point at which the Marxist logic could actively engage it. The gap which was thereby opened in his philosophy of history became manifest in Engels' growing tendency to think of philosophy of history in terms of the relations between nature and history once natural science replaced philosophy as the primary locus of a unified reality. However common he conceived the empirical foundations of natural and historical knowledge to be, Engels' own thought reveals that even he could not succeed in making the unity of nature the model for a unity in history. He returned to the subject time and again in his later philosophical works and his correspondence, where his simultaneous insistence on the necessity of a lawful explanation of all the facts and inability to see how a historical version of natural laws could explain all the facts testified dramatically to the problem that kept gnawing at him.

His aim was to make nature and history mutually convertible, but he foundered upon his recognition of a distinctive recalcitrant quality in human history. He had little difficulty in borrowing the movement from history which gave him his dialectical view of nature, but he implicitly confessed to a large difficulty in borrowing a lawfulness from nature which he now needed to give him a unified view of history. Where Marx grounded the unity of history in an overt philosophical logic appropriate to human activity, Engels had resort to a covert natural analogy antithetical to human activity. The covert quality is a matter not of our interpretation but of Engels' admission: although the interplay of "individual actions in the domain of history produces a state of affairs entirely analogous to that in the realm of unconscious nature," "the general laws of motion" which govern both realms are, in history alone, always "inner, hidden laws" which must be "discovered."[7] This acknowledgment of the gap between the event and the law which requires the latter to be "hidden" reveals the two basic and unreconciled factors in Engels' philosophy of history: his appreciation of the unique quality of the individual human act and his concomitant requirement of a unity to which it must somehow be referred. Hence the bizarre mixture of categories whereby individual acts were at once purposeful and accidental while the social results of those acts were at once blind and lawful. Both levels of human activity are "important . . . to historical investigation," and it is the function of historical law to connect them, if it is to hold sway, as it should, "both in history as a whole and at particular periods and in particular lands."[8]

There thus opened, in Engels, a gulf between nature and human history, and he could connect them only by appeal to the dialectical logic which he thought common to the understanding of both realms. But the link was ambiguous, for the dialectic was his only permitted remnant of philosophy, which he had derogated in general and which he subordinated even in this licit particular to the divergent facts of the respective realms. These fundamental terms of Engels' philosophy of history—nature, history, dialectic—set up the conflicting tendencies toward polarity and synthesis which is its main problem. For the way in which he worked out the problem we must turn to his philosophy of history itself.

Engels always held that the economic interpretation of history, devised jointly by Marx and himself, did provide a valid synthesis of the basic factors in human history. As he formulated it in terms of these basic factors, at each stage of history the mode of economic production established fundamental general conditions which acted as common "driving forces" upon the various "forms" of individual motivation to produce common historical effects, and the rationale of this process was

---

7. Engels, *Ludwig Feuerbach and the Outcome of Classical German Philosophy*, in Marx, *Selected Works*, I, 457.
8. *Ibid.*, I, 457, 459.

historical law.[9] But this formula afforded an abstract solution only, and it tended, like the other expressions of Engels' philosophy of history, to decompose whenever he elaborated upon it. Under Engels' treatment, the economic interpretation broke down in two different ways.

First, Engels' thinking suffered, as Marx's did not, from the problem of infinite regress, for his duality between the logical necessity of general truth and the invincible autonomy of individual truth was repeated within the realm of general truth itself. The realm of general truth is the realm of "the economic movement" which "amid all the endless host of accidents (i.e., of things and events . . .) finally asserts itself as necessary" by producing the historical "driving forces" common to the whole society, but this economic movement itself requires a massive kind of empirical historical study before it can play its heuristic role:[10]

All history must be studied afresh, the conditions of existence of the different formations of society must be individually examined before the attempt is made to deduce from them the political, civil-legal, aesthetic, philosophic, religious, etc., notions corresponding to them. Only a little has been done here up to now because only a few people have got down to it seriously. In this field we can utilize masses of help.[11]

Indeed, Engels even felt that he had to excuse Marx for preferring the logical over the historical method in the realm of economic analysis, and he explicitly applied to economics, ostensibly "the key to the understanding of the whole history of society," the same ambiguous relationship between contingent and necessary truths that inhabited his notion of history as such:

The logical method of treatment . . . is nothing else than the historical method; only divested of its historical form and disturbing fortuities. The chain of thought must begin with the same thing with which this history begins and its further course will be nothing else than the mirror-image of the historical course in abstract and theoretically consistent form. . . .[12]

The two methods were presumably linked by the dialectic, which was designed precisely to derive unity from heterogeneous individualities, but this simply meant that economics, far from being the key to any solution, became simply part of the wider problem that Engels had with the relating of the dialectic to history.

9. *Ibid.*, 458–59.
10. Engels to Joseph Bloch, September 21, 1890, in *ibid.*, I, 381.
11. Engels to Conrad Schmidt, August 5, 1890, in *ibid.*, I, 380.
12. Engels, "On Karl Marx's *Contribution to the Critique of Political Economy*" (1895), in *ibid.*, I, 368–69.

Second, Engels' version of historical materialism suffered from an ultimate vacillation between the logical and the empirical principles. His
general statements on the role of these principles in history as a whole
show that he thought of them in juxtaposition rather than in synthesis.
"History has its own course, and as dialectically as it may finally turn
out, still dialectic must often enough wait long upon history."[13] For a
historical event to be a consequence of dialectical law, it must be proved
that it "in part has happened and in part must happen."[14]

It was this inability of Engels' to find a source of historical unity in
either the integral force of economics or the extensive logic of the dialectic that drove him to look for it, finally, in the relations between the
economic and the other historical activities of man. His focus on these
relations marked a new stage in his search for synthesis, for the famous
concessions that he made in them to the role of the superstructure in
history show both his need to find in a reciprocating process the unity
he could not find in a monistic principle, and his stubborn recognition
of a concrete individuality in history that ultimately subverted unity in
the process as in the principle.

Engels' overt purpose, in these later glosses on the Marxist philosophy
of history, was to enlarge its scope by showing that political and ideological history had meaning for it and could be explained in terms of it.
Engels now argued that "the various elements of the superstructure"—
politics, ideology, and so forth—"also exercise their influence upon the
course of the historical struggles" and that they "react back as an influence upon the whole development of society, even on its economic development," which is the "ultimately determining" but not the "*only*
determining basis" of history. Engels insisted, moreover, that this reciprocal relationship was grounded in the very fundamentals of Marxism—
that is, in the dialectic, which "proceeds in the form of interaction" and
rejects all "metaphysical" notions of one-way "here cause and there
effect."[15]

But actually, Engels' purpose in this reassessment of historical materialism went beyond such substantive reinterpretation. This reinterpretation entailed a fundamental revision of historical method, and
Engels addressed himself both to this other dimension and to its metaphysical implications. This level of his concern reflected his interest in

---

13. Friedrich Engels, *Dialektik der Natur* (5th ed.; Berlin, 1961), p. 111.

14. Quoted in Mayer, Engels, II, 434.

15. For this discussion, see Engels' correspondence from 1890 to 1894 in Marx,
Selected Works, I, 380–94, and Mayer, *Engels*, II, 432–56.

history as a discipline and it betrayed the persistence of duality behind the formula of "interaction." For the substantive relationship of economic to political and ideological history coincided, in Engels, with the methodological relationship of rational to empirical history. Whatever the inadequacies he discerned in economic history when he focused his attention upon it alone, it acquired the exclusive properties of logical rationality and necessity when he considered it in the context of history as a whole. "Economic relations, however much they may be influenced by the other political and ideological ones, are still ultimately the decisive ones, forming the red thread which runs through them and alone leads to understanding. . . . The necessity which here asserts itself amidst all accident is again ultimately economic necessity."[16] The political and ideological elements in history, then, fill the role of "accidents," which cannot be plotted rationally, but can only be known empirically. "The further the particular sphere which we are investigating is removed from the economic sphere and approaches that of pure abstract ideology, the more shall we find it exhibiting accidents in its development, the more will its curve run in a zig-zag."[17] Thus, underlying Engels' attempt to show the comprehensive unity of the interactive process between economics and superstructure in history lay the attempt to show both the metaphysical unity between necessity and freedom and its methodological corollary of the unity between rational analysis and empirical research. That "men make their history themselves, but . . . are governed by *necessity*, which is supplemented by and appears under the forms of *accident*," was Engels' sharpened version of an early Marxian formula, and his employment of it in the later context of an enhanced superstructure indicated the larger role that he would now grant to the historical perception of man's purposive and "accidental" acts vis-à-vis the logical analysis of their unintended and "necessary" effects.[18]

But to establish the dialectical unity of history, Engels had to proceed through two distinct steps. First, he had to buttress the new dignity which he was conferring on the political and ideological superstructure as a real pole in the dialectic by conferring a parallel dignity upon its analogous principles of metaphysical contingency and methodological empiricism. With this, as we have just seen, he had no difficulty.

16. Engels to Heinz Starkenburg, January 25, 1894, in Marx, *Selected Works*, I, 392.
17. *Ibid.*, I, 393.
18. *Ibid.*, I, 392. Cf. Marx's: "Men make their own history, but they do not make it just as they please; they do not make it under circumstances chosen by themselves, but under circumstances directly found, given and transmitted from the past." *The Eighteenth Brumaire of Louis Bonaparte* (1852), in *ibid.*, II, 315.

Second, however, he had to show the logic in the interaction between each of these three principles—superstructure, contingency, empiricism —with its opposite number—economics, necessity, rationalism—and here the parallelism among the three levels broke down. Whereas the substantive relationship of politics and ideology to economics was a difference of degree, the relationships of free will to determinism and of the unique event to rational totality were oppositions of kind. On the substantive level, Engels admitted the fault of the early joint philosophy of history to be merely a matter of emphasis—"Marx and I are ourselves partly to blame for the fact that younger writers sometimes lay more stress on the economic side than is due to it"[19]—and he proposed a revised formula for the relationship of economic to political and ideological history that was essentially quantitative in its dependence upon physical analogy. Thus, on the relationship of economics to politics in history:

> It is the interaction of two unequal forces: on the one hand the economic movement, on the other the new political power, which strives for as much independence as possible, and which, having once been established, is also endowed with a movement of its own. On the whole, the economic movement gets its way, but it has also to suffer reactions from the political movement which it established and endowed with relative independence itself. . . .[20]

But the implicit methodology and metaphysics were something else again. On the level of method, his self-criticism of the early joint theory went far beyond the gradational mode of his substantive structure and took the categorical mode of opposing content to form:

> We all laid and were bound to lay the main emphasis at first on the derivation of political, juridical, and other ideological notions, from basic economic facts. But in doing so we neglected the formal side—the way in which these notions come about—for the sake of the content.[21]

Engels thought, undoubtedly, that his two judgments—the emphasis on economics and the neglect of form—were congruent, but actually they were not. If he had meant by "form" here simply a methodological synonym for the neglected superstructure, then the judgments would indeed have been apposite. But from his use of the term both here and in other contexts, it is clear that by "form" he referred not to the realm

---

19. Engels to Joseph Bloch, September 21, 1890, in *ibid.*, I, 383.
20. Engels to Conrad Schmidt, October 27, 1890, in *ibid.*, I, 384.
21. Engels to Mehring, July 14, 1893, in Karl Marx and Friedrich Engels, *Correspondence, 1846–1895* (New York, 1933), pp. 510–22.

of political and ideological events alone but to the point of their integration with the underlying economic force. He indicted for neglect of form both those who hypostatized economics and those who isolated ideology, and he defined form in synthetic terms: "As all the driving forces of the actions of any individual person must pass through his brain, and transform themselves into motives of his will in order to set him into action, so also all the needs of civil society . . . must pass through the will of the state in order to secure general validity in the form of laws. That is the formal aspect of the matter. . . . "[22]

Thus Engels' re-evaluation of "superstructure" and of "form" was not the same point attacked from two angles but two separate, sequential points. What he was saying, in essence, was this: because Marx and he had undervalued the facts of superstructure in history, they had had no occasion to proceed to the consequent basic problem of integrating these facts into the lawful economic movement. But—and this is why the distinction between the levels is so crucial—Engels now found that the solution of the first problem rendered impossible the solution of the second. After prescribing the quantitative enhancement of the superstructure in the abstract recipe of "interaction," he could not, and indeed would not, devise a formula for either the method or the rationale of its integration with its economic base. In the face of this issue, he explicitly renounced the philosophy of history for history proper, since history inhabited the substantive realm in which political and ideological facts could be juxtaposed with economic conditions without confronting the implicit philosophical antinomies of method and of metaphysics. Not only did he claim for the early Marx and Engels that "when it was a case of presenting a section of history, that is, of a practical application, there the thing was different and no error was possible," but he could now write that "the Marxist conception of history . . . puts an end to philosophy in the realm of history." Its "proof is to be found in history itself. . . . It is no longer a question anywhere of inventing interconnections from out of our brains, but of discovering them in the facts."[23] Nor did he shrink, at the end, from taking the step even beyond this position, which exalted actual history as the exclusive source of historical materialism, to the ultimate declaration of historical independence which scaled down historical materialism to a mere hermeneutic tool for the interpretation of actual history. He rejoiced,

---

22. *Ibid.,* pp. 510–12; Engels, *Feuerbach,* in Marx, *Selected Works,* I, 462.

23. Engels to Joseph Bloch, September 21, 1890, in Marx, *Selected Works,* I, 383; Engels, *Feuerbach,* in *ibid.,* I, 468.

Engels wrote in 1892, that historical materialism "finally begins to be used for what it really was—a guide to the study of history."[24]

Thus history came, for Engels, to be the only possible resolution for problems raised by his philosophy of history, and from this function stemmed its comprehensive quality. For it was precisely the inclusion of human events ranging the full spectrum from economic activities through military tactics to religious ideas that distinguished his historical works. But if Engels' history benefited from the frustrations of his philosophy of history, it had to suffer from them as well, for it reflected the philosophical irresolutions it could not resolve. His history could construct a pattern that was unified according to the distinctive criteria of its own limited realm, a pattern based upon the simple temporal simultaneity and succession of conditions and events, but, by virtue of the very assumptions that went into the history, it could only exemplify Engels' methodological inability to build the individuality of empirical observations into the generality of a logical process and his metaphysical inability to reconcile the freedom of individual actions with the determinism of collective effects. For despite Engels' nominal substitution of history for philosophy of history as the medium of synthesis, his ultimate synthesis, in both its methodological and its metaphysical versions, excluded history as categorically as the philosophy of history.

On the level of method, Engels prescribed that "historical science assimilate the dialectic," but he then defined the relationship of fact and logic in such a way as to make it impossible for "historical science" to do so.[25] When he "expelled" philosophy from history (and from nature), he was segregating rather than destroying philosophy, for he still assigned it the valid function of "the theory of the laws of the thought process itself, logic and dialectics."[26] That he did not here indicate how this philosophical logic would "discover" the "inter-connections" that were supposed to reside in the historical facts from which philosophy had been excluded was no mere neglect. It was rooted in his fundamental conviction, articulated in another context, that the only kinds of facts that could be integrated into a logical process were facts of present and future experience:

The empiricism of observation can never suffice to prove necessity. *Post hoc,* but not *propter hoc.* . . . But the proof of necessity lies in human activity, in ex-

24. Quoted in Mayer, *Engels,* II, 453.
25. Engels, *Dialektik der Natur,* p. 223.
26. Engels, *Feuerbach,* in Marx, *Selected Works,* I, 468.

periment, in labor: If I can produce the *post hoc,* it becomes identical with the *propter hoc.*[27]

It is easy to see how this logic of revolutionary activism could be applied to the experimental method of natural science, but it is easy to see too how inappropriate such a pragmatic method is to historical facts whose essence is precisely that they cannot be reproduced.

This gap between the facts of history and the laws of thought was at once confirmed by and grounded in the traces of historical metaphysics which continued to frame Engels' writing of history.[28] According to this metaphysics, the entire historical realm was necessarily condemned to the persistent tension between free will and determinism for the very simple reason that this tension could only be resolved in a kind of situation that has never yet come into existence. "Men make their history . . . not as yet with a collective will or according to a collective plan or even in a definitely defined given society," and until they do they will be governed, as they always have been governed, by a combination of "necessity" and "accident" that is Engels' terminology within history for the diremption of determinism and free will in the making of history.[29] All history hitherto, however remote or contemporary, consists fundamentally in the distinction between accident and necessity because these express in terms of historical *events* the distinction between the free individual will and the determined collective effect in the original historical *actions.* These relations hold not only for the connection between different kinds of historical events—that is, between necessary economic and accidental political or ideological events—but for the very structure of every historical event per se. For "the historical event" was itself a "resultant," "a collective mean" that was produced "unconsciously and without volition" by the "innumerable intersecting forces" of conscious and purposeful individual wills.[30] From the point of view of the individual, the event was an accident, since "what emerges is something that

27. Engels, *Dialektik der Natur,* p. 244.

28. "Metaphysics" is, of course, my label for this aspect of Engels' thought and not Engels' own, since, with Marx, he abjured metaphysics in any guise. I use it to designate that portion of their inverted Hegelianism which produced a rational schema of the historical process and an analysis of freedom and determinism and of contingency and necessity as its ultimate and formative realities. For an exhaustive philosophical analysis of the idealistic components in Engels' philosophy of history, see Rodolfo Mondolfo, *Le matérialisme historique d'après Frédéric Engels* (translated from Italian, Paris, 1917).

29. Engels to Heinz Starkenburg, January 25, 1894, in Marx, *Selected Works,* I, 392.

30. Engels to Joseph Bloch, September 21, 1890, in *ibid.,* I, 382–83.

no one willed," but from the point of view of the society, the event was a necessity, since it was a collective result determined by the collective conditions of the event, and from this collective point of view it was the intentional action of the individual will that was accidental.

But Engels never clarified the relationship between the contingency and the necessity which he thus identified in history. He did not do so for the very good reason that he believed in the cancellation of the distinction between accident and necessity, but in terms that were inapplicable to history as it has been lived and as he interpreted it.[31] This cancellation, stemming admittedly from Hegel and stipulating "that necessity determines itself as accident and that . . . this accident is absolute necessity," Engels did apply to nature, but it could apply to human society only when a future revolution would synthesize individual and collective wills—an eventuality which lay obviously beyond history.[32] Engels' repeated resort, in human history, to the concepts of "accident" and "necessity," which he rejected in both nature and the human future as false metaphysical antitheses, betrayed the fundamental character of the disjunction between the individual origins and the collective results of all historical actions in his view of man's past. All previous societies, he wrote, have been governed both by "necessity" which has appeared "under the forms of accident" and by accident as such which has "supplemented" necessity.[33]

Engels postulated both a progressive tendency toward the synthetic transcendence of accident and necessity in an expanding circle of freedom and a stubborn persistence of accident and necessity as separate identities in the continuing social limitations upon that freedom. He subscribed both to a positive relationship between accident and necessity that was teleological in character and a negative relationship that was constituent in character. But he had no theoretical solution or even formulation for the subsequent problem of how these two sets of relations were in turn related. His theoretical restraint is perhaps explicable by the ambiguous working solution he actually gave the problem in his histories when he faced it in the concrete form of individual and group actions which had no demonstrable link with the collective "driving forces" of history and in fact deviated from the individual and group actions demonstrably entailed by these forces. His solution was to treat the apparently maverick actions alternately as indifferent or as related by

31. "What can I reject more strongly than both these designations of thought?" Engels, *Dialektik der Natur*, p. 231.

32. *Ibid.*, p. 234.

33. Engels to Heinz Starkenburg, January 25, 1894, in Marx, *Selected Works*, I, 392.

dialectical negation to the main movement of history. The ambiguity was a fruitful one, for it enabled Engels to indulge freely in his passion for the specific materials of history and still to cover its descriptive details and narrative form with the logic of historical materialism.

And so we are led both by Engels' personal tastes and by his version of the Marxist philosophy of history to the history that he wrote. The foregoing considerations serve, moreover, not only as a backdrop for his historical writing but as an explanation of the surprises it contains. The mixed quality of this writing, indeed, is such as to require at least as much explanation as it provides. For if we turn to Engels' historical works with the aim of characterizing his historiography as a whole, we find that they are not simply Marxist tracts, nor are they simply empirical or scientific history—that, indeed, they are not anything simple. His history is characterized rather by the plurality of its salient traits and the divergent tendencies they denote. So divergent, in fact, are they that they even suffer arrangement into a series of contraries.

Engels wrote history primarily to illuminate the social conflicts of his own age, but he also went back through the early modern period into ancient and prehistory and immersed himself in the very different forms and issues of these eras. He wrote normative history in which he openly judged what his historical subjects did by what their social roles indicated they should have done, but he also wrote long stretches of autonomous history in which he permitted military, political, and cultural facts to speak for themselves. This differentiation held true, moreover, not only for the criteria but for the very arrangement and structure of his histories: the economic and social sections appeared at the beginning and were cast in an analytical mode, while the military, political, and cultural materials were segregated into their own later sections and were cast in a narrative mold. Again, the economic and social analysis covered long-term evolution; the rest was focused upon short-term revolution. Finally, his historical reference extended to all mankind, but his historical preference concentrated upon the German nation.

The upshot is a kind of historical writing that shares with Marx's own the schematism, the economic and social causation, the didactic purpose, the contemporary and revolutionary emphases so familiar now in Marxist historiography—and yet it has a distinctive texture of its own. The difference lies not simply in Engels' addiction to Germany in contrast to Marx's propensity for France, but in their characteristically divergent ways of executing their history. Marx's history has the texture of a plait, in which theory and fact, social structure and political events, are braided together in continuing contact. Engels' has the sound of factual nuggets jostling against one another inside a theory-ribbed receptacle.

Much of the duality that runs through Engels' historical composition is obviously explicable in terms of his own varied roles as revolutionary, social theorist, German burgher, and scholar *manqué*. Much of it is explicable, too, by the stresses which developed within his gloss on the Marxist philosophy of history. His personal tastes and his theoretical limits combined to give him a real appreciation of history as such, an appreciation that could embroil him in the methods and substance of historical inquiry without explicit reference to its ultimate Marxist meaning. He complained when he had to write history without adequate sources, and he was proud when he could claim his historical "material" to be of his own research.[34] He was clearly apologetic because his *Peasant War in Germany* "does not pretend to present independently collected material," and for years thereafter he did collect such material for the radical revision which he planned but did not live long enough to make.[35] His attraction to history was such, moreover, that it was an important dimension of all his main works. Not only was much of the *Anti-Dühring* and the *Ludwig Feuerbach and the Outcome of Classical German Philosophy* cast in the form of intellectual history, but even the early *Condition of the Working Class in England* was "originally designed to form part of a more comprehensive work on English social history."[36]

But if the factors making for a certain intrinsicality in Engels' concern with German history are obvious enough, what is not so obvious is the relationship that he postulated between this kind of history and the Marxist framework that was supposed to explain it. Unquestionably, however separate the two lines of his history—the social analysis and the political narrative—look to us, they certainly did not seem so to him. He rejected as emphatically as Marx the leading lights of the new empirical and critical history in Germany—Ranke, Mommsen, Sybel—precisely because their principle of independence for the unique political event made of history "a wild confusion of unbridled aggressions." The autonomy of empirical history was thus intellectually intolerable to

---

34. Engels to Marx, August 21, 1851, in V. Adoratsky (ed.), "Karl Marx/Friedrich Engels," *Historish-Kritische Gesamtausgabe* (Berlin, 1929), Part III, Vol. 1, p. 242; Frederick Engels, *The Origin of the Family, Private Property, and the State* (Chicago, 1902), p. 11.

35. See *Friedrich Engels*, p. 3.

36. Engels, *The Condition of the Working Class in England*, p. 3.

him, and Marx's version of the Hegelian dialectic satisfied a profound need by "bringing order into chaos" and revealing the "quiet . . . and real movement of history behind the noisy deeds."[37] But how to reconcile this need for a unifying principle with the respect for the integrity of the historical fact that found expression in the forms of his own history writing and in his agreement with the historicist principle of "the right of every age and situation to its own stage of knowledge and of society"?[38] This was the problem that repeated concretely on the historical level what Engels had failed to resolve theoretically on the level of the philosophy of history. He did solve it on the concrete historical level through the kind of history that he chose to write about. In the context of his general problem, Engels' option for the history of German revolutions becomes itself not a question but an answer.

We have already noted Engels' inability to provide a theoretical formulation of this reconciliation, but however inadequate for itself, his philosophy of history does provide the key to how he could live with the duality in his practice of history. Indeed, the fruitfulness of Engels' German revolutionary histories, both for his dilemma and for our historical knowledge, springs from the appropriateness of their subject matter to the problematic theoretical assumptions with which he organized and interpreted it. The Germans have actually been dominated in their history by the tension between an ideal unity and an actual diversity. Germany shared only partially in the unifying social effects of western economic growth; it exhibited a gap between an autocratically oriented politics and a plurally divided society; it made its tradition of national community into an illusion, detached from its real political particularism; it alienated its ambitious cultural elite from an impermeable social and political reality. In all these ways German history did epitomize in fact the fundamental disjunction between reason and reality that Engels epitomized in theory, and it is no wonder that he was attuned to this history. That Engels did understand the German past in these terms and that this understanding did fill a need in his philosophy of history are confirmed by the brief (and neglected) essay on recent German history that he wrote for the Chartist *Northern Star* immediately after his conversion to historical materialism in 1845. The historical disjunctions that must be inferred from the more sophisticated tendency of his subsequent German histories took a more primitive and obvious form here: he reserved his unitary economic and social analysis for the Euro-

---

37. Mayer, *Engels*, II, 428–29.
38. *Ibid.*, II, 446.

pean context of German developments and separated out the specifically German history into a straight narration of political conflict and cultural frustration.[39]

But to this divisiveness of his German preference Engels added the integrating influence of his option for revolutionary subjects. During most of the German past the connections both within and between each set of its tensions have been obscure, and the Germans have tended to pursue each of their compartmentalized economic, social, political, and cultural activities in apparent indifference to the others. But in times of revolution the insulation has been fretted away, and the kinds of activity which had seemed so independent became obviously implicated in a single process whose character and fate consisted precisely in the specific unfolding of the negative relationships which had for so long subsisted among them. Engels was perfectly aware of the power of revolution to expose the dialectical linkage within the apparent heterogeneity of men's usual concerns: "In history movement in the form of antitheses emerges only in all critical epochs of the leading nations. In such moments a people has only the choice between two horns of a dilemma—either-or."[40] Hence Engels' equation of revolutions with nature—" a revolution is a pure phenomenon of nature, which is led more according to physical laws than according to the rules which in ordinary times determine the development of society"[41]—takes on a historiographical meaning when we recall that for Engels it is in nature that history and dialectic have their most perfect union.

In the history of the German revolutions Engels thus found a practical form of his historical theory that managed both to incarnate the divisions of the theory and yet to escape its anomalies. For the chronological relations of historical events supplied him with a connection among the diverse facts which he could not find in the logical relations of his dialectical theory. The outstanding common feature of the historical works that he devoted to revolution in Germany was the care which he bestowed upon the delineation of political and military actions and of political and religious programs with the purpose of showing how their overt political and ideological autonomy was explicable by the conscious alienation of their individual and group agents from their real social base. What stands out in his history of the Revolution of 1848 is

39. "Deutsche Zustände," in Karl Marx/Friedrich Engels, *Werke* (Berlin, 1958), II, 564–84.

40. Engels, *Dialektik der Natur*, p. 225.

41. Engels to Marx, February 13, 1851, in Marx/Engels, *Gesamtausgabe*, Part III, Vol. 1, p. 149.

not simply his identification of the various political groups and leaders with their cognate social classes, but his analysis of the economic, political, and intellectual factors that obscured their view of their class position at that particular time, and his narrative description of the political events whose fortuitous and irrational character stemmed precisely from their social opacity. The very occasion for Engels' history of the German Peasants' War revealed its role as a synthesizer in practice of what was disjoined in theory. Engels used it to demonstrate the coherence behind the apparent incoherence of 1848 by a historical analogy that provided a limiting case of the contingency and the multiplicity necessarily infecting the acts and ideas of men who did not understand the economic and social basis of what they did and thought.

It is easy to see, in his choice of subjects, how Engels could think that history itself resolved the dilemma of the philosophy of history by manifesting social determinism in such a way as to spare the duality between necessity and freedom. But even in these choice histories Engels vacillated repeatedly between the explanation of his historical agents' false consciousness as a necessary consequence of an immature economic development and his explanation of it as a contingent product of temporary circumstances and human failings. In the last analysis, this fruitful ambiguity is precisely what is most remarkable about Engels' history: it re-echoed while it resolved the problems in the theory that spawned it.

Germany had had two revolutions by Engels' time—the Peasants' War of 1525 and the Revolution of 1848—and he wrote the histories of both. The circumstances in which he wrote them furnish an object lesson for the way in which the classic works of men outgrow the incidentals of their origin and take on a life of their own. It follows that these works have not only a content but a history of their own, and it is to the outer history of Engels' revolutionary histories that we now turn.

The editorial origins of the two volumes were similar. Engels wrote each work as a series of magazine articles. *The Peasant War in Germany* was published in the telescoped May to October (1850) issue of the *Neue Rheinische Zeitung* which Marx and Engels edited in London and had printed in Hamburg. *Germany: Revolution and Counter-Revolution* appeared sporadically between October, 1851, and September, 1852, in the socially minded Charles A. Dana's *New York Tribune*. Both works were written for reasons that were extraneous to their contents: Engels wrote *The Peasant War* just after the disappointments of 1848–49 and in expectation of a new revolutionary surge. His twin purposes were, correspondingly, to trace the genealogy of the bourgeois and petty bourgeois traitors of the recent revolution and to stimulate the hoped-for proletarian vanguard of the coming revolution. He wrote *Germany: Revolution and Counter-Revolution* because Marx, who had agreed to comment on the German situation for the *Tribune,* was too busy or too unsure of his English or too convinced that Germany was Engels' bailiwick—Marx never specified which—to do it himself. The articles were sent to Dana through Marx and were published under the latter's name, but the Marx-Engels correspondence reveals Engels' authorship and even indicates that Marx sent them along unaltered.[42] The final external similarity of the two works lies in their parallel editorial histories: both were published in volume form by Marxist disciples—*The Peasant War* in 1870 and *Germany: Revolution and Counter-Revolution* in 1896—and both have since been kept in circulation as part of the Marxist canon through divers translations and reprintings.

But if the works have followed parallel courses in their capacity as models for the historical application of Marxism, they have had divergent destinies in their capacity as contributions to European history. The divergence in their historical reputations has occurred in our own generation, for after a long period of their joint neglect by all but Marxist intellectuals like Karl Kautsky and Franz Mehring and Soviet historians like D. Riazanov[43] the postwar era has witnessed the new but limited academic use of *The Peasant War* in a non-Soviet, Marxist, professional historiography, and the new broad appreciation of *Germany: Revolution and Counter-Revolution* in professional Marxist and non-Marxist historiography alike.

The one-sided revival of *The Peasant War* stems exclusively from the

---

42. Substantive discussion of the articles is entirely absent from the lengthy published correspondence for this period. Remarks about them abound, but always in the sense of complaints about Dana's cavalier treatment of them or about the imminent deadlines requiring Engels' immediate dispatch. Together with the absence of discussion between friends who discussed everything else, this constant pressure confirms the conclusion from internal evidence that *Germany: Revolution and Counter-Revolution* was all Engels'. The one apparent exception to this was Engels' request, on April 29, 1852, for a memorandum from Marx, but characteristically what Engels wanted was not help on the historical sections of the work but on "the revolutionary prospects of Germany" and "the position of our Party," which would conclude the series of articles. Marx agreed to write such a memorandum, but he never did, pleading the pressure of family affairs as his excuse. See Marx/Engels, *Gesamtausgabe,* Part III, Vol. 1, pp. 229–392, especially pp. 343, 345, 403.

43. Thus Karl Kautsky, *Communism in Central Europe in the Time of the Reformation* (translated from German; London, 1897); Franz Mehring's edition of Engels, *Der deutsche Bauernkrieg* (Berlin, 1920); D. Riazanov's edition of Engels, *The Peasant War in Germany* (English translation; New York, 1926).

development of a Marxist academic historiography in the German Democratic Republic—that is, Communist East Germany. The official penetration of Marxism into the East German universities has introduced a new phase in the posthumous career of Engels' book because their professional historians have extended its role from a specific example of general Marxist history to the Marxist interpretation of specific history. Thereby, for the first time, the particular historical result of the work rather than its general theoretical approach has become the subject of academic discussion. A. Meusel's *Thomas Müntzer und seine Zeit* (1952), the East German translation of the Russian study by M. M. Smirin, *Die Volksreformatikon des Thomas Münzer und der grosse Bauernkrieg* (1952), and Heinz Kamnitzer's *Zur Vorgeschichte des Deutschen Bauernkrieges* (1953) have explicitly brought Engels into the historical scholarship on the Peasants' War as the progenitor of its social interpretation. Again, the recent (1952) East German re-edition of Wilhelm Zimmermann's old (1840–44) *Der Grosse Deutsche Bauernkrieg* is certainly associated with Engels' express and laudatory citation of the book as his own chief source.

That Engels' history of the Peasant War has received no such recognition among non-Marxist historians comes as no surprise, but what does need explaining is their continued failure to accord it any recognition at all beyond the dubious honor of an occasional refutation. There would appear to be three reasons for this combination of neglect and hostility in the attitude of contemporary non-Marxist historians to this work of Engels—the first technical and the other two substantive.

First, then, Engels' "material," as he himself admitted, all came out of Zimmermann, and historians do better to consult Zimmermann, where it has vitality, than Engels, where it is pap. Actually, however, they tend to consult neither of these, but rather the recent and standard Günther Franz, *Der deutsche Bauernkrieg* (4th ed., 1956), which epitomizes the results of subsequent research with its stress upon the social diversity of the peasants' revolt and its restrictions upon any uniform interpretation of the movement.

A second reason for the disregard of Engels in this field is the partial historiographical success of what he himself did obviously contribute to the understanding of the peasant revolution by "showing the religious and political controversies of that epoch as a reflection of the class struggles that were taking place simultaneously." As the very label affixed to the revolt attests and the perennial socialist interest in it confirms, the social motif of the movement is so indisputable that the kind of emphasis initiated by Engels has long since been built into all interpretations of the age. As *a* dimension, consequently, it rates no credit line.

But finally, and most fundamentally, Engels' work on the Peasant War of the sixteenth century has been particularly slighted because it ambitiously applies the economic interpretation to a pre-industrial age, an application that non-Marxist historians find singularly inappropriate. Engels posed his social thesis not simply as a dimension but as a prime cause of the peasants' revolt, and in this form non-Marxist historians have rejected it or ignored it because they have found it wrong or irrelevant. In the proportioning of causes they have tended to emphasize the primacy of state-building in triggering mass action and of religion in driving Engels' hero, Thomas Müntzer. They have also disputed the notion of a general tendency toward peasant economic and social misery, cited a mixture of progress and decline, and correspondingly made the economic and social dimensions contributory rather than primary. Although the difference seems to be one of mere proportions, the upshot is a position categorically opposed to Engels', for the contemporary non-Marxist historians see unity precisely in the politics and the religion wherein he saw diversity, and they see factual multiplicity in the economics and society wherein he saw rational coherence.

Despite its dubious status in non-Marxist historiography, Engels' *Peasant War in Germany* does remain a historical classic still worth reading. Three factors justify its longevity. First, it initiated a prominent tradition of socialist history on the era of the Peasant War, running through Karl Kautsky, E. Belfort Bax, and Roy Pascal to the current official Marxist studies.[44] It is a tradition serious enough, in the recent judgment of a respected German scholar, to rival the non-Marxist tradition and to leave the interpretation of the Peasant War still moot between them.[45] It should be added, as a subordinate consideration, that the Marxist line is not only becoming more respectable academically but has always been more convenient scholastically. Of the historical works devoted wholly or mainly to the Peasants' War, the only ones in English are those from the socialist tradition. The best of the non-Marxist tradition, old and new alike, remain in their original German.

44. For other socialist accounts of the Peasants' War (in addition to Engels' and Kautsky's, cited above), see E. Belfort Bax, *The Peasants War in Germany* (London, 1899), and Roy Pascal, *The Social Basis of the Reformation* (London, 1933).

45. Wilhelm Treue, "Wirtschafts- und Sozialgeschichte vom 16. bis zum 18. Jahrhundert," in Bruno Gebhardt, *Handbuch der deutschen Geschichte* (8th ed.; Stuttgart, 1955), II, 376–77.

This tradition is available in English only through more inclusive works in which the Peasants' War is one topic among others.[46]

The second factor which warrants the attribution of classic status to Engels' *Peasant War in Germany* is more convincing, for it bears upon an essential and distinctive quality of the book itself. In the actual working out of his economic thesis through his religious material, Engels formulated relationships of practical interests to religious ideals that are more important for the connections they make than for the putative economic primacy from which he began. Undoubtedly, Engels' early religious experience and his lifelong conviction of a kinship between religion and communism helped him to approach, in the context of the religiosity of the Peasants' War, as close as he would ever get to an integral relationship among the variegated historical activities of man.[47] The connection between the radical sects and the "peasant-plebeian" classes—the connection that embodied Engels' most penetrating historical perception—remains the one definite relationship that has been accepted by historians on both sides of the Marxist divide. In general, moreover, even if Engels' priority of social interests and his one-to-one correlation of the other religious confessions with social classes have found no such acceptance, the relevance of the social dimension to the religious conflicts of the Reformation era is beyond cavil and the discovery of how this relationship actually worked remains one of the live issues for European historiography.

Third, and finally, *The Peasant War in Germany* embodies Engels' Marxist dilemma in a form that can help every student of history to know himself. Engels himself unwittingly pointed out the lesson to be

46. For standard German accounts, in addition to Zimmermann and Franz see Adolf Waas, *Die grosse Wendung im deutschen Bauernkrieg* (Munich and Berlin, 1939), and Willy Andreas, *Deutschland vor der Reformation* (6th ed.; Stuttgart, 1959). For recent works in English with sections on the Peasants' War, see Hajo Holborn, *A History of Modern Germany: the Reformation* (New York, 1959); Harold John Grimm, *The Reformation Era, 1500–1650* (New York, 1954); George H. Williams, *The Radical Reformation* (London, 1962); *The New Cambridge Modern History:* Vol. II, *The Reformation* (Cambridge, 1958). Of the older accounts, see especially Leopold von Ranke, *History of the Reformation in Germany* (English translation; New York, 1905); Preserved Smith, *The Age of the Reformation* (New York, 1920); J. Selwyn Schapiro, *The Reformation and Social Reform* (New York, 1909); J. Janssen, *A History of the German People from the Close of the Middle Ages* (English translation; London, 1905–10).

47. See the translation of Engels' "On the Early History of Christianity" and editorial comments in Lewis S. Feuer (ed.), *Marx and Engels: Basic Writings on Politics and Philosophy* (New York, 1959), pp. 168–94, 412.

learned from the work in a later summary of the historical principles that had gone into it. When placed in juxtaposition these principles make explicit the fundamental paradox of history that Engels' work, unpretentious as it is, does exemplify. The paradox consists in the necessarily variant views of historical events taken by the men who made the events and the historian who re-creates them, and it is Engels' glory to have cast his Marxism into a sixteenth-century shape that makes clear the ultimate ambiguity of the historian's situation.

Engels, on the one hand, understood the point of view of the men who made the long stretch of pre-industrial history, and he recognized their right to put their own stamp upon that history. Because these historical subjects viewed "thoughts as . . . developing independently and subject only to their own laws," and because the determination of this thought process by "material life conditions remains of necessity unknown to these persons," the men of the pre-industrial era constrain "every social and political movement to take on a theological form."

On the other hand, however, Engels also fully recognized the right of the modern historian to read back into this same preindustrial era the knowledge of the primacy of "material life conditions," although this is a knowledge that only the industrialism of the historian's own age made possible. The historian need only perform this reinterpretation, as Engels felt he himself had, and what had been "the riddle" of the driving forces of history is thereby solved for all preceding periods as well as for his own.[48] Needless to say, Engels remained too much of a Hegelian believer in the retroactive power of knowledge to have himself been aware of the problem posed by this combination of principles. But to others not so comfortably endowed his *Peasant War in Germany* will remain a case study in the problem of how far the historian can go in opposing to his subjects' interpretations of themselves contrary interpretations stemming from subsequently acquired knowledge which the subjects did not and could not have had about themselves.

Germany: Revolution and Counter-Revolution poses no such historiographical problem. As a history of the German Revolution of 1848 in which, by the common consent of all recent historians, social interests and conflicts did in fact play a conscious and crucial role, the work has been recognized as a classic by historians of all persuasions. In part, undoubtedly, its repute and utility rest on considerations extraneous to its value as a historical study, for it functions as a primary source both for the revolution of which Engels was an intelligent contemporary wit-

48. Engels, *Feuerbach*, in Marx, *Selected Works*, I, 459, 465–66.

ness and for the revolutionary party in which he was a leading participant. But even when these functions are discounted and the question is
only of its status as a historical study, both its repute and its utility remain eminent. Its eminence does not rest especially upon its technique,
for if the materials from newspapers and other contemporary accounts
of the revolution make it superior in this respect to *The Peasant War in
Germany,* they are hardly distinctive enough to account for the precedence which it has recently enjoyed over all the contemporary and even
many of the subsequent histories of the 1848 revolution in Germany.
The eminence of the work rests rather upon the ascending role that the
social interpretation pioneered by Engels has played in the historiography of the revolution.

Down to the end of World War II the standard interpretations of the
German Revolution of 1848 centered on the political issues of liberalism and democracy, monarchy and republic, particularism and nationalism, federalism and centralism, a smaller and a larger Germany.[49] But
the postwar generation of historians, seeking to explain the futility of
German idealism in terms of its relations to practical interests, eagerly
took up Engels' social interpretation of the revolution as a scheme
which could get relevant answers out of the old material without waiting for the necessary new researches. The flexibility which we have seen
to be characteristic of Engels' revolutionary history—the separate treatment and acknowledgment given such political factors as particularism
and nationalism and to such ideological factors as the philosophies of
idealism and liberalism, combined with the confident assurance that
they were related, if only by negation, to the dimly perceived class
conflict—was perfectly suited to both the material and the needs of the
postwar historians. That the East German writing on 1848 should have
cited Engels in the style of scripture is to be expected, but a whole gal-
axy of non-Marxist historians, including even so notable a representative of the nationalist school as Friedrich Meinecke, both passed
favorable judgment upon him and relied upon his judgments, not simply as a witness or participant but as a historian.[50]

49. Especially Erich Brandenburg, *Die deutsche Revolution 1848* (2d ed.; Leipzig,
1919), and Veit Valentin *Geschichte der deutschen Revolution 1848–49* (2 vols.; Berlin,
1930–31), abridged English translation, 1848: *Chapters of German History* (London,
1940).

50. For postwar East German histories of 1848, see Jürgen Kuczynski, *Die
wirtschftlichen und sozialen Voraussetzungen der Revolution von 1848–1849* (Berlin, 1848);
Karl Obermann, *Die deutschen Arbeiter in der ersten bürgerlichen Revolution* (Berlin, 1950).
For favorable non-Marxist comments on, or citations of, Engels, see A. J. P. Taylor, *The*

Where *Germany: Revolution and Counter-Revolution* has now been superseded by new insights and researches, it has been extended rather than refuted. Even the more independent of the recent interpretations—those of Stadelmann and Hamerow that stress the role of the lower middle class in the revolution—are social interpretations that are tangential rather than opposed to Engels.[51] But the most impressive evidence of the continuing validity of Engels' work is the high value which is placed upon it in Jacques Droz's monumental *Les révolutions allemandes de 1848* (1957), now undoubtedly the standard work in the field. Droz has publicized his debt to Engels through frequent citations at crucial points—citations that are all the more impressive for the fine balance of Droz's interpretation among the social, political, and intellectual elements of the revolution.[52] But Droz has gone further and has paid Engels the supreme compliment that a historian of one generation can pay to a predecessor: one of Droz's major reinterpretations has restored to prominence the workers' revolutionary role first adumbrated by Engels and minimized by his successors. There are, to be sure, particular emphases in *Germany: Revolution and Counter-Revolution* that are unacceptable today—the wholesome condemnation of the traitorous bourgeoisie; the rigid concentration on Prussia and Austria as the only significant arenas of action; the dismissal of the Frankfurt National Assembly as the "parliament of an imaginary country" that created "an imaginary government," passed "imaginary resolutions," and was of interest only to "the collector of literary and antiquarian curiosities"; and the deprecation of Slav nationalities and cultures. These were occasions when Engels could not hold the equilibrium between the Marxism that was his key and the historical reality that was his passion. But the failure of a revolution is a sign of an actual imbalance in the historical situation, and to this extent Engels' own imbalances were appropriate to the ill-fated revolutions he so shrewdly chose to describe.

In the final analysis, the value of Engels' historical writing must be

---

Course of German History (New York, 1946), p. 77; G. Barraclough, *The Origins of Modern Germany* (Oxford, 1947), p. 416; Friedrich Meinecke, *1848: eine Sekuläbetrachtung* (Berlin, 1948), *passim;* Wilhelm Mommsen, *Grösse und Versagen des deutschen Bürgertums* (2d ed., Munich, 1964), p. 127; Koppel S. Pinson, *Modern Germany: Its History and Civilization* (2d ed.; New York, 1966), pp. 79, 106, 626.

51. Rudolf Stadelmann, *Soziale und politische Geschichte der Revolution von 1848* (Munich, 1948); Theodore S. Hamerow, *Restoration, Revolution, Reaction: Economics and Politics in Germany 1815–71* (Princeton, 1958).

52. Jacques Droz, *Les révolutions allemandes de 1848* (Paris, 1957), pp. 64, 99–100, 616, 628.

assessed by two distinct criteria. As a substantive application of historical materialism, its validity rises and falls with the factual force of economic and social interests in the historical events under consideration. From this point of view, his interpretation is relevant to both the German revolutions, but in different ways: it illuminates certain individual events of the sixteenth-century revolution and the general course of the nineteenth-century revolution.

But beyond the literal truth or falsity of the economic interpretation, Engels' historical writing has a more universal function that must be assessed by a more fundamental standard of judgment. Engels was one of those rare historians who converted a philosophy of history which conditioned history from outside of history into a historical principle which was operative within the historical process itself. By thus engaging the strands of rationality and continuity in the kaleidoscopic manifold of history, Engels put the basic issue of the philosophy of history —whether there are any constant factors in the making or knowing of history—into a form that historians cannot avoid. From this point of view, his two histories of the German revolutions are complementary: *Germany: Revolution and Counter-Revolution* is a case study in the coherence of the history that men made; *The Peasant War in Germany* is a case study in the coherence of the knowledge that the historian has of it. These variants of the issue recapitulated two whole epochs in the philosophy of history: the long previous epoch when the philosophers of history had looked for laws in history, and the epoch to come when they were to look for universals in the way historians know about history. Because Engels stood at the turning point of these two epochs, his historical works epitomize the strengths and weaknesses of any synthetic approach to the diversity of historical experience.

6 TWENTIETH-CENTURY GERMAN HISTORY

From the 16th century to the 20th, . . . the political history of
Germany had been dominated by the successive absorptions of the
various claims to human freedom piecemeal into the structure of
monarchical government without undermining the independent
authority of that government. . . . [T]he state in Germany had
become both the actual organization and the ideal symbol for the
compatible integration of . . . individual freedom into the
established order of political government and social hierarchy. . . .
It was this primal association between freedom and the traditional
state that the Nazis destroyed. . . . Dominant now is an attitude
which views the state as a morally neutral, purely utilitarian
organization of public power. . . . the central strand in the
German political tradition has been cut and all possibilities lie
open for the future.

From the Epilogue to *The German Idea of Freedom*

17 Nazism: Highway or Byway?

For those of us who were raised politically on the vicarious experience of National Socialism, its graduation into an apparently successful and overpowering regime was a cataclysm of unparalleled proportions. The movement seemed an enormous, overbearing force whose source was beyond time and the changes associated with time. It appeared not so much to grow and develop as to manifest in apparently different, but internally affinitive, ways the relentlessly consistent potentialities which had ever been in it. Nazi opportunism was well known to us, of course, but it did not so much define the movement as express it, generalizing National Socialism and equipping it to act characteristically on all kinds of objects in all kinds of situations. Nazism, in short, was a massive central reality, *sui generis*. We were uneasy about Italian fascism, saddened by the Spanish version, regretful at the east European varieties, and divided both within and among ourselves vis-à-vis the instrumental similarities of the Soviet dictatorship. But Nazism was in a class by itself, at once invincibly individual and supremely representative, an inimitable compound of Germanism, fascism, and regressive autocracy that was reducible to none of these ingredients and yet intensified each of them to its ultimate power. Thus Nazism was connected to the past and contemporary worlds sufficiently to make its impact universal, but in these connections it was ever Nazism that was the senior partner: it was not German history or fascism or absolutist tradition that made Nazism relevant to us but the other way around. Nazism abolished the limitations of time and space for us: the clutches of atavism and the tentacles of technology alike could now reach to any individual anytime anywhere. It was at once fact and symbol. It marked both the climax of German history and the point at which, as the ultimate authoritarianism, this German finality met the destiny of humanity.

Now it is no novelty for historians of modern times to see the materials of their life's experience drift into the status of recent history. With this modal change the experience toward which all things converge ac-

First published in *Central European History* 11:1 (March, 1978), 3–22. In an earlier version, this paper was delivered before the Georgetown History Forum in October 1975.

355

quires a future to which it contributes along with other antecedents of equal rank. Not only is the experience itself different in its new historical dispensation, moreover, but so is our attitude toward it: we are converted from participant into observer, and even if we were merely contemporary observers in the first place the addition in degree of intervening increments to a knowledge that had been inevitably partial and restricted brings a categorical shift in kind of our posture from a crouch within to a supervisory stance above the events in question. Yet, apart from the common enough shock of realizing that growing sections of our audience have not shared the experience with which we grew up and must be informed explicitly about contexts and assumptions we take for granted, the shift from contemporary living to recent historizing is usually not traumatic. The impact is cushioned by the osmosis which, justified by ubiquity if not in principle, takes place in both directions between the human and the professional compartments of historical man. Often enough we call events "historical" even as we live through them and cherish the conviction that if we so regard them we have achieved a comparative advantage over our contemporaries. Invariably, too, we follow the historiographical prescription to recreate the mood and circumstances of past historical events as if they were indeed a present experience, and thereby we minimize the distance between past and present from the side of the past just as our superconsciousness of the historicity of contemporary experience minimizes the distance from the side of the present.

But these modulations have not worked in the case of the Nazis. Nazism, indeed, affords a decisive instance of the categorical difference between the modalities of contemporary existence and historical event, the difference which is so often blurred in more compatible cases. To some extent the divergence between the Nazism that people experienced and the Nazism that historians describe is a matter of historians' temperament. They are revisionist by preference, and for some the focus by contemporaries of the 1930s and '40s on Nazism as the unified and unifying force of their age and as the climactic manifestation of its essential culture, whether that be defined conservatively in terms of mass democracy, liberally in terms of escape from freedom, or radically in terms of cornered capitalism—this contemporary focus has amounted to an irresistible challenge to prove the opposite in historical perspective: to assert, like Taylor, that Nazi policy was less diabolical and more ordinary than had been believed, or to assert, like Barraclough, that the Nazi episode was less central, in the modern history of both Germany and the world, than the apocalyptic sense of its attending generation assumed.[1]

To a certain extent, too, the habitual procedures of historians have wrought their own unwitting revisionism. Subject as they are to what we may call "the law of diminishing assumptions," the tendency of historians to break up a historical movement for specialized study, scientifically necessary as it may be, has the subliminal effect of suspending or diffracting the movement's collective thrust and thereby of diffusing or reducing its impact. The recent address of research to regional and local studies of Nazism is undoubtedly salutary, and the work of Allen, Peterson, and Diehl-Thiele indicates that such address need not ignore the resonance of Nazism as a whole,[2] but in any case, whatever the specific destiny of Nazi regional and local histories, they can hardly avoid becoming a subset of the generally valid historiographical proposition which stipulates that the closer we get to the detailed acts and qualities of any historical object the less possible it becomes to see anything that it did or was as such and the less we are able to say anything essential about it in general.

Even more fundamental to the historian's procedure than this penchant for variegation but equally incongruous with the original experience of Nazism is his distinctive rationalization of all human reality, whether or not it can be otherwise rationalized. To note thus the rational component of the historian's procedure is not to subscribe to the "covering-law" thesis of history's implied postulation of the rules of general logic nor to endorse the thesis that historians work with models of rationality in human behavior. It is to point out that at the very least there is a cursive kind of rationality at work in the chrono-logical ordering of any deed or attitude, however philosophico-logically or even psycho-logically incompatible with its associated deeds and attitudes it may be, and that even this minimal integrative historical reason tends to distort the anomic rational or antirational reality of the Nazi mentality. Historians are often aware of the pallid inadequacy that dims their work in contrast to the robust abundance of the life they portray, but rarely do we meet with the pervasive awareness of the mismatch between gro-

---

1. A. J. P. Taylor, *The Origins of the Second World War* (London, 1961); Geoffrey Barraclough, *New York Review of Books* 19 (1972): Oct. 19, pp. 37–43; Nov. 2, pp. 32–38; Nov. 16, pp. 25–36.

2. William S. Allen, *The Nazi Seizure of Power: The Experience of a Single German Town, 1930–1935* (Chicago, 1965); Edward N. Peterson, *The Limits of Hitler's Power* (Princeton, 1969); Peter Diehl-Thiele, *Partei und Staat im Dritten Reich* (Munich, 1969).

tesque original and methodical reconstruction so much as in the historical literature on the Nazi kaleidoscope.

Under those microscopic auspices historical reconsideration has scaled down Nazism in both its external and its internal relations. Externally, the differentiation among a plurality of incommensurable fascisms and the dissolution of totalitarianism as a political category have tended to isolate National Socialism and to divest it of the cosmic significance with which its plenary manifestation of typal qualities seemed to have endowed it. Internally, the critical dismantling of the presumed monolith into the welter of overlapping jurisdictions, internecine rivalries, personal ambitions, divided commitments, and inertial blockages, appropriately summed up in a recent title as "the limits of Hitler's power," has not only completed the destruction of the totalitarian genus but emasculated the Nazi mammoth in the name of operational reality.[3] Whether the regime be portrayed with the metaphor of a devolutionary oriental satrapy or with the unspoken vision of a Hobbesian war of all against all, the caustic historical perspective on its actual practice presents a spectacle of all-sided disorder, infecting not only non-Nazi institutions under the impress of Nazification, like the army and the bureaucracy, but also the party and even the mind of Adolf Hitler himself. The weight of the disruptive evidence is such, indeed, that the problem faced by many of the historians who use it becomes the explanation of how the "systemless" regime managed to work at all.

Were this the whole story, then the answer to our own metaphorical question would be simple: Nazism would be an experiential highway that has become a historical byway. The attention that historians pay to it would be explicable as a resultant of the interest we always have in the background of general wars, of the respectful tribute we pay to the magnified commitments of our fathers or our own youth—that is, to a prominent expression of the fascistic epoch that will never return—and of the concern with the dramatic which current historiography holds to be a crucial element in the historical enterprise. Our preoccupation would be primarily with describing Nazism in its sundry phases and features—with depicting its reality rather than with analyzing its meaning, on the assumption that like most historical byways it was literally discontinuous with both its past and its future and that whatever antecedents and effects it did have must be anonymous, bereft of any specific Nazi identity. For it is the nature of the historical tributary to be neither adumbrated nor immortalized as such, but to be signaled and perpetu-

3. Peterson, op. cit.

ated only in the appropriate currents from which it was momentarily formed and into which it definitively decomposed. In the records of history, most men, more women, and much of what they have done occupy this mortal estate. It is not a dishonorable status. Oblivion is the common destiny of mankind, and in the case of the Nazis historical disintegration is a species of normalization. It restores them to the humanity from which they so infamously distinguished themselves.

But as we all know, this is not the whole story. Nazism continues to impose itself as an important collective personality even upon the historians who denigrate both its universal representative function and the unity of its national direction. Something in it drives them to keep asking for the identifiable whole it *was*, over and above the various and discordant things its minions *did*. This provocative something is a quality in Nazism that continues to link it to our lives even now when we have become its posterity.[4] It calls for an answer to a largely unasked question: what is the meaning of a historically resurrected integral Nazism for ages outside its epoch? That there is such a Nazism is a matter of approximate historiographical consensus. That there is such a meaning is a matter of historiographical assumption. That this meaning is different from the cataclysmic meaning that contemporaries found in Nazism is a matter of historiographical necessity. That the historical meaning is proving so elusive is a matter of the idiosyncratic Nazi identity in the process of reconstruction. Perhaps we can glean something of this meaning—that is, of the historical role which we can assign to a mainline Nazism in twentieth-century culture—from the four main features of the composite Nazi portrait that is beginning to emerge.

The most striking attribute of reconstructed Nazism is one which makes a hermeneutical virtue out of its empirical defect—that is, which converts division, arbitrariness, and indecision from limiting facts upon government to positive principles of government. Especially through analyses of the Führer-idea—that is, of attitudes toward Hitler—and of the Führer-principle—that is, of the organizational corollaries of Hitler's leadership—both the proliferation of overlapping, competing authorities and the deliberate leavening of bureaucratic norms with a considerable admixture of arbitrary procedures are now seen to be consistent criteria of autocratic rule whose regularized or simplified alternatives would have meant automatic limitation and hence contradiction of

---

4. For a moving revelation of this linkage in the passage of the Nazi experience from autobiography to history, see Fritz Stern, *The Failure of Illiberalism: Essays on the Political Culture of Modern Germany* (New York, 1972), pp. xi–xv, xxxvi–xliv.

the autocracy.[5] Far from equivalents of frustration the apparent anomalies of Nazi rule have even been reduced to formulas of domination—to wit, "planned chaos," or more laboriously, "permanent improvisation within the framework of a principled divide-and-rule tactic"—a formulation which, as is so often the case with historical epitomes, is more intricate than the reality being formularized.[6] But it does convey faithfully the capacity of the reality to be so encapsulated. The characteristic means through which a historical order thus arises out of the seeming chaos of Nazi government are through the organization of personal and institutional multiplicity around certain great dualities, the assertion of Nazi subscription to both of the dual positions, and the serial demonstration of how these logical antitheses worked out complementarily in practice. There are several of these organizing dualities. What from a critical perspective appears to be indecision in assigning predominance to the various levels of administration within the party turns out to be a deliberate preservation of options between the dual sets of natural rivals—between the national leadership and the regional leadership and between the regional leadership and the district leadership (that is, between *Reichsleitung* and *Gauleitung*, and between *Gauleitung* and *Kreisleitung*).[7] What from a critical perspective appears to be a many-sided squabbling among Nazi Party, Nazified bureaucracy, cooperative army, elitist foreign service, and protectionist big business—a squabbling fragmented by the opposing pulls of ideology and practical necessity—has been telescoped into the larger issue of Party and State, with the essence of Nazism perceived in its hierarchical preservation of both. Finally, what from a critical perspective are the divergent policies which reflect the variegated inputs of Hitler's split political personality, the different party big-wigs he favored at one time or another, Old Fighters and new joiners, parvenus and traditionalists, doctrinaires and pragmatists, collectivists and egoists, are made coherent when they are pegged to the related principled duets of conservatism and revolution and of primitivism and technology. The centripetal drive which compresses multiplicity into duality and then seeks at least a relational monism behind the duality stems in part from the consciousness of the

5. See Wolfgang Horn, *Führerideologie und Parteiorganisation in der NSDAP 1919–1933* (Düsseldorf, 1972), and Joseph Nyomarkay, *Charisma and Factionalism in the Nazi Party* (Minneapolis, 1967).

6. Karl Dietrich Bracher, *The German Dictatorship: The Origins, Structure, and Effects of National Socialism* (New York, 1970), p. 213; Diehl-Thiele, *Partei und Staat*, p. 14.

7. Ibid., passim; Dietrich Orlow, *History of the Nazi Party: 1933–1945* (Pittsburgh, 1973), passim.

Nazis themselves and in part from what historians have added to that consciousness. For the Nazis, as historically reconstructed, the unity of the regime came from the unity of a single person—Adolf Hitler; for historians, the unity of the regime came also from the characteristic and flexible way in which the Nazi Party blended authoritarian and egalitarian traditions under the pressure of contemporary circumstances, as evidenced in its variable but persistent application of *Gleichschaltung*.

A second consensual attribute of historically reintegrated Nazism is its homogeneity through time. Despite the distinctions which may be and have been drawn between the movement before power and the regime in power, between the regime in peacetime and the regime in wartime, between stages of conservative legality and stages of radical violence and violation, there is also a definite historiographical tendency to see an essential continuity in both Hitler and his movement from its early years to its final denouement, whatever the circumstantial and tactical changes brought by the Beer Hall Putsch, the elision of the 25-point program, the perquisites of power, and a losing two-front war.[8] The renewed seriousness accorded to *Mein Kampf* as an ever relevant historical document and the increasing importance accorded to the larger homogeneity of aim and policy in the final years of wartime Germany are indices of an evolutionary process wherein historians see neither cycles nor developments but a persistent convergence upon the practical execution of original conceptions.[9] In short, whatever synchronic incongruities may be revealed by the Nazi record, historians are once more convinced of its diachronic consistency.

The other two cohesive attributes of historical Nazism are the constants which are deemed to hold the movement and the regime together through time. Third, then, there is the permanence of the martial mentality.[10] It is a mentality whose Manichean approach to the world as a ubiquitous war of us against them provides an overall interactive unity of domestic and foreign policy, and telescopes the different nominal phases of the regime under the uniform priority of wartime standards even in the years of nominal peace. Thus the variegations of Nazi eco-

8. For this absence of "progression" or "development" in Nazi culture, see George L. Mosse, *Nazi Culture: Intellectual, Cultural, and Social Life in the Third Reich* (New York, 1966), p. xxii.

9. E.g., Bracher, *The German Dictatorship*, p. 288; Orlow, *History of the Nazi Party: 1933–1945*, pp. 490–91; Lucy S. Dawidowitsch, *The War against the Jews, 1933–1945* (New York, 1975) pp. 14, 18, 56, 111, 151.

10. On this running theme through Nazi history, see especially Bracher, *The German Dictatorship*, pp. 149, 334, 362, 403, 489.

nomic policy, so confusing and inconclusive from the point of view of social system, have been clarified by the simple propositions that from the start of Nazi rule economic policy and economic life were dominated by the requirements of armaments and that Nazi Germany from 1933 to 1939 was a war economy in peacetime.[11] In the field of international relations, too, the usual conflict, endemic to all of Nazi rule, between the pursuit of traditionally defined interests and the application of radical racialism was bridged by the belligerent posture. It established the revolutionary primacy of foreign policy in the early years of the regime by supplying the dynamism behind the orthodox sequence of diplomatic events, and it boosted the mechanics of military occupation during the war years into so many adumbrations of the generic Nazi system to come.

The fourth and final constant attribute, which is associated with this durable role of bellicosity and with its continuous application, is the resurrection and redefinition of the ideal component in Nazism. Now the problem of what is usually called "Nazi ideology" is a tricky one, for the well-known Nazi cynicism about ideas, disdain of theory, exploitation of principles, and erraticism of program have generated both the insistence on distinctions between the Nazi leadership and following in their ideological commitments, and the skeptical acceptance of naked power and ambition as the chameleonic criteria of actions by the elite. But recently historians have been pointing out Hitler's representation of the Nazi "idea" as a crucial ingredient of his position as "leader," and they have affirmed anti-Semitism, with its premise of the general racial idea, as a fundamental, dogmatic principle, at once tenet of faith and operational ideal, that threads pervasively through Nazi thought and action from the beginning of the movement to the end of the regime.[12] The status of this idea's concomitants is variably assessed, to be sure, as befits the evidence, and to call the loosely fitting congeries of attitudes, prejudices, and well-worn notions an "ideology" is to stretch even this much abused term beyond its wonted limits. Yet this acknowledgment of a primary Nazi idea, however hybridized, balanced, or even suspended at any one moment by the countervailing pressure of political circumstance, institutional inflexibility, or traditional morality, plays a crucial historiographical role as the constant factor integrating all these

11. Renée Erbe, *Die nationalsozialistische Wirtschaftspolitik 1933–1939 im Lichte der modernen Theorie* (Zurich, 1959), pp. 3–4, 161–65, 173–74.

12. Thus Bracher, *The German Dictatorship*, pp. 249–52, and Dawidowitsch, *The War Against the Jews*, pp. 3–5, 88–91, 151, 163–169.

moments of Nazi movement and regime into a historical time series. However familiar, then, the frequent recourse to Nazi racialism may seem to those of us who grew up with it, the shift from feeling it experientially to viewing it historically entails a considerable change in its aspect. Experientially violent racism was a resultant immoral force, etiologically derivative from such destructive human drives as the need for sacrificial scapegoats and the response to alienation; historiographically, it acts as an underived persistent factor, performing the kind of empirical linkage that ideas have ever performed in history.

The combined sense of *déjà vu* and novelty which is yielded by the historical treatment of Nazi racialism is indicative of historically reconstructed Nazism as a whole. The fact is that the reconstruction has restored the coherent attributes of the original experience but has entirely altered the context and therefore limited the scope of these attributes. Whereas the original Nazism was a universal human reality, German in its agency but extensible, whether by German arms or example, to any place at any time, reconstructed Nazism is a distinctive and inimitable German phenomenon of the period bounded by the end of the first World War on one side and the end of the second on the other. The whole tendency of our research makes this fragility, this immovability, this localization of German National Socialism unmistakable.

The scholarly agreement with contemporaries on Hitler's centrality and essentiality, now in the sophisticated sense of his incorporation of the Nazi idea which was undefinable and unknowable outside of his incorporation of it and in the retrospective sense of his indispensable position above the assorted fiefdoms which composed the party organization, its formations, and the gray areas between party and traditional hierarchy, limits the life of National Socialism by the specific mortality of its leader in an especially imperative way.[13] Again, the growing tendency to characterize Nazism discursively, in terms of the shifting, often personal, spontaneous, fortuitous, and inconclusive ways in which its protagonists actually combined principled opposites, has produced portraits of the movement which are ever more difficult to envisage in other contexts and with other agents. Finally, the increasing attention to the policies of the war years, both in their domestic intentions and in their patterns of foreign occupation, has confirmed indisputably the movement's deliberate association of its destiny with that of the individual German nation and its consistent assertion of specific German over in-

13. Wolfgang Sauer, "National Socialism: Totalitarianism or Fascism?" *American Historical Review* 73 (1968): 419.

ternational fascistic interests in the list of Nazi priorities. With the recognition of Nazism's persistently martial mentality, moreover, the preferences of the war period are less and less seen to be governed by considerations of transient military necessity and more and more adjudged to be impelled by authentic Nazi aims without the modifying and camouflaging incubus of peacetime political and administrative necessities. Hence this direction of scholarship too reinforces the historical reality of a definitely outlined German, early twentieth-century Nazism, not exportable and not protractable in any literal form.

The same historical research, then, which has added so much to our knowledge of Nazism and to our sophistication about it has both affirmed its historical identity and minimized its direct impact upon us. The stress here should be on the "direct" rather than on the "impact," for the change in the status of Nazism wrought by the passage of time and the standards of historical scholarship has gone not so much to lessen its importance as to alter the character of the importance. The fact is that in the case of Nazism the passage from experience to history moves the judgment of its meaning from the immediate registration of it as such on the scale of human values to the interpretation of its connection with or expression of other, larger, more general tendencies constituent of the historical process in its antecedent and subsequent periods as well as its own. In short, where Nazism spoke to us literally in our living experience of it, it speaks to us only figuratively through movements which it insensibly abetted or symbolized in our historical understanding of it.

The most pertinent concrete issue here—the issue which exemplifies at once the historical salience of Nazism, the necessity of indirection in understanding it, and the contribution which it has thereby made to our capacity to know whole categories of homologous twentieth-century things—is obviously the issue of revolution. For revolutions by definition mark permanent turning points in history, whether through the initiation or the crystallization of qualitative change, and there is both a widespread agreement on the authenticity and essentiality of the Nazi revolution and an equally widespread incapacity to agree on just what this revolution was. From the description and the analysis of what was genuinely revolutionary in the thinking of Nazis and in the effects of Nazism, moreover, it is clear that its want of substance betokens not a failure in the historians but a necessary feature of the object being historized. We do not know what literal changes Nazism brought either to Germany or to western (and westernized) culture, not so much because of the bewildering variety attending the interpretations of the content of the actual Nazi revolution which presumably effected the changes, as because of the absence of recognizable content in the Nazi revolutionary aims which should have envisaged the changes. In other words, our vagueness about the Nazi revolution and therefore about the long-range historical role of Nazism is basically attributable neither to an indecision between substantive alternatives nor even to the frequent invocation of the gap between revolutionary idea and frustrated practice, between "true revolutionary potential" and "meager . . . revolutionary results" of an uncompleted Nazi revolution. The difficulty in identifying the abiding impact of the movement has to do rather with the hollowness of the revolutionary claims themselves.[14]

However opposed the three reigning perspectives on the revolutionary component of Nazism may be in their characterization of its revolutionary effect, they agree that the revolutionary impulse cannot be matched to this effect, nor the effect to the unprogrammatic impulse, and therefore, in essence, that what the revolution was or would have been is equally unknowable. According to one interpretation, the revolutionary motif in Nazism consisted in the regressive ideal of the racial community, an ideal addressed to a mass following of "the losers" in modern industrial society, an ideal to be realized in the construction of a corresponding national and international society—egalitarian within, hierarchical without, and harmonized by the supervening unquestionable authority of the Leader—and an ideal left continuously and suicidally unrealized in fact by the necessity and even the contrapuntal desirability which authoritative Nazis, Hitler above all, felt for collaborating with the same technical, intellectual, and industrial instruments of modern control against which the revolutionary ideal was directed.[15] According to a second interpretation, Nazism on the contrary was counterrevolutionary in its concept and revolutionary in its effect *malgré soi*, contributing through its own egalitarian tactics to a dismantling of traditional domestic hierarchies and thereby to the homogenizing triumph of a modernity it abhorred.[16] According to a third interpretation, which combines elements of both the others and probably commands a preponderance of scholarly support, the Nazis perpetrated a "double" or a "paradoxical" revolution, one in which the ideal regressive end of building a bourgeois-less, proletarian-less, Jewless alternative to modern industrial society predominated but in which the

14. Ibid., pp. 412–13.
15. Ibid., pp. 417–18.
16. Ralf Dahrendorf, *Gesellschaft und Demokratie in Deutschland* (Munich, 1966), pp. 432–40.

antithetical, but equally destructive, use of modern technological, bourgeois, and industrial instruments was a collaterally accepted revolutionary means.[17]

The common denominator of these interpretations is that the Nazis
never developed either the internal policies or the sequential ideas to
show what a society based on the revolutionary ideal of racial community would be like, economically, socially, or culturally. The fact is
that whatever interpretation of Nazism is espoused, the authenticity of
the revolutionary impulse is undeniable and the direction of the revolutionary enterprise is undecipherable. It matters not whether one accepts
the Nazis' own vision of an indefinite ideal future in which an innovative party movement would continuously direct the Nazified state administration to the ever-extended realization of an as yet unarticulated
revolution, or accepts any of the critical variants which assign the perpetuation of established norms, customs, and agencies to technical necessity, to a schizoid division between revolutionary and conservative
drives, or to a dualistic preoccupation with both primitive rootedness
and technological dynamism—in either case a combination of inherent
Nazi aversion to programmatic thinking with circumstantial diversions
from pragmatic ideation made the movement's revolutionary aims im-
penetrable and the results of the regime for the structure and quality of
German life correspondingly limited, at least until the closing months
of a war which inextricably confused the effects of a radicalized Nazism
with the decisive influence of a total defeat by an alliance of political and
social egalitarians. Class divisions, capitalist enterprise, trustification,
industrial self-government, the civil and military services all remained in
being, testimonials as much to the continuing Nazi disinterest in things
economic and their inability to develop characteristic social and cultural
lines of policy as to the pressure of international conditions and the inherent recalcitrance of executive institutions.[18]

To be sure, the party had consistently expanded its powers of social
control, both in the authority of the party administration over the regu-

17. David Schoenbaum, *Hitler's Social Revolution: Class and Status in Nazi Germany
1933–1939* (New York, 1966), pp. xxii–xxiii, 287–293; Bracher, *The German Dictatorship*, p. 330.

18. For the Nazis' failure to carry through a church revolution because of their vacillation between racial paganism as a revolutionary new religion and "positive Christianity"
as a politically controlled ecclesiastical establishment, see J. S. Conway, *The Nazi Persecu-
tion of the Churches 1933–45* (New York, 1968), pp. 2–4, 328–31. For the Nazi incapacity to develop a characteristic approach to the arts consistent with its revolutionary
self-image, see Hildegard Brenner, *Die Kunstpolitik des Nationalsozialismus* (Hamburg,
1963), passim.

lar agencies of government and in the ever increasing prominence of party formations like the Hitler Youth and the SS as mass organizations, but the nominal Nazification of Germany also brought, in some measure, a reciprocal Germanification of Nazism—that is, its dilution— with the result that the old pattern of Nazi socialization which had made the Party of Old Fighters a model nucleus of Nazi purity within an unconverted Germany and the SS a model nucleus of Nazi purity within a partially converted mass party was continued within the SS itself, with the implied admission of a merely test-tube revolution.[19]

What there was of a Nazi revolution was peripheral, negative, or formal—that is, it subverted the existence of ethnic non-Germans; it canceled the autonomy of the traditional elite organizations and it abolished all autonomous organizations of the masses; it monopolized the established levers of control over men's social actions and devised new instruments for the extended control over the individual and private sphere of men's thoughts and deeds, without coming to firm decisions on the purposes for which these controls would be used within the racial community. These features of the Nazi revolution are distinctive; they mark the German revolutionary brand of fascism off from its more conservatively oriented non-German species, and they confirm the epochal importance of Nazism; but since they have no revolutionary content of their own they also require, for the assessment of this importance, an analysis of quite different contents in which these forms reappear.

In the particular instance of revolution, then, Nazism marked the departure of modern man from the familiar substantive categories of revolution which had been established by the linear processes associating political revolutions since the Middle Ages with the norms and power of ever more populous groups and associating social revolutions since 1789 with changes in property relations. And it marked too, therefore, a fundamental shift in the way we regard revolutions. The phenomenon of a postdemocratic, so-called "legal" revolution of some popular masses against other popular masses, claiming to install a new dispensation against precisely the most progressive elements in the establishment and actually erecting the machinery for such a dispensation on behalf of an unblended medley of racial radicalism, military collectivism, and social conservatism—such a phenomenon has undoubtedly contributed much to the loosening of our categories, such as our acknowledgment of anachronism in the earlier concepts of political Right and Left, and to our capacity for understanding the asymmetrical

19. Orlow, *History of the Nazi Party: 1933–1945*, pp. 450, 479–80.

shapes of twentieth-century revolutions after the categorical social revolutions of 1917 in eastern Europe.

If we move now from the exemplar of Nazi revolution back to the general reconstruction of Nazism as such we should be equipped to perceive its figurative role in the historical process of the twentieth century and to remark too its contribution to our historiographical comprehension of that process. Over and above its obvious attestation to the end of linear progress in the political history of the west, Nazism, as the first—and indeed only—case of a total dictatorship in an advanced industrial society, patently exhibited several of the overt characteristics, both dominant and recessive, which would reappear more diffusively and less violently in all industrialized and industrializing societies. The possibilities of internal individual as well as external social control and of public machinery for positive as well as prohibitory compulsion were Nazi hallmarks that have turned out to be endemic to the mechanics of all modern societies, and so have the privatization—that is, "inner emigration"—the alienation, and the phobic outlook which have accompanied society's violative and dislocatory intrusions.

To Nazism particularly, indeed, and to our more sophisticated understanding of its social composition we owe the larger view of the lower-middle-class mentality which enables us to translate it from the specific groups which had been threatened by the process of industrialization to all groups without viable organization or vital stake in industrial society, whether advanced or incipient. Because we see now that the Nazis appealed originally to the young, to the previously uninvolved, and to the diffusively discontented as well as to the more definitely aggrieved shopkeepers, artisans, clerks, and peasants, and because we see that their original appeal broadened with success to include all the middle strata of the society which had no initiatives of their own, we sense a connection between the Nazi experience and our own. In a sense, then, the petty-bourgeois orientation which was once deemed to be an undertow to the past really was the wave of the future.

Here as in so much of history, connections become perceptible through pejoratives, and behind the recurrent accusations of "Nazi" we may grasp the important historical lesson that politics abhors a vacuum. For the facile analogies with Nazism are made whenever middle-class insecurity takes a racial form, whenever impatient authority is tempted by technical advances to transgress its prescribed limits, or whenever the partisans of a counterculture turn to violent action. We see Nazis everywhere because industrial society, with its levelings up and its levelings down, has made a petty bourgeois of everyman, save when he takes his social norms from outside the community itself. It can indeed be argued that there is a bit of Hitler in us all, although there is more of him in some of us than in others. According to this argument, it takes one to know one.

But Nazism also bears a more subtle relationship to the larger movement of twentieth-century culture, a relationship which confers on the history of Nazism a more valuable hermeneutical function than may perhaps be claimed for the study of the comparatively simple genus of industrial society through a complicated history of a particular regime in a single country. For the larger movement is one of the most difficult for nonparticipants to grasp, and Nazism is a relatively accessible manifestation of it. In the various fields of high culture during the first half of the twentieth century a series of parallel developments added up to a massive renunciation of the whole perspective on reality, the whole way of regarding the world, which had gradually permeated men's attitudes from the seventeenth through the nineteenth centuries and passed for the commonsense view of things. In physical science, in mathematical logic, in philosophies both novel and renovated, in avant-garde literature, art, music, the behavioral sciences, and even the new theorizing about history which was dignified as "historicism" at about the same time as Nazism was born—in all these varied intellectual and cultural endeavors a veritable revolution of human consciousness radically relocated the parameters of man's world and fundamentally dislocated his position in it. The commonsensical notions of a homogeneous reality composed of separate particular objects organized into a system of stable relations by a coherent set of universal laws and confronted by individual subjects who knew and acted upon it from the outside were replaced by the unfamiliar postulate of a heterogeneous, discontinuous world constituted primarily by its partial relations, subsequently differentiated into individuals as so many functions of those relations, and both known and acted upon by these individuals, therefore, from inside the partial communities which afforded the only organization and meaning in the world.

The revolution was not toward either relativism or uncertainty, as the distortions of the period's scientific labels would have it. The belief in the universal validity of truth, in its certainty, and in the capacity of the new perspective to subsume the old—this belief persisted and inspired veritable crusades. The most easily comprehensible battle cries of these crusades have been their negations, but they have also mounted campaigns *for* new open-ended visions of a higher, or sur-, reality which abolishes the autonomy of individual subjects and objects, along with the division between them, in the name of community; which abolishes the solidity of actuality and the illusoriness of imagery, along with the division between them, in the name of myth and symbol; and which abolishes the *a posteriority* of the participant and the *a priority* of the world, along with the division between *them*, in the name of emergent form.

In the morphology of culture both the kind and the age of ideas vary as one goes from the so-called higher to the popular levels of the culture, and it is hardly surprising, therefore, that particularly in the case of such a difficult and drastic transvaluation of intellectual values as was demanded on all levels of early twentieth-century culture, there was no understanding and there was even overt substantive hostility between affinitive tendencies on different levels of it. Hence to argue, as I do here, for a structural relationship between the modernism of early twentieth-century high culture and popular Nazism is neither to underestimate the Nazi abhorrence of cultural modernism nor to assert any literal affiliation between the two—as, for example, Marcuse does in his notation of a common uncritical posture toward social existence.[20] It is, rather, to argue for a common cultural matrix in the early twentieth century which impressed divers branches, levels, and directions of thinking with certain joint features; which allies the strange turns of thought so often remarked both of Nazism and of modernism; and which gives low- or middle-brow historians access to the larger-scoped and longer-lasting higher realms of the culture, from existentialism to the so-called counterculture. For in the Nazis' renunciation of the whole fabric of past thought and action, in their commitment to dynamic process and to operational truth, and in their attempts to build a whole world out of the internal relations of the racial community, to find a place for the traditional elites on a new dependent footing within it, and to cancel everything outside that community as meaningless, with no ground for existence—in all these ways Nazism articulated on its own destructive level a mental structure homologous with the period's constructive lords of the high culture and offering later observers clues to the cultural matrix behind both.

Whether by reason of their training, their language, or their audience, the assumptions of historians are generally drawn from the middle and lower levels of the culture, and therewith from ideas of relatively remote vintage. Certainly their notions about the world and their

---

20. Herbert Marcuse, *One Dimensional Man: Studies in the Ideology of Advanced Industrial Society* (Boston, 1964), pp. 123–43.

relations to it are, despite all reservations about the limits of objectivity in history, commonsensical on the Newtonian standard, and at least until very recently they have shown little interest in or influence by the high cultural revolution of the twentieth century. All the greater, then, has been the role of Nazism in adapting their approach both to the history of this century and to the general intellectual conditions incumbent upon historians writing in this century. Whether the claims which have been made for Nazism's historiographical priority can be sustained, either specifically as the first occasion for the application of psycho-history or generally as "the first systematic large-scale application of the social and behavioral sciences to a current historical problem"[21]—and there are those who would count it a mixed blessing at best if either is sustained—there can be little question of Nazism's role in flexing the explanatory concepts with which historians work, in expanding their horizons, and in sophisticating their thinking about the relations between freedom and continuity in history.

We have already seen how the concept of "ideology" has been broadened and softened to minimize the derivation of ideas from practical interests, to drop the connotation of coherent connection among ideas from the concept, and to include mental attitudes in various degrees of gestation along with formal ideas within the concept.[22] We have seen too how the concept of "revolution" has grown, through its association with Nazism, to accommodate changes, or even the agencies to enforce undecided future changes, that are indifferent to the generic transfer of sovereignty or overturn of property relations habitually associated with the concept. In the running discussion on the elements of German continuity and of Nazi spontaneity which account for the nature and the reception of the movement, moreover, we have learned something more important, historiographically, than the proportionate estimate of each element's poundage and more essential, historiographically, than our old habit of juxtaposing them and hoping that they add up to something: we have learned, through the pressure of the argument, to think of precisely *how* the discretionary contributions of the Nazis engaged with the projections from the German past and brought to actionable focus beliefs previously disparate and passive.

In general, finally, the very grotesqueness of Nazism to the bulk of

21. Peter Loewenberg, "Psychohistorical Perspectives on Modern German History," *Journal of Modern History* 47 (1975): 229–53.

22. But Mosse has retained the older concept by insisting on the coherence of Nazi ideology (see his *Nazi Culture*, pp. xxii–xxiii).

the historians who study it has purified the historical dimension of things and confirmed its indispensability to the understanding of social processes. Precisely because the Nazis tend to elude the general concepts which we borrow from other sciences and from our present living, Nazism has put a premium upon a distinctively historical reason to make at least temporal sense of what otherwise seems to make no sense at all. It is an ill wind, indeed, that blows no historical good.

But after we have said all this—after we have affirmed Nazism's historical identity; after we have recognized its subtle ties to the larger and more obscure tendencies of its period and through these ties acknowledged its persistence in the odd mix of racial, xenophobic, primitive, global, technological, and totalitarian features which these movements have carried into our own era; after we have congratulated our fellow historians for their historization of Nazism, both in the specificity of their internal descriptions and in the integration of its external connections—after we have said all this we must not neglect to state the obvious: to affirm that Nazism continues to call above history across the years to the common humanity that lives alongside the professional historian in each of us. For it is clear that historians assume an integral identity in Nazism that frequently outruns or anticipates their evidence and that can hardly be accounted for by their consciousness of Nazism's tenuous association with the larger movements of this century's society and thought.

There are two kinds of identity that are preserved from the past: one whose characteristic combination of traits—whose personality— effectuates or inaugurates larger movements that span the ages, and the other which continues to speak to us immediately, like an immortal indifferent to time, about the eternal things that affect the very core of our being. Nazism has preserved both of these identities, and we should not forget the persistent power of the second because of the attention that historians have paid to the first. In almost every inquiry into the history of Nazism there is discernible a level of concern, a steady spur of passion which floats subliminally above the sober prose, the patient description, and the dispassionate analysis, and which motivates, in the paradoxical way of scholarship, the objectivity and even empathy of the treatment through the force of repulsion. We should not need the presence of Lucy Dawidowitsch's horrific tale of the holocaust on the lists of the book clubs alongside the books on the abomination of slavery to remind us of the constant, suprahistorical meaning which continues ever to be seen in the signal demonstrations, from any age, of man's inhumanity to man, for whether by prefatory confession, conclusive accounting, running commentary, or all three, everything we write about the Nazis bears explicit as well as implicit marks of the same monstrous provocation.

"The evil that men do lives after them, / The good is oft interred with their bones," said Shakespeare's crafty Mark Antony, and the sentiment might well serve seriously as the Nazis' historical epitaph. For whether through the modest moral of "the closeness of the human comedy to human tragedy" or through the blunt acknowledgment of "the connection between the National Socialist form of government and its ideological mass crimes," all aspects of the Nazi movement and regime have acquired intimate meaning for us in the conviction of their relationship to an unprecedented kind of deliberate, official murder most foul.[23] The positive things the Nazis did—the construction of machinery for total control that could serve life-enhancing rather than death-dealing purposes—did indeed die with them. The negative things that they did—the reduction of the traditional aristocratic elites and their sanctuaries—was the National Socialist bequest to Germany. But the unforgettable evil that they did—this is their legacy to all mankind.

23. Peterson, op cit., p. xxiii; Hans Buchheim, Martin Broszat, Hans-Adolf Jacobsen, Helmut Krausnick, *Die Anatomie des SS-Staates* (Freiburg, 1965), 1:5.

18 *The Potential for Democratization in Occupied Germany: A Problem in Historical Projection*

The concepts of "potential" and "democratization" harbor a sufficient variety of meanings to require a preliminary discussion of any use which is to be made of them.

"Potential" can refer either to the possibility or to the probability that something will be done. Tempting as it is to think of this option as a matter of degree—as if the scale from a small to a large capability were equivalent to the range from the possible to the probable—a moment's reflection should suffice for us to understand that matters of degree are all matters of probability and that the two meanings of potential refer rather to two different kinds of thinking, corresponding to the categorical difference between the deductive logic of possibility and the inductive logic of probability.

"Democratization" is even more flexible, for it includes more than the whole spectrum of options, ranging from the effective will of the majority to the effective equality of civil rights and liberties, which has ever been comprehended in both the idea and reality of "democracy." It includes as well the additional choice of meanings that refers to the process of realizing democracy, a process that is the extra dimension in democrat*ization vis-à-vis* democracy. For democratization can refer either to a process whereby a people actively moves itself toward democracy or to a process whereby a people passively accepts conditions, not of its own political creation, that lead to democracy. The potential for democratization in the first of these senses would mean the capacity to bring about democracy; the potential for democratization in the second sense would mean the capacity to be brought to democracy.

The simplest way of applying such ambiguous canons of judgment would be to cut through the ambiguities by setting up an *a priori* definition of potential and a model of democratization that would fix, openly and univocally, the criteria by which the political situation of Germany after World War II should be judged. But there is good reason why such

First published in *Public Policy*, John Dickey Montgomery, ed., (Cambridge: Harvard University Press, 1968), 27–58.

a method should not be used in this case, and why an historical approach should be preferable to a theoretical analysis. The German situation under the occupation contained two distinct orders of politics—the occupants and the occupied—and the two distinct definitions of potential were respectively applicable to it. The situation contained, too, an enormous range of democratic models and a conscious choice of active or passive German participation in their achievement, and this range of models and of choice were actual issues and therefore real factors in the situation. An *a priori* hypostatization of any one definition and any one model would therefore overlie the position of a party in the situation and would to that extent distort our knowledge of the situation that we should reconstruct before we judge it. I propose, therefore, to treat the German potential for democratization not as a principle of judgment but as a subject of history. I mean not to assess directly the actual potential for democratization in occupied Germany but to describe the predominant attitudes toward it which were held by authoritative actors in the situation and which, as operational ideals, helped to create their own truth. The only judgment which will be passed here upon those historical agents and their attitudes toward the Germans will be a typically historical judgment—whether, in the light of our own subsequently acquired knowledge, the historical projection which was the basis of the dominant attitude toward the German potential for democratization was as valid as was thought.

There were, at the end of World War II, as many views on the German capacity for democracy as there were views of the democracy for which the Germans were to be judged capable, and as many opinions on the Germans' capacity to democratize themselves, whatever the judgment on their abstract capacity to carry on a ready-made democracy, as there were opinions of the Germans whose capacity was in question. Yet both the set of democratic goals and the set of judgments on the active or passive German potential for realizing them were pragmatically unified under the pressure of the immediate postwar situation. This convergence of diverse intrinsic ideas into a unified effective attitude was crucial to the judgment of the German democratic potential that came to prevail, for like any such consensus, it tended to take the form of the least common denominator, as measured by units of belief in the German political capacity.

At least three different ideas of the democracy that should be the measure of the German political potential prevailed among those responsible for planning or making German policy. Socialists, political democrats, and constitutional liberals all projected standards constructed in their own images, inquiring, respectively, into the German capacity to sustain a social revolution, equality of citizenship, and a pyramid of responsible self-governments.[1]

Cutting across this division, occasionally coinciding with its parties but more often multiplying their number, was another plane of division, grounded in the opposing opinions of the German readiness to undertake their own democratization—and opinions on this point were opposed within each of the democratic camps. Some believed that only a German central government could impose democratization, whatever the cost to temporary majorities or traditional acquired rights. Others believed that the existing German society could work toward democracy from a political *tabula rasa* on the pattern of gradual construction from grass roots. Still others believed that even the political *tabula rasa* was an excessive limitation, and that the amputation of an extraordinary and well-hated dictatorship would open the way for the spontaneous democratic evolution of the chastened political as well as social institutions of traditional Germany. And there were those, finally, at the other extreme, who believed that however capable of democracy in some form the Germans might be, they were not at all capable of democratization in the sense of doing it themselves. Theoretically, it would seem as if the socialist version of democracy would coincide with the belief in a centralistic German potential, political democracy with the German grass-roots potential, and constitutionalism with the German traditional potential, and these conjunctions did occur. But they were sharply limited by such countervailing factors as the socialist bitterness at the widespread support of Nazi antisocialism, the democrats' shock at the Germans' easy surrender of pre-Nazi democracy, and the constitutional conservatives' resentment of the Germans' *reductio ad absurdum* which embarrassed conservatism everywhere. Thus multiple permutations and combinations were formed.

Still a third plane of division, finally, was added to the diversities of views on the nature of the democracy to be aimed at and on the ability of Germans to aim at it. For these debates were waged both within each nation and between the nations, and the parties on the two levels of discussion did not entirely overlap. There was obviously some connection between the internal and the international politics on the German issue,

---

1. For the discussion of variegation in the views of Germany, see Leonard Krieger, "The Inter-Regnum in Germany: March–August 1945," in *Political Science Quarterly*, LXIV (December 1949), pp. 507–532.

for in a world as ideologically oriented as was the world in the warring 1940's, each of the major nations tended to represent in the international arena the dominant political tendency of its internal structure. Thus Russia represented socialism, the United States legalistic democracy, Britain—despite the Labor victory of July 1945—tolerant conservatism, and Gaullist France traditional nationalism. But although France was initially excluded from the councils of the great, the xenophobia which the French evinced toward the Germans was shared in some measure by the official spokesmen of the other powers as well, since they too were impelled by their outraged national interests as much as by their views on a German democracy. Not only, moreover, did these interests of state modify the democratic attitudes otherwise represented by the respective regimes, but the domestic parties which represented similar attitudes in other countries correspondingly shied away from associating themselves with the German policies of an Allied government—as American socialists, for example, opposed the Soviet plan for Germany.

But multifarious as the original attitudes towards a German democracy undoubtedly were, as destined as they were for reappearance in the subsequent divergent administrations of military governments, yet powerful factors were at work in the immediate postwar situation to effect their simplification in the decisive formulations of basic policy. For one thing, the circumstances of total defeat and the first expression of Allied consensus limited the number of those whose views had to be taken into account by excluding the Germans from the articulation of their attitudes toward democracy and toward their own active potential for it. The decisive factors, however, were those that were unifying the attitudes toward the German democratic potential both within the camp of each Ally and between the Allied powers as the necessary bases for the promulgation of a single policy toward Germany.

First, the military framework of Allied policy made for the progressive sifting of heterogeneous views of individuals and groups until the governments of the respective nations became in fact what they are often invalidly alleged to be—the spokesmen of their citizens' opinions. This process of converging an infinite plethora into a limited number of official national views has two consequences for our judgment of the German democratic potential. It defined actual standards of democratization in terms of which German capacities were judged. And it enables us to assume that these standards were formulated in the light of the historical knowledge available about Germany at that time. Thus, the officially articulated national consensus on the democratic goal for Germany was accompanied by an analogous consensus on its historically based potential to realize those goals.

Second, despite the divergent constitutional, political, and social assumptions behind the belated and hollow Allied reference to preparation for "the eventual political reconstruction of German political life on a democratic basis" at Potsdam in July-August 1945, the end of the war did provide an international consensus on the formal qualities of democracy which could serve as a measure of German developments.[2] These qualities, defined by the external relations of democracy in the Allied pronouncements, made democratization a function of demilitarization and associated democracy with pacifism (in the broad sense) and decentralization as an electoral and representative process that would permanently shift power from the militaristic elite. The identification of this elite would, of course, prove to be the joker even in this negative formulation, but there was common agreement that it extended beyond the Nazi party and its formations indefinitely into the more deeply rooted institutions of German economic, political, and social life. What is important here is that the international definition of the goal of German democracy was formulated on the basis of military and diplomatic considerations by the occupying powers. Germans and German considerations alike were excluded from the initial formulation of the goal which served as the measure for a common assessment of German potentialities. However unsubstantial such a democratic standard may be by our lights, there is nothing objectionable about it, and the convenience of a goal that was a real policy outweighs the luxury of applying our own democratic standard that would be, in terms of the situation, both more abstract and less objective.

The German potential for democratization, as democratization was conceived at the start of the occupation, may be phrased in terms of our initial categories: The possibility of democracy in Germany was certain; the probability of German democratization was almost nil.

The possibility of German democracy had all the certainty of an analytical proposition in logic, and it rested indeed on the political logic of the occupation. Democracy was a possible end because it was the actual policy of the occupants who were the sovereign power in Germany and because, on the German side, the war had the negative effect of sus-

2. See Hajo Holborn, *American Military Government: Its Organization and Policies* (Washington, D.C.: Infantry Journal Press, 1947), pp. 54, 60; and "Report on the Tripartite Conference of Potsdam, August 2, 1945," in *ibid.*, p. 198.

pending the operation of the antithetical institutions that could have made the democratic option impossible. On the Allied side, two corollaries of the joint policy made the democratic goal a German possibility: first, the distinction between German leaders and German people which made a policy of preparing the latter to realize "by their own efforts" the Allied-imposed end; and second, the agreement on a single nation state that would make possible an unqualifiedly German democracy.[3] On the German side, the visible rupture of all social organization and the ironic throwback to a state of nature, in which Germans above all had never believed, were products of a last-ditch war. A legal imprimatur was given to this final phase of the war with the formal dispossession by the Allies of "all the powers" formerly possessed by all German public authorities together with the Allied dissolution, on grounds of military security, of all institutions related to the Nazi party.[4] These were, to be sure, mere brute facts and nominal laws that broke into the German institutional crust, but their relationship to the preceding sequence of Nazi developments elevated them to a role in the logic of the German political and social system. The Nazis had begun their regime with a division of function in accordance with which they smashed mass organizations in order to replace them with their own. But they secured only the political direction of elite organizations; this they did through a combination of reliable appointments in these organizations and the authoritarian reconstitution of them. But the historical tendency of the regime was to overbear and undercut such bastions of traditional power and influence by expanding the activities of competing party organizations and—more noxiously—by founding new wartime agencies which were virtually party organs in the public sector, and which either bypassed or derogated the established authorities in the field. In either case the effect was to associate the institutions in every sector of political and social life with the Nazi regime and hence to make their postwar breakdown more than a matter of fact or fiat—to make it, indeed, the logical result of a totalitarian defeat that opened all possibilities into the future.

But the possibility that was thereby opened for an Allied-proposed democratic option in Germany must be categorically distinguished from the probability that any existing German group would realize it, for the possibility was indubitably real while this probability was, by

3. *Ibid.*, pp. 197, 198.
4. "Declaration Regarding Defeat of Germany and Assumption of Supreme Authority by Allied Powers, June 5, 1945," in *ibid.*, p. 173.

contemporary consensus, practically nonexistent. Now let us be clear about this problem of probable democratic agents, or traditions, or both. The problem is not so much the identification of potential democrats but the potential force of democrats; not so much what the democratic potential is but how much it is. Every western or partially westernized society has its democratic groupings in the populist, anti-elitist, pacific sense relevant here. In the German case, it was clear to most informed observers that social democrats in the long run, communists in the short run—that is, as virulent antifascists and as defenders of minority rights as long as they were out of power—and the unionizable working class in general were the most dependable agents of democratization in German society.

If, then, the problem of the German democratic potential were only the identification of German democrats, then in principle the occupants might simply have encouraged the prompt and selective organization of political and social organizations and designated the social democracy or a socialist-communist coalition their primary agent of democratization—a pattern that the Russians were in fact to follow. Nor, in principle, need we quibble about the exclusiveness of these agents. The existence of anti-Nazi groupings within the traditional institutions associated as such with the Nazi regime—the Confessional Church and the conservative civilian-army network which had been connected with the name of Karl Goerdeler and the events of July 20, 1944 are the obvious cases in point—their demonstrated willingness to work with socialists, at least, against Nazism, and their political planning for a non-Nazi, normalized Germany were usable criteria for expanding the German agencies for democratization beyond a socialist political and proletarian social base. From this view of the problem, the Soviet misuse of German agents and the western postponement of their use are not relevant. They would be attributable to variants in the occupants' interpretation of democracy, prejudices—on all levels of the occupation—about the class origins or social goals of the democratic agents, and the countercurrents of military security, international diplomacy, and local administrative necessity that competed with democratization within occupation policy. All of these were indeed factors, and crucial factors—but they bear rather on the Allied potential for German democratization than on their notion of the German potential for it, and that is another story.

But if we ask not who was thought most likely to succeed, but how likely was thought the success of those most likely to succeed, then we return to a level of consensus and open up the problem of German potential as such to considerations that go beyond the barren principle of *chacun à son goût*—a blind alley which, as Peirce has taught us, is death to truth-finding. For the Allies' tacit agreement, legislated jointly albeit executed distributively, to consummate what John Montgomery has tellingly called an "artificial revolution" was tantamount to a negative decision upon the power of German democratic agencies. This decision reflected a common judgment upon both their more remote and recent pasts, as well as on their immediate present.[5] At the root of this cumulative judgment was the consciousness of the sequence that had made Nazism a postdemocratic era in a different way than the occupation had become a post-Nazi era. The Nazified system of institutions was cracked from the outside, whereas the democratic system of institutions had been smashed from within. This meant that if the occupants only assumed the monopoly of power against which the democratic agents had been obviously impotent, these agents would still be confronted with overcoming Nazified institutions, however disorganized, when they had already shown themselves weaker than Nazis without institutional bastions. Or, to put the judgment alternatively, the German democrats seemed doubly impotent: If German institutional life were simply permitted to resume, after the suspension imposed by the pattern of conquest, diminished only by the dimension of National Socialist government, the unfavorable political consequences of the Nazi regime for democracy would certainly persist; if the historic democratic agents were permitted to substitute their own characteristic institutional controls during the hiatus, there was no reason to think that these controls, and the democrats with them, would not fall before the Nazis again as they had done before. Nor could a circumstantial interpretation of the original impotence in terms of national disgrace and depression, whatever its validity, amend this judgment, since the reconstruction would have to take place under analogous circumstances of occupation and reparations.

The negative judgment upon the German capacity for democracy at the start of the occupation was thus grounded in the conviction that an antidemocratic continuity ran through the changing times and conditions of modern German history—a continuity of a span and momentum sufficient to leap over the institutional gap opened by total defeat

5. John D. Montgomery, *Forced to be Free: The Artificial Revolution in Germany and Japan* (Chicago: University of Chicago Press, 1957), pp. 1, 4, 5. Note that Montgomery applies the term only to the Western Allied occupation, *vis-à-vis* the Soviet participation in "permanent revolution" (pp. 7, 177–180), but the purpose of his distinction, to differentiate between the two executions of policy, is not mine here, since my context is its joint declaration.

and through the backwash of the Nazi collapse, and to deposit a negative charge upon the future of German democracy. The conviction postulated a three-stage process, integrated by the constant subordination
of democratic to undemocratic groups through the overt changes in
German political systems. What was obviously predicated of these
groups in this process was that through the transfers of specific identities in the succession of political generations their essential characteristics, molded by constant relations, held fast, so that the same roles that
manifested democratic debility before the Nazis persisted, with their relationships merely magnified, through the Nazi transformations, and
remained unconvulsed by the cataclysm of fascist defeat and Allied occupation. Let us look more closely at the operation of the process
through these three stages—assuming still, from the coherent relationship between the knowledge and the policy, that the historical and contemporary analyses of Germany along these lines were made true in
practice through the Allied policies which were framed in light of them.

1. Given the ideological issues of World War II, the heightened prestige of the social sciences—and particularly of anthropology—during
the generation between the wars, and the prominent role of German-
born scholars in Allied intelligence agencies, the racially tainted ethnic
interpretation of German history in evidence during World War I could
not supply the interpretive constant for the second. The constant that
did become standard was derived not from any putative source of German behavior—not, that is, from any national characteristic either in
primitive or sophisticated conception—but from its durable conditions. These conditions were found in either one or in both of two dimensions, which could be propounded disjunctively or conjunctively
but which in either case intersected as common long-range limitations
upon the efficacy of German democratic movements. The first of these
dimensions was geography, justifying still, as it long had, the principle
of "primacy of foreign policy" as a basis for the distinctive orientation
toward security and power in German institutions; but now it was used
pejoratively to stress its negative effects on human rights and their proponents. The German situation in the center of Europe, open to invasion from both east and west and actually invaded many times from
both east and west, had been adduced to rationalize the subordination
of individual and popular rights to governmental power, on the ground
that the right of defence against the foreign aggressor was the most indispensable of all rights; but now, in the context of a German war of aggression, it was easy to endorse the institutional facts while reversing
their meaning.

But the second dimension of continuity—the socioeconomic—was by far the more novel, the more far-reaching, and the more instructive. Not that it was novel in itself, for it reached back, either directly or through the detours marked by Veblen, Sombart, and Weber, to Marx and Engels, but it was novel in its forward extension to include the contemporary stage of German capitalism, in the broad acceptance of its validity (revealing the fact that Marxism is always more acceptable when it is applied to someone else's country). This socioeconomic dimension—as the duality of its lineage might indicate—was relatively indifferent to the familiar problem of infrastructure and superstructure *vis-à-vis* their combined deterrent effect upon German democracy. Whether the primary motive force was taken to be the distinctive rhythm and structure of German economic development that conditioned the forms of German politics and culture, or whether it was taken to be the political structure and cultural pattern that channelled the distinctive rhythm and forms of German economic development, the stress was not on such a motive force but on the permanence and the pervasiveness of the syndrome that the relationship produced. The relationship, in substance, was this: German economic growth has kept supplying new dominant social groups as supporters of authoritarian political regimes, and the effects have been to modernize authoritarianism, to spread authoritarian relations through the society, and to strengthen socially while alienating politically the subordinate social groups—and their cultural analogues—simultaneously produced by the same economic growth.

Now the advantages of this syndrome over constants such as national character or even geography were: First, it was multiform and hence could catch contrapuntal movements like democracy which the coarser mesh of a simple constant merely sifted out; and second, it was developmental and hence could account for the democratic movement in its changing forms, whereas for constants such changes were both inconsequential and unintelligible. These qualities of the syndrome were advantages because they corresponded to the actual character of the democratic movements whose historical strength was being assessed. For what needed explanation was not any uniform absence or impotence of the democratic tradition, but rather the cyclical abortiveness of its successes and the progressive destiny which matched the ever increasing scope of its successes with the ever-increasing scope of its subsequent frustration.

On the first count, what had to be accounted for was not simply the steady subordination of liberal and democratic to authoritarian regimes through most of German history, but the familiar cycle of democratic failures, marked by the Peasants' War of 1525, the Revolution of 1848, the Revolution of 1918, and the Weimar Republic, which demonstrated both that the democratic movement did possess a genuine social force in Germany and yet that it remained subordinate to authoritarian groups not merely because of inferiority in physical power—suspended in revolutions and republic—but precisely because of inferiority in social force.

On the second count, what had to be explained was the undeniable growth of the democratic movement through time in terms of number, wrested concessions, and the scope of initial successes—a growth which yet left that movement no closer to the control of German public life than it had ever been. That German history, if considered simply from the point of view of democratization, did in fact show a linear progress toward that end admitted of little doubt. Peasants and artisans, led by individual ex-priests, could gain only local and monthly gains for their vague goal of self-governing communes in 1525. By 1848 a whole class of intelligentsia was providing the intellectual leadership, a considerable middle class and a small contingent of proletarians joined the peasant and artisan revolutionary force, and the effect was a *de facto* national sovereignty that hung on for almost a year before being displaced by the regular governments with which it had been juxtaposed. In 1918 a politically organized and committed group of socialist intellectuals followed the massive movement of a giant working class, abetted by peasants and artisans in uniform and unopposed by an *attentiste* bourgeoisie and a neutralized aristocracy, in a revolutionary success. In the face of this triumph the political establishment simply disappeared, and the result was the *de jure* government of Germany for some 14 years under the most democratic constitution in western experience.

And yet it was equally undeniable that from a comparative rather than a linear point of view each democratic gain had been overmatched by a larger gain in favor of the nondemocratic, authoritarian forces in German state and society. What was most lethal in this proportion was the increasing success of the counter-revolution in appropriating not only the social force of the uncommitted but sections of the appeal, the groupings, and the force of the revolutionary groups themselves. This success was lethal not only because it proved a sure tactical means of defeating democratic revolution, but even more because it presaged the permanent authoritarian appropriation of the practical promise and support of democracy. The process was barely in evidence during the Peasants' War, when the reactionary social goals and the sectarian implications of the revolutionaries sufficed of themselves to alienate the larger towns and the Lutheran reformers, but even here the stream of princely conversions to the Protestant cause during the half-century following upon the military triumph of the princes seems to have been motivated at least in part by a shrewd policy of diverting the religious tributary of social unrest. The military triumph of the counter-revolution after 1848 was sealed for some 70 years by the authoritarian adoption of constitutionalism, nationalism, and industrialization in combinations that divided the bourgeoisie and pacified the lower middle classes. The most far-reaching achievement of the German democracy, finally—the Weimar Republic—was met by a Nazi movement that not only smashed it far more thoroughly than popular institutions had ever been damaged before, but carried the original democratic impulses of antiestablishmentarianism, populist nationalism, and social welfare to extremes that seemed to brook no future alternative.

To explain these developments by the eccentric rhythm of the German socioeconomic process—the long centuries of relative stagnation followed by the accelerated telescoping of industrial revolution, small-scale capitalism, and large-scale capitalism from the middle of the nineteenth century—would account for both the belatedness of German democracy and the expansion of its claims and its support, but it would not in itself account for the constant quotient of its failures. Nor did it make any difference, for either the achievements or the limits of this process, whether the rhythm was conceived along Marxist lines as an original economic fact or along Weberian lines as a politically and culturally conditioned economic function. Either way the process could supply continuity to the evolution but not constancy to its effect. To make it fully explanatory, a single crucial relationship was added to the process, a relationship equally applicable to both versions of it. Economic development on the one hand and political and cultural movements on the other were conceived as independent variables, and their respective effects upon the German society as disjunctive. By virtue of this relationship the rise of German democracy could be explained for different periods either by the social effects of economic growth or by the social response to the politics of international competition and the ideas of cosmopolitan culture, but their repeated frustration could be explained by the continuing incongruity of the two orbits.

Thus when the increment of social mobility in the political power of the western nations and the advancing realization of cosmopolitan liberal ideals in the west combined to foster liberalism in early nineteenth-century Germany, its limits were set by the laggard pace of economic growth. When the massive growth of industrial organization in the late nineteenth and early twentieth centuries ushered in the welfare state under the aegis of mass democracy, German democratization was stymied by the militaristic consequence of diplomatic conflict and by the bitter ideological divisions which reflected the accumulation of contemporary and unresolved past domestic political issues. The first of these stages was manifest in Engels' interpretation of early nineteenth-century German history, the second in Max Weber's influential exposition of the early twentieth-century German dilemma, which made a democratic component in the state the necessary consequence of industrial capitalism but at the same time posited an equally inevitable limit to democratic control as a consequence of the authoritarian and bureaucratic requirements of the power-state. The crucial demonstration of the relationships which had been thus theoretically indicated lay in the reality of the Weimar Republic, whose fall was seen as the frustration of constitutional democracy by the fateful intersection of the social possibilities of democratic politics with the political influence of authoritarian social elites still entrenched in army, bureaucracy, business, and agriculture.

From the dissynchronous process of German history, two conclusions were drawn, one militating against the probability of an historical projection toward democratization, the other leaving open the possibility of democratization by mutation.

The negative conclusion was this:

The interpretive habit, native to western analysts, of associating democratic groups with progress and undemocratic groups with regress, could not be applied to Germany, and consequently the impetus of the technological process, together with its social implications, that we have tended to identify with progress, could not be a factor in planning for Germany. Social progress and social regress, political democracy and political authoritarianism all performed as independent variables and entered into various combinations with one another. This principle had two corollaries.

First, political authoritarians have often associated economically and socially progressive groups and policies with their preservation of economically and socially regressive fundamental institutions, just as political democrats have associated economically and socially regressive aims with the dynamic populism of their basic commitment. On the first count, the Nazi juncture of revolutionary and conservative appeals was the most extreme example of what had many precedents in German history. On the second count, the internal vacillations of the Centrist

(Catholic) democracy and the social paralysis of middle-class democrats in general during the Weimar Republic perpetuated the separation between the political and social components of democracy that had appeared as early as the Peasants' War and as fatefully as the fateful revolutionary split of 1848.

The second corollary was the invalidity of any attempt to project a German political effect from the putative ramifications of a general economic and social process. Hence it could be and was admitted that as individuals Germans were not essentially different from other human beings and that as a society Germany participated in the economic industrialization and the social democratization that have become the hallmarks of western civilization; but it was held just as strongly that in their political posture and in the social organization connected with it autonomous factors operated that gave a distinctive form to German operations in these areas. Since the tendency of the modern economic and social process has been generally held to be toward democratization, the persistence of a distinctive German dimension has meant the neutralization of this tendency.

The positive conclusion inferable from the broad lines of German history was this:

Because the historical frustrations of German democracy have been actual intersections of autonomous processes rather than functions of a single process of its own, there is no more a predictable necessity for this frustration than there is a predictable probability of its realization. All that could be said was that the repeated failures of German attempts at democratization have left existing democratic groups with no forward thrust toward future democratization. The historical view postulated no necessity for the incongruity of the German social and political orbits and no bar to a future congruity: it postulated only that the democratic groups had been shaped by the historic incongruity and gave no reason to hope for a change in pattern.

But the historical point of view sketched above went one step beyond implying the possibility of an open future to recognize, from history, a possible source for a future change of pattern. The overt hostility to foreign influences, recurrently manifest in the outbreaks of xenophobia which dot the course of German history, was the obverse of a German receptivity to which it was an anxious and violent response. However distinctive the German form which they ultimately assumed, time and again techniques and ideas from the west had upset the tensile order into which the authoritarian elite had integrated the mobile elements of the society, and increasingly through time a new order had

been established only through the appropriation of the foreign incur-
sions by the German institutions of social and political control. The alternation of repulsion and accommodation to international movements
was such as to preclude any notion of a necessary domestication of international standards of democracy, but it was also such as to render not
impossible a new German initiative stemming from it.

2. The assessment of the German situation at the start of occupation
had also to reckon with the chance that the cataclysm of Nazi totalitarianism had so altered the structure of the German state and society that
the conclusions from a German historical tradition had become irrelevant. There were three plausible interpretations of the relationship between Nazism and the structure of German life, and each implied a
different conception of the Nazi impact upon the German potential
democratization.

First, as lords of a new-fangled totalitarian state the Nazis atomized
German society for the purpose of instituting their own integral system
of controls over its naked individuals, with the effect of terminating the
autonomy of all historic German institutions. The implication of this
interpretation was that all historical bets were off and that there was no
way of knowing what would succeed the Nazi demise.

Second, in contrast to this political interpretation, the stock Marxist
interpretation which saw in Nazism the last desperate stage of capitalism viewed the course of the Nazi regime in terms of the developing crisis brought on by the fatal contradictions of an overripe economic and
social system. According to this interpretation, the Nazi terror manifested the climactic convulsion of the exploitative system whose less extreme frustrations of democracy had made up the bulk of German
history, so that the demise of the Nazi regime could only mean the end
of contradictions and the conjunction of social revolution with people's
democracy.

It should be noted that however different in substance these two interpretations may have been, they were formally homologous and had
formally similar implications for the German democratic potential.
Each of these interpretations postulated the primacy of one process in
Nazism—i.e., the political and the economic-social, respectively—
deemed Nazism the terminal extreme of that process, and presumed
from this termination of the traditional tensions within the process the
essential irrelevance of the German past to the German potential for
democratization. For the interpretation in terms of political totalitarianism, democratization would be a matter of future institutional con-

struction on the basis of the *tabula rasa* that would be left by the removal of Nazis from public office. For the interpretation in terms of an overripe capitalism, democratization would be a matter of the social transformation that must follow the removal of the elite groups and institutions of which Nazism was a function. Obviously these inferences were never drawn in so pure a form, since they were always modified by actual memories of the German past, but still we can recognize in them the logic that actually came to prevail behind the respective zonal occupation policies.

Temporally prior to these approaches, however, a third interpretation of Nazism prevailed, which is placed finally here only because, as a hybrid of the two categorical positions, it is most easily explained in terms of them. This hybrid may be viewed as a kind of resultant, the interpretation of Nazism that was the prevalent assumption in the early phase of planning for Germany in the light of a joint east-west policy, but it is independently important for our purpose because its corollary on German democratic potential was categorically different from the corollaries associated with either of the interpretations it seemed only to mix.

The hybrid interpretation viewed Nazism as both totalitarian and capitalistic, but it viewed these functions not in terms of an integral process but rather as a continuation and intensification of the traditional German disjunction between the political and social processes that would leave the German democratic potential as heavily mortgaged as before. This interpretation indicated the necessity of redefining totalitarianism to signify the unlimited intensity of dominion within an extensively limited political sphere while recognizing the persistence of other centers of social power outside that sphere.[6] The implication of such an analysis for the democratic potential of Germany was to show how the Nazi system both increased the possibility and diminished the probability of post-Nazi democracy. On the one hand, the structure of the Nazi regime opened new possibilities for German democracy by virtue of the naked privileges which the Nazi division of function with the traditional elites assigned to the latter. On the other hand, the Nazi destruction of all the foci of democratic activity would leave the democrats with little physical probability of actually overcoming the organiza-

6. E.g., Franz Neumann, *Behemoth: The Structure and Practice of National Socialism* (2nd. ed.; New York: Oxford University Press, 1944), pp. 387, 398; H. R. Trevor-Roper, *The Last Days of Hitler* (3rd ed.; New York: St. Martin's Press, 1956), p. 5.

tional advantage of the extant elitist institutions after the fall of Nazism without either a spontaneous revolutionary organization or a decisive push from an outside power.

The pattern of German resistance to Nazism which became visible in the events and repercussions of July 20, 1944, seemed to confirm this third interpretation.[7] Unlike the pattern of resistance in the nations of occupied Europe, where the center of gravity lay on the left, in the cadres of communists, socialists, and radical intellectuals, and tailed off into smaller and looser groupings of the nationalistic right, in Germany the organizing core was formed within the protected institutions of the army, bureaucracy, and Confessional Church, with tenuous links to small and inactive socialist circles. From this movement four conclusions about the particularity of the German situation under Nazism seemed warranted: first, that in Germany Nazism had left only the traditional privileged institutions and their German elite capable of political action; second, that this elite could resume its tradition at least to the extent of striving for popular support in terms of its conception of national interest; third, that this conception of anti-Nazi national interest was not democratic but Burkeian in its combination of traditional ideal and contemporary utility, and hence was a throwback to what was best in German conservatism; and fourth, that the movement remained a conspiracy and did not become a revolution, confirming thereby the continuing abstractness of the possibility of democracy.

For what was distinctive about this German resistance, in comparison with other European resistance movements against Nazism, was entirely political and social. Obviously the difference was not ethical, for the integrity of the German conspirators' moral reprobation of the Nazis was at least as pure as any underground's in Europe. Nor was the presence or absence of nationalism the distinguishing factor that it superficially appeared to be. Although the nationalism which was the overt organizing principle for the disorganized democrats of occupied Europe seemed in the German homeland to be monopolized by the Nazis and therefore to be unavailable to the German conservative opposition, in fact this opposition also appealed to the idea of the permanent nation in its effort to unite various vested interests against the Nazi interloper. The German resistance fought in the overt forms of corporate interest for the cause of formal nationalism—that is, against the Nazi imperilment of the long-range institutions which their leaders

7. See Franklin L. Ford, "The Twentieth of July in the History of the German Resistance," *American Historical Review*, LI (July 1946), pp. 609–626.

identified with Germany—whereas the other resistance movements fought in the overt forms of nationalism for the cause of social democratization. The European resistance was antifascist as much as it was anti-German and used Nazism as a catalyst for the renovation of democracy. The German resistance was not nearly as antiauthoritarian as it was anti-Nazi, and it sought to pull down Nazism in order to restore unchallenged hierarchy. The contrast between the resistance movements did not lie in the presence or absence of nationalism, which, however different its function, was operative in both cases—it was a contrast of democratic potentials.

3. In addition to German tradition and the impact of the Nazi regime, there was a third potential source of German democracy—the reflex response to the military defeat of Nazism. Certainly there were precedents aplenty for the apparently spontaneous generation of democratic movements from the defeat of authoritarian regimes. In the German case itself—to omit the more notorious instances of the Paris Commune and the three Russian revolutions—the wildcat socialist revolution of 1918 that replaced the monarch-constitutionalism of the defeated Hohenzollern Empire with the political democracy of the Weimar Republic seemed a particularly apt parallel. Such events obviously bear some relationship both to the general history that developed the identities of the parties and to the structure of the immediate regime that set up the conditions of their activity, but the distinctive quality of such events is their origin from neither persistent movement nor contemporary regime—factors which become operative in the development of the event—but from the mere fact of the regime's military defeat. In such events, moreover, not only is the immediate response to this fact unpredictable, but the subsequent activities of historically familiar groups in the new conditions may themselves resist anticipation in terms of prior categories.

Hence the dour expectations which were the conclusions from the assessment of both the more remote German past and the recent Nazi chapter of it did not preclude the possibility that the Nazi military defeat might crystallize movements unrecognizable in advance. One important factor, indeed, spoke for the analogy of the post-Nazi situation with the precedents of spontaneous popular revolution. Although the evidence was not—and is not—at hand to warrant a general judgment that the commitments of total war make the internal loyalty to any regime a function of the military outcome, the available evidence did seem to support the hypothesis that modern authoritarian regimes are particularly involved with the security they provide and are therefore

particularly susceptible to the results of their military policies. From the
circumstances of the Nazi movement's rise and consolidation and from
what was known of the German wartime mentality, it could be presumed that for an indeterminate number of Germans the regime was of
this authoritarian type, not essentially different in kind from other
political regimes but vastly superior to them in the effective provision
of economic, military, and—through its hegemonial international
position—psychological security. From this point of view, the disaffec-
tion which began with the diplomacy of risk in 1938 and climaxed in
the darkening months of 1944 could be a harbinger of a widespread revulsion against those who had defaulted on the promise of security.
Such revulsion could submerge not only Nazism but the whole type of
authoritarian politics built on such a promise.

As a matter of fact, no such groundswell appeared in the aftermath of
defeat. But although the fact is certain, its meaning is not. Nor can it
ever be, for the pattern of piecemeal defeat and immediate occupation
blocked the communication, assemblages, and activities necessary to
make any movement of either masses or organized groups a reality even
if it had been otherwise prepared. We are reduced to the speculative enterprise of projecting probabilities from the situation in the isolated lo-
calities, a projection which must inevitably be distorted by the truism
that the form of a political arena goes far to shape the reality that fills it.

The distortion, moreover, may be particularly significant, for the local image is itself not quite uniform. In general, apathy was the rule, an
outer lethargy and inner emptiness so pervasive as to indicate not simply a state of shock in the face of catastrophe and the deadening routine
of daily exercise in the face of a crushing struggle for survival, but a political withdrawal so profound as to mark the Nazi experience off from
any authoritarian analogy. However utilitarian the commitment to Nazism may have been, the regime's novel success in identifying its own political aims with the very possibility of German public utility and in
exterminating all alternative associations with such benefits made its
failure appear as the failure of politics as such. As the Nazi governments
disappeared they were not replaced by other local governments or by
revolutionary governing committees; they simply left behind admin-
istrators who persisted in their technical functions and old non-Nazi organization men who themselves claimed democratic status but whose
organizations had long since disappeared.

But not everywhere. We may leave aside the self-styled "Executive
Government (*Geschäftsführende Reichsregierung*)" of Admiral Dönitz
which controlled the Flensburg area in Schleswig-Holstein for some

two weeks after May 1, 1945, since Dönitz had been appointed by Hitler himself and his government of Nazi officials actually functioned as "a kind of liquidation office of the 'Third Reich'" during its short existence.[8] Nor need we dwell upon the informal revival of old party and trade union connections, since these were resuscitations from the past to be expected from the removal of the Nazi terror. The important exception to the image of local apathy was the sporadic appearance of the so-called "antifa" (i.e., antifascist) committees in sundry cities and towns. Analogous in orientation and function to the European resistance movements at the time of liberation, albeit local rather than national or even regional in organization, the "antifas" were ostensibly formed on the united-front principle that would not so much unite as transcend all former political divisions in the fight against the survivals of Nazism, but they were actually run by communists, a communist-social democratic coalition, or socialists open to cooperation with communists. They were ostensibly nonpolitical, devoted to the urgent practical issues of the purge and reconstruction as necessary public preconditions of politics, but actually they interpreted both of these putatively technical aims institutionally to include far-reaching measures of socialization and democratization. They were ostensibly informal associations, but they actually operated as municipal governments where they could seize control and as a kind of pressuring citizens' council where they could not.

The antifa movement did not survive long under the occupation. All the occupying powers—Soviet Russia included—preferred more regular and traditional forms of political, and nonpolitical, organization, and the antifas quickly ran into the sands of history, whence nary a trace of them is to be found. Unlike the rest of Europe, moreover, where the resistance organizations suffered an analogous literal fate in favor of a more orthodox dispensation, in Germany they have not even survived as a political symbol. And yet their meaning for immediate postwar Germany remains a tantalizing question. Omitting the issue of communist inspiration or participation for our diagnostic purpose as an instance of the genetic fallacy, we must avow the antifas to have been novel, reconstructive, and democratic in their programs, and both activist and politically committed (despite their protestations) in reality; we must avow them too to have gotten the jump, when they appeared, on the elite groups and to have been disbanded finally by occupying rather than German powers. But we must also avow them to have been small

---

8. Fritz Rene Allemann, *Bonn ist nicht Weimer* (Cologne, 1956), pp. 15, 16.

in membership (aside from the reportedly impressive cases of Leipzig and Bremen) and, for their influence, more dependent upon an anticipated collaboration with the occupying authorities than upon any clear evidence of support from a German population whose own organizations were in temporary eclipse. The antifas clearly could no more have become long-range democratic institutions than such supraparty councils or soviets ever have been able to, but whether they could have triggered new departures in German politics must remain an open question.

We are left only with the certainty that the occupying powers did not see in them the kind of German democratic movement that could alter the negative judgment of the German democratic potential based upon the pattern of the German past and the effects of the Nazi regime. Ostensibly in concert but actually in tandem, the occupying powers proceeded to enact their judgment that the Germans were capable of democratizing themselves only upon an initiative and under conditions that would come from without; only in this way, they thought, could the frustrating treadmill of the German past be stopped.

What, we must now ask, have we learned since these contemporary judgments about the German potential for democracy under military occupation were made?

Of the three segments of the German past—remote, recent, and immediate—which entered into the judgment of German democratic potential at the start of occupation, subsequent research and analysis have added to our knowledge in an inverse order of relevance: They have added nothing to the third, information to the second, and substantial knowledge to the first.

1. The brief period between defeat and occupation has suffered the usual fate of unproductive brevities in history and has been telescoped into its more eventful precession and succession. It is the kind of elision in history that will probably remain recoverable only in the form given it by the testimony of contemporary observers.

2. Despite the spate of diplomatic, military, and biographical narratives and of formal analyses of political structure that have been so prominent in the postwar literature on Nazism, there is now also a considerable body of studies that is more directly relevant to our problem. If we characterize this relevance as the delivery of information rather than insights, it is not to characterize these studies as such—since they have enriched our understanding as well as our fund of facts about National Socialism—but to characterize the relationship that they do bear, and perhaps must bear, to the problem of democratization. Obviously,

the investigation of a regime that was the very antithesis of what we mean by democracy can by its very nature add little but a contextual or dialectical relief to this problem. But if the conclusions are therefore incommensurable conceptually with the idea of democratization, these same conclusions are highly appropriate as epitomes of recent circumstances and conditions bearing upon democratization.

We may identify three fields of such relevant research—the history of the Nazi accession to power, the operational analysis of Nazi institutions, and the inquiry into German social attitudes in the Nazi era. This research has, as its common academic concern, the interaction between politics and society, the general field within which the problem of German democratization also falls. But, more important, the substantive results of these researches can be grouped into two main tendencies which bring new support to the two main assumptions of the immediate postwar judgment on the German potential for democratization: the actual persistence of the traditional antidemocratic syndrome, and the unprecedented possibility of breaking it.

The first tendency demonstrates the reality of internal divisions within the Nazi regime and their necessary counterpart in the limitations of the regime's control over German society. This is the moral both of the most searching historical works and of the most intensive of the institutional analyses, which share an emphasis on the essentially political character of the Nazi regime and the implication of its restricted social impact. Thus the monumental histories both of Karl Bracher and of Ernst Nolte agree, from radically different approaches, on the essentially suprasocial character of Nazism.[9] The less dramatic but more pointed analyses of Nazi political institutions in social operation extend the implications of these histories by showing that the political, rather than the social, changes that accompanied the establishment of Nazism apply as well to its effects. Studies of such widely separated fields as Nazi cultural activity and economic policy indicate parallel patterns. In the arts, in literature, in education, independent studies register a standard pattern: a joint purpose of total control and sponsorship of a new National Socialist culture; divisions and struggles within the Nazi hierarchy for personal pre-eminence and debates about the character of the Nazi culture; and the resolution of the struggle by *ad hoc* as-

9. Karl Dietrich Bracher, Wolfgang Sauer, and Gerhard *Schulz, Die nationalsozialistische Machtergreifung* (Cologne, 1960). See Bracher's convenient summary in Fritz Stern (ed.), *The Path of Dictatorship* (trans. John Conway; New York: Praeger, 1967) pp. 113–131; and Ernst Nolte, *Der Faschismus in seiner Epoche* (Munich, 1963), and *Die faschistschen Bewegungen* (Munich, 1966), esp. p. 105.

signments of competence based on mutual surrender of new Nazi
culture as an aim of policy. The net effect of successful control over
deadened but unreconstructed German culture was the uncreative and
persistent inertia of the traditional.[10] At the other end of the social
spectrum, the main lines of the relationship between Nazi policy and
the German economy are sketched in the same genre according to the
recent studies, for their general tendency is to stress the persistence of
long-range economic trends under Nazism and the essential imperviousness of the economy to characteristically Nazi regulation.[11] All
these researches refer the traditional conflict between German politics
and society to internal division within Nazi politics itself and leave German society at the end of the Nazi regime not very different from what
it was at the start.

If we may label research along this line to be works in socialized politics, then we may collect the other main tendency in the recent study of
Nazi Germany under the rubric of political sociology. However variable
the particular findings within this category, they share two qualities
which point in a direction quite contrary to the tendency of the studies
in socialized politics. First, the political sociologists explain the Nazi regime in terms of the universal qualities of "industrial society"; and second, they maintain that in these terms the Nazis manifested and
perpetrated a revolution which transformed the traditional structure of
German society. Precisely how they performed these functions is a matter of some dispute. Hannah Arendt is prominent among those who see
in Nazism a manifestation of the hollowness, rootlessness, and restlessness of industrial mass society, whereas others, like Seymour Lipset, see
it as a manifestation of petty-bourgeois reaction against the hollowness,
rootlessness, and restlessness of industrial mass society.[12] The interpretation of the regime's revolutionary consequences has been similarly
varied. For Ralf Dahrendorf, the Nazi commitment to tradition was

10. See Hildegard Brenner, *Die Kunstpolitik des Nationalsozialismus* (Hamburg,
1963), pp. 1–118, *passim;* Dietrich Strothmann, *Nationalsozialistische Literaturpolitik*
(Bonn, 1963), pp. 427, 428; Rolf Eilers, *Die Nationalsozialistische Schulpolitik* (Cologne,
1963), pp. 135–140.

11. Arthur Schweitzer, *Big Business in the Third Reich* (Bloomington: Indiana University Press, 1964), esp. pp. 502, 503; Burton H. Klein, *Germany's Economic Preparations for
War* (Cambridge, Mass.: Harvard University Press, 1959), pp. 78–81, 236, 237; *Die
deutsche Industrie im Kriege, 1939–1945* (Berlin, 1954), pp. 40, 41; Enno Georg, *Die
wirtschaftlichen Unternehmungen der SS* (Stuttgart, 1963), p. 144.

12. Seymour Martin Lipset, *Political Man: The Social Bases of Politics* (Garden City,
N.Y.: Doubleday, 1960), pp. 134–149; Hannah Arendt, *The Origins of Totalitarianism*
(New York: Meridian Books, 1958).

merely ideological, and the practical effect of the regime was the consummation of a social revolution that dissolved the traditional ties in the German social structure, aligned it, for better or worse, with the modern industrial societies, and thus abolished the distinctively German pattern of historical authoritarianism.[13] But this particular process is not required for this result. In an equally recent analysis, David Schoenbaum has found the same social revolution composed of quite opposite proportions: of an "objective social reality" that perpetuated the traditional class relationships and of a Nazified "interpreted social reality" which produced the revolution.[14] The variations indicate the speculative character of the studies along this line—the empirical studies are still immersed more in methodology than in substance[15]—but they do bring to bear upon German Nazism what we have learned since the war about the social ramifications of industrial growth. The effect is to stress the fundamental conditions to which the Nazi rulers had to conform, or which, at most, they could exploit.

How does this subsequent knowledge about Nazi Germany affect the judgment of the German democratic potential at the end of the regime? Its net result has been not to amend the judgment but rather to lessen somewhat the relevance of the Nazi regime to the judgment. This diminution stems not only from the mutually neutralizing conflicts between the main lines of the research but from the one point of their formal agreement—that the Nazi regime was even less monolithic and totalitarian than had been assumed and that any judgment about German politics and society must rest even more than had been assumed on longer-range structures and trends stretching back into the remote past and forward into the imminent future.

3. The recent studies of the remoter German past have tended in general to confirm the judgment on both the existence of and the rigid limitations upon democratic forces in Germany, for they have started from it and supplied a solid and projectable knowledge of process to what was originally based on observation and conjecture. The relevant historical research has gone along three lines, each identifying a process in the development that frustrated the realization of past democratic pos-

13. Ralf Dahrendorf, *Gesellschaft und Demokratie in Deutschland* (Munich, 1966), pp. 431–448.

14. David Schoenbaum, *Hitler's Social Revolution: Class and Status in Nazi Germany, 1933–1939* (Garden City, N.Y.: Doubleday, 1966), pp. 298–301.

15. E.g., Karl Martin Bolte, *Sozialer Aufstieg und Abstieg: Eine Untersuchung über Berufsprestige und Berufsmobilität* (Stuttgart, 1959), esp. pp. 1, 214, 227, 228; and Wolfgang Zapf, *Wandlungen der deutschen Elite* (2nd ed.; Munich, 1966), pp. 207–211.

sibilities. First, the history of liberals and socialists has been explored to show how the general relationships of the German political and social structure were internalized into the essential divisions and inherent limitations upon the evolution of liberalism and socialism toward democracy.[16] Second, in the large literature devoted for obvious reasons to the history of German authoritarianism, a small but significant segment has been addressed to the process of "revolution from above"—that is to say, to the realization by authoritarian means of ends that elsewhere were realized by democratic means.[17] But most to the point, perhaps, has been the third line of research, which has treated the critical confrontations of democracy and authoritarianism in German theory and practice, showing the interplay of democratic divisions, authoritarian accommodations, and authoritarian rejections actually working in different instances of democratic defeat.[18]

The closest thing we have to a synthesis of the recent knowledge bearing on the German historical incapacity for democratization is Ralf Dahrendorf's *Gesellschaft und Demokratie in Deutschland*. It starts frankly from the question, "Why has the principle of liberal democracy found so few friends in Germany?" and develops an explanation that in effect merges into one cogent and demonstrable "syndrome" of persistent social structure the loose and descriptive duality of a dissynchronous politics and society. In effect it confirms the immediate postwar judgment that Nazism and its defeat brought to German society new possibilities for democratization that were not of its own

16. On liberalism and democracy, see esp. Rudolf Stadelmann, *Soziale und politische Geschichte der Revolution von 1848* (Munich, 1948); Theodore S. Hamerow, *Restoration, Revolution, Reaction: Economics and Politics in Germany, 1815–1871* (Princeton, N.J.: Princeton University Press, 1958); Theodor Schieder, *The State and Society in Our Times* (trans. C. A. M. Sym; New York: Hillary House, 1962). On socialists, see Carl E. Schorske, *German Social Democracy, 1905–1917* (Cambridge, Mass.: Harvard University Press, 1955).

17. See esp. Rudolf Stadelmann, *Deutschland und Westeuropa* (Schloss Laupheim-Württemberg, 1948), pp. 11–33; Ernst Fraenkel, *Deutschland und die westlichen Demokratien* (2nd ed.; Stuttgart, 1964), pp. 13–31. See also the recent Bismarck literature, esp. Otto Pflanze, *Bismarck and the Development of Germany, 1815–1871* (Princeton, N.J.: Princeton University Press, 1963).

18. On postliberal neoconservatism, see esp. Fritz Stern, *The Politics of Cultural Despair* (Berkeley: University of California Press, 1961); Klemens von Klemperer, *Germany's New Conservatism* (Princeton: University Press, 1957); Arnim Mohler, *Die konservative Revolution in Deutschland* (Stuttgart, 1950). On the fateful clash of authoritarianism and democracy, see esp. Karl Dietrich Bracher, *Die Auflösung der Weimarer Republik: Eine Studie zum Problem des Machtverfalls in der Demokratie* (3rd ed.; Villingen/Schwarzwald, 1960).

making and that could not be realized without a social reorganization not yet in being.

A final question remains. Since every actual situation must have been potential at one time, has the present actuality of Germany any retrospective bearing upon the potential for democratization at the start of the occupation and consequently upon the validity of the dominant views toward it? Even if we assume that Germany currently is an authentic democracy and thus waive discussion of whether there is in fact a democratic actuality for which a potential should be reconstructed, the answer must be in the negative, for the simple reason that today's Germany has developed not from the original postwar potential of the Germans but from an intervening process that incorporated influences from outside the German orbit and thus became another potential, charged with the thrust of new actualities. Thus the course of the occupation manifested two tendencies of interest to us in this context: One confirmed the original judgment of the German potential by actualizing it; the other reflected the acknowledgment of a new German potential as a response both to changed conditions and to changed notions of the democratization which defined the nature of the potential.

First, then, the Allies confirmed their judgment of the German potential for democratization by the most foolproof of methods—by legislating it into reality. The original judgment had made democratization a possibility through the Allied power to initiate a permanent break in the continuity of authoritarian institutions and thereby to alter the fundamental conditions of German social and political life. Undeniably this became fact. In the east the social revolution; in the west, the initial extent of Nazi disenfranchisement, the pyramidal pattern of political reconstruction, and standards of competitive free enterprise: All these were clearly responses to action by or presence of the occupying powers. Included among the stimuli of these responses were the respective democratic styles of the occupying powers. Unquestionably the types of democracy represented by the occupying powers were crucial determinants for both the western and eastern types of democracy that developed in Germany. Even inadvertently, moreover, the occupying powers were responsible for the conditions which would make German democratization a real possibility as it had never been before: By taking over the burdens of military security for zones and then the republics of Germany, they undermined the potential functions of a military elite and the general rationale of traditional authoritarianism.

Thus the Allies, perhaps even more literally than they had intended, made their original judgment on the German democratic potential come true: They had assessed as minimal the probability that any German group could achieve significant and long-range democratic results until new conditions supervened which these groups could not themselves directly effect. Both by their own innovations and by prolonging the suspension of German controls until they could be born amid new surroundings, the occupying powers confirmed their negative judgment of the German potential by preparing the circumstances for a new one.

Secondly, the subsequent German potential that produced the current German regimes developed out of the new actualities that were themselves produced by the conjunction of Allied actions and the inexorable change of circumstance. How different the new potential had to be from the old is patent from the alteration of the basic condition: The national unity which was deemed a necessary condition of the original potential—not, in this context, that Allied diplomacy demanded it, but because it was thought that German democratization was impossible if national self-determination were frustrated—gave way to the two Germanies which have furnished the framework for whatever democratization has become actuality.

The shift encompassed, moreover, not only the conditions of German political activity but the character of the democratic ends by which its potential was assessed. As international relations worsened and the German institutional net was, in its varying forms, knit or reknit, the occupying powers insensibly scaled down their criteria of democratization to mean the practical cooperation of Germans with the respective occupying power and, especially in the west, to include an acknowledgment of the actual direction the Germans were taking. The coincidence of these two aspects in the attitudes of the occupying powers meant that as the Germanies moved toward independence, their potential for democratization was reassessed into a judgment of the Germans' capacity to continue to do what they had started to do. Where the judgment of the original potential had posited the widest gulf permitted by the limits of possibility between the goal of democracy and the German actuality, the judgment of the subsequent potential brought the democratic goal and the German actuality into such intimate relations as to make the German potential for these kinds of democratization very probable of realization indeed.

But perhaps the most significant change in the standards for assessing the German potential has come from the alteration which the postwar era has brought to the connotations of democracy not only in Germany but in general. The democracy which was the measure of the German potential in 1945 was the culmination of two centuries' development which fused constitutional, national, and social ideals into a single political system. But the ambiguous democracies that subsequently developed in the Germanies may be viewed as test-tube cases of the tendencies toward institutional formalism, government by pressure groups, and civic privatization that lately have infected the democratic model everywhere. The moral for planned political change would seem to be this: A society's potential for democratization is not identifiable as definite qualities, groups, or institutions, but as a process in which the planners must not only measure continuously the changing tendencies of their charges but take continuous account of their own measuring rod as well. In politics as in science, allowance must be made for the participation of the observer.

Leonard Krieger: A Bibliography

1949

"The Inter-regnum in Germany: March–August 1945." *Political Science Quarterly* 64 (December): 507–32.

1951

"The Idea of Progress." *Review of Metaphysics* 4, no. 4 (June): 483–93.

1952

"The Intellectuals and European Society." *Political Science Quarterly* 67: 225–47.

1953

"Marx and Engels as Historians." *Journal of the History of Ideas* 14, no. 3 (June): 381–403.

1957

The German Idea of Freedom: History of a Political Tradition. Boston, Mass.: Beacon Press.
"The Horizons of History." *American Historical Review* 63, no. 1 (October): 62–74.

1960

"History and Law in the Seventeenth Century." *Journal of the History of Ideas* 21, no. 2 (April–June): 198–210.
"The Uses of Marx for History." *Political Science Quarterly* 75 (September): 355–78.

1961

"European and American Liberalism." *Amerikanische Gelehrtenwoche an der Ludwig-Maximilians-Universität, 19–24 Juni 1961.* Munich, 1962. Pp. 129–42.
"Nationalism in America." Ibid., pp. 143–54.

1962

"Stages in the History of Political Freedom." *Liberty: Nomos IV* (Yearbook of The American Society for Political and Legal Philosophy), ed. Carl J. Friedrich. New York: Atherton Press. Pp. 1–28.

"Nationalism and the Nation-State System, 1789–1870." In *Chapters in West-ern Civilization*, 3rd ed., vol. 2. New York: Columbia University Press. Pp. 103–39.

1963

"The Idea of the Welfare State in Europe and the United States." *Journal of the History of Ideas* 24, no. 4 (October–December): 553–68.

"Comments on Historical Explanation." In *Philosophy and History: A Symposium*, ed. Sidney Hook. New York. Pp. 136–42.

1964

"The Distortions of Political Theory: The Seventeenth Century Case." *Journal of the History of Ideas* 25, no. 3 (July–September): 323–32.

1965

The Politics of Discretion: Pufendorf and the Acceptance of Natural Law. Chicago: University of Chicago Press.

History: The Development of Historical Studies in the United States (with John Higham and Felix Gilbert). Englewood Cliffs, N.J.: Prentice-Hall.

"Kant and the Crisis of Natural Law." *Journal of the History of Ideas* 26, no. 2 (April–June): 191–210.

1967

"Power and Responsibility: The Historical Assumptions." In *The Responsibility of Power: Historical Essays in Honor of Hajo Holborn*, ed. Leonard Krieger and Fritz Stern. Garden City, N.Y.: Doubleday. Pp. 3–33.

Series editor, Classic European Historians. Chicago: University of Chicago Press, 1967–76.

Volume editor, Friedrich Engels, *The German Revolutions*. Classic European Historians. Chicago: University of Chicago Press. (The Editor's Introduction to this volume is published above as chapter 16.)

"History and Existentialism in Sartre." In *The Critical Spirit: Essays in Honor of Herbert Marcuse*, ed. Kurt H. Wolff and Barrington Moore, Jr. Boston: Beacon Press. Pp. 239–66.

1968

"The Potential for Democratization in Occupied Germany: A Problem in the Historical Projection." In *Public Policy*, ed. John Dickey Montgomery. Cambridge, Mass.: Harvard University Press. Pp. 27–58.

"Culture, Cataclysm, and Contingency." *Journal of Modern History* 40, no. 4 (December): 447–73.

"Official History and the War in Vietnam: Comment." *Military Affairs* 32: 16–19.

1970

Kings and Philosophers: 1689–1789. New York: W. W. Norton & Co.
"Note on Hajo Holborn's Unfinished Business." *Central European History* 3 (March): 172–75.

1971

"Nationalism and Modern Germany." In *Perspectives on the European Past,* ed. Norman F. Cantor. New York: Macmillan & Co. Pp. 209–41.
"Comment on Monroe Beardsley's 'Inevitability in History.'" *Philosophic Exchange* 1: 25–27.

1972

"Introduction." In Hajo Holborn, *History and the Humanities* Garden City, N.Y.: Doubleday. Pp. 1–10.

1973

"The Autonomy of Intellectual History." *Journal of the History of Ideas* 34, (October–December): 499–516.
"Authority." In *Dictionary of the History of Ideas,* vol. 1. New York: Charles Scribner's Sons. Pp. 141–62.

1975

An Essay on the Theory of Enlightened Despotism. Chicago: University of Chicago Press.
"Germany." In *National Consciousness, History, and Political Culture in Early-Modern Europe,* ed. Orest Ranum. Baltimore: Johns Hopkins University Press. Pp. 67–97.
"Elements of Early Historicism: Experience, Theory, and History in Ranke." *History and Theory,* Suppl. 14: *Essays on Historicism,* 1–14.

1976

"The Historical Hanna Arendt." *Journal of Modern History* 48 (December): 672–84.

1977

Ranke: The Meaning of History. Chicago: University of Chicago Press.
"The Idea of Authority in the West." *American Historical Review* 82, no. 2 (April): 249–70.

1978

"The Heavenly City of the Eighteenth-Century Historians." *Church History* 47, no. 3 (September): 279–307.
"Nazism: Highway or Byway?" *Central European History* 11, no. 1 (March): 3–22.

1980

"Historicism's Revenge." *Annals of Scholarship* 1, no. 2 (Spring): 15–30.

1981

"Contemporary American Liberalism." *TriQuarterly,* no. 52 (Fall): 31–42.

1982

"Samuel Pufendorf." In *Deutsche Historiker,* vol. 9, ed. Hans-Ulrich Wehler. Göttingen: Vandenhoeck & Ruprecht Pp. 7–22.

Introduction to *Essays on Culture and Society in Modern Germany* (The Walter Prescott Wells Memorial Lectures), ed. Gary D. Stark and Bede Karl Lackner. Published by Texas A&M University Press for the University of Texas at Arlington. Pp. 3–14.

1984

"The One That Got Away" (Comments on the historical Descartes). *Proceedings of the American Philosophical Society* 128, no. 3: 248–51.

1986

"The Philosophical Bases of German Historicism: The Eighteenth Century." In *Aufklärung und Geschichte: Studien zur deutschen Geschichtswissenschaft im 18. Jahrhundert,* ed. Hans Erich Bödeker. Göttingen: Vandenhoeck & Ruprecht. Pp. 246–63.

1989

Time's Reasons: Philosophies of History Old and New. Chicago: University of Chicago Press.

Index